Revolution Revisited

Behind the Scenes in East Germany, 1989

Nancy and Jim —
I appreciate your interest
and support over these many years
as I've been researching and
writing this book.
I hope you enjoy this history
of our time. May it bring back
memories of your trip to Germany
and elsewhere.
Love,
Pat
November 2014

Patricia J. Smith

Dog Ear Publishing
Indianapolis, Indiana
2014

First published by Dog Ear Publishing
4010 W. 86th Street, Ste H
Indianapolis, IN 46268
www.dogearpublishing.net

dog ear
PUBLISHING

ISBN: 978-1-4575-3252-8

Library of Congress Control Number: has been applied for

This book is printed on acid-free paper.

Printed in the United States of America

For Bill, Mark, and Jennifer

for inspiration, support, and love

Table of Contents

Appendices

Maps and Illustrations

Tables and Figures

PREFACE:

Accidental Encounters with History

In a way, this story began fifty years ago when I first crossed into East Germany and East Berlin from the west. I had just completed my freshman year at the University of Kansas (KU) and had the opportunity to spend the summer studying German at KU's summer language institute in Holzkirchen, West Germany, twenty miles south of Munich. For me, a teenager from a small Kansas farming community, Moundridge, the trip opened up my world. The year was 1964.

Three Kansas girls explore Berlin, 1964. From left: Patricia, Trisha, and Terry with Berlin bear.

Just three years earlier East Germany had built the Berlin Wall, separating East Germany from the west. The previous summer—1963—the young, charismatic John F. Kennedy had visited the Wall. There cheering crowds greeted the newly elected U.S. President as he promised West Berlin citizens to defend their rights and uphold U.S. commitments. Just five months later, Kennedy would be assassinated.

The next summer–1964–the West German government provided money for us Kansas language students to travel from Holzkirchen to Berlin and gave us each 25 marks

Author's passport stamped at Checkpoint Charlie,
July 19, 1964

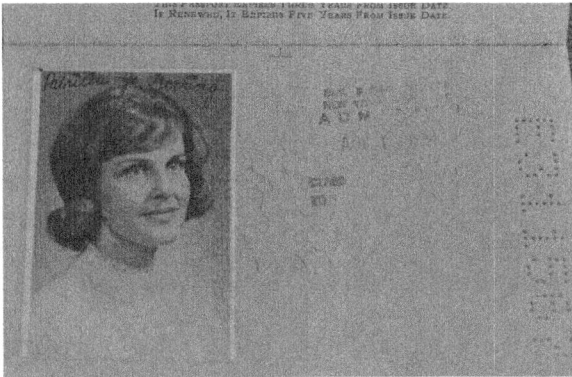

Author's passport stamped in New York, 1964

a day for spending money.[1] Traveling by chartered bus, we first experienced Cold War politics at Hof, the border town between East and West Germany. There border officials ordered us off the bus, and we spent several hours standing on the side of the road in the hot sun as guards systematically searched our bus before allowing us to proceed on the transit highway toward West Berlin. A bus tour of Berlin—West and East—introduced us to the two cities standing at the flash point of the Cold War and to the political and economic systems that each represented.

In our free time, my roommates, Trisha and Terry, and I decided to explore further, so we three young, naïve Kansas girls took the subway and crossed into East Berlin. We explored and returned to our group in West Berlin without incident; however, the trip whetted my appetite for further travel and to learn more about this intriguing country behind the Iron Curtain.

Back at KU, I succumbed to the joys of research in musty library stacks, reading copies of FBIS (Foreign Broadcast Information Service) reports of the Central Intelligence Agency (CIA), community power structure studies, and survey research, and I changed my major from German to political science. Coinciding with my graduate and undergraduate years during the 1960s, movement politics entered campus life. Civil rights, voting rights, the assassination of

Checkpoint Charlie, July 19, 1964
Photo by Patricia Smith

Sign at Checkpoint Charlie: "You are leaving the American Sector"
Photo by Patricia Smith

Martin Luther King. The peace movement and Vietnam. The environmental movement and antinuclear protests. The student movement. The women's movement.

Decades later many of these same issues and movements would fuel the East German revolution of 1989, but I would not return to East Germany for many years.

After graduation, life intervened. Graduate school. Marriage. Moves. Jobs. Family. Then, almost 25 years later—in 1986—I had the opportunity to travel in the Soviet Union and Eastern Europe with a singing group from the Pacific Northwest, and I returned to East Germany and East Berlin for my first visit since 1964. Gorbachev had recently come to power in the Soviet Union, and signs of change were everywhere.

Every morning in Moscow I left my hotel and walked freely for several hours throughout the city—something unheard of just a year earlier—and our singing group staged an impromptu mini performance at St. Basil's. In Poland I visited a candlelight vigil honoring the slain oppositional priest Jerzy Popiełuzko and joined thousands of Poles at Czestochowa's Black Madonna, where Solidarity leader Lech Wałęsa and the Polish Pope John Paul featured side by side had inspired a nation to protest. But Cold War politics were still in place, and as our group crossed through (unreformed) Czechoslovakia by night train, Czech officials took all our transit visas, including those for our return trip through the country. We had to spend the next day at the Czechoslovak embassy in Budapest securing new visas—an easy source of western currency for Czechoslovakia.

I spent much of the train ride between Prague and Berlin standing in the corridor, talking with a young East German woman and hearing stories of unrest in her country. After our group sang in East German churches, we usually were invited to receptions where we had the opportunity to talk with church members. We heard about dissatisfactions, Gorbachev, pressures for reform.

*   *   *

The trip renewed my interest in East Germany and the political transformations occurring within the Soviet bloc and sent me back to graduate school at the University of Washington in Seattle to get a PhD in political science with a focus on East European politics. I wanted to learn more about what was going on—to make sense of the political changes I had witnessed as I traveled throughout Eastern Europe.

In 1988, I returned to the Soviet Union and East Germany, this time with my husband, Bill, and a group affiliated with the United Methodist Church Board of Global Ministries promoting peace and disarmament. We met with Soviets and East Germans. That summer, I met a number of people who wanted to leave their countries but were prohibited from doing so. Alex wanted to leave Russia, we learned later, after he took my husband and myself book shopping, and he especially wanted a sponsor in the United States. In Tbilisi, Georgia, a German-speaking woman approached me on the street—she thought I was perhaps German—and wanted to meet and talk with me, but at our planned meeting later, security police in the hotel lobby scared her off. I talked with her daughter by phone afterward and learned that the woman wanted to leave the Soviet Union, but she was too frightened to meet me again. In Tallinn, Estonia, I met a Jewish couple and their son who wanted to emigrate because they were persecuted in the Soviet Union. A young man at a reception for us American visitors in a church in Karl-Marx-Stadt (now Chemnitz), East Germany, passed a note to me saying he wanted to leave East Germany—to emigrate—but he wasn't allowed to do so.

In summer 1989 I returned alone to East Germany and studied German at the College of Economics in East Berlin. I flew into West Berlin and planned to cross by foot through Checkpoint Charlie, the best-known border crossing at the Wall into East Berlin. As I waited in line for the passport check and customs, the thought crossed my mind that officials might find contraband in my luggage. I almost always travel too heavy, and my suitcase and carry-on were stuffed with German dictionaries, grammars, and books on German verbs, along with research materials. Among them were copies of *Der Spiegel*, the often controversial West German weekly news magazine known for its investigative reporting and usually banned in East Germany. However, I passed the inspection without problem. The biggest problem was finding a taxi to take me to my dormitory in East Berlin's Karlshorst neighborhood (also the area where most Russian troops were stationed). I walked, pulling my suitcase and carry-on, for most of an hour before I found a street with taxis.

At the language institute we students and staff celebrated the French Revolution and the American Revolution and Independence on the Fourth of July.

At the party we sang "We Shall Overcome"—initiated by the East German head of the language institute—and I was surprised to hear that students from so many countries knew the song. Each country group put on a small program for the closing gathering. We Americans sang "Wild Thing," a song Jimi Hendrix of Seattle made famous at the Monterey Pop Festival two years before.

That summer I also became aware of the Stasi, the pervasive and infamous East German security police. One day I had decided to cut class and visit East Berlin's famous museums on Museum Island in the city center. From my dormitory I walked the several blocks to the U-Bahn (subway) station and waited for the next train. As soon as I sat down I noticed two of the student workers from the snack bar in our dormitory sitting across from me. One asked me where I was going, and I said I was taking the day off to visit museums. We rode together to Alexanderplatz, where we all exited. I headed down Unter den Linden toward the museums, and they walked with me. When I turned off toward the Pergamon Museum with its famous Pergamon Altar and Ishtar Gate of Babylon, I asked the two if they wanted to come with me, but they declined. I knew that at least one of them was a Stasi informer, because earlier that week he had been out with my friend Armando, an Italian communist, and under the influence of alcohol confessed that he had to go home to write his reports.

A highlight of my summer in East Berlin was meeting East Germans Maureen and Fritz plus Heidi and Harry through Armando who had already spent many vacations in East Germany. These two families would become my good friends and would provide supports of all kinds during my many trips to Berlin over the next 25 years.

After a month studying German in Berlin, I rented a car, picked up my husband, Bill, and teenage daughter, Jennifer, at the Vienna airport (my son Mark was away at college), and we began our 1989 road trip through Eastern Europe. Although we spent several days at Lake Balaton, Hungary, we did not realize the significance of the thousands of East Germans also there at the time; many hoped to cross into Austria—and they and other would-be emigrés would soon destabilize East Germany.

Then on to other legendary East European cities: Budapest, Sarajevo, Dubrovnik, Belgrade. At the Hungarian–Romanian border we waited for hours to cross into Romania—reputedly the country with the most hardline dictator-ship in Eastern Europe—in a line of cars that stretched for miles. The border guard, a middle-aged woman with a friendly smile, surprised us. She chuckled when she saw my *Russian in 10 Minutes a Day* book—said there was no way I could learn Russian in 10 minutes a day. We wanted to spend the night in Timisoara, but we didn't have reservations, so she offered to call ahead. Thanks to her help, we got the last hotel room in the city. We arrived late, driving through unlit, potholed streets. At the hotel they showed us to our room with a flashlight, and we fell into our beds in the dark. The next morning we woke to find that we had missed the hot water, which was already turned off for the day. We toured Timisoara briefly, long enough for me to get a warning not to take photographs. Just four months later the Romanian revolution, the only violent East European revolution of 1989, would start in Timisoara, and Nicolae Ceaus-escu would be deposed, convicted, and shot before the year ended. Later, after I finished my doctorate, I would teach political science and international relations at Romanian universities in Timisoara and in Cluj-Napoca as part of the Civic Education Project's program to take western social science courses and methods to universities in Eastern Europe and the Soviet Union.

After a summer in East Germany and Eastern Europe, I returned to Seat-tle in fall 1989, and while I was studying for and writing my general exams for my doctorate, demonstrations erupted throughout East Germany, and the Berlin Wall fell.

In spring 1990 I returned to East Berlin and spent several months there with friends. Every night we sat around the table with a bottle of wine, dis-cussing what had happened, what the future might hold. During the day I researched and searched for a dissertation topic. I had planned to study politi-cal change in East Germany, but the dramatic events of the past year argued for a new focus. The changes kept coming. Round Tables. The first and last free East German elections. Pressures for reunification with West Germany.

In summer 1990 I again studied German in East Berlin. While I was there, I witnessed Economic and Monetary Union on July 1, 1990.[2] Overnight, all East German products disappeared from the shelves of grocery stores, replaced by West German products. Economic and Monetary Union was quickly followed on Octo-ber 3, 1990, by reunification of political, governmental, and other systems as East

Germany was absorbed into the much larger and stronger West Germany. Now East Germany was part of the Federal Republic of Germany [*Bundesrepublik*].

During the summer I decided on the focus for my dissertation and fellowship application, and I met Marianne Schulz, then a sociologist at Humboldt University, who would become my advisor in East Germany and a good friend and support over the years. Although one American professor wanted me to study Neo-Nazis and their rise in East Germany after 1989, I couldn't imagine spending several years researching and writing about them, given their anger and negativity—and their focus on things I didn't believe in. All the events I witnessed led me to focus on the role of political groups and movements in the revolution of 1989, and I looked forward to interviewing activists and learning about their goals and activities that enabled them to change the world.

In Berlin, I heard stories of revolution and conducted preliminary research for my dissertation. An IREX (International Research and Exchanges Board) Fellowship with an affiliation at Berlin's Humboldt University supported a year in Germany, enabling me to interview more than sixty East German activists and others associated with the revolution of 1989 and to conduct archival research on East German groups and social movements.

In 1995 I published my PhD dissertation, *Democratizing East Germany: Ideas, Political Groups, and the Dynamics of Change* (Seattle: University of Washington). The comparative politics dissertation focused on political activism in three East German cities—Berlin, Leipzig, and Erfurt. In 1998 I published *After the Wall: Eastern Germany since 1989* (Boulder, CO: Westview Press), an assessment of the reunification process and eastern Germany's progress since reunification. Over the past 20 years, I have returned repeatedly to eastern Germany, where I continued my research and again interviewed activists from 1989.

I wrote *Revolution Revisited: Behind the Scenes in East Germany, 1989*, because I was inspired by the fearlessness of these activists as they took to the streets, inviting injury and arrest. Their beliefs that people can and do make a difference, their seemingly small local actions that ultimately changed the world, and their insistence on nonviolence moved me to want to know more.

I also wrote this book because English speakers in the west have seldom heard the story of these East German activists. Because the government controlled the press, media coverage of the 1989 demonstrations was limited. In addition, Leipzig, the center of revolutionary activity, was several hours by car or train from Berlin, where most international media coverage originated. Moreover, because calls for German reunification began shortly after the Berlin Wall fell, the emphasis quickly shifted from the demonstrations. In less than a year, East Germany was absorbed into the structures of the much larger Federal Republic of Germany—West Germany.

However, reunification was never the goal of most East German groups. They wanted a reformed, more democratic East Germany.

Another reason their story has seldom been told in the west is because explanations for the East German demonstrations and the fall of the Berlin Wall frequently focused on the contributions of the U.S., President Ronald Reagan, and West German Chancellor Helmut Kohl. Such explanations ignored the roles of small groups and ordinary people in the East German revolution of 1989. [See Appendix B explaining the East German Revolution of 1989.]

As I complete this book, my experiences with a divided Germany have come full circle. I was born the day after FDR died in 1945—as the Yalta talks and the victory of the allies in Europe ended WWII and divided Germany into sectors. I traveled to East Germany for the first time in 1964, shortly after the Berlin Wall was built, and since 1986, I have returned to the region almost every year. Now I'm again focusing on East Germany as I recount the experiences of small groups of courageous men and women seeking justice and democratic rights in a closed political system—activists who managed to create a revolution that changed not only their country but also the entire world. *Revolution Revisited: Behind the Scenes in East Germany, 1989,* is their story.

INTRODUCTION:

Prelude to Revolution

Whatever you can do, or dream you can, begin it. Boldness has genius, power, and magic in it. Begin it now.

—Johann Wolfgang von Goethe, Faust

In fall 1989, millions of television viewers throughout the world watched night after night, transfixed, as the people took to the streets in East Germany. Few could imagine the momentous events that would change the course of world history before the year's end. On November 9, 1989, the Berlin Wall fell, and East Germans streamed into West Berlin and West Germany. The world had changed.

Most of us know this part of the story. We know that the Wall had symbolized the division of Berlin, Germany, Europe, and the world into two hostile blocs. The Wall stood as the flash point of the Cold War, arguably the defining epoch of the twentieth century, with the United States and its NATO allies on the one side—the west—and the Soviet Union and its Warsaw Pact member countries on the other—the east. When the Berlin Wall fell, it signified the beginning of the end of communist control in Eastern Europe and set in motion actions that would end the Cold War.

But what many don't know is where that story begins—and that this major world change had its humble origins in a small group of activists not from Berlin but from the city of Leipzig, East Germany's second largest city about 100 miles south of Berlin.

During the first half of 1989, various Leipzig groups staged a series of small-scale public protests to highlight their demands for democratic reforms and to gain more supporters for their causes. Activists in Leipzig came from about twenty groups, most organized originally under the protective roof of the church, [3] the only non-state-affiliated organization allowed any, if limited, freedom to operate in East Germany. Later these groups moved away from the church, challenging the state from the streets. Following the model of Gandhi and Martin Luther King, Leipzig activists practiced nonviolence and promoted peaceful change.

1

Most group members were tied to like-minded "alternative thinkers" in other cities in East Germany and saw themselves as part of peace, environmental, or human rights movements. Some groups focused on study and discussion, while others focused on action. Some groups worked openly, others conspiratorially. Only a handful of the groups were self-consciously oppositional, but as the year progressed, members from other groups increasingly joined in activities and demonstrations that challenged the position of the state.

These activists achieved the rights and freedoms they desired by acting as if those rights already existed. When they met illegally, they exercised freedom of association. They joined together in unauthorized demonstrations to promote freedom of assembly. They published illicit *samizdat*[4] materials to promote freedom of the press and freedom of information. They spoke out at unsanctioned gatherings and sang and played at unauthorized festivals to promote freedom of expression, free speech.

Thomas Church, home of the world-renowned boys' choir
founded in 1212
Photo by Patricia Smith

This small group of committed activists dreamed of a better East Germany, a better political system, a better world. But they did not stop with dreams. They strategized, organized, and worked to turn their dreams into reality, and by autumn 1989 their small-scale protests promoting democratic reforms had grown to massive demonstrations involving hundreds of thousands and ultimately brought down the state.

*   *   *

Leipzig seemed an unlikely venue for political

Sign for Auerbach's Cellar, restaurant made
famous by Goethe's *Faust*
Photo by Patricia Smith

opposition and revolution. A city of slightly more than 500,000 inhabitants in 1989, Leipzig's population was a little more than half the population of Berlin. Leipzig had not fared well under almost forty years of communism. As an industrial center and one of the most polluted cities in East Germany and Eastern Europe, Leipzig had air that burned eyes and nostrils. Chemicals spewed from nearby Espenhain's oil, gas, and mining industries. Sewage ran through the canals of the Weisse Elster, the Pleisse, and the Parthe Rivers, making Leipzig's water unfit to drink.

The once proud city of Goethe, Schiller, Bach, and other great German writers and musicians, Leipzig in the post-World War II period had been devastated by neglect. Berliners, with access to the perks of power and influence, generally fared much better economically than Leipzigers. As the capital and showplace of communist East Germany, Berlin had received most of the money for building and renovation. For Leipzigers, only traces remained of better years in earlier times, like concerts at St. Thomas Church by the world-renowned boys' choir, founded in the year 1212, or meals at Auerbach's Keller (cellar), the restaurant made famous by Goethe's *Faust* and still patronized by Leipzigers and visitors from throughout the world. Almost all commercial buildings and apartments in Leipzig suffered from deferred maintenance, and abandoned buildings dotted the landscape.

The city's design almost encouraged demonstrations, however. Streets from every part of town led to the city center, like spokes on a wheel, and Leipzig's central ring, a series of connecting boulevards, surrounded the central city. Potential demonstrators from Leipzig could reach the center quite easily by foot, bicycle, auto, or inexpensive public transportation—no matter where they lived. Leipzig's central train station, one of the largest in Europe, stood on the

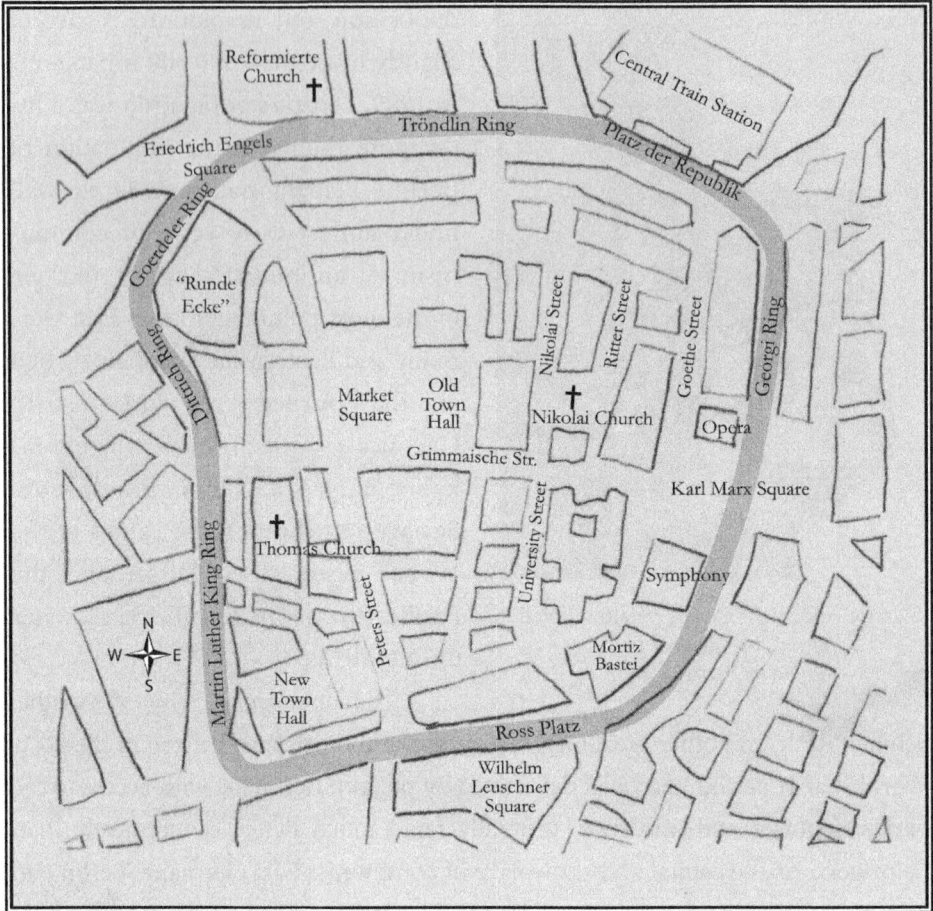

Map I-1 Sketch of Central Leipzig, 1989

Map of central Leipzig showing ring streets and key locations

northeast section of the ring, making it relatively easy for activists from through-out East Germany to reach Leipzig as the demonstrations escalated throughout Leipzig's hot fall of 1989.

In early September—a mere two months prior to the fall of the Berlin Wall—a handful of demonstrators marched in Leipzig following what had become a tradition of Monday night peace prayers. These mostly young group members had experienced the injustices of the East German political system, and they felt they needed to take action. Monday after Monday the number of demonstrators grew—hundreds, then thousands, later tens of thousands, hundreds of thousands of peaceful demonstrators taking part in candlelight vigils, carrying banners demanding free elections, free assembly, free speech. Proclaiming "We are the people!" and demanding nonviolent change.

The demonstrations quickly spread throughout East Germany—to Dresden, Karl-Marx-Stadt, Berlin, Plauen, Erfurt, Jena, Weimar, Wittenberg—by the end of October reaching more than 160 East German cities and towns. These popular uprisings climaxed with massive demonstrations on November 4 in Berlin involving one million participants and on November 6 in Leipzig, a city of 500,000 people, with 500,000 demonstrators. Three days later, the Berlin Wall fell.

* * *

Each chapter in Part I of *Revolution Revisited* focuses on one event or activity carried out by Leipzig activist groups during the first half of 1989—events that drew an increasingly larger base of participants into the movement for democratic reforms. The Rosa Luxemburg demonstration in January organized by Leipzig human rights groups initiated the demonstration cycle, and human rights groups played critical organizational roles in almost all the early protests. Next, demonstrations during the trade fairs drew a large group of emigration protestors (those who wanted to leave East Germany) into the movement. The Monday night peace prayers at Nikolai Church moved demonstrators from the church to the street. Election monitoring brought critical Marxists and communist party members into the movement for a more democratic East Germany. Environmentalists became more oppositional as they participated in the Pleisse memorial march, and the Alternative Church Congress involved a much larger proportion of church members in critical and oppositional activities.

In Part II of *Revolution Revisited,* these major groupings joined together in the huge demonstrations that ultimately brought down the East German state. Despite infiltration by East Germany's pervasive secret police and ongoing threats from security forces, the demonstrators practiced nonviolence and the demonstrations remained peaceful.

* * *

Revolution Revisited: Behind the Scenes in East Germany, 1989, tells the inspiring story of this small group of activists who mobilized the movement for democratic reforms, brought down the East German state, and changed the world. The book focuses on one year—1989—in one city—Leipzig, East Germany. By the end of the year, the group-initiated nonviolent demonstrations had prevailed. Erich Mielke, head of the infamous East German security police, the Stasi, later commented, "We were prepared for everything except for candles and prayers."[5]

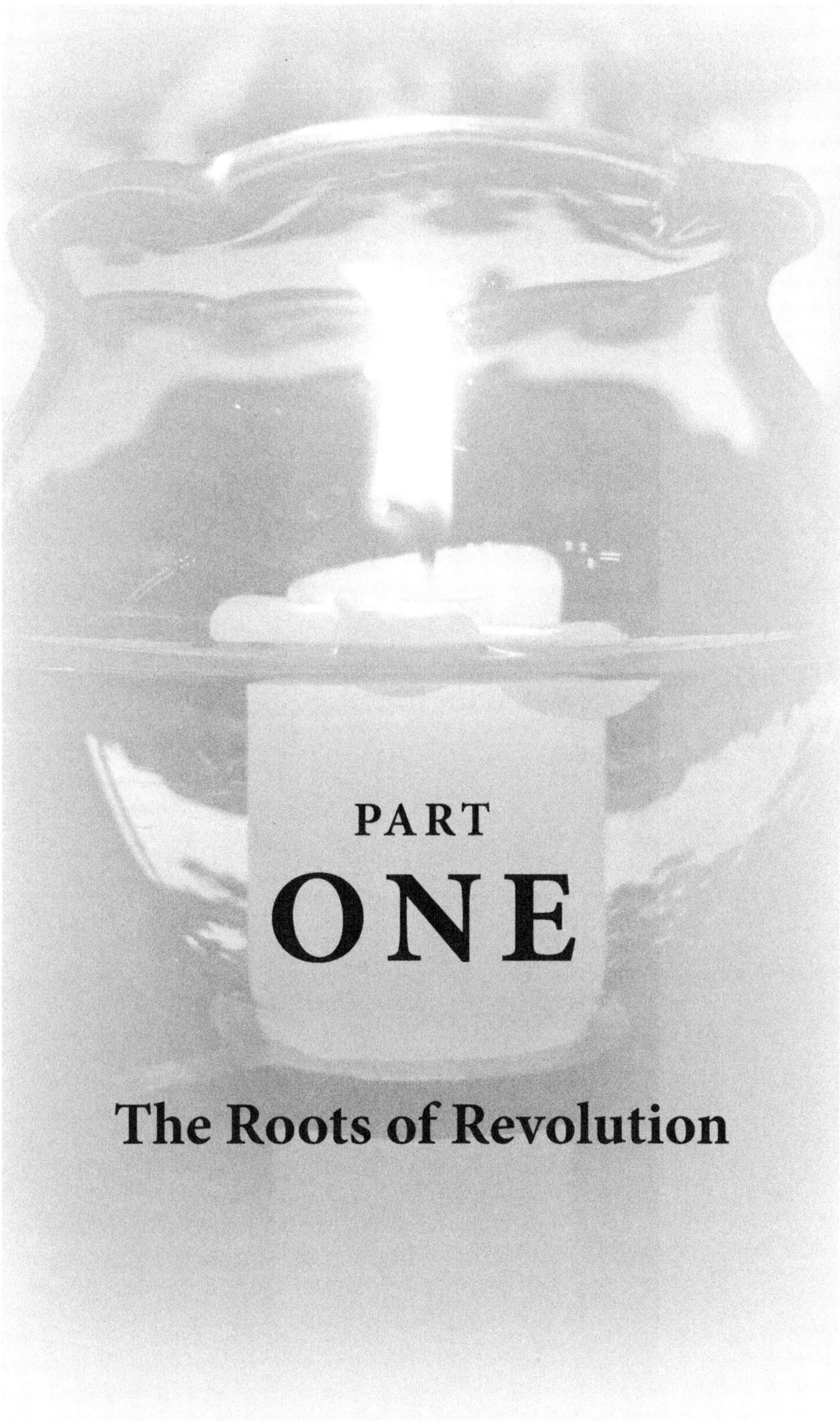

PART ONE

The Roots of Revolution

CHAPTER 1

Seizing the Initiative:
The Rosa Luxemburg Demonstration, January 15, 1989

Freedom is always freedom for the one who thinks differently.

—Rosa Luxemburg,
Cofounder, German Communist Party

We simply had to demonstrate with our own bodies that we wanted democratic rights and that we were prevented from getting them. Therefore some of us had to go to jail to demonstrate the injustice of the system. . . . And then others fought to get us out of prison. . . . That was right, because it brought a strong measure of believability. That's how the group dynamic functioned. . . . This had a huge solidarity effect.[6]

—Jochen Lässig,
Initiative Group Living, Leipzig

A Call to Action

Just after midnight on January 12, 1989, a small group of young women and men rushed to deliver their flyers to mailboxes in Leipzig's inner city and in several nearby suburbs. They knew they needed to work quickly. The handbill called for Leipzigers to meet for a silent demonstration honoring Rosa Luxemburg and Karl Liebknecht (the martyred cofounders of the German Communist Party) at 4:00 p.m. on Sunday, January 15, on Market Square in front of Old Town Hall. Both the handbill and the demonstration were illegal, and once authorities learned of their actions, these activists faced almost certain arrest.[7]

News of the flyers first reached the police shortly after 3:00 a.m. when a woman heard noise below in the entry hall of her apartment building and telephoned them. But by the time police discovered the illegal action, almost half of the 10,000 flyers had reached their intended destinations.

Producing any flyer, let alone 10,000 copies, strained the resources of the young activists. To prevent such unauthorized publications, East German authorities limited access to typewriters and mimeograph machines, ink, and even paper. There were almost no photocopy machines in East Germany in 1989, and an individual could purchase only a few sheets of paper at a time. To trace unauthorized publications back to their source, the Stasi, East Germany's notorious secret police, collected samples of text from typewriters just as they collected fingerprints from individuals and wiretapped their residences. Printing 10,000 copies required an enormous effort from the few group members involved—securing the supplies, typing up multiple stencils (one stencil could produce only several hundred copies), and cranking the mimeograph machine handle 10,000 times. Additionally, the fact that every step in producing and distributing the document challenged the state's control over information and expression put these activists at great risk for arrest.

The arrests began almost immediately. In two days, police held eleven group members in custody. The Stasi had infiltrated most of Leipzig's groups and identified the 11 as participants in the leafleting action.

Mimeograph machine
Photo from GMRE Inv.-Nr.: 03000

Signed by the group called the Initiative for the Democratic Renewal of Society and the brainchild of three recently founded human rights groups in Leipzig, the flyer urged East Germans to stand up for their rights—for freedom of expression, assembly, and the press as guaranteed in Articles 28 and 29 of the East German Constitution. The Initiative called for citizens to end their apathy, to stop conforming, and to work for the democratic renewal of East Germany by holding a silent demonstration parallel to the annual state-sponsored Rosa Luxemburg demonstration scheduled for January 15—a counterdemonstration.

In a state and society where conformity was valued and rewarded, the Initiative for Democratic Renewal's call for a counterdemonstration directly challenged the East German authorities. The flyer had not only been printed illegally, but it called for an unauthorized assembly, and it expressed ideas that threatened the state.

Through an elaborate system designed to create "a new socialist citizen," the state pressured East Germans to conform. In East Germany and elsewhere in the Soviet bloc, citizens were expected to join state-sponsored organizations and participate in state-sponsored activities like the annual Rosa Luxemburg demonstration and May Day parade in support of socialist workers, and most did. Reports suggest that in East Germany as many as 90 percent of those eligible for membership did belong to the pertinent mass association.[8] Organizations in the East German National Front, a coalition of state-affiliated organizations, included the Federation of German Trade Unions, the Free German Youth, the Cultural Federation, and the Women's Federation, along with the five state-affiliated political parties, with the Socialist Unity Party (SED) or communist party in the leading role.[9] Mass organizations and structured educational programs as well as sports and work-related activities all served to socialize East Germans. Acceptable behavior fell only within a narrow range, and nonconformists and challengers were ostracized and excluded from the benefits of the system, including good jobs and access to a university education.

The process of socialization was especially critical in East Germany because *socialism* was the key element that distinguished East Germans from West Germans, a separation reinforced by the 12-foot-high, 100-mile-long Berlin Wall between the two countries. At the time of their founding in 1949, both Germanys shared a common history, ethnicity, religion, and culture, including the recent Nazi period. Consequently, in the years following World War II, as the Cold War intensified, each new state attempted to differentiate itself from the other, and both attempted to tie themselves more closely to their respective blocs. East Germany followed the Soviet model for building a socialist state and a planned economy, while West Germany followed the western model of representative government and a market economy. Within each Germany—East and West—government structures and socialization programs were set up to mold their subjects into productive citizens and members of society. The state-sponsored Rosa Luxemburg demonstration was an example of this kind of government program.

In the flyer, the young authors of the Initiative for Democratic Renewal pointed out that the state had distorted Rosa Luxemburg's message. They argued that the state required East Germans to conform by joining state-sponsored demonstrations, when what Luxemburg represented, instead, was nonconformity and the right to voice differing opinions. In her writings and in her life Rosa Luxemburg had fought for freedom of expression and, especially, for the freedom of individuals to think independently. Luxemburg's famous quotation, "Freedom is always freedom for the one who thinks differently," even gave name to participants in alternative movements in East Germany—*Andersdenkenden,* or alternative thinkers—nonconformists who struggled to voice differing opinions in a conformist society.

The organizers in Leipzig modeled the 1989 Rosa Luxemburg protest after a similar, highly publicized protest in Berlin on January 1988. Unlike participants in the official Rosa Luxemburg parade, oppositional group demonstrators in Berlin carried unauthorized banners with slogans emphasizing that Luxemburg represented freedom and alternatives, rather than the conformity demanded by the East German state. The day of the protest in Berlin, state authorities arrested more than 120 demonstrators, and in the following weeks, a number of others were arrested, including some of the most prominent leaders of East Berlin's oppositional movement.

The Berlin arrests in 1988 had elicited a wave of support throughout East Germany. Vigils had been set up in numerous churches, and protest meetings had been held nightly. Contact telephone networks were activated across the country to coordinate solidarity efforts, and within days, solidarity demonstrations had been held in more than thirty East German cities.[10] Information concerning the arrests quickly reached groups elsewhere in Europe, who activated international contact networks and publicized the arrests. In response, hundreds of dissidents from throughout Eastern Europe signed a petition protesting the crackdown on East German activists.[11]

Groups in Leipzig also organized nightly candlelight vigils in support of those arrested in Berlin. As the number of participants grew, the vigils moved to Nikolai Church, revitalizing Leipzig's tradition of Monday night peace prayers. Attendance swelled at subsequent Monday night services at Nikolai Church— from more than 300 participants on January 18, 1988, to almost 1000 the next month as Leipzigers learned the fate of the Berlin activists. Many of those attending the services were emigration group members or would-be emigrants, and the 1988 Rosa Luxemburg affair led to many new applications for visas to leave East Germany and reinvigorated emigration groups.

Meanwhile, in East Berlin, church and state officials worked to resolve the crisis. Instead of long prison sentences, a negotiated settlement secured the release of many prominent oppositionists—many of them parents of young children. But against their will, many were sent into temporary exile abroad—to West Germany and Britain—rather than sent to prison in East Germany.[12] With the loss of so many prominent leaders, the Berlin movement floundered. Activists from throughout East Germany who had rallied in support were left without a focus or cause. Disappointed that their leaders had at least symbolically joined the emigration groups—East German citizens choosing to leave rather than to stay and fight for internal changes—the Berlin opposition withered, and the hub of oppositional activity shifted from Berlin to Leipzig.

Several Leipzig group members in Berlin at the time had participated directly in solidarity efforts for those arrested during the January 1988 Rosa Luxemburg affair and during the Stasi break-in at Zion Church two months earlier. The firsthand experience these Leipzig activists gained in Berlin proved invaluable for organizing subsequent events in Leipzig later in 1988 and throughout 1989. Leipzig activists seized the initiative and set up Leipzig as the center for revolutionary activity in East Germany. Already in January 1988 after the arrests and forced emigration of many Berlin activists, Leipzig activists began planning for a 1989 Rosa Luxemburg demonstration in Leipzig.

*   *   *

The 1989 leaflet prepared by the Initiative for Democratic Renewal in Leipzig called attention to the lack of reforms in East Germany, despite reforms throughout the Soviet bloc, and called on citizens of Leipzig to take action. When Mikhail Gorbachev came to power in 1985 as general secretary of the communist party of the Soviet Union, he began campaigning for political, economic, and social reforms. Gorbachev's programs—*glasnost* (openness), *perestroika* (restructuring), and *democratization*—helped legitimize calls for democratic reform in East Germany and other Soviet satellite states. By January 1989, Poland and Hungary had already implemented major changes, in some cases providing models for reform in the Soviet Union.

Gorbachev's Reforms*

Glasnost
> Policy promoting more openness and transparency in government. Encouraged open discussion of social and political issues and freer dissemination of news and information. *Glasnost* is the Russian word for "publicity." In East Germany, the equivalent term was *Öffentlichkeit*.

Perestroika
> Policy encouraging restructuring of the economy, government, and bureaucracy. Emphasized decentralization and reducing the central government's role in the economy and in government. A move away from central planning and toward a market economy.

Democratization
> Policies to make the political system more democratic. Promoted multiple candidates for elections (but not necessarily a multiparty system) and freer, fairer, and more transparent elections. Encouraged more citizen participation and some expansion of personal freedoms and human rights.

*Introduced after Mikhail Gorbachev assumed power in the Soviet Union in March 1985

East German citizens supporting Gorbachev's proposals hoped that at last East Germany, one of the last holdouts in Eastern Europe, would change, but the country's mostly old and conservative leaders continued to resist. East German communist party and government leader Erich Honecker reportedly told Gorbachev: "We have done our *perestroika,* we have nothing to restructure."[13] Honecker's argument that East Germany had already made the necessary economic reforms had a hollow ring in Leipzig, however. Wherever Leipzigers looked, they saw crumbling buildings and polluted air and water.

Leipzig Human Rights Groups

The three major human rights groups that organized the 1989 Rosa Luxemburg demonstration in Leipzig were Working Circle Justice, Working Group Human Rights, and Initiative Group Living. All founded in the late 1980s, they worked together on a number of projects, including the Initiative for Democratic Renewal, which was responsible for producing and distributing the leaflet

Leipzig Human Rights Groups

Initiative Group Living (IGL)

> **Work Areas/Themes:** Conscientious objection to military service; environmental protection; restructuring government and society; emigration

> **Key Members:** Michael Arnold, Uwe Schwabe, André Botz, Fred Kowasch, Jochen Lässig, Gesine Oltmanns

> **Tactics:** Open, public action; invited arrest

> **Founded:** 1987

Working Circle Justice (AKG)

> **Work Areas/Themes:** Free elections; a true multiparty system; representative democracy; emigration; media/press freedom

> **Key Members:** Thomas Rudolph, Kathrin Walther, Rainier Müller, Susanne Krug, Bernd Oehler, and Katrin Hattenhauer; earlier, Jochen Lässig and Gesine Oltmanns

> **Tactics:** Worked conspiratorially; used international media; prepared written documents to publicize programs and action in *samizdat* in East Germany and internationally, e.g., in *Die Mücke*

> **Founded:** 1987

Working Group Human Rights (AGM)

> **Work Areas/Themes:** *Öffentlichkeit*; freedom of expression; freedom of information; freedom of the press; issues related to military service and conscientious objection

> **Key Members:** Christoph Wonneberger, Frank Richter, Steffen Gresche (who later emigrated to West Berlin), Johannes Fischer, Oliver Kloß, Christoph Motzer, and Wolfgang Sarstedt

> **Tactics:** Contrasted what the state said in relation to various human and civil rights with actual practice; publicized human rights violations in international media

> **Founded:** 1986

prior to the 1989 protest. However, the three groups had separate identities and tactics and approached even joint projects quite differently.

More than half of the 11 activists arrested in Leipzig after the January 12, 1989, leafleting action belonged to Initiative Group Living (IGL)—among them Uwe Schwabe, Michael Arnold, Jochen Lässig, Frank Sellentin, André Botz, and Gesine Oltmanns. As prime organizer of the Rosa Luxemburg demonstration, the group called attention to problems with the political system and to restrictions on their basic civil rights—on their ability to speak freely, to assemble, and to print and distribute information. The organizers also wanted to highlight the fact that East German leaders continued to resist reform, despite Soviet leader Mikhail Gorbachev's calls for *perestroika, glasnost,* and *democratization.*

Initiative Group Living (IGL)

IGL used the symbolic Rosa Luxemburg march to highlight the group's primary goal—*Öffentlichkeit*—openness and public action, analogous to Gorbachev's *glasnost.* Members of IGL staged public demonstrations, held open meetings, signed their names and addresses to published documents, and made themselves visible to other Leipzig and East German citizens as well as to state authorities. For Gesine Oltmanns, public discussion and action represented a critical part of her work in IGL: "*Öffentlichkeit* was always very important for me. I saw myself as a person who wanted to reach the people. I wanted to provoke them to speak their own minds."[14] This visibility made group members likely targets for arrest as they challenged laws and publicly stood up to authorities.

The group's emphasis on public action differentiated IGL from most other groups in Leipzig and East Germany and represented a point of tension among groups. Fearing arrest, many East German groups avoided public action. Some feared arrest because they felt they could not carry out group activities and responsibilities if they were arrested. Others had to care for young children. Members of IGL, however, consciously staged public action to highlight their grievances—and to challenge authorities to arrest them.

Most members of IGL did not have significant prospects for the future in terms of education or employment, and because, like Jochen Lässig or Uwe Schwabe, they had little or nothing to lose, they did not fear arrest. In fact, many

---

*Öffentlichkeit**

- defined as "openness," "transparency," "publicity," "public opinion," "public sphere"
- similar to Gorbachev's *glasnost*
- a primary goal of most East German groups
- term brought into discussion in Germany years earlier by West German Jürgen Habermas**

East German group goals and tactics re. *Öffentlichkeit* included
- expanding the sphere of acceptable opinions, making space for alternative ideas
- promoting a human rights agenda when associated with freedom of expression, assembly, and the press
- "publishing" and distributing underground *samizdat* newsletters, journals, and books
- signing names with addresses and telephone numbers on documents (thereby risking arrest)
- using the western media to publicize group activities such as demonstrations and to call attention to government human rights violations, violence, and arrests

*See discussion of *Öffentlichkeit* in Patricia J. Smith, *Democratizing East Germany,* PhD dissertation (Seattle: University of Washington, 1995), 89–90.
**Jürgen Habermas, *The Structural Transformation of the Public Sphere*, published originally in German in 1962.

---

felt that public action, arrests, and prison time helped establish their legitimacy and might have a snowball effect on the movement, promoting "solidarity" and inspiring more action. Some members felt it was necessary to put their bodies on the line to demonstrate that they were being prevented from achieving their basic democratic rights.[15] According to Jochen Lässig, time in prison had a tremendous effect personally and as a solidarity effect for members of the group: "After going to prison, things went twice as well. Also, my personal life changed uncannily in a positive direction from my time in prison. Whoever was in prison had a higher value immediately afterwards."[16]

Freedom of expression and human rights were always at the top of IGL's agenda, as they focused on four work areas—conscientious objection to military service, headed by Uwe Schwabe; environmental protection, André Botz; restructuring government and society, Michael Arnold; and emigration, Fred Kowasch. Reflecting its loose organization and style, IGL seldom took formal votes on issues. Lässig remembered, "Decision-making in the group often occurred quite spontaneously with lots of discussion over political issues. *Glasnost* played a large role. . . . Discussions took place every day, sometimes continuing for days and even weeks."[17] The group also had a more formal decision-making structure, however. The four subgroups each met weekly, and after that, speakers from the subgroups would also meet to make decisions on behalf of the entire group.[18]

By meeting outside of church facilities, IGL and other human rights groups differentiated themselves from most other groups in Leipzig and in East Germany, and because they were not constrained by the church, the groups had more freedom and flexibility to initiate oppositional programs and take more radical actions. According to Uwe Schwabe, IGL "attempted, through public action outside the church, to make people aware of what was happening. . . . When we planned an action, we didn't always think out fully what we would do as a follow-up. We were the Kamikaze group."[19]

Members of IGL usually met in private homes,[20] and several members lived together communally in a dilapidated building at Zweinaundorfer Str. 20 in a neighborhood several miles east of Leipzig's center. Michael Arnold remembered, "We had this great room where, most importantly, we could smoke. We also had lots of fun there. . . . We didn't want to let ourselves be intimidated. . . . It was a time between great tension and euphoria, whenever we once again succeeded in bringing out the state powers."[21]

Working Circle Justice (AKG)

On January 12 police also arrested Rainer Müller, a member of Working Circle Justice, another key human rights group in Leipzig.

Working Circle Justice was less spontaneous than IGL and maintained more radical long-term goals such as western-style democracy, support for a multiparty system, and the abolition of the leading role of the communist party. Founded in December 1987, Working Circle Justice had 12 very active members, and by the summer of 1989 the size of the main group ranged from 35 to 60.

Swords to Ploughshares, Micah 4:3,
badge of peace movement

In his early twenties in 1989, Müller had participated in groups for years, and as part of the speakers' circle, he was a key decision-maker of Working Circle Justice.[22] Raised in Borna, a small town 20 miles southeast of Leipzig, Müller developed a reputation as a difficult student, and by ninth grade he had already stepped out of the system. As part of East Germany's independent peace movement, in the early 1980s he had protested by wearing the controversial "Swords to Ploughshares" badge with its biblical reference to Micah 4:3: "and they shall beat their swords into plowshares, and their spears into pruning hooks."[23] He also had refused to take part in the state-promoted *Jugendweihe* ceremony, the state-sponsored ceremony for 13- or 14-year-olds promoted as an alternative to the church's confirmation.

In school Müller was known as a questioner, challenging his teachers and the curriculum in civics and other classes. For political reasons, he was not allowed to take the *Abitur*, the East German examination and certificate that indicated high school completion and served as a ticket for college, and Müller's teacher reported that he had never before seen anyone with the best grades in his class denied the *Abitur*.[24] Without access to higher education, Müller first apprenticed as a bricklayer but later took a special exam and was admitted to theological study at Karl Marx University. However, he lost his permission to study at the university when he refused military service. Müller maintained contact with others in East Germany who had refused to serve in the military, and these became important connections for his oppositional activities.

Totally committed to the political opposition and to changing the system, Müller never considered leaving East Germany. Instead, he worked for change from within. "I had the strength to stay," said Müller. "We didn't want our country to fall apart. To everyone engaged in resistance as I was, it was clear that we stood with one

Rainer Müller in front of boarded-up building, Mariannenstraße 46
Photo by Frank Sellentin/Archiv Bürgerbewegung Leipzig e. V.

leg in prison. We couldn't, wouldn't do things halfway. Since we knew that sooner or later we would end up jail, we had no fear."[25]

The group also regularly published information about their activities and those of other Leipzig oppositional groups in *samizdat* periodicals. This information was in turn published in the *samizdat* newsletters of other East German groups. In addition, AKG periodically sent information through clandestine channels to publications in West Germany and East Europe, including the periodicals *Ost/Mittel Europa, Forum für Kirche und Menschenrechte,* and various publications of the Greens.[26] A particularly important publication, *Die Mücke,* produced jointly with Working Group Human Rights, outlined the action programs of Leipzig human rights groups. *Die Mücke* appeared in four separate *samizdat* journals and was also published in four issues of the West German *Ost-West Diskussionsforum.*[27]

In contrast to IGL's relatively loose organization, Working Circle Justice (AKG) had a much tighter and more hierarchical organizational structure and required more of its members. As speaker Thomas Rudolph emphasized, if members "didn't participate in the work of the group, they weren't considered

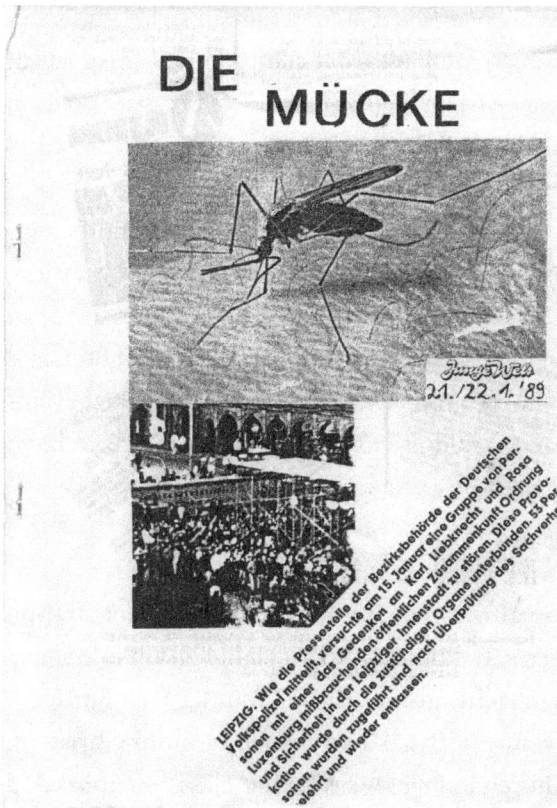

DIE MÜCKE

21./22.1.'89

Die Mücke, samizdat publication of Leipzig
human rights groups
Source: Archiv Bürgerbewegung Leipzig e. V.

part of the working circle."[28] The group also had a different decision-making structure than most groups. According to Rudolph,

Working Circle Justice did not follow a grassroots model where everyone had the opportunity to speak out on issues and decisions were made through consensus. In our group responsibility was delegated upward, and the speakers' circle composed of five speakers made decisions on behalf of the group. The speakers were competent and responsible, and they also assumed responsibility for contacts outside the group.[29]

Generally the most active members of the group were members of the speakers' circle, which included Kathrin Walther, Susanne Krug, and Bernd Oehler, along with Müller and Rudolph.

Working Circle Justice used pressure from outside Leipzig and outside East Germany to accomplish its goals.[30] An important tactic involved publicizing activities of Leipzig oppositional groups and information about arrests and solidarity action in the international media. Because the government-controlled East German press, radio, and television seldom published or broadcast stories on East German groups, Working Circle Justice and a few other oppositional groups took their reports on activists through clandestine channels to western media outlets in an attempt to inform East German citizens and the broader international community about East German groups.

The tactic was a point of controversy even among human rights groups in Leipzig. Some felt that using the international media compromised the goals of groups that favored a reformed East Germany rather than a western-style political system. Others felt that the international media was generally a tool of the west and that its coverage frequently trivialized or distorted events that took place in East Germany. Jochen Lässig of IGL spoke about a "great misunderstanding from the outside" and argued, "The media showed only what it wanted to show."[31] Nevertheless, contact with the western print, radio, and television media represented an extremely important tactic of Working Circle Justice for publicizing conditions and events in Leipzig.[32] Throughout 1989 the group would continue to publicize events through the international media and would use its international contacts to build solidarity and to secure the release of those arrested.

Working Group Human Rights (AGM)

A third group involved in organizing the Rosa Luxemburg demonstration was Working Group Human Rights, the oldest human rights group in Leipzig and a group tied closely to human rights groups throughout Eastern Europe.[33] In September 1986 a group of young activists had formed around Christoph Wonneberger, pastor of Lukas Church in Leipzig's working-class neighborhood of Volksmarsdorf east of the city center. Active members of the group besides Wonneberger included Frank Richter, Steffen Gresch (who later emigrated to West Berlin), Johannes Fischer, Oliver Kloß, Christoph Motzer, and Wolfgang Sarstedt, who was later identified as a Stasi informer.

A key figure of the opposition and one of the persons in East Germany most connected to a wide variety of groups (e.g., church, draft resisters, peace, human rights), Christoph Wonneberger had been observed by the Stasi since the early 1970s. Under pressure from church and state authorities for his work with the independent peace movement and his central role in creating the model for peace prayers in East Germany, the impetus for Leipzig's Monday night peace prayers, Wonneberger had moved to Leipzig from Dresden's Weinberger Church in 1985.[34] Forty-five years old in 1989 and viewed by many as the grand old man of the Leipzig opposition, Wonneberger regularly made space available at Lukas Church for controversial groups and activities that were not allowed to meet elsewhere.

Destroyed apartment building with Lukas Church in background
Photo by Frank Sellentin/Archiv Bürgerbewegung Leipzig e. V.

Wonneberger's earlier involvements and connections to various church and alternative groups throughout East Germany enabled Working Group Human Rights and other Leipzig groups to tap into a number of already well established contact networks. An early conscientious objector and peace activist, Wonneberger maintained contact with numerous activists from these groups throughout East Germany and beyond.[35] Through his contacts with oppositional pastors and others, Wonneberger had access to literature of the East German and East European opposition, as well as to West German groups, and he set up a *samizdat* library in Lukas Church to make these documents available to Leipzig activists.

For Wonneberger, a lasting memory that informed his activism was his visit to Prague as a young man in August 1968. There he had witnessed Soviet tanks and troops, supported by Soviet bloc member states Bulgaria, Poland, and Hungary, attacking activists and other citizens and crushing the Czechoslovak reform movement, Prague Spring.

Working Group Human Rights promoted freedom of expression and especially the freedom to hold differing opinions. According to Wonneberger, "The group's most important goal was *Öffentlichkeit*"—to fashion a public space for ideas and action—"so that one could do something."[36] Within the group, members focused on various human rights themes. Besides freedom of expression, these included freedom of information, freedom of the press, and issues related to military service and conscientious objection. The group's first project was a public meeting on freedom of expression held May 24, 1986, in Michaelis Church.

Working Group Human Rights pushed for consistency in what the state said in its policies and what it did in regard to East German citizens. An important tactic the group used was to call attention to the state's rhetoric in relation to various human and civil rights and to contrast this with actual practice. Groups would point to violations of rights guaranteed under East German laws and would publicize these violations throughout East Germany and in the international media. The three Leipzig human rights groups joining in the Initiative for Democratic Renewal used this tactic for the Rosa Luxemburg demonstration, and they would use it repeatedly as they organized demonstrations and other public action throughout 1989.

*   *   *

Leipzig oppositional groups took this tactic a step further and regularly called attention to the East German state's violation of United Nations and Helsinki human rights provisions.[37] When East Germany failed to uphold basic human rights by arresting activists for distributing flyers and participating in the January 1989 Rosa Luxemburg demonstration, the Conference on Security and Cooperation in Europe (CSCE) was convening Helsinki follow-up meetings in nearby Vienna. Using their underground and various third-party connections, East German human rights groups contacted foreign ministers and others attending the conference to report the arrests and violations of Helsinki, and they also informed other East European human rights groups and public officials in east and west of the events in Leipzig.

The Role of the Church

To escape the expectations and demands of the state, many retreated into a "niche" society, finding satisfaction in family and friendship groups. Others found their niche—an alternative to what the state promoted—in the church, the only organization allowed in East Germany that was not affiliated with the state.[38]

Unlike in many other communist states where the church was prohibited, in East Germany a complicated church-state relationship allowed churches to continue, and more than six million people belonged to East German churches, almost 40 percent of the population. Joining the church, however, put people on a certain path, or "track," subjecting them to discrimination and disqualifying them from various perks of joining the system. Many children raised in Christian families were excluded from state universities and could not find jobs except in church-related positions—or if one found a job, it was hard to advance without communist party membership. Within the church, too, there were limits to what an individual or group could say or do, as Leipzig group members had learned.[39]

Although many Leipzig group members had been pressured to join the Free German Youth and other state organizations, most had resisted, struggling against pressures to conform. Rather than confront what they viewed as an unjust system, many found refuge in the church. Some had refused to participate in the *Jugendweihe*, as had Rainer Müller. Still others had refused to serve in the military. As Jochen Lässig of Leipzig's IGL emphasized, "We were all outsiders. We were all from religious or intellectual backgrounds, or anarchists, or from some other alternative milieu, and we were fully disconnected from the system."[40]

Kathrin Walther, one of the organizers of Leipzig's Rosa Luxemburg demonstration, had initially participated in state-sponsored youth programs including Young Pioneers and Free German Youth. However, she left the state-affiliated groups and joined Leipzig's Working Group Human Rights when she was only 16 years old.[41]

According to Walther, she got involved with alternative groups in the church's youth program [*Jugendgemeinde*] because it was important for her to be able to think about things differently and to not have to conform. Walther went further, however. While participants in alternative movement groups tended to step out of society, stop conforming, and join others with similar ideas and interests, a few like Walther moved to oppositional groups that directly challenged the state. According to Walther, the basic question that led to her involvement in human rights groups, among the most oppositional in East Germany, was "Do you want democracy or not? I joined the opposition (I protested) because I wouldn't accept that a person in East Germany could not express herself freely and had no chance to advance in society without joining the communist party."[42]

Solidarity with the Arrested

On the morning of January 14, members of Working Circle Justice and Working Group Human Rights set up an information center in Lukas Church to work for the release of the 11 activists arrested for distributing flyers, and members began notifying groups throughout East Germany. Primary organizers of this contact network included Thomas Rudolph, Kathrin Walther, and Susanne Krug of Working Circle Justice, and Frank Richter of Working Group Human Rights.

Contact Bureaus

Church-based telephone networks were critical to the solidarity efforts of East German groups, given the difficulty many East Germans had in getting access to telephones. Because telephones were controlled in East Germany, only one in six East German families had a telephone, and the waiting list for a phone was years long, so private individuals had limited access to telephones, and when they had phones, the phones were usually monitored by the Stasi. The problem was even more severe for activists, most of whom were personally under surveillance.

From the offices of Lukas Church, Kathrin Walther, along with others, organized solidarity actions to press for the release of those arrested.[43] Walther, one of the youngest oppositional group members, worked behind the scenes to coordinate the efforts of these contact networks of Leipzig human rights groups throughout East Germany and internationally. (Although Walther's parents did not try to prevent her involvement with oppositional groups—her father had been a communist party member but was critical of the East German regime—they did request that she not stand in the front row of oppositional activities and face probable arrest before she reached adulthood.)

Kathrin Walther's telephone log from January 19, 1989, containing information about calls she made that day for the oppositional network, illustrates the wide variety of contacts Leipzig groups could call on.[44] These ranged from local group members; to East German groups in human rights, peace, and environmental movements; to pastors and church officials within East Germany; to activists in other East European countries; to members of western political parties and other organizations.

Oppositional Networks

Various networks linked human rights groups and other oppositional groups together. Members of the clandestine oppositional network that coordinated group efforts within Leipzig included the three Leipzig oppositional human rights groups, Working Circle Justice, Working Group Human Rights, and Initiative Group Living, as well as several more oppositional members of other groups. A steering committee composed of leaders from these groups met regularly to plan and coordinate an oppositional program.[45] Although these groups never agreed on a common program, a consensus did develop among them on the importance of human rights issues and on the importance of action programs to promote their goals.[46]

Beginning in mid-1988, members of Working Circle Justice coordinated a network of oppositional groups in the southern part of East Germany, inviting them to Leipzig once a month. About 25 groups from the regions of Saxony and Thuringia participated in the oppositional network, as well as groups from Magdeburg, Berlin, and other cities. The network provided organizational information that coordinated the programs of oppositional groups throughout East Germany.[47]

With the support of the contact network of this so-called Saturday Circle, Leipzig activists succeeded in publicizing the Leipzig arrests throughout East Germany and in the international arena, linking them to a broader oppositional movement.

The International Media and Other International Contacts

Thomas Rudolph, a member of Working Circle Justice and one of the masterminds of the Leipzig opposition, favored conspiratorial action and seldom participated in demonstrations. Instead, he spearheaded the media efforts of Leipzig's oppositional groups, especially as they publicized events in the international media. Highlighting East Germany's failure to conform to international standards of freedom and human rights, these organizations discredited the East German government and pressured it to change policies and to release political prisoners. Although human rights groups in other East European states—Poland, Czechoslovakia, Hungary—had successfully used international publicity for years to protect group members or to secure their release from prison, most East German groups opposed this tactic.

For some East German human rights groups and for Thomas Rudolph of Working Circle Justice, however, the international media constituted a critical element of the groups' strategy. "One can't bring down a dictatorship as an individual fighter, but only with a disciplined, effective team. We had various, clearly defined assignments,"[48] said Rudolph, describing the network developed by Working Circle Justice to deliver news and photos from Leipzig and other East German groups to their contacts in the international media. He called these contact networks an *Ameisentransport*—an ant brigade.

This transport usually involved Katherine Walther of Working Circle Justice and Frank Richter of Working Group Human Rights taking materials from Leipzig to East Berlin by motorcycle. There, Susanne Krug, also a group member from Leipzig, delivered the documents to contacts from the Associated Press or the German Press Association. The contacts in these organizations then carried the documents over the border from East Berlin and East Germany to the west.[49]

This system, employed in January 1989 in conjunction with the Rosa Luxemburg silent march, would be utilized over and over during 1989. By fall, the system provided well-established lines of communication from Leipzig to international news services in the west.

The Stasi thought agents from the west had infiltrated East German groups to promote unrest. They never grasped the fact that, instead, East German group members themselves—key among them Rudolph and Walther in Leipzig—were the source of the information as they sought out western politicians, organizations, and journalists to publicize stories of East German unrest.[50]

Using UN and Helsinki Human Rights Agreements

While the Rosa Luxemburg events unfolded in Leipzig in January 1989, high-level government officials from 35 countries, including western democracies, attended the follow-up meetings to the Helsinki human rights agreements of the Conference on Security and Cooperation in Europe convening in Vienna. These leaders publicly condemned the actions of East Germany. U.S. Secretary of State George Schulz confronted his East German counterpart, Oskar Fischer, about the arrests of human rights demonstrators in Leipzig for exercising their civil rights guaranteed under Helsinki.[51] Letters and telegrams protesting the actions of the East German government in Leipzig poured into Vienna from Europe and America, demanding the release of those arrested.

Meanwhile, in Berlin, East German leader Erich Honecker also received communications protesting attempts to criminalize East German citizens and to deny them their basic rights. The director of the Heinrich Böll Foundation telegraphed, "It is shocking that citizens of East Germany were once again arrested for simply exercising their constitutionally guaranteed rights and then were prevented from freely expressing their opinions."[52] Leipzig District Attorney Lehmann also received letters and telegrams. An open letter from the Green Party in Gladbeck, West Germany, stated, "We protest the ongoing attempt to criminalize and intimidate critical citizens. Preventing that kind of action is in your interest so that East Germany doesn't become the laughing stock of the international community."[53]

January 15, 1989

Despite the arrests earlier that week and the continued detention of 11 group members in Leipzig, on January 15, 1989, hundreds of protesters defied authorities and gathered for the Rosa Luxemburg demonstration on Market Square near Old Town Hall.[54] Fred Kowasch of Initiative Group Living spoke briefly to the group from the entrance to the underground Trade Center Hall, emphasizing that they had gathered to show that fundamental freedoms guaranteed in the East German constitution were not being upheld. Kowasch closed his speech by again quoting Rosa Luxemburg: "Without unrestricted freedom of speech, press and assembly, public life dies."[55]

Old Town Hall and Market Square
Photo by Patricia Smith

Fred Kowasch at Rosa Luxemburg Demonstration, Market Square
Private photo

Rosa Luxemburg Demonstration, January 15, 1989
Private photo

When Kowasch finished speaking, the gathering headed south toward Braustrasse and the Karl Liebknecht memorial. Others joined the unauthorized protest, forming a group of about 800 demonstrators. Several hundred of the protestors headed south from Market Square down Petersstrasse in the direction of the New Town Hall and Dimitroffplatz (Dimitroff Square). When they reached Floßplatz, they encountered armed police.

Security forces had mobilized, taking positions in several central Leipzig locations.[56] Standing shoulder to shoulder with nightsticks in hand, police and other armed forces blocked the intersection. Supported by dogs and water cannons, they stood ready to maintain public order and security as they encountered the unauthorized demonstration consisting of mostly young "enemies of the state." Before the demonstrations ended that day, security forces had arrested 53 demonstrators, dragged them into police wagons, and taken them to jail to await their charges.

In spite of the show of force, however, not all security personnel had been prepared to take action against the demonstrators that day. Some questioned how they could carry out what they were being asked to do—to take action against East German citizens who didn't necessarily do anything wrong. One Leipzig soldier assigned to a unit backing up police that day wrote, "I stand here as a policeman, but I have to do things as a soldier that I can't in good conscience do."[57] The reluctance of security forces to attack their fellow East German citizens participating in peaceful demonstrations—perhaps even family and friends—would play out repeatedly throughout 1989.

The next day, January 16, Fred Kowasch was also arrested for his part as speaker at the demonstration that had gathered on Market Square the previous day. Other group members arrested for their roles in Leipzig's unauthorized demonstration also heard their charges.[58] Michael Arnold, Jochen Lässig, Uwe Schwabe, Gesine Oltmanns, and others involved in the leafleting action were charged under Article 214 of the East German penal code for "impeding state or social activity." If convicted, they would face up to three years in prison just for passing out leaflets. Carola Bornschlagel was charged under Article 217 for "riotous assembly" and faced up to two years in prison. Several other persons involved in the oppositional group network coordinated by Leipzig activists were questioned by the Stasi and warned to discontinue their activities or to face arrest for "association to pursue illegal aims and purposes," a charge carrying up to five years in prison and up to eight years for those viewed as leaders. Others charged for printing or distributing leaflets faced fines of from 300 to 500 marks, exorbitant fines in relation to their small salaries.

Follow-up and Release of the Arrested

Leipzig groups instituted follow-up actions almost immediately to demonstrate solidarity with the arrested. On the evening of January 16, more than 500 people attended a prayer service in Lukas Church to support those arrested in the Rosa Luxemburg silent demonstration on January 15 and in the days leading up to it, but church officials reacted differently.

After the arrests, Superintendent Friedrich Magirius of the Leipzig-East church district and Superintendent Johannes Richter of Leipzig-West sent out communications to pastors and churches in Leipzig encouraging them to mention those arrested during worship services, though they did not support the group-organized Rosa Luxemburg demonstration. The superintendents argued that they could not support groups because the Lutheran Church did not support the materialistic worldview of Luxemburg and Liebknecht, and because "political demonstrations cannot be an acceptable form of witness for the church."[59] In Dresden, the bishop of the church office for the state of Saxony, which included Leipzig, also separated himself from the groups and supported the superintendents. Tensions between groups and church leaders in Leipzig would continue throughout 1989, even though later in the year many church members and leaders would join demonstrations and other group-organized activities (and some church leaders would claim credit for organizing and promoting them).

The statements by church officials refusing to support the groups triggered responses from church-related groups throughout East Germany. One letter from eight Berlin groups challenged the Leipzig superintendents' and bishop's positions. Citing Christ's story of the good Samaritan, the Berlin groups argued that the role of the church was to stand behind all who suffer, including those who think differently and those released from prison.[60] The Gospel of Christ sometimes requires that Christians stand up and take public action, they said.

Protests using the human rights provisions of the Helsinki accords also had their impact. Leaders from Europe and the United States attending the Vienna meetings of the Conference on Security and Cooperation in Europe had called for East Germany to release the prisoners arrested during the Rosa Luxemburg affair. As a result of the many-faceted protests from east and west, all those arrested during the Luxemburg affair were released from Leipzig's Beethoven Street prison by January 20.

Called to task and embarrassed by the international publicity, Honecker and East German authorities vowed to control future demonstrations in Leipzig, using whatever force was required.

* * *

The three Leipzig human rights groups had succeeded. Joining together as the Initiative for Democratic Renewal, they had planned and carried out a public demonstration and called attention to problems in Leipzig and in East Germany. They had organized solidarity efforts, sending news of the demonstration and arrests through Leipzig and throughout East Germany—and they had successfully used international meetings and the international media to publicize the Luxemburg demonstration.

These groups had demonstrated that they had the courage and the organizational abilities to confront the East German state. They had succeeded in bringing their demands for freedom of expression, assembly, and the press into the public arena. Through this first group-organized demonstration of 1989, Leipzig human rights groups provided a taste of what later months would bring as they continued to confront East German authorities and publicize their demands for democratic reforms. With the Rosa Luxemburg demonstration, these Leipzig human rights groups had established a pattern that would be followed again and again in the months ahead—first in Leipzig and later throughout East Germany.

CHAPTER 2

Joining Forces:
Emigration Groups and Freedom of Movement,
March 13, 1989

We recognized early in comparison to most groups that it was necessary to work with emigration groups—that groups in the area would be strengthened by working together. [61]

—Jochen Lässig,
Initiative Group Living, Leipzig

No one in Initiative for Peace and Human Rights was allowed to travel in Eastern Europe. We lived in a completely closed land. [62]

—Regina (Lotte) Templin,
Initiative for Peace and Human Rights, Berlin

Many East Germans simply wanted out.

The first Rosa Luxemburg affair in Berlin in January 1988 not only galvanized the human rights activists but also energized emigration—or "exit"—groups and individuals who wanted to move abroad. Those wanting to emigrate saw how the state had handled the leading members of Berlin opposition groups. Those group members had been arrested, and many had been sent out of the country to West Germany and Great Britain as the result of a negotiated settlement between church and state officials. Would-be emigrés attempted to link their fates to these Berliners, hoping to increase their own chances to emigrate. They hoped that East German authorities would also send them out of the country to quiet their protests. Consequently, the forced emigrations in Berlin unleashed a flood of new applications and reapplications for emigration throughout East Germany, overwhelming state officials. Hoping to defuse the situation, state authorities did decide to allow thousands to emigrate; however, the strategy backfired and resulted in even more exit applications.

During 1988 and early 1989 emigration from East Germany to West Germany increased dramatically. East Germany's Interior Ministry reported that the number of those illegally crossing the border to West Germany increased 87.6 percent during 1988. West Germany's Interior Ministry reported that 29,031 persons had legally left East Germany and moved to West Germany during 1988, and 9,718 had fled illegally.[63] And still, only a small percentage of those who wanted to go were allowed to leave or managed to cross the inner German border or the Berlin Wall illegally. In the first half of 1989 alone, 125,429 East German citizens filed *new* applications to emigrate; thousands more had filed earlier, in a country with a population of only 17 million. During those six months, however, about 40,000—only a small proportion of all applicants—received permission to leave East Germany. These poor odds for receiving a visa led many applicants to look for new methods to call attention to their cause.

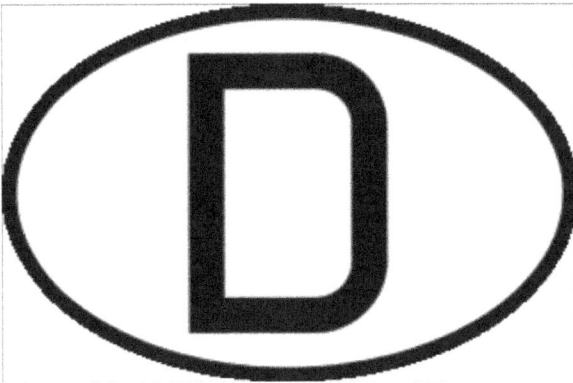

"D" vehicle registration symbol for *Deutschland*
(West Germany)

Increasingly, those wanting to leave their East German homeland identified themselves publicly.[64] Some attached white flags to their car antennas. Others changed the "DDR" for *Deutsche Demokratische Republik* (East Germany) on their car plates or on decals to a simple "D" for *Deutschland* (West Germany). In 1988 posters appeared displaying a red heart with drops of blood and the words "let's go," or the given names of persons wanting to emigrate. Signs appeared in windows of homes with a large letter A for *Ausreise* (emigration) printed on them.

Applications for emigration listed many reasons for wanting to leave East Germany and move abroad.[65] One of the most frequent was the increasingly long waiting time to buy a car—four, six, and up to ten years for an East German *Trabant*—and problems getting repairs and keeping vehicles running. Applicants also complained about the scarcity of fruits and vegetables, the shortage or absence of fashionable clothing and modern consumer goods, and the high costs of these items relative to wages and salaries. Also mentioned frequently were the shrinking opportunities for travel outside East Germany. Many complained about inadequate housing, certainly no surprise in Leipzig where decaying buildings dotted the city. Others pointed to broader societal and political problems: waning trust in socialism and growing discontent with the environmental situation in East Germany.

For many people who had stepped out of the system for various reasons, the situation in East Germany had become intolerable. Some who wanted to emigrate were misfits who for many reasons found it impossible to fit in and to meet the expectations of East German state and society and then were penalized for not conforming. These included gays and lesbians, alternative artisits and musicians, and individuals who for political reasons had poor educational and career opportunities. All were dissatisfied with their country and had given up hope that East Germany could or would change.

After applying for emigration visas, many found life in East Germany even more difficult, almost unbearable. Applicants paid heavy penalties. Frequently they couldn't go to school or get jobs, or their children couldn't succeed in school. They were pariahs, outcasts rejected by state and society and by most other East German groups, so the decision to apply for a visa to leave East Germany was a difficult choice. But difficult, too, was the decision of Leipzig groups like Working Circle Human Rights and Initiative Group Living to join forces with emigration groups and support their activities.

Members of other church-related alternative and oppositional groups also complained about conditions in East Germany, but their complaints generally differed dramatically from those articulated by would-be emigrés. Rather than centering on material goods, demands of most group members wanting to stay in East Germany centered on expanded civil rights and basic freedoms, environmental concerns, and issues related to peace and justice. So, while the grievances of emigration groups set them apart from most groups and church members, their concerns did begin to resonate with a cross-section of East German society: factory and office workers, medical personnel, bus drivers, artists. Many of these dissatisfied citizens belonged neither to groups nor to churches, and most had little or no access to the perks of power and influence. Most kept their complaints silent and retreated to the company of family and friends. But in Leipzig during 1988 and 1989, both emigration groups and opposition groups took their grievances into the public arena in an attempt to reach a broader base of dissatisfied East Germans.

The next major demonstration in Leipzig would take place in March of 1989, and this demonstration would involve both emigration groups and opposition groups.

A Divided Germany, Emigration, and the Berlin Wall

Emigration had played a role throughout East Germany's history, with mass exoduses occurring on repeated occasions.[66] Thousands fled the country in the late 1940s after World War II as the communists consolidated power and nationalized industries. Large numbers of health professionals left in 1950–51 with the nationalization of health care, and more than 20,000 farmers fled to the west when East Germany began collectivizing farms. Thousands more left in 1953 during the workers' uprising that started in Berlin and spread to more than 400 cities in East Germany before Soviet authorities sent in troops and tanks to quell the unrest. Numbers of emigrants spiked again in 1960–61 as East Germans fled to the west, fearing the closing of the East German borders. And in just one month, August 1961, prior to and during the construction of the Berlin Wall, 47,433 East Germans left the small country with a population of only 17 million. Later, shortly after the Helsinki accords were signed in 1975, from 100,000 to 200,000 East Germans applied for exit visas.[67]

Throughout the 1950s and into the early 1960s East and West Germans could move relatively freely between East and West Berlin; however, as West Berlin and West Germany prospered, economic pressures and currency issues led many East Germans to move west. In the late 1950s East Germany, with the support of the Soviet Union, constructed a barbed-wire fence with guard towers and closed the inner German border separating East Germany from West Germany, but Germans from East and West Germany could still move freely between East and West Berlin, which lay inside the borders of East Germany, and transit highways from Berlin allowed travel between West Berlin and West Germany.

In the early 1960s East German leaders decided that they had to do something more to stem the migration of East Germans and the flow of currency to the

Inner German border
Photo by Rainer Kühn/Archiv Bürgerbewegung Leipzig e. V.

Watch tower, Potsdam, East Germany
Photo by Rainer Kühn/Archiv Bürgerbewegung Leipzig e. V.

A Divided Germany and the Cold War

The sites of spy novels and real-life intrigue, Berlin and East Germany stood on the front lines of the Cold War for almost half a century. When Roosevelt, Churchill, and Stalin met in Yalta in 1945 to plan for the peace treaties ending World War II in Europe, a central concern was what to do about Germany, the aggressor in both World War I and World War II. They felt a divided Germany would mean a weakened Germany, and they drew boundaries that divided Europe and Germany into four zones. The four powers—the United States, Great Britain, France and the Soviet Union—each controlled a sector, and Berlin was also divided into four sectors.

The occupying powers went about trying to shape the four sectors, or occupation zones, in their own images. As the Cold War heated up, conflicts between east and west intensified. Already in 1948, the Soviet Union attempted to cut off supplies to West Berlin, which lay in the heart of the Soviet occupation zone, by blocking all land and river access to the city. In response, the United States, along with Great Britain and France, instituted the Berlin airlift and managed to supply West Berlin with food and other goods for almost a year.

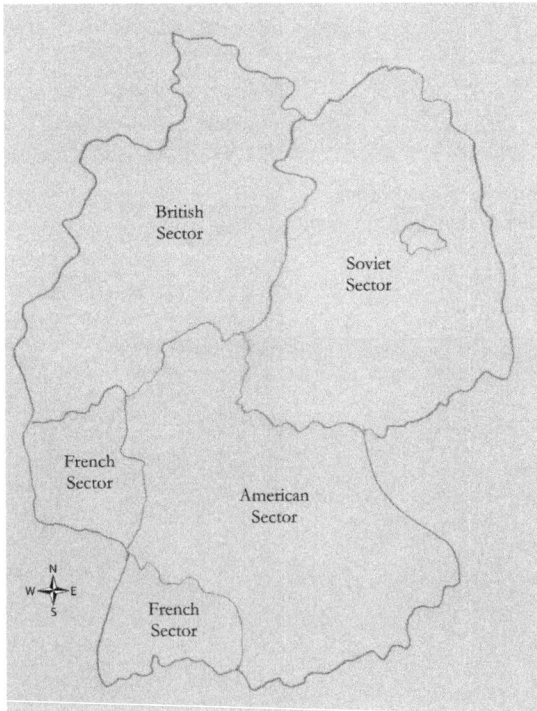

Map 2-1 Germany, 1945
Map showing Germany divided into four sectors, 1945

In 1949, the two Germanys declared their independence—the German Democratic Republic (GDR), or East Germany, formed from the Soviet sector, and the Federal Republic of Germany (FRG), or West Germany, established from the U.S., British, and French sectors. Berlin, which

A Divided Germany and the Cold War (continued)

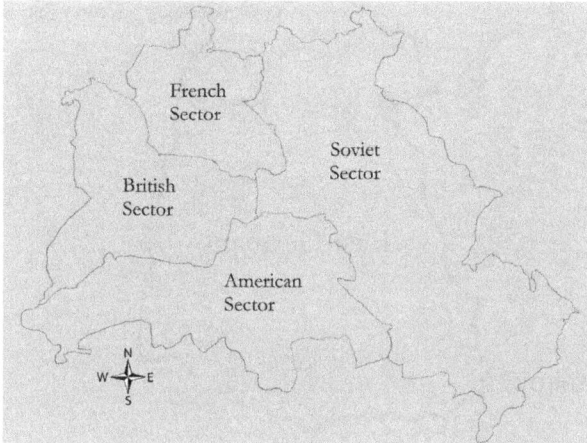

Map 2-2 Berlin, 1945
Map showing Berlin divided into four sectors, 1945

lay totally inside the territory of East Germany, was divided into East Berlin and West Berlin. The former Soviet sector of Berlin formed East Berlin, which was designated the capital of East Germany, while the U.S., British, and French sectors formed West Berlin. However, the western allies chose Bonn, which lay in western territory on the Rhine River almost 300 miles west of Berlin, as the capital of West Germany. The great powers tried to tie the German states into their respective areas of influence and to organizations in their respective blocs—West Germany to the North Atlantic Treaty Organization (NATO), created in 1949, and East Germany to the Warsaw Treaty Organization or Warsaw Pact, created the same year.

The Cold War, the great 20th-century standoff that divided the world into two blocs, centered on these two states—East Germany and West Germany—and on their contrasting political and economic systems. In the east, the Soviet Union promoted a communist, authoritarian political system and a command economy. In the west, the three western powers—the United States, Great Britain, and France—promoted a democratic, parliamentary style government and a free market economy. The Berlin Wall stood as the symbol of the Iron Curtain dividing east and west and as the flash point for Cold War tensions.

Throughout the history of the East German state, most East German citizens experienced a closed, oppressive system dominated by an extensive state apparatus. With the building of the Berlin Wall in 1961, the state became even more obtrusive. Berlin's and East Germany's location on the international divide between east and west placed pressures on the state to keep the domestic situation under control. Although the power of the East German state was backed up by a strong Soviet presence, the Helsinki accords in the mid-1970s put pressures on East German leaders to reform. Later changes in the Soviet Union under Gorbachev in the mid-1980s renewed pressures on Erich Honecker and other leaders and began destabilizing East Germany.

Map 2-3 Germany, 1961
East and West Germany in 1961; map shows fence around East Germany

west. Erich Honecker, at the time a young Central Committee member (and later party and governmental head of East Germany), was put in charge of closing off access to West Berlin. During the night of August 12–13, 1961, troops in East Berlin systematically tore up streets leading to West Berlin and replaced them with a 100-mile-long barbed-wire fence, effectively closing off free passage between East and West Berlin, and cutting telephone wires as well.[68] Overnight, 60,000 East Berliners were cut off from jobs and many more were prevented from visiting

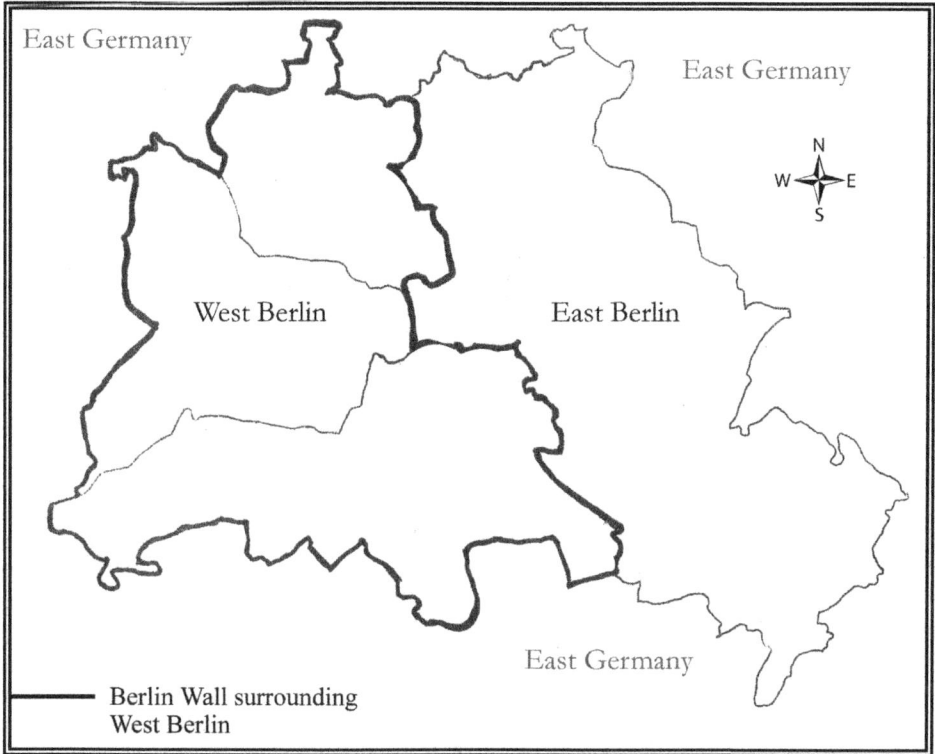

Map 2-4 Berlin, 1961
Map shows East and West Berlin, with Berlin Wall around West Berlin

family and friends in West Berlin. Over the years, the fence was increasingly fortified with barbed wire and concrete, and by 1965 a reinforced concrete wall—the
Berlin Wall—ran through the center of Berlin, dividing the city and completely
surrounding West Berlin. By the 1970s the Berlin Wall stood 12 feet high and was
fortified with 350 guard towers and 20 bunkers. Although the Wall prevented East
Germans from crossing into West Berlin and the west, westerners could continue
to travel between West Berlin and West Germany on the transit highways crossing East Germany.

In addition to these physical barriers, travel restrictions also controlled the
flow of East Germans to countries in Eastern and Western Europe. With a
barbed-wire fence around the perimeter of East Germany separating it from
West Germany to the west, Czechoslovakia to the south, and Poland to the east,
East Germany was a completely closed-in land.

Berlin Wall at Brandenburg Gate, 1964
Photo by Patricia Smith

Berlin Wall with barbed wire and no-man's-land, 1964
Photo by Patricia Smith

State authorities occasionally loosened travel regulations, sometimes in an attempt to portray East Germany more positively in the international realm or as part of efforts toward *détente* or other international initiatives. For a few older activists ratification of the Helsinki accords of the Conference on Security and Cooperation in Europe in 1975 did loosen travel restrictions.[69] Wolfgang Ullmann, a theologian, had studied in Göttingen, West Germany, from 1950 to 1954[70]; however, from 1960 through 1975, Ullmann was not allowed to travel outside East Germany, despite invitations from conferences abroad. Later, after the ratification of Helsinki, he was again allowed to travel outside the country. His trips abroad, including one as guest lecturer in the United States in the early 1980s, caused Ullmann to question why East Germany walled itself off from West Germany and the rest of the world. He kept asking himself, "What is really wrong here? What is wrong with this country?"[71] In the late 1980s Ullmann spearheaded a group, *Initiative Absage gegen Praxis und Prinzip der Abgrenzung,* questioning the division of Germany, and in 1989, Ullmann cofounded the East German citizens movement group Democracy Now.

*   *   *

In December 1988 East Germany issued revised travel regulations that took effect in January 1989. For some East Germans—especially for seniors and for those with relatives living in West Berlin or West Germany—the revised regulations loosened restrictions and also provided for a system of appeals.[72] Under the new regulations authorities were instructed to approve requests for visits by close relatives to celebrate important birthdays, as well as many visits for births, weddings, anniversaries, sickness, or death.[73] The new travel regulations also gave authorities discretion relating to visa applications and, in this sense, permitted discriminatory treatment, so this discretion was a benefit for some but a disadvantage for others.

For many, the new regulations made travel outside East Germany increasingly difficult. Although the stated intent of the regulations was to liberalize travel conditions, many complained that the new regulations were actually *more* restrictive, because authorities interpreted the rules more strictly and did not allow as many exceptions to the rules as they had in the past. And because persons who had applied to permanently leave East Germany suffered repercussions for applying, for them, travel outside East Germany became almost impossible. These East Germans were confined within the boundaries of East Germany, a country slightly larger than the state of Ohio—41,748 square miles—surrounded by tall barbed-wire fences and protected by border guards in watchtowers.

Although East German regulations officially allowed citizens to travel freely within Eastern Europe without a visa, in actuality, authorities required visas even for travel to Hungary, Bulgaria, Romania, and Poland. Prior to 1989 many activists had never been allowed to travel outside East Germany, including Czechoslovakia, where most other East Germans could travel without a visa.[74] Later in 1989 East Germany would also close the border with Czechoslovakia for all citizens.

Most activists who had traveled abroad previously saw their travel privileges ended once the state learned of their political involvements, and they were forbidden to travel, not only to the west, but also in the east bloc—and because most activists from other countries in both east and west could not travel in East Germany (because of East Germany's or their own state's regulations), restrictions on travel severely limited direct contact among groups across borders. Lotte Templin described the situation for members of her group, noting, "No one in Initiative for Peace and Human Rights was allowed to travel in Eastern Europe. We lived in a completely closed land."[75] The clergy, however, often enjoyed travel privileges in east and west.

Group activists and Evangelical Church authorities publicly criticized the new East German travel restrictions and called for the state to extend travel possibilities in line with the Helsinki agreements of the Conference on Security and Cooperation in Europe.[76] Church demands included allowing visits to friends and relatives without special reasons, tours for youth and other groups, and exchange visits between church parishes and sister cities. In addition, emigration groups continued to press for liberalized travel regulations that would allow them to more easily leave East Germany.

The Second Leipzig Demonstration

The March 13 demonstration of emigration groups and others wanting to leave East Germany—the second public event promoted by Leipzig human rights groups in 1989—initiated a new cycle of activism in Leipzig. During the march, political and oppositional groups promoting changes in East Germany joined forces with group members wanting to emigrate.[77] Would-be emigrés voiced their dissatisfaction with conditions in East Germany and emphasized that they had given up hope that East Germany would change and implement fundamental political, economic, and social reforms, so now they demanded freedom of movement—freedom to travel and to leave East Germany.

March 13, 1989, fell on a Monday during Leipzig's spring trade fair week. Group members intentionally staged the demonstrations to coincide with both Leipzig's trade fair, an important institution since the Middle Ages, and the Monday night peace prayers, which had seen increased participation since the group-organized Rosa Luxemburg demonstration in January. By choosing March 13 to demonstrate, groups also could take advantage of coverage by the international media, which was allowed in Leipzig only during the spring and fall trade fairs.[78]

On the evening of March 13, 1989, more than 650 persons attended the peace prayers at Nikolai Church, including many members of emigration groups wanting to publicize their demands to be allowed to leave East Germany. East German authorities were also aware of the significance of these days each year during the trade fairs, and they attempted to abort, or at least disrupt, the demonstrations. Before the March 13 protest, Stasi personnel had gone around the city, threatening persons who had turned in applications to emigrate.[79] Some were taken to the Stasi headquarters and asked to sign documents promising that they would not participate in the demonstration. The threats generally had no effect, however. These would-be emigrés had already considered the possible consequences, and most were willing to go to prison to publicize their demands. The Stasi offered others the opportunity to emigrate, on the condition that they leave the country before March 13.

After the peace prayer service around 1,300 demonstrators gathered in the courtyard of Nikolai Church in central Leipzig.[80]

Almost immediately after leaving the Nikolai Church courtyard, the demonstrators encountered security police, some dressed in civilian clothes and others uniformed, who attempted to dissolve the demonstration with force (850 armed forces had been assigned to detail the city). The Stasi also tried to prevent journalists and photographers from carrying out their work. During the demonstration Gunter Schröder unfurled a sign with the words "Freedom to Travel Instead of Arbitrary Actions of the Authorities," and he was immediately detained. On the perimeter of the demonstration, Michael Arnold of Initiative Group Living and Wolfgang Sarstedt of Working Circle Justice had already been arrested for distributing flyers. The demonstration lasted about half an hour before security forces dissolved the group. Perhaps because the international media was in town and the state did not want to look bad in the light of international publicity, there were no beatings that day.

West German television had managed to film the demonstration, despite attempts by the Stasi to prevent them. When the footage played in the news that evening, West Germans could view the unrest in East Germany. East Germans, too, in most areas of the country could watch the illegal demonstration in Leipzig on West German television.

When news of the incident reached the west, the government of West Germany protested the actions of the East German security police and disruption of a peaceful protest march.

*   *   *

The flyer that Leipzig human rights group members distributed to journalists that day was a declaration of Working Group Emigration, a subgroup of the Leipzig human rights group Working Circle Justice. Pointing to the stagnation in politics, culture, and the economy, the flyer called "the flood of those wanting a emigrate" "a mirror of societal conditions."[81] Articulating the human rights group's support for the demands of emigration groups and individuals, the flyer also called for other East Germans to join emigration groups in publicizing problems in East Germany rather than ignoring them and retreating into their private spheres—East Germany's "niche society."

The declaration laid out an ambitious civil rights agenda that the group intended to carry out in support of emigration. Emphasizing that the ability to leave one's country is a universally recognized human right, the declaration argued that attempts to leave East Germany should not lead to repression. The group planned to gather information and to develop policies about other pressing issues, including environmental problems, the militarization of East German society, and local elections.[82]

Some Leipzig groups supported those wanting to emigrate and urged churches and groups to take them seriously, but others were reluctant to associate themselves with emigration groups. Those wanting to stay and reform East Germany were not always willing to join forces with those trying to leave.

In fact, most alternative and oppositional groups in East Germany felt that emigration groups and individuals who wanted to emigrate had a negative effect on their own group's programs and goals and undermined the movement for change in East Germany.[83] They were therefore reluctant to allow would-be emigrés to join their own groups. Because most alternative and oppositional groups worked for changes in East Germany, they felt others should do the same, rather than lobby for the right to leave the country. When would-be emigrés joined other groups, they often proved unreliable, because if the opportunity came to emigrate, those people would not carry out previous commitments to the group;

so, at least initially, alternative and opposition groups seldom associated themselves with emigration groups and preferred not to have persons wanting to
emigrate among their members.

Emigration Groups in Leipzig

The same strained dynamic was present in Leipzig. Most alternative and
oppositional groups there felt that the would-be emigrés hurt the movement as
a whole and gave their own groups a bad name. Nevertheless, two Leipzig
groups took a different approach from most other groups in East Germany.[84]
Recognizing the potential in joining forces, oppositional groups Working Circle Justice and Initiative Group Living decided to cooperate with emigration
groups and to incorporate emigration issues into their programs. Both groups
also allowed those wishing to emigrate to join their groups and organized separate subgroups concentrating on the emigration issue.

Working Circle Justice/Emigration

The first to join forces was Working Circle Justice because, as Rainer
Müller noted, "the political situation posed a real problem for the 100,000 persons who wanted to leave East Germany."[85] Working Circle Justice struggled
with how to integrate the emigration subgroup into the larger group structure
and how to deal with emigration issues.[86] Working Circle Justice frequently published documents to support its programs, among them materials on the emigration problem.[87] Using these publications to inform other groups about the
issues, Working Circle Justice distributed the information in Leipzig through
personal contact, at meetings of groups, and by mail to individuals and other
groups in East Germany and abroad. It also advocated on behalf of those wanting to emigrate within the church and group milieu and assisted emigration
groups through its media efforts, as it did with the flyer for the March 13
demonstration.

Publicity was a key element for Working Circle Justice, and emigration groups
as well as opposition and other groups benefited from its media contacts and connections to groups abroad. Joining forces with emigration groups allowed oppositional groups to tie into the frequently spectacular media coverage focusing on
persons exiting or trying to leave East Germany, e.g., fleeing through the Berlin

Wall or crossing a fortified border. Such widespread media coverage was often not available for other East German groups, because the western media did not always view their activities as newsworthy.

On March 12, the day before the joint demonstration, members of Working Circle Human Rights had paraded past the trade fair area on bicycles while East German leader Erich Honecker visited. Western journalists covered the action, and although state security forces observed the event, they made no arrests. Working Circle Human Rights had staged the bicycle parade to accustom the Stasi to public gatherings such as demonstrations and the bicycle parade.[88]

Publicity was also important to these would-be emigrants, and thanks to Thomas Rudolph of Working Circle Justice, joining forces considerably improved their media efforts. Rudolph made emigration demonstrators aware of the need to approach the media when confronted by Stasi or police forces, and to make their names and addresses known. Beatrix Nietzschmann, one of the participants in the March 13 demonstration, later publicly thanked Rudolph for his effort because, prior to joining forces, emigration groups weren't really conscious of what they needed to do. "It was tremendously important," said Nietzschmann, "that people who were imprisoned didn't disappear."[89] Before meeting with human rights groups, emigration group members didn't realize how political arrests usually proceeded, and group members credited Rudolph's efforts with publicizing their cases and speeding up the emigration process.

Initiative Group Living/Emigration

Initiative Group Living also cooperated with emigration groups and welcomed them as members. As Jochen Lässig noted, "We recognized early in comparison to most groups that it was necessary to work with the exit groups—that groups in the area would be strengthened by working together."[90] While Leipzig oppositional groups had only several dozen members, Leipzigers wanting to emigrate numbered in the thousands, so by joining forces, they would substantially increase the number of activists and their public presence. The two types of groups had some similarities. Both emigration groups and human rights group members had demonstrated their willingness to take public stands on issues, to demonstrate openly, and to risk arrest.

Folk Singer Stephan Krawczyk in Leipzig
Photo by Christoph Motzer/Archiv Bürgerbewegung
Leipzig e. V.

Leipzig church Youth Bureau located next to
St. Thomas Church
Photo by Patricia Smith

One of the Leipzig human rights group members most involved with emigration groups was Gesine Oltmanns.[91] Oltmanns' involvement with Leipzig groups began in earnest with the arrests of popular singer-songwriter Stephen Krawczyk and his wife film director Freya Klier in conjunction with the January 1988 Rosa Luxemburg protests in Berlin. In November 1987, just two months before their arrests, Krawczyk had performed at Michaelis Church in Leipzig. After the Stasi break-in, arrests, and destruction of equipment at Berlin's Environmental Library, also in late November of 1987, Oltmanns decided that she had to do something to change conditions in East Germany. So after the Rosa Luxemburg arrests in Berlin in January 1988, Oltmanns joined with other group members to staff the contact network at Leipzig's church Youth Bureau located next to Thomas Church to show solidarity with those arrested.

Raised in Olbernau in the Erzgebirge southeast of Leipzig, Oltmanns had moved to Leipzig in 1983 hoping to study biology. After several applications had been rejected, presumably because she grew up in a parsonage and had ideas too closely tied to the church or to other alternative movements,

Oltmanns worked at various jobs, among them for the post office and a music publisher. Oltmanns herself had applied for a visa to emigrate to the west in 1988. However, in spring of 1989 she decided she wanted to stay in East Germany and to work to change the country from within. Consequently, she withdrew her application to emigrate, to the astonishment, and even anger, of the authorities. Her reasoning: "I felt that things were changing."[92] Oltmanns continued to work openly and to promote programs that challenged East German authorities into fall 1989.

Gesine Oltmanns initially joined Leipzig's Working Circle Justice where she focused on emigration issues. Quickly immersing herself in oppositional group work, Oltmanns headed the subgroup Working Group Emigration and served as one of the four members of the larger group's speakers' circle, the decision-making body. In November 1988 Oltmanns and members of Working Group Emigration prepared a document, "Explanation Concerning the Peace Prayers, November 10, 1988," and advocated on behalf of emigration groups. They criticized the decision by Pastor Christian Führer of Nikolai Church banning would-be emigrés from participating in the meetings at Nikolai Church. In the document they argued that these would-be emigrés were not simply persons wanting to emigrate meeting under the group's auspices but were regular members of Working Group Emigration, the subgroup of the larger Working Circle Justice. Therefore, it was entirely appropriate for these persons to participate in the group-sponsored meetings inside the church to discuss problems related to emigration. The document ended by noting that, because emigration was such a pressing problem in society, groups needed to continue to hold meetings to discuss the subject.[93]

In December 1988, Gesine Oltmanns left Working Group Justice and joined Initiative Group Living, favoring the latter group's emphasis on public action rather than conspiratorial activities.[94] There, Oltmanns, a strong proponent of *Öffentlichkeit* and working openly, helped emigration groups organize public demonstrations and worked with others in Initiative Group Living to set up public programs.

Kaden's Circle

Klaus Kaden, a pastor who moved to Leipzig in November 1987 and lived in the parsonage next to Michaelis Church, headed the Leipzig Evangelical Church's Youth Bureau and worked extensively with Leipzigers who wanted to emigrate. Kaden's responsibilities included Working Group Environmental Protection, a church-affiliated group that met at the Youth Bureau. Just two months after he arrived in Leipzig, Kaden's involvements with persons wanting to emigrate intensified as several members of the environmental group became closely involved with opposition groups and their activities.[95]

Despite Kaden's concerns, the meeting between environmental and oppositional groups did lead to his close involvement with persons wanting to emigrate. He sympathized with their plight, noting, "You have to keep in mind that people who had applied for an exit visa were treated very badly: they had to wait up to five years for an official response; their children were not allowed to go to a post-secondary school; teachers were fired from their jobs—all in all, it was a very tough position to be in."[96] After the meeting, Kaden requested permission from Bishop Johannes Hempel, head of the Saxony Church District in Dresden responsible for Leipzig, to set up a group supporting persons who wanted to emigrate. Hempel approved the idea and asked only that Kaden keep the group's activities within the confines of the church.

This new group, known as Kaden's Circle, met regularly with Kaden throughout 1988 and 1989. Kaden himself grew more attuned to the views of those wanting to emigrate, feeling increasingly that East Germany couldn't be reformed. Later, after Leipzig's revolutionary autumn, Kaden would argue, "It was really the pressure of the would-be emigrés, particularly in Leipzig, that brought about the peace prayers and led to all these political activities. Of course the grass-roots groups supported this process, they gave it a particular content, and ultimately pushed it forward, there is no question about that."[97]

Working Circle Hope

Christian Führer, the head pastor at Nikolai Church, had also worked with emigration groups since 1988, when he formed Working Circle Hope (*Hoffnung für Ausreisewillige*) for those wanting to emigrate.[98] After the 1988 Rosa Luxemburg arrests in Berlin, an increasingly larger group of persons wanting to emigrate had attended the peace prayer services on Monday nights at Nikolai Church, and by February more than 1000 attended most services. On February 19, 1988, more than 900 persons attended a meeting organized by the church to discuss living and staying in East Germany. There Führer offered Nikolai Church as a contact point for persons wanting to emigrate. At the meeting Working Circle Justice circulated a petition for signatures on a letter to Erich Honecker demanding new regulations for emigration, and two of the initiators of the petition action were arrested. Solidarity action after the next peace

---

Leipzig Emigration Groups

Kaden's Circle

   Leader: Klaus Kaden, head of church Youth Bureau

   Tactics/Objectives: Provide support for persons wanting to emigrate

Working Circle Hope

   Leader: Christian Führer, head pastor, Nikolai Church

   Tactics/Objectives: Provide support for persons wanting to emigrate

Working Circle Justice—emigration subgroup

   Key Member: Gesine Oltmanns

   Tactics: Prepare and distribute documents about goals, program; assist with publicity, media work; combine forces of emigration and opposition groups

Initiative Group Living—emigration subgroup

   Key Members: Fred Kowasch, Gesine Oltmanns

   Tactics: Organize demonstrations and other public programs; combine forces of emigration and opposition groups

prayers for those arrested resulted in more arrests. The Stasi put pressure on Führer to discontinue his work with emigration problems, but he refused, feeling that the state could not do much to him as pastor of one the most important city churches in East Germany.[99]

*   *   *

Throughout 1989 emigrations from East Germany affected more and more families personally. With tens of thousands of (mainly young) East Germans trying to leave the country, most knew a friend or relative who wanted out. In some cases, the emigration or proposed exit of a son or daughter prompted parents to join demonstrations or movements for reform. More than one person decided for personal reasons to get involved or to increase involvement for changing East Germany, as did Konrad Elmer, later a cofounder of the East German Social Democratic Party. When his daughter told him she wanted to leave the country because she was unwilling to live her life like his generation had, Elmer decided it was time to make a serious commitment to changing East Germany.[100] Personal experiences as well as the mass emigrations highlighted for the broader population that, for many, conditions in East Germany were intolerable and that changes were necessary and perhaps even possible.

The March 13 demonstration represented a significant step forward in Leipzig activism as emigration groups and opposition groups joined forces. In Leipzig, unlike in most East German cities, leaders of opposition groups recognized the advantages of joining forces with emigration groups. The relatively small number of opposition and alternative group members willing to demonstrate publicly made common cause with the tens of thousands of applicants for emigration who had already identified themselves publicly as critics of the political system. Together, these groups formed a critical mass of demonstrators in Leipzig in spring of 1989 that demanded public attention. However, even the renewed energy and activism apparent in these joint demonstrations could hardly predict the thousands of would-be emigrés in West German embassies and consulates—in Berlin, Prague, Budapest, Warsaw—by late summer. By joining forces and making common cause with this long-dissatisfied segment of the population wishing to leave East Germany, Leipzig groups formed a much larger critical mass of activists.

Media coverage spread stories of unrest across East Germany and abroad. Courier systems comprised partly of former East German activists who had emigrated to West Berlin helped link Leipzig and other East German groups to the western media. For years, West Berlin radio and television stations, along with Voice of America, beamed newsworthy coverage from the west into East Germany. Later, East German groups managed to get group-published materials to their media contacts in the west, and the western stations broadcast information from East German groups as part of their coverage. Finally, in late fall 1989, the more limited domestic coverage from East German television and the press helped keep civil rights and emigration issues in the forefront.

*   *   *

After the March 13, 1989 demonstration during the spring trade fair in Leipzig, demonstrators in the front rows watched themselves on the evening news and waited for the Stasi to knock on their doors. They knew that authorities would be able to identify them from the television news footage filmed by western news crews, so it was only a matter of time before they would be arrested.[101]

CHAPTER 3

Moving from the Church to the Street: Monday Night Peace Prayers, April 10, 1989

I grew up in a church family and, as a Christian, it was important that I lived in a way that supported my beliefs. I couldn't not participate. . . . I felt that it was important to be able to say to my children, "I did something. I worked to change the system."[102]

—Brigitte Moritz,
Working Group Peace Service, Leipzig

The intention of the groups was to popularize the peace prayers and to build a larger following for group ideas and activities.[103]

—Jochen Lässig,
Initiative Group Living, Leipzig

The peace prayers prepared the people to carry out the revolution without violence.[104]

—Brigitte Moritz,
Working Group Peace Service, Leipzig

The 1988 Rosa Luxemburg protests and the solidarity efforts on behalf of those arrested in Berlin revitalized Leipzig's Monday night peace prayers, a tradition that started in 1982 to pose alternatives to East Germany's increasing militarization. But the reinvigorated peace prayers and the demonstrations that followed in the streets threatened to destabilize fragile church-state relations. The state put pressure on church authorities to rein in the political groups and to depoliticize the peace prayers or to cancel them. Tensions peaked in summer 1988 when Leipzig's Superintendent Friedrich Magirius banned Pastor Christoph Wonneberger—who had conceptualized the original peace prayers in 1982—and grassroots groups from the peace prayer leadership.

In a letter dated August 25, 1988, and sent while Wonneberger was on vacation, Magirius informed Wonneberger that he was released from his responsibilities for the peace prayers and would no longer be involved in the services.[105] Magirius had previously censured Wonneberger for his handling of the

last service before summer recess, June 27, 1988, when the peace prayer congregation raised 1000 marks to help Jürgen Tallig, a Marxist pro-democracy
protestor, pay off the fine he received for painting pro-democracy signs.[106] In
response to the letter from Magirius, Wonneberger criticized the increasingly
close relationship between church and state, saying, "The state expects the
church, too, to be an administrative organ of the state power structure. But,
please, without me."[107]

Magirius defended his decision. He noted, "Difficulties arose when the
groups used the church primarily for a political platform."[108] He argued that the
Biblical method, which included references to Jesus and brought societal problems together with the Biblical word, needed to be followed in the services, and
that the Monday peace prayers ought to allow people to bring their concerns
before God and not only provide political information. While the church provided an open door for all, Magirius argued, it should not serve only as the
meeting point for the opposition. He added that church members in small
parishes were critical of the Leipzig peace prayers and the oppositional positions
often taken by groups.[109]

Magirius's plan backfired, however. He had inadvertently placed Leipzig
groups in a position where they could play an even more public role. When
groups weren't allowed to express their concerns inside the church, they set up
a makeshift podium in the church courtyard so people could speak from the
street.

After Magirius and the church council prohibited groups from participating in the leadership and from bringing forward their concerns during the peace
prayers, a number of the more oppositional group members attempted to disrupt the services. Some carried posters and banners protesting their exclusion
with slogans such as "Stop the church hierarchy" or "The church people are the
same as the ones outside." Others covered their mouths with bandages printed
with the words "Gag Order" in German, protesting Magirius's demand that they
not speak in the services. Still others raised their concerns after the services in
the courtyard of Nikolai Church—issues such as the exclusion of groups from
the peace prayers, the state's censure of church newspapers, police disruption of
a silent march in Berlin, and calls for solidarity with various groups and their
members.[110]

Demonstrators at Nikolai Church protest their exclusion from peace prayers. From left, Udo Hartmann, Frank Selentin, Rainer Müller, Anita Unger, and Uwe Schwabe. *Photo by Christoph Motzer/Archiv Bürgerbewegung Leipzig e. V.*

By the spring of 1989—after a nine-month ban—the groups were again allowed to lead the peace prayer services. On April 10, Leipzig's activist groups and Pastor Wonneberger once again participated in the organizing committee and regained their forum inside the church. But the demonstrations had already moved into the streets.

Churches in East Germany

In Leipzig, the tension between groups and the church stemmed in part from church-state relations. Regularly, the state pressured church leaders to control oppositional pastors as well as groups promoting controversial programs.

Across East Germany, the Evangelical (Protestant) Church and most other churches played roles quite different from the roles of churches in many Soviet bloc countries where churches were banned. More than six million people of East Germany's 17 million claimed church affiliation. As the only non-state-sponsored organization allowed relatively free operation, churches provided

important alternatives outside the framework of state structures, and throughout the 1970s and 1980s the institutional church played an increasingly important role in East German society.

With more than five million members, almost one out of every three East
Germans claimed connections to the Evangelical Church, the largest denomination in East Germany. In 1978 the Evangelical Church and the East German
state reached an agreement allowing the church relatively free rein in return for
not actively opposing the state. The church agreed, in the words of Bishop
Albrecht Schönherr, to be "not a church against socialism, nor a church alongside socialism, but a church in socialism."[111] Under the agreement the church
attempted to work with and influence the state but not be co-opted by it.
Expanding its role, the church took an activist stance on a number of social and
political issues, including human rights, the environment, peace, and, in the late
1980s, political reform. For a wide variety of groups, the church played a critical role. By allowing them to meet under its auspices, the church facilitated the
growth of grassroots groups, both church- and nonchurch-related, that could
never have developed initially outside the church's meeting spaces and protection.

Despite efforts of the church to create free space and to provide alternatives to the ideas and programs of the state, the church's agreement with the state
forced it to walk a narrow line. When the church overstepped this line, the state
pressured the church to moderate its stance—or to pressure pastors, church
members, and groups to censure their statements and actions. Nevertheless, the
church did succeed in providing considerable operating space outside the close
oversight of the state.

The Evangelical Church was a differentiated institution with members
representing a wide range of opinions and political stances. Comprised of eight
church regions (*Landeskirchen*) corresponding to the old (and current) state
(*Land*) boundaries of Germany and connected through the Federation of Evangelical Churches (*Kirchenbund*), the Evangelical Church structure was quite
decentralized, with the different regions and districts operating relatively independently. The approximately 7,000 individual parishes served by more than
4,000 pastors also enjoyed considerable autonomy.[112] Further differentiation
existed because the Evangelical Church incorporated two different theological

traditions—the Lutheran, which tended to follow rather than challenge the dictates of the state, and the Reformed, which allowed and even encouraged a Christian to stand up to an unjust state.[113]

Pastors, too, represented different traditions and held diverse positions on various issues, including how they viewed the state. Ehrhart Neubert of the Evangelical Church Federation staff and an important chronicler of the church and groups, estimated that of the 4,500 Evangelical Church pastors in East Germany, 20 percent were critical, 60–70 percent were cautious, and 10 percent were state-conforming.[114] These critical East German pastors played a crucial supportive role for groups and facilitated group organization, and a number of critical pastors were directly involved in oppositional activities.

The state of Saxony and Saxony-Dresden, the church district where Leipzig was located, was a religious stronghold in East Germany.[115] The Saxony area was a relatively conservative church area composed primarily of Lutheran churches, and although Lutheran church theology did not encourage churches to stand up to the state, the conservative churches in Saxony had a tradition of not cooperating with the state. Also, discrimination against church members was more prominent in some areas of the country, including in Leipzig.[116]

The Catholic Church in East Germany, with more than one million members, was generally less active in social and political issues than was the Evangelical Church. Nevertheless, the Catholic Church did view itself as providing alternatives to positions promoted by the East German state and especially an alternative to a materialistic environment. In 1983, the Catholic Conference of Bishops in Berlin took stands on peace and disarmament similar to those of the Evangelical Church, challenging the state and indicating its willingness to become more involved in controversial issues.[117] Although the Catholic Church did not actively shelter alternative groups composed of nonchurch members, as did the Evangelical Church, a number of Catholic groups developed around thematic areas such as peace.

Other denominations in East Germany, although much smaller than the Evangelical or Catholic churches, nevertheless represented a significant alternative for persons not conforming to positions promoted by the East German state. Some of these denominations, such as the Seventh-Day Adventists, with an estimated 25,000 to 30,000 members, were openly oppositional and severely persecuted by the state. The New Apostolic Church, the third largest denomination in

East Germany, with approximately 100,000 members, was an eschatological movement that viewed institutions other than the church as run by Satan.[118] Other smaller denominations were to an extent tolerated by the state, although their members frequently suffered discrimination because of their beliefs, and many of these churches periodically challenged state positions on issues such as peace. For example, in the 28,000-strong Methodist Church in East Germany, more than half of the members registering for the draft registered as conscientious objectors in the 1980s.[119]

East German denominations and church traditions tended to keep quite separate; however, in 1983 at the World Council of Churches meetings in Vancouver, British Columbia, the assembly adopted a proposal initiated by East German churches that led to a broad-based ecumenical program in East Germany and throughout the world. In East Germany, the process began in 1986 and continued through 1989. During that period, delegates within East Germany from the Catholic Church and most Protestant denominations would consider and vote on a number of reform-oriented proposals. Ultimately, delegates would take initiatives based on their deliberations back to local congregations. This ecumenical process exposed church members from throughout East Germany to many group-promoted ideas for democratic reform that would resonate during the revolutionary autumn of 1989.[120]

*   *   *

In the early years of the East German state, many church members had experienced often extreme forms of discrimination, and some discrimination against church members continued through 1989. Throughout the state's history, Christians experienced discrimination in education and employment. Also, the military service question and the lack of alternatives for conscientious objectors affected many East German Christians.

With the implementation of the 1972 law on public events, the state limited churches' freedom of assembly by restricting public meetings.[121] Public events had to be announced to the local police, and churches also had to notify police of youth meetings. Some churches resisted, however. In the Saxony-Dresden church region, including in Leipzig, churches frequently refused to notify the state, although violations could result in heavy fines. These restrictions caused churches to question what was "religious" and the extent to which the law and notification requirement violated constitutionally guaranteed freedom of religion.

The usually confrontational relationship between church and state changed dramatically, however, with the March 6, 1978, church-state agreement.[122] Rather than try to limit the church's freedom of assembly, the state tried to gain the church's cooperation in carrying out the goals of the state. The agreement also dealt with the treatment of individual Christians and was intended to lessen discrimination on the basis of world view or religious confession.

After the 1978 agreement and throughout the 1980s, the East German state pressured local church leaders to discipline particularly oppositional pastors and to moderate the positions taken by groups meeting under church auspices, indicating that this disciplinary action was required to continue good church-state relationships. A Stasi report noted that the state feared the inability of the church leadership to control oppositional pastors.[123]

Because independent associations or organizations were not allowed in East Germany and only the church had managed to secure some autonomy, most grassroots groups met under the protective roof of the church. Besides more explicitly religious groups, East German churches allowed a range of groups to meet within their facilities, including peace, environmental, and, occasionally, human rights groups.[124]

The church's protection had its limits, however—both in what the church would allow within its walls and in the extent it was willing to support those with different views and agendas. In addition, the Stasi had numerous informers within churches, including among the clergy, and the state pressured the church whenever it went too far. So, under state pressure, the church leadership regularly disciplined "out of line" members, clergy, and groups that met inside the church.

Conscientious Objection to Military Service

In 1962, in the context of the newly built Berlin Wall and increasing Cold War tensions, East Germany passed a military conscription law that required all able-bodied East German men between 18 and 26 to serve eighteen months in the East German military.[125] At the time the draft began there was no alternative service option for conscientious objectors—persons objecting to military service on ethical or religious grounds—and the East German government viewed those who refused to serve as enemies of the state. However, many East Germans, especially in the churches, opposed the new draft requirements and the increasing militarization of society and had concerns about parallels to Germany in World War I and World War II.

Although the conscription law was amended in 1964 to provide young men an option to serve as construction soldiers, many conscientious objectors in East Germany felt that this was not a real alternative because it involved quasi-military aspects that they opposed. Construction soldiers were required to wear military-style uniforms only slightly different from those of regular conscripts. They might be assigned to build military barracks or carry out other military-related jobs, in addition to their more civilian-related roles such as working in natural disasters. Although construction soldiers were not required to carry weapons, they had to pledge to "protect the socialist state against all enemies and achieve victory."[126]

Many young East Germans did choose to serve as construction soldiers rather than in the regular military. Others, however, felt they could not in good conscience serve as construction soldiers alongside military troops or construct installations for defense purposes. So opposed to war and military action were these conscientious objectors that they felt they could not serve at all, so they made the difficult choice to refuse all military service—to become draft resisters (*Wehrdiensttotalverweigers*)—and to accept the consequences.[127]

In East Germany the penalties for such choices were harsh. Construction soldiers received black marks in the official files kept on all East Germans and frequently found access to higher education, certain careers, and advancement possibilities limited.[128] For draft resisters, those refusing to serve in the military in any capacity, the penalties were harsher and usually involved prison terms. Prior to 1964 this meant a mandatory 18 months in prison and sometimes more than two years. Those who had refused military service and thus had been imprisoned had to carry East German identity cards marked PM12 (a designation also given to persons who had applied to emigrate), which indicated they had served a prison sentence and denoted them as "unreliable elements."

Such a choice and subsequent time in prison had profound effects on many conscientious objectors for the rest of their lives. With poor education and job possibilities, most conscientious objectors—construction soldiers and draft resisters—worked in church-related jobs or menial jobs where they could find them. In addition to severely limiting educational and employment opportunities, this designation meant they were not allowed to travel abroad.[129]

Nevertheless, by the mid-1970s an estimated 10,000 East Germans had served as construction soldiers.[130] Evangelical churches in East Germany set up extensive programs through the Youth Bureaus of each district to counsel young people about their options relating to military service. Churches also assisted young men returning from service as construction soldiers as well as those who had refused to serve.

After terms in alternative service or in prison, many of these conscientious objectors supported each other, keeping in regular contact with other construction soldiers and draft resisters through periodic (quarterly, biannual, or annual) meetings held throughout East Germany. In Königswalde in Saxony, for example, construction soldiers met annually initially, and, later, every six months.[131] These networks provided important contacts throughout East Germany for questions related to peace and military service, and solidarity developed among these conscientious objectors as a result of their shared experiences.

Christoph Wonneberger, the pastor who initiated the peace prayers, was linked into many of these networks. Born in 1944, he was 18 when the initial conscription law passed. He had served as a construction soldier as a young man, and over the years he kept in regular contact with other construction soldiers and draft resisters. Later, as a young pastor in the church's youth work in Dresden, he counseled young men about their military service options and was connected to a network of other counselors. In the late 1970s and early 1980s Wonneberger, arguably the most important person in East Germany's peaceful revolution,[132] initiated a program for a social peace service as an alternative to military service. The peace prayers developed out of that initiative.

The Independent Peace Movement in East Germany

The militarization of society that took place in East Germany in the late 1970s and early 1980s provided an impetus for church involvement in peace groups and in the independent peace movement. In early years much of the emphasis was on alternatives to military service, especially after military conscription was introduced in the early 1960s with no option for conscientious objectors. In the late 1970s and early 1980s the peace movement's importance within the East German church grew. Events leading to a reinvigorated peace movement included the state prohibition of the symbol and phrase "swords to ploughshares" used by members of the independent peace movement in East Germany,[133] the development of the West European and West German peace movement, and the proposed stationing of NATO missiles in West Germany and Warsaw Pact missiles in East Germany. The church began promoting an "education for peace" program.

*   *   *

With 400,000 Soviet troops stationed in the country and one out of every 40 persons in East Germany a Russian soldier, it was difficult to ignore the military presence.[134] In addition to the Soviet presence, the East German military was 167,000 strong, including 116,000 in the army, 37,000 in the navy, and 14,000 in the air force.

Military troops were backed up by local police, as well as by the ever-present forces of the Ministry for State Security or the Stasi. Figures released before the 1989 revolution indicate that the ministry employed approximately 17,000 full-time staff members, including 8,000 uniformed officers.[135] Reports released in the post-revolutionary period when the Stasi files were opened contained much higher numbers, however, including up to 85,000 official staff.[136] These official Stasi forces were supplemented by a huge contingent of informers—100,000, according to official reports—although unofficial estimates of informers go as high as one million, and the Stasi collected files on as many as five million East Germans.[137] The presence of the Stasi and other security forces provided a psychic as well as a tangible reminder to East Germans that there were limits to the opinions they could express and the actions they could take.

A critical aspect of the acculturation process promoted by the East German state was to reinforce the image of the west as militaristic and as the enemy.

This "image of the enemy" (*Feinbild*) was particularly directed at West Germany but also included portraying the United States and her NATO allies as the enemy. The west was painted as imperialistic and warmongering—as the enemy of peace—in contrast to peace-loving and socialist East Germany and the Soviet Union. Increasingly, East German church members, particularly those involved in peace groups, opposed the efforts of the state to portray the west as the enemy, to promote a "war" mentality, and to expand military education.

Over the years the state intensified its pressure on youth to choose state-sponsored youth organizations over church groups and confirmation. The *Jugendweihe* ceremony and pledge, initiating East German youth, male and female, at around age 13, required them to defend East Germany against the imperialist enemy in the west. Several paragraphs of the pledge they took follow:[138]

> Dear young friends!
> Are you prepared, as young citizens of our German Democratic Republic, true to the Constitution, to work and fight with us for the great and noble cause of socialism and to cherish the revolutionary heritage of the people? Answer me:
> *Yes, we pledge!*
>
> Are you prepared, as true patriots, to deepen friendship with the Soviet Union, to strengthen the brotherhood with the socialist countries, to fight in the spirit of proletarian internationalism, to protect peace and to defend socialism against every imperialist attack? Answer me:
> *Yes, we pledge!*

Such efforts by the state to socialize young children into a militaristic mindset energized church peace groups. In fall 1978 a new round of protests developed in response to state actions. The East German state had introduced military instruction as a required course for ninth- and tenth-graders and provided summer camps with military training for both girls and boys.[139]

Throughout the country, church-based groups as well as more official church bodies produced studies and held meetings to counteract the increasing militarization of society. The initiative for a social peace service and the peace prayers, highlighting what one person or one group could do, developed in this climate.

Proposal for a Social Peace Service

With proposed changes in military service requirements, another wave of pressure for a real alternative to military service developed within the Evangelical Church. The requirement to serve in the military reserves became a critical concern for those wanting an alternative to military service.[140] In prior years the state had called up more and more men to serve in the reserves, which required 8 to 12 weeks' service, and many East Germans in churches and in the peace movement protested the requirement. For those who had originally done their service time in the regular military, the law required that they also fulfill their reserve obligations in a military unit, so there was no option to serve as a construction soldier in the reserves if their original service had been with a military unit, and the penalty for refusing to serve in the reserves was six to eight months in prison.

These changes in conscription led to a proposal for a social peace service, a true alternative to military service, where those drafted could work at jobs within the community, e.g., in hospitals or nursing homes.[141] The initial proposal came from Christoph Wonneberger, then pastor of Weinberg Church in Dresden (1977–1984), several colleagues working with church youth, and members of a peace circle at his church. Under the Open Work (*Offene Arbeit*) counseling program,[142] part of the Saxony church district's youth ministry, Wonneberger and other pastors and church workers developed an extensive program to counsel young men about their options related to military service.

The proposal was sent to contacts around the East German peace community in the form of a chain letter, with each recipient asked to make several copies and send the letters on to others. In this way, organizers could circumvent state control over paper, ink, typewriters, and duplicating machines. The proposal resonated with many East German church members, especially those involved in the peace movement, and members of grassroots church groups reacted with overwhelming support. Within several months of the proposal's introduction, more than 5,000 people had signed the initiative, and peace groups planned local, regional, and East German-wide meetings in support.

Hoping to receive official church support, Wonneberger and his colleagues also took their proposal to the church leadership for the Saxony region, but

Exhibit of Initiative Group Living for
a social peace service as an alternative to military service
*Photo by Christoph Motzer/Archiv
Bürgerbewegung Leipzig e. V.*

Bishop Johannes Hempel and President Kurt Domsch refused to approve it. Instead, Saxony church leaders kicked the proposal up the church structure to the central offices of the East German Evangelical Church (*Kirchenbund*), where Bishop Albrecht Schönherr and lay head of the church Manfred Stolpe also refused to endorse the initiative. Church district leaders throughout East Germany followed suit and rejected the initiative, including several regions that had initially supported the proposal for a social peace service.

Concerned about the widespread public support for the proposal, state authorities had pressured church leaders to take action against the initiative for a social peace service. Otherwise, the church-state relationship would be negatively affected, they threatened.[143] Thanks in part to state coercion, the official church structure did not pass the initiative.

Nevertheless, support for a social peace service continued at the grassroots level. Several years later Leipzig's Initiative Group Living held a meeting featuring information and an exhibit on the proposed social peace service.

Peace Prayers

In the face of opposition from church leaders and state authorities, Wonneberger and his colleagues involved in the Dresden Peace Circle drew back from plans for an East German-wide movement for a social peace service. They decided to decentralize their activities and to adapt the concept for the local level by holding weekly peace prayers in Dresden. Following Wonneberger's model, they held their first service on February 4, 1982.[144]

Wonneberger drew inspiration for his proposal for the peace prayers from a model of church meetings in Essen, West Germany, that was influenced by liberation theology and third world problems in the late 1960s.[145] He had learned about the group as a young man when he had listened to their services on West German radio programs broadcast into East Germany. Wonneberger's model for peace prayers was also influenced by Martin Luther King and the American civil rights movement.

Grassroots peace groups continued to support the proposal for a social peace service, now in its new, more decentralized form as peace prayers. In several cities, groups carried out small-scale actions to publicize the peace prayers and the earlier initiative through posters, postcards, and exhibitions. Throughout East Germany, congregations initiated peace prayers following Wonneberger's model for the services. Later, this model would play a critical role in the fall 1989 revolution as peace prayer services provided a gathering point and inspiration for demonstrations in Leipzig and throughout East Germany.

The broad grassroots support for a social peace service and, later, for the peace prayers, concerned state authorities. In turn, church leaders continued to pressure Wonneberger, threatening that if he didn't back off, his job would be affected.[146] Even after the proposal for a social peace service was dropped and the peace prayers were promoted instead, harassment continued.

On February 17, 1982, the Stasi in Dresden picked up Wonneberger and interrogated him for several hours. They demanded that he give up his petitions containing names of those supporting the initiative for a social peace service, but Wonneberger refused. A thorn in the side of church and state authorities, Wonneberger continued with his peace work in Dresden until he was moved to Leipzig in 1985.

Peace Prayers in Leipzig

Following Christoph Wonneberger's model, youth pastors for Leipzig and for the Saxony region initiated peace prayers in Leipzig in 1982. The first services were held at Nikolai Church in the Leipzig city center, and they continued on Mondays at 5 p.m. at that location through fall 1989 and beyond.[147] The peace prayers in Leipzig had had a checkered success, however, and attendance fluctuated over the years. Often sparse, participation increased periodically in response to state repression, international tensions, or solidarity efforts.

In 1985, in an effort to revitalize the peace prayers, Leipzig church Superintendent Friedrich Magirius set up a coordinating committee that gave church-based groups a role in organizing the peace prayers. Composed of both church and group

Nikolai Church exterior
Photo by Patricia Smith

Courtyard of Nikolai Church
Photo by Patricia Smith

leaders, the Synodal Committee for Peace and Justice[148] was designed to coordinate group work within the church district and responsibilities for the peace prayer services in Leipzig.[149]

According to Magirius, this form of church-group committee was a specialty of Leipzig and did not exist elsewhere in East Germany. As part of their involvement with this committee, Leipzig groups participated in the planning and shared leadership of the traditional Monday night peace prayers in Nikolai Church, and during the committee's existence about 20 groups had been involved in leadership roles. However, from the beginning Magirius had excluded several groups from the organizing committee because he viewed them as too oppositional, too controversial.[150]

Christoph Wonneberger's involvement with the Leipzig peace prayers began in 1985 with his participation on the peace prayers coordinating committee.[152] At that time the Leipzig peace prayers were practically defunct and church leaders hoped that Wonneberger as initiator of the concept for peace prayers, along with the newly created coordinating committee,

Christoph Wonneberger extinguishing candles, Lukas Church
Photo by Martin Jehnichen/Archiv Bürgerbewegung Leipzig e. V.

could help revitalize the Leipzig service.[153] Then in 1986 the church leadership assigned Wonneberger responsibility for coordinating the peace prayers, and groups continued participating in the planning and leadership of the services.

After the East German-wide Ten Days of Peace (*Friedensdekaden*) meetings in 1987, Wonneberger called for Leipzig groups to meet at Lukas Church, his parish, on December 15, 1987. There the group assessed the weaknesses of the peace prayers in Leipzig as they currently stood. Stasi reports on the meeting indicate that Wonneberger felt that the peace prayers dealt with problems in a "too loyal and too superficial" manner and that the results were "too ineffective."[154] Wonneberger offered various concepts for broadening the services and for making them more practical and more effective. The meeting led to a politicized peace effort in Leipzig and to a new emphasis in the peace prayers on human rights and democratic change.[155]

Nikolai Church interior
Photo by Patricia Smith

When groups participated in organizing and leading the services, they featured themes that group members viewed as important, such as alternatives to military service and education for peace. Groups also put up posters and other information in the Nikolai Church foyer so persons attending the services could learn about group meetings, solidarity demonstrations, and other issues of concern.

As Uwe Schwabe of Initiative Group Living noted, "Concerning my motivation to take part in the peace prayers, it seemed to offer a real opportunity to inform people, to articulate political positions. We felt that it was part of the task of the church to articulate these things. It was their job. It was part of liberation theology that we learned from Martin Luther King, Jr. So it seemed a very legitimate means, this nonviolent approach which came out of the peace prayer meetings."[151]

But not everyone in the church felt that way.

This politicization of the services led to Superintendent Magirius's letter prohibiting the groups from participating, and, as described earlier, his decision moved the groups out of the church and onto the street.

*   *   *

The relationship of the church to groups and the role of groups in the peace prayer services divided the clergy in Leipzig. Klaus Kaden, the pastor in charge of Leipzig's Youth Bureau, was generally supportive of groups; however, some of the particularly oppositional statements by group members in the services shocked him.

For example, at a service in June 1988 organized by Solidarity Church, group members directly criticized the state and party leadership, and organizers also brought in a hard rocker who dressed in leather and sang blatantly political lyrics. Kaden felt that the service "had nothing to do with a 'prayer' anymore. Group organizers had overstepped the boundaries and had clearly pushed it to a breaking point."[156]

Magirius's ban on group participation caused Kaden to reflect on his support for groups, and in some cases he felt that groups went too far.[157] Kaden recalled a meeting between groups and church officials in October 1988 after Magirius had banned groups from participating. There, Jochen Lässig, a member of the oppositional Initiative Group Living and a theology student, had challenged Bishop Hempel about whom the church served and who could participate. Reflecting his Protestant background and the importance of the individual in religious decisions, Lässig asked, "Who gave you the right to tell us what is and what is not in accordance with the Gospel? You are in no position to do that."[158] Hempel responded, "I heard what you had to say. It affects me a great deal, but you are right."

Kaden later told Jochen Lässig, "This cannot go on like this. I can't assume responsibility for this kind of thing; this no longer has anything to do with a religious service." Kaden felt it was very important that "we *actually* had religious services in the church. This was not only important in symbolic terms, but also in our relationship to the state. Besides, I think we owed that much to our beliefs and our reputation."[159]

Kaden agreed with Magirius's decision to exclude groups from the peace prayer leadership, feeling that the clergy needed to get more involved and take more responsibility for the peace prayer services. However, he disagreed with the way Magirius handled the decision—made without the participation of other church leaders, carried out in a blatant authoritarian manner, and informing group members and Wonneberger with a letter rather than in a meeting.[160]

*   *   *

In February 1989 the Nikolai Church council had decided to allow groups to again take responsibility for planning and leading the peace prayers, after they had been excluded for more than six months. April 10, 1989, the day of the first service when Wonneberger and the groups resumed responsibility, marked a new era for the Leipzig peace prayers. The experiences of Leipzig groups in the street had politicized them. Throughout 1989 as groups took responsibility for the peace prayer services, attendance swelled. On April 10, 1989, more than 900 persons attended this first service again led by groups after their exclusion,[161] and throughout the spring 500 or more persons attended almost every peace prayer service. After many services increasingly large groups of demonstrators spilled out of Nikolai Church, into the church courtyard, and onto the streets of central Leipzig.

The Monday evening peace prayers, regularly scheduled services that had taken place in Nikolai Church since 1982, provided a focal point for group organizing, and groups intentionally promoted demonstrations following the services as a means of building a mass base supporting fundamental changes in East Germany. "The intention of the groups," according to Jochen Lässig of Initiative Group Living, "was to popularize the peace prayers and to build a larger following for group ideas and activities."[162]

Leipzig Peace Groups

At least two peace groups played significant roles in the Leipzig group scene. Members of both groups participated regularly in the activities of most Leipzig groups, and they periodically organized their own public events. One of the Leipzig peace groups, Working Group Peace Service, participated in the church synod's coordination committee for the peace prayers, while the other group featured below, Women for Peace, had been excluded.

Working Group Peace Service

An early Leipzig group, Working Group Peace Service (*Arbeitsgemeinschaft Friedensdienst*) was founded in 1981–82 by a circle of 12 personal friends.[163] The east/west military confrontation, and particularly the proposed stationing of missiles by NATO in West Germany and by the Soviet Union in East Germany, provided an impetus for the group's beginning. The group originated shortly after Wonneberger's initiative for a social peace service had gained prominence in Dresden and throughout East Germany. Several group members had refused military service and served as construction soldiers.

   All members of Working Group Peace Service viewed themselves as Christians, and key members included Brigitte Moritz, Matthias Sengewald, and Katrin Sengewald. Group members had participated in the peace prayers coordinating committee and regularly planned and took responsibility for leading the Monday night peace prayer services in Nikolai Church, which they always organized around a particular theme. According to Brigitte Moritz, members saw themselves as part of the European-wide peace movement. "We didn't really view ourselves as opposition, but we weren't satisfied with the current situation and wanted to change East Germany."[164]

   Every year the group concentrated on a particular theme and promoted its work by publishing information on the topic under church auspices for broader distribution. The group also prepared information and exhibits for various gatherings. As part of the Leipzig church district's Youth Bureau, Working Group Peace Service had primary responsibility every year for planning the program for the East German-wide Ten Days of Peace workshops that involved groups from all over East Germany.

   For an early Ten Days of Peace event organized around the slogan "Justice—Disarmament—Peace," the Leipzig group supplemented the official materials prepared by the central administration of the Evangelical Churches in East Germany with their own materials. Group-initiated subjects included war toys, civil defense, and social peace service—the controversial proposal for an alternative to military service. During these ten days, exhibits and programs were presented in several Leipzig churches and raised a number of provocative issues. The largest gathering was held on closing day in Nikolai Church, with more than 800 youth attending and reflecting on the theme "walls." Since these early meetings in Leipzig, the Stasi had kept close watch over the annual Ten Days of Peace meetings in Leipzig and throughout East Germany.[165]

   Brigitte Moritz played a central role in Working Group Peace Service as well as in the Leipzig group scene as editor of *Kontakte*, an informational newsletter of Leipzig church-based groups.[166] The publication provided extensive information about group activities in Leipzig and other cities and played a critical coordinative and communication role within Leipzig and in the broader East German group milieu. *Kontakte* was published twice monthly, and 100 copies of the publication were distributed to Leipzig groups and sent by mail to other groups throughout East Germany.[167]

Part of Moritz's work was with Christoph Wonneberger in Lukas Church, and there she was involved in a number of controversial activities initiated and carried out by Leipzig groups. Since 1984, the Stasi had Brigitte Moritz under surveillance using the code name "Julia," also the name of Moritz's daughter, who was three years old at the time.[168] The church hierarchy disapproved of Moritz's involvements in controversial activities, and Saxony church bishop Johannes Hempel once chastised her for her group work, saying, "You [group members] are only five percent. What that means is: 'Don't make so much noise; the church community wants to have its peace.'"[169]

Moritz became involved personally in promoting ideas and activities that challenged the state because, as she recounted, "I felt that it was important to be able to say to my children, 'I did something. I worked to change the system.'"[170] For Moritz, the group experience was central and rewarding: "I grew up in a church family and, as a Christian, it was important that I lived in a way that supported my beliefs. I couldn't *not* participate. I always earned very little, but in the groups I experienced much more than I would have otherwise."[171] "Essentially we were only a courageous minority that ultimately was able to work under the protective shield of the church."[172]

Women for Peace

The Leipzig group Women for Peace (*Frauen für den Frieden*) originated in 1984–85 with about 15 members, including Gabriele Heide, Brigitte Moritz, Ute Leukert-Kämpf, Marianne Ramson, and Katrin Sengewald.[173] The formation of the Leipzig group by a number of women with children who were concerned about the future followed the founding of the first Women for Peace group in Berlin in 1982. Major themes of the group centered on military service, the education system, and *Öffentlichkeit,* and a method for promoting *Öffentlichkeit* was to hold public forums on various issues—to open up the discussion to a broader segment of the population.

Women for Peace viewed the picture of the enemy promoted by the East German state as especially detrimental to children. To counter this, the group promoted reform of the education system and worked especially to change the concept of others as "the enemy." Protesting against education for hate in state kindergartens and schools, the group published a critique of a proposal for a state kindergarten system that it distributed widely among women's groups throughout East Germany.

Gabriele Heide's involvement with groups and the peace movement began in 1982 with the publication of the new military defense law and its provisions for the draft. The law required that all men serve 8 to 12 weeks in the military reserves every year and, in case of a national emergency, women between the ages of 18 and 50 would be drafted, a particular concern for Heide, the mother of two children. Educated as a social worker and employed in the Evangelical Church's youth programs, Heide engaged herself personally and within the group for reforms in the East German educational system.

According to Heide, "We viewed ourselves as opposition from the beginning and promoted a political agenda."[174] Women for Peace also saw itself as part of the alternative movement worldwide. In these senses, members viewed themselves as connected to other women's groups and to oppositional and alternative groups in East Germany and in the international arena.

Because of its critical stance, Women for Peace was one of four groups that Superintendent Magirius had excluded from the coordinating committee for the peace prayers, and the group had difficulties finding rooms for its meetings and for group-initiated programs. However, Women for Peace was tied into the network of oppositional groups in Leipzig formed around pastor Christoph Wonneberger, who supported grassroots groups and especially critical groups. According to Heide, "Wonneberger didn't play a strong, directive leadership role but rather served as an integration figure who wanted to make it possible for all groups to meet."[175]

Leipzig Peace Groups

Working Group Peace Service (AGFD)

> **Work Areas/Themes:** Alternatives to military service, reducing tensions between east and west; military education in schools

> **Key Members:** Brigitte Moritz, Matthias Sengewald, Katrin Sengewald

> **Tactics:** Exhibits and programs on peace issues; organized Ten Days of Peace meetings

> **Founded:** 1981–1982

Women for Peace (Frauen für den Frieden, FfdF)

> **Work Areas/Themes:** Military service issues, educational system reform

> **Key Members:** Gabriele Heide, Brigitte Moritz, Ute Leukert-Kämpf, Marianne Ramson, Katrin Sengewald

> **Tactics:** Prepared documents and programs on issues related to peace, promoted nonviolence, viewed self as opposition

> **Founded:** 1984–1985

Church-State and Church-Group Relations

In Leipzig, the tension between groups and the church stemmed in part from church-state relations, and, as mentioned, the state regularly pressured church leaders to control pastors and groups promoting oppositional or controversial programs.[176] Over the years the state had periodically pushed church officials, including both President Domsch and Bishop Hempel of the Saxony Church District in Dresden, to discipline Pastor Christoph Wonneberger, first in Dresden and later in Leipzig. Already in May 1987, Bishop Hempel had sent a letter of warning to Wonneberger, demanding that he not support group activities such as the planned evening featuring the controversial singer and group supporter Stephan Krawczyk.[177]

The state also pressured Leipzig Superintendent Magirius to prevent Wonneberger, whose Stasi code name was "Lukas," from allowing groups to use the facilities in Lukas Church for controversial activities,[178] and in fall 1988, Magirius took away Wonneberger's responsibility for the peace prayers. In his defense, when I asked about state pressures, Magirius answered, "Stasi reports were not always written fully—they were selective and presented a false picture."[179] But Wonneberger complained to me, "The church leadership was not always fair. A person always had to fight for everything, and groups certainly couldn't do everything under the roof of the church."[180] The Stasi report on church politics in Saxony added that Wonneberger felt that the church leadership could not afford to take legal proceedings against him, so he continued to support political groups.[181]

Most group members viewed Christoph Wonneberger, pastor of Lukas Church and cofounder of the oppositional Working Group Human Rights in Leipzig, as supportive of their programs.[182] He facilitated the meetings of the informal network of Leipzig oppositional groups and made Lukas Church available for meetings and programs of a wide variety of groups, over the long term and for all types of activities, including controversial programs.[183] Solidarity efforts using contact telephone lines, the alternative church congress, and oppositional group networks all periodically used the facilities at Lukas Church.[184]

Sign, "Open for All," in front of Nikolai Church
Photo by Patricia Smith

When another pastor would not allow a group to meet because of an especially controversial program, the group would frequently turn to Wonneberger. He complained, "Most other pastors in Leipzig didn't have an ear for anything hot, and they wouldn't support groups in their more controversial activities."[185] Wonneberger noted that despite the sign "Open for All" in the church courtyard, Nikolai Church was not always available, especially for oppositional groups. The church may have been "open for all, but not for everything,"[186] commented Won-neberger.

Rolf-Michael Turek, pastor of Markus Church in the Leipzig-Reunitz area of south Leipzig from 1984, also had good working relationships with most Leipzig groups. He supported group activities by periodically allowing groups to use church meeting rooms, mimeograph equipment, and telephones, as he did with the contact network for the Rosa Luxemburg solidarity efforts.[187]

Group relations with a number of church officials and pastors were strained. In Leipzig, at least seven pastors were Stasi informers.[188] One of the most difficult relationships for groups was with Matthias Berger, pastor of Erlöser Church. As head of the church-group coordinating committee respon-sible for the peace prayers, he played a significant role in relation to groups. However, as a Stasi informer with the code name "Carl," Berger undermined many group-initiated activities.[189] Brigitte Moritz, a member of the coordinating committee, called Berger "a little James Bond."[190] Human rights activist Uwe Schwabe recalled that several years after the coordinating committee formed in 1985, Berger had recruited Initiative Group Living, a group not founded until 1987, into the synod committee and then attempted to influence the group.[191]

Superintendent Friedrich Magirius viewed himself as a group supporter, partially as a result of his own earlier experiences as director of the group Wit-ness for Peace (*Aktion Sühnezeichnen*) in East Germany.[192] Most group mem-bers, however, did not consider Magirius supportive, especially after he took away group responsibilities for the peace prayers. While groups promoted demonstrations as a legitimate form of action,[193] Magirius called the demon-strations "a form of action not appropriate for the church."[194] He also criticized other group activities, such as a program by Stephan Krawczyk, who "sang only political and not Christian songs," as more political than Christian.[195] Because Magirius and the official church leadership tried to prevent these and many other controversial activities from occurring under church auspices, the rela-tionship between many groups and Magirius was frequently strained.[196]

Some Leipzig groups had a history of difficult relationships with the church, and some group members expressed considerable anger about the church's role in relation to groups. Thomas Rudolph characterized the relation-ship of Working Circle Justice with the church as "tense, strained." A grassroots

group not affiliated with a particular parish, Working Circle Justice was politi-
cally independent, but it did use the church's meeting rooms.[197] Rainer Müller,
another member of Working Circle Justice, viewed the church as playing a negative role in the changes in East Germany. He commented, "The church should
be ashamed of what it did in East Germany. It was made up of lots of weak people, and it didn't really create free operating space for groups or others."[198]

An important function played by the church was to protect group members from the state and from probable arrest. This was particularly important for
groups like Women for Peace, where all members were mothers with young
children, and many were single mothers. As Gabriele Heide of Women for Peace
noted, "We couldn't be jailed for our activities because we needed to care for our
children, and we relied on the church for protection in this regard."[199] Although
Women for Peace also had a strained relationship with the church leadership,
was excluded from the church-group coordinating committee, and had contin-
ual difficulties finding meeting rooms and church supporters, the group had
good relationships with Christian Führer, head pastor of Nikolai Church, and
Christoph Wonneberger.[200] Not all group members in Leipzig agreed that the
church's protection was important. Rainer Müller of Working Circle Justice
complained, "The church's protection was a mixed benefit, because the church's
support came with conditions that sometimes prevented groups from carrying
out their programs."[201]

In assessing the influence of the church on groups, Jochen Lässig of Initiative Group Living ranked group contact with the church leadership as *the*
most significant aspect of the group-church relationship. According to Lässig,
"This influence was a negative factor—although the *key* factor in moving the
groups away from the church."[202] The groups' negative relationships with the
church leadership forced them to move away from the church and resulted in
their taking independent actions that challenged the state and led to the revolution of 1989. Lässig points to the August 1988 letter from Superintendent
Magirius prohibiting the groups from participating in the peace prayers as the
key incident in raising the activity level of groups and leading to the East German revolution, because it pushed the groups out into the street.

Peace Prayers and Demonstrations in 1988 and 1989: Prelude to Revolution

The Monday night demonstrations in Leipzig provided for most armchair observers a visual symbol of the 1989 East German revolution. Most western observers who followed the 1989 revolutions in Eastern Europe can recall scenes from Leipzig's fall candlelight demonstrations with hundreds of thousands of East Germans marching around Leipzig's central ring. The media often referred to the protests as spontaneous, but these demonstrations were far from spontaneous. The demonstrations were the culmination of group activities by a small but growing core of Leipzig activists that intensified over a period of several years.[203]

Although the traditional Monday peace prayers at Nikolai Church provided a central location and a starting point for moving toward the Leipzig Ring—the broad, demonstration-friendly streets that circled the city—these demonstrations were neither church-sponsored nor church-promoted.

As Uwe Schwabe of Initiative Group Living explained later, "The demonstrations had to come away from the church because the leadership didn't want us to express all our political ideas there. So we looked for another way, and the other way was to stand outside the church and inform people. . . . [B]oth ways were used to try to inform people and move them, the peace prayer meetings and the demonstrations. These demonstrations were legitimate means, in my opinion, during the time of the GDR [East Germany]. . . . Now there are other ways, but then about the only way one could publicly express one's ideas was to go out on the streets in a demonstration."[204]

In large part, the answer to the question "Why Leipzig?" stems from the move away from the church on the part of several Leipzig groups and on these groups' initiation of a number of significant activities outside the protective walls of the church. Only as groups moved away from the church did they consistently organize and participate in political actions that directly challenged the East German state. When groups again assumed leadership of the peace prayers in April 1989 after being banned for more than six months, they had developed a new venue for promoting political change—the streets.

The peace prayers would resume in September 1989, after the summer recess. Despite pressures from the state not to continue, the church leadership responsible for the peace prayers decided to allow the services to go ahead.[205]

However, when the peace prayers reconvened on September 4, 1989, the fall trade fair would be in Leipzig, bringing the international media to town along with thousands of visitors.[206]

Although only several hundred demonstrated after the Monday services in early September, the number of supporters increased every week—7,500 by the end of September, 75,000 in early October. And by November, half a million people circled the Leipzig Ring, peacefully demonstrating their support for more freedom in East Germany.

CHAPTER 4

Proving Election Fraud:
Local Election Monitoring and Protests, May 7, 1989

That is the paradox of the epidemic: in order to create one contagious movement, you often have to create many small movements first.[207]

—Malcolm Gladwell, *The Tipping Point:*
How Little Things Can Make a Big Difference

There was no democracy. Our actions were the creation of a democratic platform.[208]

—Jochen Lässig,
Initiative Group Living, Leipzig

Without the May election campaign, there would have been no fall demonstrations and no revolution.[209]

—Martin Böttger,
Initiative for Peace and Human Rights, Berlin

Many East German citizens had long suspected that election results reported by the East German state were fraudulent, and in 1989, activists in most major cities in East Germany set out to prove it, something no one had ever done before. East German groups organized an election-monitoring campaign for the May 7, 1989, local elections held throughout the country.[210] The idea for the monitoring campaign came from grassroots groups, both Christian and non-Christian, and also involved Marxists, artists, and anarchists.[211]

To recruit observers for the election-monitoring campaign in Leipzig, the church-based group coalition distributed mimeographed notices to group members and friends. The notice requested that observers attend a training session at Markus Church in Strasse der Befreiung at 7:30 p.m. on May 2, five days before the election, to discuss the monitoring program and to receive their precinct assignments.[212] Although the notice indicated that at least 90 persons would be needed to observe the vote, hundreds showed up, and on election day more than 300 participated in the church-group coordinated monitoring effort, observing the election in 250 polling places located outside the city center. For their parallel monitoring effort, the group Dialog and Perestroika had recruited about 100 people to observe voting in the Leipzig city center, and they succeeded in observing the election in 83 of 84 voting stations.[213]

Officially, the East German government maintained that elections were democratic, and voting was one of the most important rights and obligations of citizens. In theory at least, elections were free with secret ballots, and all citizens' votes were deemed equal.

Critics, however, pointed to a "democratic deficit" in East German elections. The ballot, a list with only one candidate for each position, was prepared by party officials and did not offer voters a choice. Elections did not involve a true multiparty system because in its "leading role," the communist party controlled the candidates on the ballot and the outcomes. In practice, ballots were not secret, because voting booths were seldom available, and all citizens were expected to vote in favor of the party list—to vote "yes."

Nor could voters freely choose to vote or not vote. State authorities viewed voting as an obligation in East Germany's socialist democracy and linked voting participation to support for the East German government and political system at all levels. Authorities expected almost 100 percent turnout, and published election reports customarily showed that around 99 percent of eligible citizens had voted. But an increasing number of East German citizens suspected that election results published by state and local authorities were not accurate.[214]

To achieve such high levels of participation, election authorities resorted to extraordinary measures. Election workers carried portable ballot boxes, labeled "flying urns" for the portability and shape of the receptacles, to elderly or ill voters. In later years, as participation in elections dropped, authorities resorted to more extreme measures to get out the vote. For example, applicants for emigration to the west received warnings that their visas would be denied if they failed to vote. Election authorities within a precinct went so far as to compile a list of persons whom they expected would not vote. Then on election day, election workers would carry portable ballot boxes around the city to private residences of citizens who had not voted by noon that day. East Germans who wanted to boycott the election as a protest learned that it was best to take a trip out of the city on election day.[215]

Despite the fact that voting was required of all adults, throughout the 1980s a growing number of East German citizens protested against the system by not voting. The largest groups of nonvoters were clergy and other church members, construction soldiers, oppositional group members, and emigration group members and individuals who wanted to leave East Germany.[216] During the last years of East Germany, authorities viewed this growing number of would-be emigrés boycotting elections with particular concern.

In addition to participating in elections, East German citizens were expected to vote for the slate of candidates put forward by the communist party in the "leading" role, along with the other four parties involved in the National Front. Although the ballot contained some candidates from the bloc parties, communist party and state authorities had preapproved all candidates, and the ballot did not include a choice among candidates. To vote "yes" in an election—the expectation of authorities—voters simply folded their ballots and dropped them into the ballot box. Given this widespread practice of simply folding the ballot rather than making an active choice, East Germans would sarcastically refer to the process of voting as "ballot folding" (*Zettel falten*) rather than as voting.[217]

To vote against the proposed slate of candidates—to vote "no"—involved considerable risk. Although election authorities did provide some voting booths so that it was theoretically possible to vote in secret, using the voting booth drew negative attention. Using voting booths identified the voter as not supporting the state, at a minimum, and perhaps even as actively opposing the state.

The procedure for voting in secret was also cumbersome. To use the voting booth, a prospective voter had to sign a special register kept by election authorities. If a voter signed the register and used the voting booth, the voter would be put under surveillance after the election, and repercussions often followed. Authorities would send information about the person's election behavior to the voter's work, party, or Free German Youth group, and as a result, the voter might be denied a promotion or admission to a university program or some other special privilege. The information that identified persons using a voting booth was also sent to local authorities and to the Stasi.[218] Nevertheless, an increasing number of East Germans protested against the election system by using voting booths.

Others voted "no" more publicly, rather than in secret, by striking through the names of one or more candidates on the ballot or by marking an "X" through the entire ballot.

Sometimes East German authorities—in an effort to have elections run smoothly—offered certain perks or benefits to potential election boycotters. A potential boycotter might receive a new apartment or repairs to an existing apartment. Or an applicant for emigration to the west might suddenly find his or her application approved. In fact, just prior to the May 7 local elections, authorities approved the applications of 1,700 Leipzigers who wanted to emigrate.[219] These emigrants were required to leave Leipzig immediately, before they had the opportunity to boycott the election or to vote against the party list, so their numbers would not appear in the election results compiled on May 7 by Leipzig group members or by the state.

East Germans were widely aware of election irregularities, and most also knew or at least suspected that party and state authorities falsified election results. Until the May 7 local elections, however, no one had attempted to prove election fraud.[220] To do so required considerable coordination. Such an endeavor required a plan and the implementation of the plan by a number of groups.

*   *   *

In Leipzig, three human rights groups—Working Circle Justice, Working Group Human Rights, and Initiative Group Living—and the Marxist group Dialog took the lead in organizing the election-monitoring effort. Group members would observe the elections in local precincts on election day in Leipzig and in other cities throughout East Germany.[221] At the close of voting, observers would count both the total number of ballots cast in each precinct as well as the "no" votes. After group observers in each city compiled their results, couriers would take the local data to Berlin, where group members would tally the results from throughout East Germany. The objective of the election-monitoring campaign was to compare the state's election results with the groups' figures. If the numbers differed substantially, the groups would have proved that numbers had been falsified. In that way, they would prove election fraud.

The Context for Democratic Reforms

Many older activists in East Germany point to Czechoslovakia in 1968—the major movement for democratic, economic, and cultural reform referred to as the Prague Spring—as the backdrop for their own involvements in alternative or oppositional groups. By late 1967 reform-minded intellectuals in Czechoslovakia had gained control of the communist party, and in January 1968 they replaced party and government leader Antonin Novotny with reformist leader Alexander Dubcek. Important political reforms included eliminating the principle of democratic centralism, curbing police power, removing censorship, guaranteeing civil rights, and allowing citizens to form associations and petition the government.[222] However, several Soviet bloc leaders from Eastern Europe and the Soviet Union feared their own abilities to retain control of their governments and populations if the Czechoslovak reforms succeeded and spread. The leaders convened the Warsaw Treaty Organization and decided to end the Czechoslovak reforms militarily. On August 21, 1968, 500,000 Warsaw Pact troops and tanks—from the Soviet Union, East Germany, Bulgaria, Hungary, and Poland—invaded Czechoslovakia, forcibly ending the Prague Spring. This military action established the so-called Brezhnev Doctrine (named for the Soviet leader in power at the time) and articulated the right of Warsaw Pact troops to intervene militarily in the affairs of Soviet bloc states to protect them from internal or external threats.

Both the reforms initiated in Czechoslovakia and brutal repression of the reform movement had a major impact on many citizens throughout Eastern Europe. A major lesson of 1968 concerned the limits of reform.

More than thirty years later, with Gorbachev's rise to power in the Soviet Union, democratic reforms once again became conceivable in the Soviet bloc, and Gorbachev's proposals for *glasnost, perestroika,* and new thinking stimulated reform movements in the Soviet Union and other East European states. Gorbachev's reform efforts suggested that the Soviet Union would allow major democratic reforms in East European satellite states and that Soviet troops would not intervene. Soon, on July 7, 1989, at a meeting of communist bloc states in Bucharest, Romania, Gorbachev would formally announce the end of the Brezhnev Doctrine.[223]

Already in early 1989, significant political reforms had occurred in Hungary, the Soviet Union, and Poland.

Hungary

- January 11, 1989. The Hungarian parliament in Budapest decided to allow a multiparty system and reassessed the uprising of 1956, calling it a "popular rebellion."[224]
- March 1989. Hungary's communist party and the political opposition began discussing Hungary's transition to parliamentary democracy.[225]

Soviet Union

- March 26, 1989. For the first time, voters in Soviet elections for the Chamber of Deputies, the lower house, could choose from among several candidates—the first multiparty elections in the Soviet Union.

Poland

- February 6 to April 4, 1989. The Polish Round Table, composed of representatives of the Polish government, on the one hand, and the banned trade union Solidarity and other opposition groups, on the other, began talks.[226] The Polish Round Table established a model for government–opposition talks in East European states.
- April 5, 1989. The Polish Round Table announced an agreement to hold free elections for the Polish parliament in June 1989.[227] Oppositional parties could participate, giving Poland contested elections and a multiparty system.
- April 17, 1989. The Polish government legalized Solidarity, by then a broad-based movement for reform.[228] Lech Walesa, leader of Solidarity, would later be elected president of Poland.

Meanwhile, several East European states continued to resist reform. In hardline Czechoslovakia, prominent Czech writer and opposition leader Vaclav Havel was sentenced to nine months in prison on February 21, 1989.[229] His arrest unleashed a wave of solidarity protests throughout the east bloc. As in Czechoslovakia, leaders in Romania, Bulgaria, and East Germany continued to resist Gorbachev's reforms. Gorbachev grew to dislike Erich Honecker and publicly made a number of comments that served to undermine Honecker's position and hold on power in East Germany. Lumping Honecker together with Todor Zhivkov in

Bulgaria, Gustav Husak in Czechoslovakia, and Nicolae Ceausescu in Romania, Gorbachev called them a "Gang of Four"—a group of inflexible east bloc leaders unwilling to make necessary reforms.[230]

East German activists, however, drew support for democratic reforms from Gorbachev's statements and actions and from reform efforts throughout the Soviet bloc. Campaigns of civil resistance sprang up throughout Eastern Europe, featuring popular opposition to one-party rule and manipulated elections. In this context, East German civil rights groups and other alternative groups made plans to monitor the May 7 elections.

*   *   *

Some signs of reform were visible even within the seemingly conservative communist party structure. Even though officially East Germany's communist party did not support Gorbachev's reforms, significant portions of its membership and of affiliated organizations in the National Front, especially young people and intellectuals, supported such reforms.[231] For example, the 1988–89 issue of the orthodox *Deutsche Zeitschrift für Philosophie* contained an article by Alfred Kosing of the central committee's Academy of Social Sciences on the need for reforms. Kosing argued that the reforms that had taken place in East Germany were not enough and that it was necessary to carry out reforms in all spheres—political, social, cultural, and educational—in addition to economic reforms.[232]

Over the years various ideas and events created discussion and dissension within the party. Many members left the communist party in 1968 after the Warsaw Pact invasion crushed the Prague Spring. Prominent East German oppositionist Wolfgang Templin had been a part of the Trotskyite left opposition, but in 1983 he stepped out of the communist party and became active in peace and human rights groups.[233] The November 1988 banning of the Russian periodical *Sputnik*, because it contained materials reassessing history that state authorities viewed as threatening, led to widespread dissension within the party and sparked the beginning of a new exodus.[234] Others stayed in the communist party through 1989 but became increasingly disillusioned and critical as the aging East German leadership refused to implement meaningful changes.

Elections and the Political System: A Democratic Deficit

Following the model used throughout the communist bloc, the East German state maintained a strong presence in almost all aspects of political life. Directed democracy guided by the principle of democratic centralism provided a top-down approach to political and governmental affairs.[235] Party leaders held both party and government positions and sent directions down through the hierarchy to the local level. The communist party played the "leading role" in the political system, and the other four recognized bloc parties—the Christian Democratic Union, the Liberal Democratic Party of Germany, the National Democratic Party of Germany, and the Democratic Farmers' Party—followed the lead of the communist party.[236]

Historically, these parties had represented various segments of East German society. The communist party represented workers, under communist theory the most important element in the socialist state—in East Germany as in the Soviet Union and throughout the communist bloc. The other four parties represented churches, the middle class, nationalists, and farmers.[237] In East Germany's nominally multiparty system, only about 12 percent of East Germans belonged to the communist party.[238] However, this was not a multiparty system of equals. Because the communist party played the leading role among the parties, candidates for all offices had to be acceptable to communist party and state officials.

East Germany, along with other socialist countries, also developed a system of mass organizations to involve the East German population in political affairs. The state put considerable pressure on its citizens to belong to pertinent organizations—associations for trade unions, cultural affairs, youth, women— and most complied, at least by joining if not by participating actively. These mass organizations along with the five political parties comprised the National Front, the body assigned responsibilities for encouraging civic participation and community spirit as well as for organizing and promoting elections in East Germany.[239]

Organizations in National Front

Mass Organizations
Federation of German Trade Unions (FDGB)
Free German Youth (FDJ)
Democratic Woman's League of Germany (DFD)
Cultural Association (Kulturbund)
Peasants' Mutual Aid Association (VdgB)

Political Parties
Socialist Unity Party (SED, communist)
Christian Democratic Union (CDU)
Liberal Democratic Party of Germany (LDPD)
National Democratic Party of Germany (NDPD)
Democratic Farmers' Party (DBD)

Scharf, *Politics and Change in East Germany,* 25.

Protesting Elections in East Germany

The effort to monitor elections had started several years earlier, in 1986, with an effort to prove election fraud by observing ballots for the East German parliament (*Volkskammer*) elections in several precincts in Berlin-Friedrichshain.[240] These earlier election activities document group organization and planning but provide little evidence of any coordinated organizational efforts. Nevertheless, these election activities provided background and experience for the May 1989 East German-wide election-monitoring campaign. Oppositional and church groups involved in election activities included human rights, peace, ecology, emigration, and others. In addition to these groups, the May 6 election-monitoring campaign included Marxist groups and other group and party members closely tied to the East German communist party and state.

The attempt to prove election fraud in East Germany in 1989 actually combined several types of election protests. In addition to monitoring the election, some activists protested by refusing to participate—by boycotting the election. Clergy and other members of various religious groups had used election boycotts regularly throughout East Germany's history.[241] Most election boycotts involved more personal protests, however, usually unaccompanied by publicity,

in contrast to the May 1989 election monitoring campaign's intent of publicizing the results and thereby discrediting East German elections.[242]

Other proposals for reforming elections, such as the one from Pro
Humanitas, a recently founded group composed of persons wanting to leave
East Germany, attempted to get group-supported candidates on the ballot, a difficult proposition, given the state's procedure of compiling its own list comprising only "acceptable" candidates.[243] In January 1989, a loose coalition of several
Berlin groups sent church peace and environmental groups "A Letter to Christians," encouraging them to nominate independent candidates.[244] Also, the
Peace Circle of Erlöser Church in Berlin sent out a countrywide call for groups
and individuals to participate in election meetings and to nominate their own
candidates, and Network Ark called for the development of a Green (pro-envi-
ronment) list with candidates from peace, environmental, and human rights
movements to challenge the official state list of candidates.

On April 15, 1989, after attempts to get group-supported candidates on the
ballot failed, the Working Circle of Solidarity Church/Regional Group
Thuringia sent out leaflets calling for an election boycott, and they were joined
by several other groups. Earlier, Solidarity Church had prepared a detailed
analysis of East German election laws that outlined four valid election options
available for East German citizens: voting "yes" for the recommended slate of
candidates (not a protest vote), voting "no" for all the recommended candidates,
casting an invalid ballot (i.e., participating in the election but not making any
decision for or against a candidate), and refusing to participate in the election by
staying away.[245]

Several official church bodies, including the synods of several church
regions, complained about the absence of full democratic participation in
East German elections—a democratic deficit. Already in fall 1988 the
Magdeburg synod of the Evangelical Church discussed the election issue,
calling for a more secret ballot through the regular use of private voting
booths and for the freedom to participate or not participate in elections. In
April 1989, a month before the local elections, the Saxony church synod,
which included Leipzig, passed recommendations for churches in the synod.
Because attempts to run independent candidates for elections had failed and
the elections offered no real choice, citizens should either participate and

vote in voting booths or choose not to participate and stay away from the elections. These recommendations represented a direct challenge to the East German election process and to the state on the part of the Evangelical Church
synod in Saxony.[246]

Other East German groups worked together on plans to get out the "no"
vote. As one of the organizing groups, Network Ark, recommended in its publication *Arche Nova*, because the state would not allow groups to propose their
own candidates, "a more meaningful protest vote is to strike out all candidates
of the National Front rather than not vote at all."[247] After some internal disagreement, however, Network Ark hedged. Their editorial board changed its
position and in the April 1989 issue of *Arche Nova* advised its members to follow their own consciences, noting, "Finally, it will be the personal decision of
each individual, whether s/he actively participates in the election or not."[248] So,
as the May 7, 1989 election approached, the election-monitoring campaign represented only one of several types of election protests, and a number of individuals, groups, and church bodies continued to favor an election boycott.

Monitoring the Election in Leipzig

Two coalitions of groups monitored the elections in Leipzig: human rights
groups within the church, on the one hand, and Marxists and communist party
members, on the other.[249] The involvement of Marxists and party members was
significant because they and church-based groups seldom joined forces to carry
out common programs. Working together on election monitoring set a precedent for future cooperative action and expanded the base of groups and individuals involved in activities challenging the East German state and political
system. Also, by participating in election monitoring—a project directly challenging state authorities—Marxists and communist party members signified
widespread dissatisfaction with social democracy as practiced in East Germany.
Because communist supporters generally benefited most from the perks of politics, they had more to lose from engaging in public protest.

Nevertheless, a number of persons with links to party and mass organizations joined the monitoring effort.[250] Many volunteers came from the university,
primarily students, and from the medical community and related professions. A
number also came from publishing, arts communities, and critical intellectuals.

Many welcomed this first opportunity to actually do something concrete, since they had supported *glasnost, perestroika,* and social reforms for a number of years. The task of the Marxist groups was to count votes in 84 precincts in central Leipzig.

A key organizer of the Marxist, university student, and party member coalition was Jürgen Tallig, cofounder of the Leipzig group Dialog.[251] The group, which promoted a more democratic socialism, had originated in response to Gorbachev's reform program in the Soviet Union. Tallig had previously worked as a bookseller and had organized cultural events including discussion circles, book readings, and artists' evenings. However, he had lost his job for political reasons, and in 1989 he worked as a psychiatric nurse.

In February 1988, Tallig, along with several friends, had painted pro-Gorbachev slogans in the pedestrian tunnel under Wilhelm Leuschner Square. After a week-long search, the Stasi had arrested Tallig as he attempted to hang a pro-democracy poster on the information kiosk in front of Moritz Bastion, and he was fined 2,000 marks for damages.[252]

Following Tallig's arrest and fine, Leipzig church-based groups demonstrated their solidarity with Tallig and his public actions in support of democratic reform. At the last peace prayer service before the summer recess in 1988, Initiative Group Living, along with Pastor Christoph Wonneberger, raised 1,000 marks to help Tallig pay off his fines. This support by church groups on behalf of an activist not associated with any church represented an important step in the Leipzig activist community: church-based groups had joined with Marxist and communist party reformers, thereby increasing the base of protestors in Leipzig.

Although the collection for Tällig increased group solidarity, church officials disapproved of the supportive action and Superintendent Magirius called the collection "an illegal collection." This action was a major factor leading to Magirius banning the activists from participating in future peace prayer services and relieving Christoph Wonneberger of his responsibilities for the peace prayers, as was mentioned earlier.

The second coalition of groups monitoring the election in Leipzig included Initiative Group Living, Working Group Human Rights, and Working Circle Justice. This second election-monitoring group involved several hundred persons, mostly from Leipzig human rights and other oppositional groups.

Their task was to count votes at election stations in almost 250 Leipzig precincts outside the city center.

Although all three human rights groups participating in the election monitoring favored a more democratic East Germany, their more specific goals differed, as did their preferred tactics. Though members of Initiative Group Living played a central role in organizing and monitoring the May 7 elections, IGL group members also organized a parallel action—a demonstration in Market Square. This demonstration not only allowed them to publicize the monitoring campaign but also provided an opportunity for those who had protested the election by not voting to publicly express their concerns about the lack of true democratic choice in East Germany.

Earlier that year, according to Pastor Rolf-Michael Turek, several church workers had attempted to get the church synod in Leipzig independently involved in monitoring the elections, i.e., without the support of groups.[253] In an attempt to recruit volunteers, they had sent out personal letters to representatives in local district churches; however, from 120 letters sent out, only 10 persons responded. It was clear that there was not enough interest for the church to carry out an election-monitoring program by itself—that would have to take place outside the church—so they gave up on that effort. Instead, a few church members joined with group organizers in the monitoring program, and several churches offered their equipment and rooms to support the group-initiated election project.

On May 6, the evening before the election, Working Circle Justice held a seminar in Reformierte Church for election observers and other election protesters. The meeting focused on what protesters should do if they were arrested and interrogated.[254] Many of the organizers had been arrested previously and, along with those of oppositional colleagues in Eastern Europe, their experiences prepared them for dealing with these situations. In Leipzig, an important part of the lessons of groups was nonviolence.

Election Day

On election day, May 7, when the elections ended, group representatives observed the official counting of ballots in the various precincts. The group observers counted "no" votes—ballots in which all candidates on the officially

approved slate had been crossed out. The observers then took their results from
the various precincts to election stations set up and staffed by group members
where the results were tallied.

The three human rights groups that initiated the election-monitoring
campaign in Leipzig set up a small election office in the seminary on Paul List
Street where they could compile the election results.[255]

Michaelis Church, north of the center, served as another of several bureaus
for coordinating Leipzig's election results. From there, Kathrin Walther telephoned regular updates on the progress of Leipzig's election monitoring to
Susanne Krug and Thomas Rudolf, who represented Leipzig groups in East
Berlin for the national monitoring campaign. At the end of the day, Kathrin
Walther and other group organizers in Leipzig relayed the final election results
from Leipzig to Berlin, where group organizers compiled the results from cities
throughout East Germany.

As in most group-initiated actions, these members of Working Circle Justice had responsibility for press reports about the East German-wide election
monitoring campaign. In addition to publicizing the election returns, this small
East German media group—Leipzig's underground press—sent out reports on
election protests from May 6–8, on election irregularities, and on Stasi and
police action and arrests. They kept in regular contact with the western press
through their contacts with journalists accredited in East Berlin.[256]

*   *   *

Markus Church, in the Leipzig-Reunitz area, served as another election headquarters for Leipzig's group-coordinated election observers.[257] The location of the
Markus Church offices at the conjunction of several public transportation lines supported group activities, since members could easily reach the church. Also, the
church offices regularly served as a communication center, because information
posted in the church office's window was visible from the street. Pastor Rolf-Michael
Turek allowed groups to use church telephones and mimeograph equipment, and he
also opened the church library to groups, where they had access to controversial
materials, including several dozen underground publications.

After votes were counted, results from each voting station in Leipzig were
carried to Turek at Markus Church. There he compiled sheets from each

precinct and typed up the results on the church's typewriter. He then sent out the results to other churches in the Saxony district and throughout East Germany.

Other Election Day Activities

In addition to participating in the election monitoring campaign, Initiative Group Living and several other Leipzig groups independently organized a gathering and demonstration for 6 p.m. on election day.[258] Several days before the election, group members had distributed handbills throughout the city calling for major changes in East Germany's election system. Organized as the Initiative for Democratic Renewal, these group members had encouraged citizens *not* to participate in the election but rather to meet in Leipzig's Market Square on May 7. Demonstrators were asked to bring a blank white sheet of paper to symbolize that they rejected existing election laws and election practices.[259] At the demonstration, protesters could toss their blank "ballots" into a ballot box on the square. West Berlin's Radio Glasnost also publicized the notice of this May 7 demonstration in Leipzig.[260]

Aware of the initiative, the Stasi had tried to prevent groups from placing their handbills in mailboxes. Nevertheless, on election day, more than 1,500 persons assembled in Market Square. After several speeches, about 1,000 demonstrators left the square and began marching through the streets of Leipzig's center. Security forces broke up the demonstration and shoved protesters into police wagons standing by at the scene.[261] State authorities detained 120 demonstrators and arrested 72 (in addition to those they had detained leading up to election day).[262] The Stasi report on the May 7 elections credited Initiative Group Living with primary responsibility for the election-monitoring campaign and the demonstration, noting that the organizers were under constant surveillance but did not appear at the demonstration.

The day after the elections, Monday, May 8, Initiative Group Living had responsibility for conducting the peace prayers at Nikolai Church, and at the services they reported on the previous day's events. Afterwards, an estimated 550 persons again attempted to demonstrate against election fraud. Twelve persons were arrested but were later released.[263]

Election Results

The day after the elections, May 8, state election authorities published offi-cial overall election results throughout East Germany in the party newspaper *Neues Deutschland*. Surprisingly, the state published results lower than 99 per-cent. The report claimed that 98.77 percent of eligible voters had voted and 98.85 had voted in favor of the party list—a "yes" vote.

Participation and votes of 98 percent were still much higher, however, than what group election monitors had observed. Precinct by precinct the group-tal-lied results from cities throughout East Germany confirmed that in some areas, participation ranged from 70 to 85 percent rather than almost 99 percent, and "no" votes averaged 7–8 percent, rather than the less than 2 percent reported by the state.[264]

In Leipzig, the Marxist-led coalition counted the vote in 83 of 84 precincts in the center, Leipzig-Mitte.[265] They reported that 91.6 percent of eligible voters participated in the election, with 90.9 percent voting for the slate of the National Front and 9.1 percent voting against. This contrasted with official state figures showing a participation rate of 98.5 percent and a "yes" vote of more than 96 percent (less than 4 percent voting "no"). Differences were even greater in other election districts monitored by groups, but groups were unable to compare exact numbers because authorities failed (declined) to publish the results for other areas. In an attempt to undermine the results obtained by election observers, Leipzig authorities published only city-wide totals for the rest of the city.[266]

The results in other East German cities were similar to those in Leipzig, but in some locations, much more dramatic. For example, in the Weißensee dis-trict of Berlin, groups monitored the election and vote count in almost all precincts. Official state election results reported 43,042 votes, but group observers in 66 of 67 precincts tallied only 27,680 total votes, only about 65 per-cent of eligible voters, indicating that in Weißensee a large number of potential voters boycotted the election. Election officials reported only 1,011 "no" votes, while group observers counted 2,260 "no" votes, more than double the "no" votes reported for Weißensee by state authorities in *Neues Deutschland*.[267] Sim-ilarly falsified results were observed and reported in Weimar, Naumburg, Pots-dam, Dresden, Erfurt, Jena, and the Berlin districts of Pankow, Prenzlauerberg, and Friedrichshain.[268]

For Rolf-Michael Turek, the results that day were "shocking." He noted that, for example, in Berlin's Prenzlauerberg the falsified results meant that instead of the official state results of 98.14 percent "yes" votes, according to group statistics, only 88.58 percent had voted "yes." "For East German times, that [more than 10 percent voting against the party slate] was an almost unbelievable result."[269]

The May 7 elections from Leipzig and throughout East Germany finally proved what many East Germans had long suspected. Group election observers had provided evidence that the state had falsified election results. For the first time, East German citizens had documented election fraud.

Follow-up Activities and Significance

The follow-up to the May 1989 local elections took various forms throughout East Germany. Groups publicized the results from the group-organized monitoring campaigns widely and organized demonstrations and other protest actions. In reaction to the falsified reports, a number of groups prepared reports documenting the fraudulent elections, and in many localities, groups sent letters of protest to local and state election authorities.[270] Also, a joint statement was prepared and signed by members of 18 groups from Berlin and other East German cities.[271]

In addition, four Leipzig groups—Working Group Human Rights, Working Circle Justice, Initiative Group Living, and Young Seminarians Leipzig—produced, signed, and distributed a declaration (*Erklärung*) protesting election fraud. Primary authors of the document were Thomas Rudolph and Kathrin Walther of Working Circle Justice and Frank Richter of Working Group Human Rights. Documenting the results obtained by group members monitoring the election returns, the proclamation concluded that "about 10 percent of the valid votes in Leipzig were cast against the recommended slate of the National Front"—that almost 10 percent of Leipzig voters had voted "no."[272] Furthermore, election monitors had observed other irregularities. These included ballot boxes with broken seals, missing ballots, and ballots correctly crossed through but counted as "yes" votes. Given these irregularities, the declaration concluded that in reality even more citizens had voted "no" during the election than the monitors had documented.[273]

The Marxist group carried out its own election protest. When authorities failed to publish the election results for Leipzig in the *Leipziger Volkszeitung*, the regional party newspaper for the Leipzig area, group members pressed local officials for election results. Members of the group Dialog sent letters of protest to local officials and telephoned various authorities in an attempt to get election results for all precincts in Leipzig, but group members received no satisfactory answers.[274]

Members of Dialog paid a price for their election protests. Participants in the election-monitoring campaign suffered repercussions at their workplaces, and communist party members were forced out of the party.[275] However, the election monitoring campaign also had positive effects for these critical Marxists. Proof of election fraud provided the impetus for a number of long-standing communist party members to leave the party and for some to move into active opposition. Following up on the heels of the *Sputnik* affair, the election-monitoring campaign brought a new wave of protests and defections within the communist party and led to massive resignations throughout fall 1989.

*   *   *

In Erfurt, the follow-up to the election deception was quick and decisive, and, as was the case with most group action there, took place primarily within the organizational structures of the church. On May 11, 1989, the Erfurt Association of Ministers of the Evangelical Church sent a letter protesting election fraud to the National Council of the East German National Front, the state body with election responsibilities. Detailing the differences between the official election tallies and those counted by group election observers, the association called for a reconsideration of the conduct of the Erfurt election and, if necessary, a new election.[276] The state responded to the demands only verbally, calling for a meeting between representatives of the ministerial association and the mayor of Erfurt, the head of the city election commission. State and city election authorities viewed the church's letter as an insult, however, and refused to recognize the petition, even declining to put their response in writing.

The next step for church officials was to prepare a proclamation detailing the election-monitoring process and the results. This proclamation, along with the letter sent to the National Council containing the initial charges of election fraud, was read from the pulpit of all Erfurt Evangelical churches on May 27, 1989. Calling for "more democracy and openness," the proclamation emphasized that if the state engaged in dialogue with its citizens and allowed more openness, the controversy would die down, but that if they did not, it would intensify.[277] This proclamation from the pulpit helped to legitimize group demands for openness and democracy and spread those demands to a broader segment of the population as represented by the Evangelical Church.

Aribert Rothe, Evangelical Church youth pastor and one of the organizers of the election-monitoring campaign in Erfurt, pointed to the central role of the church as a communication structure, noting that "proclamations from the pulpit were a political tool of the church." According to Rothe, "the election protests in Erfurt tied all the churches together. From that point on, they were no longer so cooperative with the state."[278]

*　*　*

In East Berlin, groups attempted to keep election fraud in the public eye by demonstrating on the seventh of every month, but police repeatedly put down the protests and arrested demonstrators. On June 7, protesters gathered in Alexanderplatz in central Berlin and placed a black funeral urn representing a ballot box in the square.[279] The sign accompanying the urn contained the words "Here lies democracy." Police had blocked streets and alleys leading to the site, and that day Berlin police arrested 150 demonstrators and took them to the Stasi prison for questioning. The protestors were later released, but many received heavy fines. The next day, 1,500 activists gathered at Gethsemane Church to protest the arrests and fines.

On July 7, Berlin groups again attempted to protest election fraud, but more than 1,000 police and military troops in civilian clothes blocked the streets leading to Alexanderplatz.[280] Police also prevented riders from exiting the subway at all Alexanderplatz stops. That day only a few demonstrators reached Alexanderplatz. Those arrested were quickly released.

Networks

A lesson of the election-monitoring campaign lies in its diversity. A wide variety of interlocking networks, informal as well as institutional, contributed to its success. This overall organizational picture was almost invisible to outside observers, and even those intimately involved in the organizational efforts were aware of only the broad outlines of the campaign in any one community or even within any group. However, these varied organizational efforts, from loose and informal to more structured and institutionalized, all contributed to the overall goal—to prove that the East German state falsified election results.

In Erfurt, networks were primarily church-related, and church leaders were actively involved or at least supportive of alternative activities such as the election-monitoring campaign. This contrasted with the situation in Leipzig and Berlin, where similar or related activities were organized primarily outside church networks. Both activities—the election-monitoring campaign and the later demonstrations—involved East German-wide participation. These examples highlight the importance of interconnections among a variety of groups and illustrate how a movement, because it involves such diverse actors, often plays itself out quite differently in different contexts. Although both the election monitoring and the fall demonstrations lacked a centralized leadership core organizing and directing activities from above, both provide evidence of looser coordinative elements that made possible the spread of revolutionary conditions throughout fall 1989 in East Germany.

The monitoring campaign was also important for building a broad group consciousness in East Germany, because it tied together activists from cities across the country and from various types of groups, and it raised the activity levels of groups. The monitoring program and related events incorporated activists with a long history of involvement as well as people who had previously *not* participated in oppositional activities. In addition, the election-monitoring activities carried the message of groups to the broader populace and helped promote a broad dissatisfaction. This led to increasing legitimacy problems for the East German state.

In Leipzig, the election-monitoring campaign was especially significant because it involved not just opposition group members who had long fought the system. Marxist groups and other critics from within the communist party and the National Front also participated. And the Marxist group Dialog was not just an organizer but also an active participant in this widely publicized oppositional activity. The addition of critical communist party members and other Marxists to the relatively small group of other activists in Leipzig provided a potential that could be mobilized in the future for other oppositional activities and demonstrations.

The proof of election fraud had far-reaching effects on group members, church members, party members, and other East German citizens unaffiliated with groups or churches. Proving election fraud lent credence to East German groups as they continued to advocate for democratic reforms. The election campaigns served to spread the concerns of groups to the broader populace—to many people who had previously not identified with the concerns and demands of groups—and even to some who viewed group members as a fringe element in society. Because elections affected almost everyone in East Germany, by organizing and publicizing the election-monitoring campaign, groups spread messages concerning democracy, justice, freedom, and basic civil rights to an increasingly receptive audience.

CHAPTER 5

Publicizing Environmental Devastation:
The Pleisse River Memorial March, June 4, 1989

Here in Leipzig there was a very active scene. From January 1989 on there were about 500 people actively involved—people who were simply always there.[281]

—Gabriele Heide,
Women for Peace, Leipzig

It's not about a revolution with weapons. Rather, it's a small revolution in thinking—a revolution promoting openness, cooperation, and shared responsibility.[282]

—Michael Arnold,
Initiative Group Living, Leipzig

The second largest city in East Germany, Leipzig was known not only as the most polluted large city in the country but also as one of the most polluted in all of Europe. Signs of ecological disaster were everywhere. The Pleisse River ran the length of the city, but the river was essentially dead and carried sewage and industrial runoff along its route.[283] The smell from the Pleisse was so bad that since the 1950s much of the river had been channeled underground as it wound its way through Leipzig.

Gone were the days when Leipzigers enjoyed sitting in riverfront cafes, riding in flat-bottomed gondolas, and hiking through nearby meadows. Industrialization had changed all that. Now smog habitually covered the city. Pollution spewed from Bitterfeld north of Leipzig and from Espenhain to the south. The name practically synonymous with pollution and environmental disaster, Bitterfeld housed East Germany's massive photochemical industry, and Espenhain, in the heart of East Germany's brown coal region, featured aging power plants and open-pit mines. Whichever way the wind blew, it almost always carried pollutants to Leipzig, and many mornings Leipzigers woke to windowsills covered with soot.[284] According to Gisela Kallenbach of Leipzig's Working Group Environmental Protection, "The pollution was there to see, to smell, and even to taste. Under certain weather conditions the smog that came over us was so thick that we had sulphuric acid on our tongues."[285]

Bitterfeld, just 15 miles north of Leipzig, was a symbol of environmental devastation in East Germany. Located in the heart of East Germany's chemical and mining industry and with a population of 20,000, Bitterfeld was sometimes described as the "cesspool of Europe." Widely known as one of the most polluted cities in East Germany, Bitterfeld was ranked by some as among the most polluted cities in the world.[286] Bitterfeld enterprises—coal mines, chemical plants, power plants—suffered from the same problem as industrial complexes in most of East Germany. They were deteriorating and lacked modern technology to reduce pollution. Dust from open-pit mines and gases from chemical factories polluted the air. Nitrates from fertilizers and particulates from smokestacks polluted the water and soil. Sometimes a person could barely see to drive, as ash and soot covered the land, the buildings, and the roads. Reports released after 1989 documented that "more than a pound of particles per square yard per month" fell on some areas in the region.[287]

Five miles north of Bitterfeld lay Wolfen, site of East Germany's largest photochemical plant, where 12 smokestacks spewed chemicals throughout the region. The wind regularly carried the pollution to Leipzig, 20 miles south. During the communist era, the pollution of Bitterfeld and Wolfen was easy to observe, but state authorities prohibited the publication of environmental data. Reports published the next year, 1990, after the revolution and after data became available, revealed the extent of environmental damage in the region and documented what all East Germans already knew.

Residents of the Bitterfeld-Wolfen area suffered from a broad range of health problems. The widely held perception was that the average life expectancy was five years lower in the Bitterfeld area than elsewhere in East Germany. However, that, too, was hard to prove because the state did not publish data on the health of East Germans for fear that it would portray East Germany in a bad light. But East Germans could observe the unhealthful conditions and the impacts on residents of the region, and some environmental group members decided to take action.

In an effort to expose children from the area to more healthful conditions, groups from the Ecological Working Circle of the Dresden church district developed a program to give children from the heavily polluted Bitterfeld region a month at the seashore during their summer vacations.[288] In part, this concrete action program provided a more healthful environment for children living in heavily polluted areas. However, the program was also symbolic, highlighting the problems of pollution in East Germany and the lack of government response. Beginning in 1983 with 10 children, by 1985 the Dresden group had already raised enough money to send 200 children on a month's vacation in a healthier environment. The program had succeeded both in helping children and in spreading its message about environmental problems. In order to raise the money to send 200 children away for a month, the relatively small number of Dresden group members had spread the message to a much larger number of supporters among group and church members.

The theme of environmental damage was still taboo, however, and the government criminalized private research reports and attempts by East German citizens to draw attention to environmental problems. Nevertheless, in response to the state's position, the major goal of most East German environmental groups, including Leipzig groups (and ultimately, the efforts of church groups), was to bring environmental problems into the open and to influence change. Key among their demands was freedom of information. Groups called for accurate information about the environment, the release of state reports and environmental data, and the right to publicize problems. As they promoted *Öffentlichkeit,* groups challenged state lies about the environment. Because everyone could observe the environmental destruction throughout East Germany, these demands often resonated beyond group members to the broader East German public.

Environmental networks connected a relatively large number of groups and group members throughout East Germany (and because groups focused mostly on local problems, the environmental movement was not centralized— even though it did become a widespread East German movement). Records from the church's Environmental Research Center in Wittenberg listed 58 environmental groups in 1988.[289] A Stasi report in June 1989 estimated there were 39 environmental groups and 23 mixed peace and ecology groups in East Germany but suggested that these represented only the political core and that the number of groups and members was increasing.[290] Andreas Passarge, a member of the

environmental Network Ark, estimated that by 1989 there were 40–50 environmental groups in Berlin alone.[291] Moreover, information compiled after the revolution suggests that many more groups operated in large and small cities
throughout East Germany than the Stasi or the coordinator of any one network
knew. Documenting the revolution in Saxony, Michael Richter reported that in
1989 in just one of district in Saxony, Karl-Marx-Stadt, there were more than 43
environmental groups.[292]

This growing environmental awareness fueled dissatisfaction with other
aspects of government and society. By fall 1989 East Germans ranked environmental problems as a major reason for changing their country. As a *Der Spiegel*
poll, cited later in the *Los Angeles Times,* documented: "East Germans' desire for
a better environment ranks second only to their desire for democracy."[293]

Chernobyl

The Chernobyl nuclear disaster on April 26, 1986, in the Soviet Union
(north of Kiev in today's Ukraine) energized East German environmental
groups and raised public concern about environmental problems. Widely
viewed as the worst nuclear power plant disaster in history, the explosion
released radioactive material over the western part of the Soviet Union and
throughout most of Europe. Berlin lay just 600 miles west of Chernobyl, and
even though radiation spread throughout the country, East German authorities
withheld information about the accident from the East German population,
concealing reports and failing to warn citizens of potential dangers posed by the
accident. Although the East German press did mention the accident, the government called it an incident that did not pose any problems for East Germany.

The facts about the disaster in Chernobyl itself were difficult to ascertain, in
part because the Soviet Union withheld information. Estimates of deaths ranged
from 30 to 600 to 16,000, depending on the source.[294] Soil contamination affected a
wide area, and a Greenpeace press release from Kiev on April 3, 2011, noted that
studies conducted 25 years after Chernobyl still found contamination in a number
of food products typically consumed by Ukrainians—milk and milk products, blue-
berries, mushrooms, and root vegetables such as potatoes and beets.[295]

In 1986, given Chernobyl's relatively close location, East Germans feared
that radiation released by the nuclear reactor posed health and safety hazards,

and they worried especially about contamination of their food and water. Despite the government's assurance that Chernobyl did not affect East Germany, reports from other sources contradicted this. Some showed that radioactive contamination spread over 40 percent of Europe, including throughout Germany. The Chernobyl disaster also raised concerns about the safety of East Germany's aging nuclear energy plants, five Soviet-style nuclear reactors. Authorities tried to reassure East Germans that their own nuclear plants were safe because they were newer and had a different design, but the population was not convinced. Reports coming from West Germany differed dramatically from theirs, and East Germans grew increasingly skeptical about their own news. Because the government had failed to inform them about the Chernobyl accident in a timely manner and to provide them with accurate information, East Germans felt betrayed by the state.

The Chernobyl nuclear disaster stimulated the growth of East German environmental groups both in terms of new members and more intensive involvements. Environmental group members recognized the necessity of bringing ecological issues into the open and influencing change. Chernobyl also led many previously uninvolved East Germans to realize that the situation had to change. Some, like Roland Quester in Leipzig, joined environmental groups, where they hoped they could make a difference.[296]

Just days after the Chernobyl disaster, Quester participated in the state-sponsored May Day parade in Leipzig for the first time—but as a protester rather than as a state supporter. Quester and a friend smuggled a bedsheet into the demonstration. When they were in the midst of the crowd, they unfurled their freshly painted sign, revealing the words "Nuclear Power—No Thanks."[297] The demonstration had proceeded only about 50 feet when Quester was stopped by the Stasi, arrested, and later interrogated by authorities. This was Roland Quester's first obvious contact with the Stasi, but one that would be followed by many others. From then on, the Stasi observed Quester and his activities using the code name "Green." Shortly after the experience, Roland Quester joined Working Group Environmental Protection.

Working Group Environmental Protection

Founded in 1981, Working Group Environmental Protection (*Arbeits-gruppe Umweltschutz, AGU*) was the most important environmental group in Leipzig. Although the group had only 10 to 20 members prior to 1986, the Chernobyl nuclear disaster prompted Roland Quester and a number of others to join. By September 1989, Working Group Environmental Protection had approximately 80 members, with about 30 members regularly and actively involved.[298] Most group members worked on group environmental projects in their free time, and they contributed money to publish research materials and the group's environmental newsletter *Streiflichter.*[299]

Organized as part of the Evangelical Church's Youth Bureau, Working Group Environmental Protection carried out its programs primarily within church structures. With a number of church members among its membership, the group had mostly good relationships with various levels of the church, as compared with groups composed primarily of non-Christians or groups consciously promoting oppositional programs. These included relationships with the church leadership and pastors as well as with many church workers.[300]

The irony here was that Working Group Environmental Protection did not generally receive much support from church leaders, though this may have been due to state pressure. Stasi reports released after the 1989 revolution document that as early as 1986 government authorities pressured Superintendent Friedrich Magirius to stop church services and activities planned around the theme "movement without automobiles" by a Leipzig environmental group.[301]

Key members of Working Group Environmental Protection included Roland Quester, Gisela Kallenbach, Ralf Elsässer, Nikolas Voss, and Christian Mathes. In May 1987, several radical members, including Uwe Schwabe, Jochen Lässig, and Michael Arnold, had split off from the environmental group and formed Initiative Group Living to carry out a more action-oriented program.[302]

The primary goal of Working Group Environmental Protection was to improve the environmental situation in East Germany, particularly in Leipzig.[303] In Leipzig, this meant, especially, improving air and water quality. According to Gisela Kallenbach, in part this goal involved "making the population aware of environmental problems, and in part it involved doing something ourselves, informing ourselves, and influencing changes."[304]

Leipzig Environmental Group

Working Environmental Protection (AGU)

Work Areas/Themes: Ecological issues, freedom of expression, freedom of information, lifestyle reform

Key Members: Roland Quester, Gisela Kallenbach, Ralf Elsässer, Nikolas Voss, Christian Mathes

Tactics: Research, education on environmental issues; small-scale actions such as tree plantings, transportation without autos; group not particularly oppositional, but some members in opposition

Founded: 1982

Through a variety of group, church, and personal networks, Working Group Environmental Protection had access to extensive information about the environment and most other issues, as did many other East German groups. Most information important to environmental discussions came from the church-based Environmental Research Center in Wittenberg and other environmental groups in East Germany, from the East German human rights and peace movements, and from West German groups.

Working Group Environmental Protection also worked for a reformed socialism with expanded democratic rights, including freedom of expression and assembly. Other key themes for the group were ecological issues and lifestyle reform, involving reduced consumption and a simplified lifestyle (such as tree plantings and weekends without autos).[305] Members struggled with group decision making and attempted to develop a good process.[306] In the early years decisions involved the entire group, but because as many as 80 persons sometimes participated, the process was very slow. In later years, a leadership group with representatives from subgroups was set up to make decisions in the interim. Quester viewed this decision-making mechanism as "as democratic as practicable, because 20 persons can do what isn't possible for eighty."[307]

Gisela Kallenbach

An early member, Gisela Kallenbach joined Working Group Environmental Protection in 1982. "I have three children, and I felt that if they were to have a future, I needed to do something,"[308] Kallenbach noted. "I didn't want my children to ask me, 'What have you done?'" Her initial awareness of the extent of environmental devastation in East Germany occurred in the early 1980s on a vacation in the Iser Mountains (*Isergebirge*), where, for the first time, she saw woods that had been totally destroyed by pollution.[309]

Woods destroyed by pollution
Photo by Martin Jehnichen/Archiv Bürgerbewegung Leipzig e. V.

Because Kallenbach had been raised as a Christian, almost by definition she was opposed to some aspects of the state. She had been confirmed as a Christian and therefore had not participated in the state's *Jugendweihe* dedication ceremonies. Kallenbach also raised her children as Christians and had not allowed them to join the state youth organizations, Young Pioneers or Free German Youth, or to take part in the *Jugendweihe*. When her oldest child came home with a note from the teacher saying he wanted to participate in a Pioneer outing with the rest of his class, Kallenbach said no and organized an outing for those in the class who were not members of Young Pioneers. In her children's school she developed a reputation as uncooperative, and by the time her twins were old enough to join Young Pioneers, Kallenbach was not even approached for permission.[310]

With an educational background in science and as a laboratory assistant, Kallenbach later earned her credentials as a chemical engineer. Beginning in 1970, Kallenbach worked in a research institute for water supply and treatment,[311] and she brought years of scientific education and experience to her group-based environmental activities. For Working Group Environmental Protection, Kallenbach carried out various research projects in her area of specialization and helped organize a number of programs to take the group's environmental information to a broader public.

Gisela Kallenbach viewed herself as critical but not oppositional:[312] "I wasn't a revolutionary who wanted to bring down East Germany."[313] She continued to protest against what she viewed as injustices. Particularly galling for Kallenbach were the restrictions placed on information about the environment.[314] The East German government banned discussion of problems and failures in the environmental realm, operating under the watchword "What is not allowed is forbidden."[315] Kallenbach also fought for the right to information in other arenas. For example, in November 1988 she sent a letter to the Ministry for Culture in Berlin, protesting the banning of Soviet films.[316] Citing the right of East German citizens to information, Kallenbach requested that the authorities explain their reasons for the government ban.

Over the years Kallenbach had taken part in a number of activities that marked her, at a minimum, as critical of the East German political system.[317] At her work Kallenbach had challenged the system in a number ways, but she managed, nevertheless, to keep her position. At the waterworks research institute Kallenbach and several colleagues decided to post a pamphlet containing environmental data from their work on the hallway walls. They wanted to describe the actual environmental situation based on research in their areas of expertise and to point out what society needed to do to change the situation.[318] Institute leaders reacted with anger and quickly removed the pamphlet from the walls. Years later when Kallenbach had a chance to review her Stasi file, she learned that after this incident she had been under ongoing Stasi surveillance. Her code name was "Emerald," for the green eye shadow she frequently wore at that time, she presumes.[319]

Roland Quester

Roland Quester joined Working Group Environmental Protection in 1986 shortly after his Chernobyl protest.[320] In 1987 Quester had been in Berlin during the Stasi break-in at Berlin's Environmental Library, and he gained organizational experience working with Berlin activists. Returning to Leipzig, Quester and several movement colleagues set up a contact network to inform group members throughout East Germany about the Berlin events and to build solidarity for those arrested.

Supported initially by his "baby year" (a state stipend allowing mothers and fathers leave from work during a child's first year) and by other group members, Quester worked in the group's office as one of the only paid employees in East German groups. Later, the group paid Quester 100 to 200 marks a month, which he supplemented with modeling for the university art department and other odd jobs. The small salary allowed him to leave his job as cabinetmaker and to concentrate on group work full time. As staff for Working Group Environmental Protection, Quester prepared *Streiflichter,* the group's newsletter, organized "Green Evenings" (lectures, exhibitions, and other programs on environmental issues), and established Leipzig's Environmental Library.

Quester's involvements in oppositional activities included organizing and participating in the first and second annual Pleisse marches in 1988 and 1989, the May 1989 election-monitoring campaign, and contact groups demonstrating solidarity with activists arrested in various group programs. Unlike some members of Working Group Environmental Protection, Quester had made a personal decision to leave the protection of the church and to participate in the Monday night demonstrations and other public protests that marked him as oppositional.[321]

As a youth, Quester had already developed an oppositional stance. He had grown up in a Christian home and had participated in the church's confirmation, refusing to take part in the state's *Jugendweihe* ceremony, and because of his questioning had to sit alone at the back of the class during civics lessons.[322] In the army Quester spoke out against the rules and was consequently not allowed to study engineering as he had hoped. He carried his opposition into the civil rights arena, refusing to vote for the state-approved list of candidates and using the voting booth to signify his opposition to state-controlled elections.

While Working Group Environmental Protection tended to emphasize study and education, a position represented by Gisela Kallenbach, some members such as Roland Quester linked themselves with other groups that emphasized oppositional programs and public action. Quester viewed Working Group Environmental Protection as "part of the worldwide ecological movement."[323] But Kallenbach saw the group in the international context only to the extent that it was part of the World Council of Churches' ecumenical Conciliar Process for

Peace, Justice, and Preservation of Creation, which she viewed as important because it spread many group and movement ideas to church leaders and to the mainstream of the church.[324] (See Chapter 6.) Quester was tied more into environmental and, to an extent, oppositional circles, while Kallenbach's environmental group contacts were primarily within church circles and other church groups.

Moving toward Opposition

Working Group Environmental Protection had taken a relatively cautious stance in its early years, but after Klaus Kaden assumed leadership of the church's Youth Bureau in 1987, many members became involved in more explicitly political activities.[325] Several individuals within the group, including Quester, helped organize and participated in illegal demonstrations and other activities promoted by more openly oppositional groups.[326] Moreover, although Working Group Environmental Protection did not view itself as particularly oppositional, to spread awareness about environmental ideas and problems, members of the group had organized several illegal activities including the Pleisse River marches that automatically brought them into conflict with state authorities.

Although the state did not view most environmental groups as particularly threatening or oppositional, especially as compared with human rights groups and some peace groups, the state kept tabs on Working Group Environmental Protection, its members, and its activities. Stasi spies had infiltrated the group, and reports of environmental group activities even reached the East German leadership in Berlin. In a report to East German leader Erich Honecker and Politburo members Egon Krenz and Kurt Hager, Stasi chief Erich Mielke reported, "The hostile, oppositional forces acting in ecological groups are trying to collect, analyze and publish data about the environmental situation which will disgrace the name of [East Germany]."[327] How the international community viewed East Germany was a foremost concern of East German leaders, but Mielke did admit that groups might actually be looking for solutions to ecological problems.

The Environmental Movement in East Germany

Coordinating Environmental Groups

A number of groups and networks played roles in coordinating environmental groups in East Germany from the movement's origin up to 1989. However, in 1989, Leipzig's Working Group Environmental Protection, a part of the Leipzig church district's Youth Bureau, played a central role. As staff of the group and editor of *Streiflichter,* Roland Quester provided groups within Leipzig as well as throughout the country with information about group activities. He also kept in contact with persons in other cities who coordinated other environmental networks. In addition, Quester was tied into networks of oppositional groups both in Leipzig and throughout East Germany.

The Evangelical Church's interest in environmental issues began years before the origin of independent environmental groups.[328] Especially influential was the publication in 1972 of *The Limits to Growth* by the Club of Rome, but even prior to this several church synods had begun to discuss environmental issues. Because the East German state restricted information on environmental issues, the Evangelical Church used its various academies to help fill the void. These academies researched various issues and regularly brought together scientists and church members in forums to provide alternative sources of information on the environment.[329] In 1974 the Evangelical Church set up the Environmental Research Center (*Kirchliches Forschungsheim*) in Wittenberg under the direction of Hans-Peter Gensichen. This center provided information on the environment and coordinated environmental groups throughout East Germany. Nevertheless, for a variety of reasons, the Wittenberg institute backed away from its leadership and coordination roles in the mid- to late 1980s, in part because of increasing state pressure on churches to control critical members and to curtail their activities.[330]

As the Wittenberg institute's role declined, several competing groups and networks stepped up to provide leadership and coordination for East Germany's loosely structured environmental movement. To an extent, two Berlin-based environmental groups and networks filled the void: the Environmental Library (*Umweltbibliothek*) and the Green Network Ark. Leipzig's Working Group Environmental Protection also vied for the role of coordinating environmental groups throughout East Germany.[331]

Various environmental groups joined sides in a dispute over what kind of organization and what specific organization, if any, should coordinate environmental groups. Some of the more oppositional members of environmental groups had criticized the Wittenberg Research Center for not taking a more proactive leadership role in the environmental movement. As Aribert Rothe, a member of the Erfurt group Oasis and a supporter of Network Ark, recalled, "Gensichen provided information but was not courageous enough." [332] So, in an attempt to coordinate environmental groups throughout East Germany, several Berlin environmental group members set up Network Ark and organized regional contacts throughout East Germany.

But Network Ark was controversial. Gensichen criticized Ark, calling it too centralized and not tied enough into church structures.[333] In addition, many groups throughout East Germany viewed Network Ark as too centralized and directive, and they resisted its efforts to coordinate the movement. Network Ark also suffered from the "Berlin problem" and was not very important or effective in Leipzig or the Saxony region.[334] According to Quester, "Leipzig groups viewed Ark as an attempt by a few people in Berlin to direct activities of groups in East Germany, but local groups wanted to do things for themselves—to emphasize their grassroots origins and local problems."[335] Network Ark was a bureaucratic organization and wanted regions and cities to fit into its centralized structure, and the resistance in Leipzig was part of the ongoing tension between the capital city and other cities.[336]

In contrast, many groups in Leipzig and Saxony had a much more positive relationship with the Environmental Library in Berlin, a more open organization. As Roland Quester noted, "In 1988 we [members of Working Group Environmental Protection] developed strong, intense contacts and received lots of support from the Environmental Library in Berlin."[337] However, Berlin's Environmental Library informally coordinated many different types of groups, not just environmental groups, despite its name, so after the Wittenberg research institute retreated from its leadership role for environmental groups, Leipzig took over many of its functions. Leipzig's Working Group Environmental Protection played a loose coordinative role especially for *environmental* groups throughout East Germany, particularly groups that resisted working with Network Ark.[338]

Several newsletters focusing specifically on environmental issues helped coordinate environmental groups in East Germany and provided information about events of interest. *Arche Nova*, the publication of Network Ark, concentrated on environmental problems and group activities in East Germany as well as throughout Eastern Europe. The Environmental Library's newsletter, *Umweltblätter*, a much broader publication than most other church-related or *samizdat* publications, served as a primary source of information for and about all types of groups throughout East Germany.[339] Working Group Environmental Protection's newsletter *Streiflichter* contained information about environmental groups and their activities, but it also included information about the activities of other types of groups.[340]

Using Networks to Spread Information: *Pechblende*

Despite the attempts of East German authorities to control environmental information, in 1988 Michael Beleites succeeded in publishing *Pechblende: Der Uranbergbau in der DDR und seine Folgen,* an exposé on uranium mining in East Germany and its effects.[341] Researched and written by Beleites, the publication and distribution of *Pechblende* highlight the difficulties involved in publishing critical data in East Germany.

In a later book Beleites recorded his experiences researching and publishing *Pechblende* and dealing with the Stasi, which tried to prevent the book's publication.[342] A Stasi report described *Pechblende* as "cheap, superficial, church propaganda material, which the church organizations characterize as vital, human, protecting the environment, life-preserving, future looking, and so forth." The same report described Beleites as "a potential enemy of the state."[343]

The publication of *Pechblende* illustrates the dense network within group and Evangelical Church structures that could be activated to produce and distribute controversial or oppositional materials and information. As the son of a pastor and baptized by Heino Falcke, Erfurt provost and strong supporter of East German groups, Beleites was personally well connected within church networks—in East Germany and internationally—in spite of (or sometimes because of) his challenging and controversial stances on the environment.[344]

Beleites finished the manuscript in October 1987. However, it was not until spring 1988 that he found supporters willing to serve as editors for the document, when the Environmental Research Institute in Wittenberg and Working Circle Doctors for Peace in Berlin signed on as co-editors.

Publication posed other problems. The Berlin doctors' group did not have access to mimeograph equipment, the machine at the Wittenberg Research Institute was broken, and the Federation of Evangelical Churches in Berlin declined to get involved printing materials for other church agencies. Finally, Beleites and his coeditors located an offset press at an apprentice printing facility of the Evangelical Church in Magdeburg to print the pages with graphics. They found an old mimeograph machine in the basement of Samariter Church in Berlin to reproduce the rest of the pages, and Beleites spent a week in the church basement, turning the handle of the antiquated machine to print the approximately 50,000 pages.

In addition to this network of church-related connections throughout East Germany, international networks also proved invaluable to the production and distribution process. Because the quality of mimeograph and printing supplies was so poor in East Germany, members of the West German International Physicians for the Prevention of Nuclear War (IPPNW) provided the medical circle in East Berlin with higher quality ink and mimeograph supplies. They also contributed a stapler and staples, because no stapler available in East Germany could staple more than 15 pages.[345]

Distribution of the 1,000 copies of *Pechblende* throughout East Germany relied on a variety of church-related networks. On June 2, 1988, Beleites carried 100 copies of the document to Gera, and distribution commenced from Berlin, Wittenberg, and Gera. Originally, Beleites and the editors had intended to distribute and incorporate the materials in the World Environment Day programs held on June 5 in churches across East Germany. But after state officials put pressure on both Sebastian Pflugbeil of the East Berlin medical group and Hans-Peter Gensichen of the Environmental Research Institute, they decided to change their mode of distribution and not begin until June 8. Instead of sending copies of the study through the mail, they decided to hand-deliver the copies to church workers who could personally deliver them to interested groups and individuals. Pflugbeil distributed a number of copies, sold for five marks each, at the Erfurt Church Congress meetings (*Kirchentag*). An individual from Dresden who had picked up copies from Pflugbeil in Berlin distributed the pamphlet through the Church Research Institute in Wittenberg. Another colleague in Zwickau who had received his copies from Beleites delivered the document in the south-central part of the country. In addition, church and group publications, including Letter No. 17 from the Wittenberg Institute and *Arche Info 1/88* from Network Ark, carried information about the pamphlet and how to obtain copies.[346] Copies of the document were also distributed in the west, and the study received broad coverage through the western press.[347]

Environmental Action in Leipzig and Beyond

In 1988 as the center of movement activities shifted from Berlin to Leipzig, the type and intensity of group involvements changed as groups moved beyond the tree plantings and cleanup to public action.

Significant environmental action programs in Leipzig and the surrounding region included the first and second Pleisse River memorial marches, "a Mark for Espenhain," and demonstrations against environmental devastation in the Bitterfeld photochemical area.

First Pleisse River Memorial March, June 5, 1988

The first Pleisse River Memorial March, a major group-organized event highlighting environmental problems, took place on June 5, 1988, in conjunction with World Environment Day and involved approximately 230 activists. Organized by Leipzig groups Initiative Group Living, Working Circle Justice, and Working Circle Solidarity Church/Leipzig, along with some of the more oppositional members of Working Group Environmental Protection, the demonstration aimed to raise awareness that Leipzig firms and other industries upstream had polluted the Pleisse River. The groups wanted to press for cleaner water in Leipzig. This group-organized public demonstration was not supported by Leipzig churches and provides a relatively early example of independent group activity outside the church.[348]

Although organizers had avoided calling the event a demonstration, East German authorities nevertheless tried to stop the unauthorized event. The Stasi tried to blame pastors, and city authorities put pressure on Leipzig church leaders to rescind the invitations and cancel the event. However, because no names were listed on the invitations and no groups or pastors took credit for organizing the event, pastors were not disciplined. Church officials would not allow groups to announce the upcoming Pleisse March during the peace prayers at Nikolai Church, and at churches where signs announcing the event had been posted, church officials demanded that pastors remove the signs. A representative of Superintendent Friedrich Magirius approached group member Uwe Schwabe of the Pleisse organizing committee and demanded that he contact everyone who had received an invitation to the event and withdraw the invitation. But Schwabe refused. State authorities also contacted Schwabe along with Roland Quester of Working Group Environmental Protection and warned them not to take part in the demonstration. Willing to risk arrest, Schwabe and Quester ignored the warnings and joined other activists at the Pleisse Memorial March.

Dissension between groups and the church escalated. One pastor charged the group organizers with trying to "practice revolution," arguing that the groups were not really concerned about the pollution of the Pleisse. Michael Arnold of Initiative Group Living responded to the charge. "It's not about a revolution with weapons," he wrote. "Rather, it's a small revolution in thinking—a revolution promoting openness, cooperation, and shared responsibility."[349]

Bottle of water from Pleisse River
Photo from GMRE/Tobias Hollitzer (Inv.-Nr.: 17226)

Despite limited publicity because church officials had not allowed organizers to announce the event through church channels, at 2 p.m. on June 5, 1988, more than 200 activists gathered at the sports center on Teichstrasse near Connewitz Crossing in south Leipzig. The demonstrators walked along the Pleisse River for about an hour. At one point several group members put a probe into the water where the river ran above ground and tested the water quality. Also, group members had placed three signs containing information about the Pleisse River in Clara Zetkin Park. Although the Stasi and other security officials were visible throughout the demonstration, they did not make any arrests, perhaps because of other events in the same vicinity.

Afterward, oppositional group members assessed the effectiveness of this first Pleisse River demonstration. The group had been extremely successful in that they managed to organize a public demonstration outside of church facilities and without church support. Members acknowledged, however, that the number of participants in this first Pleisse Memorial March was much too small. In comparison to the 230 people attending the Pleisse demonstration, the game preserve festival held that same day and organized by sports clubs affiliated with the mass organizations of the communist party had attracted more than 15,000 participants.[350]

The first Pleisse River Memorial March highlighted a problem for East German groups—the fact that most group members were not viewed positively by many East Germans.[351] In East Germany, group members, and especially oppositional members, corresponded to the early adapters of an idea or a product in innovation theory.[352] They were the vanguard leading the way, but they were also the fringe at the margins of society. They needed to reach a much larger proportion of the population than the several hundred activist group members currently involved in Leipzig. If groups wanted to achieve their goals to bring about peaceful but revolutionary change, they would need to broaden their appeal. Already by July 1988 organizers of the first Pleisse event had decided to hold a second Pleisse memorial march the following year, and they hoped to attract a much larger group of participants.

A Mark for Espenhain

The weekend following the first Pleisse march, groups organized another event designed to raise environmental awareness. A Mark for Espenhain would prove to be one of the most significant environmental programs in East Germany because it involved not only environmental group members but also a broad cross-section of church members and because it raised concerns about environmental devastation not only in the Leipzig area but also throughout East Germany.[353]

In Rötha, a town about 15 miles south of Leipzig, the environmental group Christian Environmental Seminar had attempted for years to get state and plant authorities to take action and clean up the deteriorating power plant in nearby Espenhain that spewed pollution throughout the region. Since 1983 the Rötha group had invited environmental groups from around East Germany to an annual

View of the briquette factory in Deutzen
*Photo by Christoph Motzer/Archiv Bürgerbewegung
Leipzig e. V.*

Power plants in Espenhain
*Photo by Martin Jehnichen/Archiv Bürgerbewegung
Leipzig e. V.*

worship service for the environment, with the primary aim of calling attention to the environmental devastation created by the plant in Espenhain. But the group had had little success.[354]

In 1988 the Environmental Seminar group broadened its campaign, working with the Dresden Ecological Working Group and organizing A Mark for Espenhain. The immediate objective was to raise money to renovate the brown coal processing plant in Espenhain in order to improve air quality in the region.[355] On July 12, 1988, at a worship service in Deutzen in the heart of the environmentally devastated brown coal area near Borna and Espenhain, the Dresden Working Group publicized a call to action. While acknowledging the contribution of the power plants to the energy needs of East Germany and to the life and well-being of its people, the group emphasized that these gains came at a price—"the catastrophic burden on nature and on human life in the industrial region."[356] The declaration of the groups called for East Germans throughout the country to sign a petition and to contribute one mark each to demonstrate their solidarity with the residents of the Borna-Espenhain region. By signing, East Germans would signify that they were prepared to take responsibility for changing their own lives and to work for ecological restructuring in their own local areas.

That month the groups also publicized the program through the Saxony church district's fourth annual "Week of Responsibility for God's Creation" in Dresden and took their program to churches and environmental groups throughout East Germany. To make their case, group members had prepared text and photos documenting the catastrophic situation in Espenhain. Declaring their solidarity with persons suffering because of environmental conditions in the region, the group called for an East German-wide action program. They emphasized, "'A Mark for Espenhain' is a sign that here and now something must happen. 'A Mark for Espenhain' is a symbolic contribution, the beginning of improved conditions in Espenhain and a challenge for the entire society to become involved."[357]

Leipzig groups supported the effort and by November 13, 1988, Leipzig groups responded en masse to the call for Espenhain. More than 500 group members gathered at Reformierte Church in Leipzig for the daylong event to commemorate "A Day for Espenhain" and to educate themselves about environmental problems in Leipzig and in the surrounding region.[358]

Leipzig group member Rainer Müller had been involved in a number of environmental efforts for many years, both as an individual and as a group member. Growing up in Borna, he had an early awareness of environmental problems in the region. In the late 1980s Müller had organized several boycotts protesting strip mining in the region and the deteriorating power plants in Espenhain. In 1988 at a worship service for International Day of Peace in Borna's Marienkirche, Müller called for a boycott of the brown coal open-pit mining in the region and for an end to the destruction of the environment.[359] Adapting the text "Say No" (written by German poet, author, and critic of the Nazi dictatorship, Wolfgang Borchert after he returned from World War II), Müller added a third line: "Say no when your homeland is being destroyed."[360]

On June 11, 1989, 800 people attended the seventh annual Environmental Worship Service convened in Rötha. There, groups first learned about secret plans for the construction of a nuclear power plant in Börln. Organizers also announced that the petition supporting the East German-wide environmental action A Mark for Espenhain had already been signed by 25,000 East Germans and raised more than 25,000 marks.[361] By the end of 1989, more than 80,000 persons would sign the petition demanding that authorities renovate or shut down the hazardous plant, and East German groups would raise 80,000 marks. Authorities would close the plant in January 1990.[362]

Second Pleisse River Memorial March, June 4, 1989

Initiative Group Living had been planning the second Pleisse memorial march since the first march the year before.[363] Organizers aimed to involve not only group members but also a broader base—atheists, artists, church members not associated with groups—by highlighting the fact that environmental issues involved everyone in society. The intention of the organizing group, a combination of environmental and human rights groups calling themselves Working Circle World Environment Day, was to gather a group of demonstrators on June 4 who would walk the length of the river through Leipzig.[364] Participants would observe the conditions of the river as they walked along its banks, using the centuries-old religious practice of the pilgrimage.[365]

Along with the demonstration itself, the plan for the daylong event involved services at two different churches to begin and end the activities, a program featuring films and slideshows, and exhibits on environmental issues.[366] Event flyers invited people to the church services, rather than to the demonstration, because it would be more difficult for the state to prohibit more explicitly religious events without destabilizing fragile church-state relationships than to prohibit a demonstration, not typically considered a religious occasion.[367]

The organizing group decided to apply to government authorities for permission to hold the march, and Klaus Kaden, as head of the church youth bureau and sponsor of its environmental group, turned in the application. The organizers agreed to make several concessions in order to receive official permission, and they temporarily stopped publicizing the event as they waited for word on the application. Nevertheless, on May 25, only 10 days before the scheduled Pleisse demonstration, government authorities rejected the organizing group's application. As reasons, authorities listed the following: organizers could not guarantee they could maintain order and security during the event, they had advertised the event in the *Umweltblätter* in Berlin, and they could not exclude the possibility of misuse of the event by "certain elements." The Pleisse Memorial March was not permitted and was therefore an illegal event.

Nonetheless, plans for the march moved forward.

Security forces also attempted to disrupt plans for the Pleisse march. Already on May 22 the Stasi had begun close surveillance of Leipzig groups organizing the June 4 Pleisse demonstration and the Leipzig street music festival scheduled for the following week on June 10. Authorities stopped and questioned organizers of the events as well as persons not part of the planning group, and a number of group members were detained, arrested, and/or beaten.[368] In the days leading up to the Pleisse demonstration, authorities forced 63 group members to sign papers indicating that they been warned not to participate in the illegal demonstration or they would face charges. A number of Leipzig residents who had applied for visas to leave East Germany were told they would receive permission to leave the country if they did not participate in the demonstration. Kaden, too, was warned that he faced consequences if he went ahead with plans for the unsanctioned demonstration. When the Pleisse events began on June 4, 19 group members were already under house arrest.[369]

Nevertheless, at 10 a.m. on Sunday, June 4, about 1,000 persons gathered for the worship service at Paul Gerhardt Church in the Connewitz area in south Leipzig, just a few blocks from the Pleisse River. Kurt Nowak from the theological faculty at Karl Marx University spoke about the history of the Pleisse and concluded his message by calling for the healing of the river, of society, and of mankind. [370] At the end of the service, youth pastor Klaus Kaden announced to the group that state authorities had refused permission for the memorial march but that the demonstration would proceed as planned, and Kaden called on each person to make his or her own decision about whether to participate in the demonstration. He then invited everyone to the closing worship service that evening at Reformierte Church, located on Tröndlin Ring on the northwest edge of the city center.[371]

That day security officials brought out a massive display of force. Six hundred police, Stasi, and other security forces surveyed the demonstrators. Fearing that Leipzig officials would not be able to control the situation, East German authorities had sent a contingent of Stasi from Berlin to support their Leipzig counterparts.[372]

The march itself involved more than 500 demonstrators—people who had made the personal decision to join the illegal march and risk arrest.[373] Among them that day was Brigitte Moritz, a member of Working Group Peace Service.

Although Moritz didn't view herself as particularly oppositional, she remembered the significant decision she made that day. She and several friends had arrived at the worship service early, and they stood in the church discussing the upcoming march. Moritz recalled, "We talked about it the entire time—the march was illegal, but in spite of that we wanted to participate."[374]

After the worship service, the demonstrators broke into several groups as they left Paul Gerhardt Church and headed toward the Pleisse. After 500 meters police disrupted one group and arrested 50 persons. A second group stayed together and reached the district communist party headquarters, where they made an unplanned stop because police there formed a human chain and blocked their progress. In response, demonstrators spontaneously staged a sit-down strike on the steps of the communist party building. About 40 persons from a third group reached Reformierte Church unhindered, where they joined other participants for the evening's events.

Pleisse River Memorial March in Clara Zetkin Park
Photo by Christoph Motzer/Archiv Bürgerbewegung Leipzig e. V.

Despite arrests earlier in the day, more than 400 people attended the evening service at Reformierte Church[375] conducted by pastors Klaus Kaden and Harald Wagner of Solidarity Church.[376] The exhibits and the program at Reformierte Church included a slide show on pollution in the Espenhain brown coal region, a video on environmental devastation in the Bitterfeld chemical and mining area, and an exhibit on the Pleisse River, supported with copies of a study on the Pleisse compiled by environmental groups. Working Group Environmental Protection also made part of its Environmental Library available to those attending.[377] That evening, in the face of threats from state authorities not to get involved, 437 participants signed a petition demanding that government authorities implement measures to improve water quality in the Pleisse.[378]

As participants left Reformierte Church, they could see seven police wagons with uniformed officers and a number of security personnel in civilian clothes in the side streets, but no additional arrests were made that evening. Overall, 84 demonstrators had been arrested in connection with the second Pleisse memorial march.[379] Later, state representatives confided in church officials that the fears they had had prior to the event had not materialized. Nevertheless, the state levied fines as high as 500 marks on a number of participants in the Pleisse memorial demonstration. The charge: participating in "a prohibited event" in south Leipzig.[380]

After the second memorial march, group members implemented measures to spread information about the successful event throughout East Germany and into the international arena. Group organizers set up a telephone contact line at Lukas Church to report on the events and to organize solidarity actions on behalf of those arrested. Members of Working Group Human Rights and Working Circle Justice contacted the western press, and group members Kathrin Walther and Frank Richter carried press photos of the Pleisse activities to contacts in Berlin for publication in the western press.[381]

The Pleisse memorial demonstration and subsequent arrests elicited broad support in Leipzig. The next evening, June 5, 1989, the largest group ever attended the Monday night peace prayers in Nikolai Church—1,250 people.[382] Surprisingly, there was no police action following the peace prayers that evening, perhaps because Bishop Hempel from the synod office in Dresden participated in the services.

Die Pleiße

WASSER

Heft I/4. Juni 1989

Herausgegeben vom christl. Arbeitskreis Weltumwelttag Leipzig

Die Pleisse, samizdat publication
documenting environmental
problems in Leipzig
Source: Archiv Bürgerbewegung Leipzig

Working Group Environmental Protection produced a 40-page booklet, *die Pleisse,* documenting events and issued as a special issue of *Streiflichter.*[383] One thousand copies, selling for five marks each, were distributed in Leipzig and throughout East Germany. Because of state controls on printing equipment, paper, and other supplies, production of the booklet was a massive undertaking. It required 40,000 sheets of paper, a scarce item in East Germany, and 40,000 turns of the mimeograph machine handle. Because the editors wanted to produce a high-quality document, ink and mimeograph stencils had been secretly secured through family and friends in the west. All this was accomplished under Stasi observation, "thanks to the work of many individual Leipzig citizens who overcame their fear and involved themselves in the problems of their city and their country."[384]

Later, organizers evaluated the second annual Pleisse march. They acknowledged that because part of their intent had been to inform people about conditions in Leipzig and about their protest, they should have carried signs or banners during the march. They also decided that until the condition of the Pleisse improved, they would continue to research and to call for changes, and they would work to involve more people in their activities.[385] But overall the groups had succeeded in their efforts. The second Pleisse River Memorial March highlighted a new level of environmental activism in Leipzig and demonstrated that groups could organize significant events outside the walls of the church.

CHAPTER 6

Confronting the Church and Bringing the Church Back In: The Opposition's Alternative Church Congress, July 6–9, 1989

Groups recognized that it was important to discuss the themes that groups deal with in the churches—among the broader church population.[386]

—Gabriele Heide,
Women for Peace, Leipzig

Together we had set ourselves in motion. What was special about that moment was that, already at this one demonstration in the run-up to October 1989, many people who didn't come out of the narrow circle of the basis groups—but many other people—had joined us.[387]

—Kathrin Walther, Working Circle Justice, Leipzig
Organizer of Alternative Church Congress

Epidemics are, at their root, about this very process of transformation. When we are trying to make an idea or attitude or product tip, we're trying to change our audience in some small yet critical respect: we're trying to infect them, sweep them up into our epidemic, convert them from hostility to acceptance.[388]

—Malcolm Gladwell, *The Tipping Point:
How Little Things Can Make a Big Difference*

Oppositional groups and church groups may have come together for the Pleisse Memorial March and on other environmental matters, but the relationship between the church and political groups was still strained. After the second Pleisse march, these relations hit a new low.

The day after the Pleisse Memorial March, East Germans awoke to the shocking news that the Chinese government had crushed the pro-democracy movement in Beijing's Tiananmen Square the previous day. During the night of June 3–4, 1989, the Chinese government had used troops and tanks to brutally attack thousands of students and other demonstrators advocating for expanded political rights and democratic change. Although numbers varied according to the sources, reports suggest that as many as 5,000 demonstrators were killed, 10,000 arrested, and 30,000 injured in the savage police and military action.[389] In East Germany, televised reports of the Tiananmen Square massacre were shown repeatedly on state television, and East Germans were shocked to see the Chinese government attack its own citizens.[390]

Even more shocking to East Germans was their own government's response to the Tiananmen Square massacre. The official state response published in *Neues Deutschland* supported the Chinese government, arguing that Tiananmen was a necessary answer to the "counterrevolutionary rebellion" of a minority.[391] Reporting the position of the East German government, Egon Krenz, a member of the Politburo and secretary of the Central Committee, emphasized that East German leaders believed the Chinese government had acted properly in suppressing this threat to domestic order. Also supporting the Chinese government action, the East German legislature (*Volkskammer*) maintained that what had happened was "an internal matter of the Chinese People's Republic."[392]

Particularly galling to East German citizens, the government continued to publicize and justify the Chinese government's attack on the pro-democracy demonstrators. In late June East German television showed a documentary film about Tiananmen Square. Titled *The Counterrevolutionary Rebellion in Peking on June 3 and 4, 1989,* the film showed original footage of the massacre.[393] The government's support for the Chinese actions further decreased the legitimacy of the state and heightened tensions in Leipzig and across the country. East Germans increasingly feared that their own government would resort to a "Chinese solution" to quash future protests in order to maintain domestic order.

In response to the Tiananmen Square massacres Leipzig groups organized a number of protest activities.[394] On June 18 members of Solidarity Church and Working Circle Justice held a prayer service in Reformierte Church, where they provided information about the events in China. Many groups gathered petitions supporting the Chinese students and protesting against government actions and sent these, along with letters of complaint, to state officials and church leaders. For example, 44 Leipzig theological students sent a petition to the Saxony church district to gain support for the protest movement. Throughout the city students wore jackets displaying Chinese flags and black bands indicating mourning to signify their solidarity with Chinese students.

Youth Bureau reader board: "China," a reference to the Tiananmen Square massacre
Photo by Bernd Heinze/Archiv Bürgerbewegung Leipzig e. V.

Tiananmen Square also spurred protests in state and party organizations. Several workers at the Leipzig headquarters of the communist party complained about the East German government's support for the Chinese government, and they were fired or demoted.[395] Throughout Leipzig, members continued to resign from the communist party in protest of government actions, just as they had after the May 7 local elections. From January 1 through June 15, 1989, almost a thousand (997) communist party members in Leipzig chose to leave the party, and party authorities terminated the membership of another 695 Leipzigers.

Most East German citizens—not just group members—were appalled by both the Chinese government actions and the East German government's response, and groups regularly called attention to the government's position on China as a tactic to elicit broader societal support for political changes. Many East Germans not associated with groups pointed to events in China as a personal turning point—a time when they decided that East Germany had to change and that they needed to personally take a stand. Consequently, later that year when Egon Krenz was selected by party officials to lead East Germany, his legitimacy had already been undermined within large segments of the population. His statements on China as well as his participation in the state deceptions surrounding the May 1989 local elections meant that, from the start of his term, many East German citizens did not trust him.

The state's reaction to Tiananmen Square shocked almost all East Germans, because they could not imagine that their government would even consider a Chinese-type massacre as a legitimate method for maintaining order. Tiananmen Square raised fear levels among East German demonstrators, because their government's response to the Chinese government's action signified East Germany's willingness to quell the unrest with tanks and troops. On the other hand, this recognition strengthened East German activists' resolve and renewed their efforts to keep demonstrations nonviolent.

To prevent a Chinese solution, groups would work tirelessly to promote and maintain nonviolence during all the Leipzig demonstrations.[396] Peace prayers and group meetings all emphasized nonviolence. Nevertheless, as the number of demonstrators increased, fears of violent crackdowns also increased as state authorities threatened to use massive force to maintain control. Could a Chinese solution be avoided? Or, as in Peking in 1989 or Prague in 1968 when guns and tanks had been turned on demonstrators, would the East German government resort to a Chinese solution?

In June 1989 the Saxony district synod passed a resolution protesting the actions of the Chinese government in Tiananmen Square and affirming solidarity with the Chinese people. The Saxony synod also sent a proposal to the Federation of Evangelical Churches requesting that it express these concerns using its ecumenical connections with China.[397] Clearly, by summer 1989, the demands of the church had broadened and many church concerns increasingly converged with group agendas.

Leipzig's Alternative Church Congress

It was in this highly charged atmosphere that the Evangelical Church convened its annual Church Congress in Leipzig July 6–9, 1989.[398] When the church gave in to state demands to exclude the political groups from the conference, Leipzig groups responded quickly.

Only twice before, in 1954 and 1978, had Leipzig been the site of the official Church Congress for the Saxony region,[399] and now in 1989 organizers of the official event planned for another massive gathering of church members. Planning for the 1989 congress had begun years earlier. The event was viewed as particularly significant because church leaders wanted to incorporate a major celebration of the Protestant Reformation in the program. But in 1989 as church-state relations continued to deteriorate, the state used its leverage on church officials. As part of the agreement to allow to the Church Congress to take place in Leipzig, state officials placed a number of conditions on the organizers, and the church submitted to the state's demands:[400] the church must hold the congress on the periphery of Leipzig rather than in the city center, organizers must restrict the participation of western politicians and journalists, and they must exclude East German alternative and oppositional groups.

Christoph Wonneberger first heard about the church's decision to exclude groups from the Church Congress in January 1989 when he was in Karl-Marx-Stadt (now Chemnitz) for a meeting of various groups from the Saxony region. As Wonneberger remembered, he responded immediately, saying, "If that's the case, then we have to do something else. And then I spontaneously called it 'Statt Kirchentag.'"[401] In this way the Alternative Church Congress was conceived—with statt meaning "instead of" or "alternative" and Kirchentag referring to the Church Congress held by the regional synods of the Evangelical Church in East Germany.

According to Kathrin Walther, a member of Working Circle Justice and a primary organizer of the Alternative Church Congress,[402] "Wonneberger had already built Lukas Church in Leipzig into an important oppositional center by this time, and when church officials refused to allow groups to participate in the official Church Congress, Wonneberger said, 'People, then let's do it ourselves. . . . We'll organize an Alternative Church Congress at Lukas Church.'"[403] "There, parallel to the Church Congress we organized our own program with the participation of all groups—all grassroots groups from throughout East Germany that we were in regular contact with," and "everyone presented their own exhibits."[404]

With the support of his church council, Wonneberger regularly made Lukas Church available for controversial activities of groups.[405] Youth pastor Klaus Kaden assessed Wonneberger's contribution: "[T]he great thing about this man is that he always made it sound very casual: 'Well, if these young people

Alternative Church Congress with participants on
steps of Lukas Church
*Photo by Christoph Motzer/Archiv Bürgerbewegung
Leipzig e. V.*

want to organize something on their own, don't you think that we can provide some facilities for them?' or 'Don't worry so much about the consequences. Why don't we give them a chance? What can go wrong anyway?'—that's just how Wonneberger is."[406]

The Stasi had infiltrated the organizing committees of both the official Church Congress and the Alternative Church Congress, and surveillance continued from the planning phases throughout the July events.[407] Stasi personnel monitored communications by mail and by telephone. They installed listening devices in meeting rooms used by the congresses. Stasi informants followed "ecumenical" guests at the official meetings as well as participants in the alternative meetings and bugged their hotel rooms. Journalists and their reports were also under regular, ongoing observation by the Stasi. Because the state viewed the Alternative Church Congress at Lukas Church as potentially the most disruptive, Stasi personnel worked hand in hand with police to monitor the activities at Lukas Church.

More than 2,500 persons showed up for the events at Lukas Church, [408] more than anyone had expected. According to Christoph Wonneberger, "There was an unexpectedly large number of people there and they were very interested in working together. . . . You could say, everything that had been forbidden was freely distributed."[409] The "marketplace of possibilities" that weekend featured

Banner for Alternative Church Congress at Lukas Church;
Jochen Lässig with guitar
Photo by Martin Jehnichen/Archiv Bürgerbewegung Leipzig e.V.

controversial themes and materials excluded from the official Church Congress proceedings. Group offerings included concerts, readings, lectures, discussions, panels, and exhibits on various topics including human rights questions, Solidarity in Poland, Tiananmen Square, the ecumenical Conciliar Process, alternative art and culture, and other themes.

One small exhibit displayed photos of police violence against participants in the street music festival held the previous month in Leipzig, in which musicians highlighted their lack of freedom.[410] (See insert about the street music festival.) The festival had been held in spite of being prohibited by local authorities; 300 to 500 people had attended each performance, with an estimated 2,000 involved throughout the day, and there had been 114 arrests.

Leipzig Street Music Festival, June 10, 1989

On June 10, less than a week after the Pleisse Memorial March in Leipzig and the Tiananmen Square massacre in China, oppositional groups in Leipzig held another activity designed to publicize the lack of democratic rights in East Germany. Throughout East Germany, musicians and other artists were licensed by the state and were governed by tight restrictions over who could perform and where. Musicians and other artists were prohibited from assembling freely and from working as they chose, and in Leipzig, unlike in many other cities throughout Europe, musicians were seldom allowed to perform in outdoor venues for festivals or other occasions.

Organized primarily by the Leipzig's Initiative Group Living, the street music festival brought together musicians, theater troupes, and other participants and audiences from throughout East Germany. By joining together and celebrating publicly throughout the day in Leipzig's Market Square, participants would act as if the right to assemble freely already existed. The key organizer was Initiative Group Living member Jochen Lässig, a theology student and musician who made his living by playing guitar in the streets, alleyways, and passages of Leipzig's city center.

Street music festival on Leipzig's Market Square
Photo by Rainer Kühn/Archiv Bürgerbewegung Leipzig e. V.

Leipzig Street Music Festival, June 10, 1989 (continued)

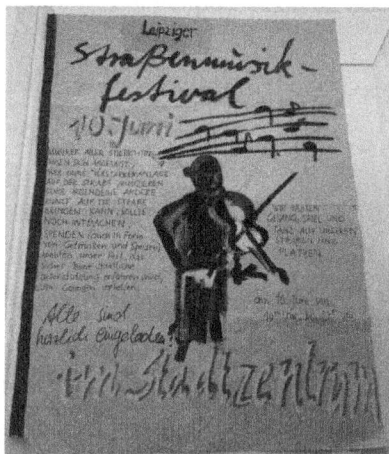

Poster for street music festival
*Source: Archiv Bürgerbewegung
Leipzig e. V.*

Although prohibited by local authorities, the Leipzig street music festival nevertheless drew huge crowds of participants and observers.[411] Organizers had sent 500 invitational letters to groups throughout East Germany and distributed handbills in Leipzig, and approximately 15 theater and music groups from around the country participated in the event. Despite attempts by security forces to prevent residents of other cities from entering Leipzig, many did manage to reach the city center. From 300 to 500 people attended the festival at any one time during the day, with an estimated total number of more than 2,000 persons involved.[412] At least 114 persons were arrested during the daylong festivities.[413] Persons attending the street music festival feared that the massive security force presence would mimic the events of Tiananmen Square just one week earlier and turn violent. However, despite the 114 arrests, relative calm prevailed.

Afterward, a photo journal of the day's events was produced, documenting the activities of participants and observers as well as of Stasi and police forces.[414]

Events in China provided a cautionary tale for pro-democracy groups in Leipzig and in East Germany. The legitimate fear of East German protestors—that the state would employ massive force and violence against the demonstrators to crush a public gathering—had not yet materialized in East Germany. Security personnel had used limited force against demonstrators and arrested a relatively small number of organizers and protesters during the street music festival. But the fear remained. Tiananmen Square had reignited concerns that East German leaders might still use the Chinese solution to control demonstrators and to maintain order throughout the country.

During the Alternative Church Congress meetings, Working Group Human Rights and Working Circle Justice publicized a declaration protesting the increasing use of violence by state authorities in Leipzig and demanding a more democratic society.[415]

Exhibits at the Alternative Church Congress
Photo by Bernd Heinze/Archiv Bürgerbewegung Leipzig e. V.

One panel featured prominent members of the East German opposition, a representative of the Helsinki Federation for Human Rights, and a legislator from the West German Social Democratic Party (Erhard Eppler) discussing "our common European home" and the future of the two German states. Group members also assembled a collection of more than forty publications, many covering controversial themes such as election fraud.

In contrast, at the official Church Congress, none of the pressing issues of the day—the focus of the Alternative Church Congress—were featured in the events.[416] In an attempt to avoid controversy and comply with the demands of the state, organizers of the official meetings censured themselves by adopting a narrower and more explicitly Biblical focus. In their scripture-based proceedings, no one was exposed to the market of possibilities put together by the grassroots groups. Nor did participants have the opportunity to grapple with critical themes and demands for change confronting the East German government and society.[417]

Tensions built throughout the weekend. Because grassroots groups had been excluded from the official events, many people expected that groups would stage some sort of public action at the closing meetings of the official Church Congress at Scheibenholz racetrack.[418] An estimated 60,000 to 70,000 persons gathered at the racetrack on Sunday afternoon, July 9, for the closing services.[419] On that final day, organizers of the event had stationed officials throughout the

Closing ceremony of official Church Congress
Photo by Bernd Heinze/Archiv Bürgerbewegung Leipzig e. V.

Banner with "Democracy" in German and Chinese
Photo by Bernd Heinze/Archiv Bürgerbewegung Leipzig e. V.

stadium so they could maintain control in case of disruptions. Additionally, Stasi and other security forces in plain clothes sat among church members in the stands, representing as many as one in every five persons of those attending the closing ceremonies.[420] An event organizer reported that the organizing committee had ordered inexpensive identification badges from the printer for official delegates to wear at the closing event, but when the order was delivered, it contained 20 percent fewer badges than they had ordered, leading organizers to conclude that the Stasi had taken the missing badges for their own employees.[421] Hoping to take photographs to identify oppositional group members in case a demonstration materialized, the Stasi even employed a low-flying helicopter to circle above the raceway grounds.[422]

That afternoon a number of group members excluded from the official event gathered outside the racetrack. They had planned an unauthorized demonstration through the raceway grounds to remind Church Congress participants of recent events in Tiananmen Square and to call for more democracy in East Germany.[423] Group members carried a megaphone and two large banners. One read "Never again—election fraud,"[424] and the other contained the word "Democracy" written both in German and in Chinese script. [425] Earlier that week civil rights activist and member of Working Group Justice Rainer Müller had gone to the Deutsche Bücherei (German Library) to find the Chinese symbols for democracy so that he and a friend could paint them on a sign.[426]

The several hundred group members participating in the demonstration moved simultaneously as they entered the racetrack grounds, linked together with dozens of colorful streamers wound around each other and protecting the sign in the midst of their group.[427] According to Kathrin Walther, who remembered carrying the second sign in memory of the victims of Tiananmen Square,[428] "We wanted to take the sign to the stage, because the events of Tiananmen Square weighed heavily on us, and because there was a similar situation in East Germany where things had escalated and we didn't know how it would play out. We didn't know if the state powers in East Germany would run us down as the Chinese rulers had on Tiananmen Square. So the sign was a symbol of our fear and also a reminder that we couldn't allow it to come to that in East Germany."[429]

Some church officials tried to stop the demonstrators, but other organizers said, "Why don't we let these young people go ahead and demonstrate,"[430] and they allowed the protestors to move into the stadium. Although the group was prevented from reaching the speakers' platform, the protest inside the raceway had had a greater effect than group members could have hoped. Before they left the racetrack grounds, more than 1,000 participants in the official Church Congress, and as many as 1,500 according to some estimates, left the stands and joined the demonstration. Still carrying their signs, the expanded group of demonstrators continued to parade through the racetrack grounds.[431] Then, as Kathrin Walther recalled, "This huge cluster of demonstrators linked together with streamers held high above their heads left . . . the stadium and headed toward the city center."[432]

But the Stasi wouldn't let them get there.

Later, Kathrin Walther recalled the emotional moment at the racetrack when other church members had joined the group-organized demonstration. "Together we had set ourselves in motion. What was special about that moment was that, already at this one demonstration in the run-up to October 1989, many people who didn't come out of the narrow circle of the basis groups—but many other people—had joined us. . . . They had decided, 'Since 'I'm for that,' we have to do something, and I'm going with you.'"[433]

Walter continued, "Those were Church Congress participants, who probably had never previously attended an alternative conference or had any connection with grassroots groups. That was something very moving for us." At the same time, it placed a tremendous responsibility on the group organizers "to see that things went well and that these people who had decided to become involved in the demonstration would not be injured."[434] Group members were well aware of the potential for violent confrontations and the necessity for working to ensure that the demonstrations in Leipzig would not end tragically as they had in Tiananmen Square.

Bringing the Church Back In

Although groups had to move away from the church initially to take the kind of radical action necessary to create a revolution in East Germany, later they also needed to bring the church back into the discussions and the political process. By summer 1989 the Evangelical Church represented an expanded base of participation and support for the political groups, and the church's incorporation into the movement for change denoted a significant broadening of the movement. So groups attempted to bridge the gap. According to Gabriele Heide of Women for Peace, "Groups recognized that it was important to discuss the themes that groups deal with in the churches—among the broader church population."[435]

During late 1988 and 1989, a number of Evangelical church leaders, synods, and other meetings had considered ideas and programs for reform that had constituted part of most group agendas—ideas viewed by many church members as quite radical. At the June 1988 regional church congresses in Görlitz, Erfurt, Rostock, and Halle, delegates debated a document on 20 theses for reforming and restructuring East Germany prepared by Pastor Friedrich Schorlemmer and his parish in Wittenberg. Included were proposals to reform the election system and to abolish the leading role of the communist party.[436] Following the May 1989 local elections, several church districts sent letters protesting the fraudulent election returns to local and state authorities.[437]

The Conciliar Process for Justice, Peace, and the Preservation of Civilization

Among the most significant of the programs bringing concerns of groups to the broader church membership was the so-called Conciliar Process. In East Germany, the ecumenical Conciliar Process for Justice, Peace, and the Preservation of Creation brought together clergy and lay members including group activists from a wide range of religious communities. Involving a series of meetings held over several years in the late 1980s, the Conciliar Process represented an important step in building church support for a broad range of ideas endorsed by political groups, including many that were critical to the East German revolution.[438] Consequently, by September 1989 the climate within much of the church was changing, and protest inside and outside the church was becoming more acceptable.

The Conciliar Process for Justice, Peace, and the Preservation of Creation had its roots in the World Council of Churches Conference in 1983 in Vancouver, Canada.[439] There, the East German delegation proposed the idea for a worldwide but locally based program for churches to struggle with questions relating to justice, peace, and the environment, along with other issues. Solidarity with persons in other countries represented a key concept, and the entire program promulgated by the Conciliar Process pointed to the interdependence of peoples and to the need to take responsibility for oneself and others.[440] In this sense, the Conciliar Process aligned itself with and supported various political groups in East Germany that saw themselves as part of international peace, environmental, human rights, third world, women's, and other movements. Almost all issue areas of the Conciliar Process focused on problems in both a global and a local context. For example, the section on energy use looked at high per capita use of energy in the industrialized world, including East Germany, in comparison with the dramatic energy needs of the third world, and then proposed a responsible worldwide energy policy as well as specific steps for East Germany.[441]

The ecumenical structure of the Conciliar Process was important. For the first time in East Germany, representatives of almost all faith-based communities met together to discuss social concerns. Churches represented in the process included the Evangelical Church (the largest church in East Germany, with representatives from seven regional districts); a number of smaller Protestant denominations, including Methodists, Mennonites, Society of Friends, and

Seventh-Day Adventists; and Roman Catholic, Russian Orthodox, and Old Catholic churches.[442]

In East Germany, the Conciliar Process began in February 1986 with the formation of the organizing committee composed of Erika Drees, Heino Falcke, and Christof Ziemer. In late 1987, the organizing committee issued invitations to all East German churches and church-based groups, asking them to send the organizers suggestions related to the themes of justice, peace, and the preservation of creation as well as ideas about how the process should work.[443] The letter generated a huge response, and by January 1988 the organizing committee had received more than 10,000 suggestions.[444] The Conciliar Process involved extensive local church participation, as church members and group representatives met together in local areas throughout East Germany to discuss proposals for 12 thematic areas relating to peace, justice, and the environment. Later these recommendations, including many far-reaching suggestions for societal renewal, were discussed and formalized in national conferences. Three ecumenical gatherings—February 1988 in Dresden, October 1988 in Magdeburg, and April 1989 again in Dresden—brought together representatives from throughout East Germany to discuss and vote on proposals. Then the recommendations adopted by these joint meetings were taken back to local churches for discussion and implementation.[445]

Many controversial issues reached the Conciliar Process agenda, including a number of recommendations that had been part of groups' agendas for years and challenged the current political and social situation in East Germany. These included calls for expanded political rights for everyone, separation of state and party functions, free and secret elections with a choice among candidates, freedom of expression and assembly, freedom to travel and to emigrate, and access to information on societal problems and other issues. In the environmental discussions, the lack of relevant information was pointed to as a major problem, and the recommendations called for more *Öffentlichkeit* and free access to information.[446] The final recommendations incorporated numerous ideas and programs promoted by East German political groups. Consequently, as the representatives and leaders of churches took these recommendations back to their own local congregations, more and more people in church communities were exposed to ideas promoted by groups—ideas that now had received the endorsement of the churches.

Nevertheless, many group members criticized how the Conciliar Process played out in Leipzig. Many groups had been excluded or had chosen not to participate in the process, in part because of extremely strained church-group relations in the city and the region during this period. Some Leipzig groups, particularly human rights and civil rights groups, had adopted increasingly radical programs challenging the East German state and promoting a more democratic state and society. Their views had brought them into conflict with the Leipzig church leadership, and groups viewed Leipzig church leaders such as Superintendent Friedrich Magirius as influencing the Conciliar Process from the background and excluding the positions of the most critical groups from the agenda.[447]

Group members complained that many groups had been shut out of the process. In fact, only three of the almost eighty grassroots groups in Saxony were allowed to participate in each of the three main topics of the Conciliar Process— peace, justice, and the environment.[448] These critical groups felt that the positions of state-conforming groups such as the Christian Peace Conference, a church-based group that the communist government viewed as "progressive" or supportive of the state,[449] dominated the Conciliar Process. Stasi reports published after 1989 document that the state did try to exclude the most oppositional groups from the process and to involve, rather, the groups most supportive of the status quo, and the Christian Peace Conference was one of only six East German groups allowed to participate in high-level meetings of the Conciliar Process.[450]

In contrast, Joachim Garstecki, writing in the Afterword to the official publication on the Conciliar Process, pointed out that fully one quarter of the 146 delegates participating in the three East German-wide ecumenical gatherings came from groups.[451] Also, many of the issues suggested by groups were incorporated into the themes discussed throughout the process. He also noted that even though some groups were disappointed or excluded, many group members at all levels of the process worked intensely on a number of different themes, and many of their ideas were incorporated into the consensus of the larger group.[452]

Garstecki argued that the Conciliar Process also helped to build a working relationship between religious communities and alternative groups. Delegates to the final meetings—ecumenical gatherings—pointed out what a "normal" part of the process the contribution of the groups had been and how seriously the final gathering had considered these in the final consensus.[453] As Garstecki wrote, "The groups participated actively in the Process, broadening the basis for later consensus. Representatives of institutions also discovered that group members weren't just a disruptive factor, but they had the potential for serious work."[454] The Conciliar Process was important for groups, for churches, and for relationships among the various participants.

The Conciliar Process also succeeded in improving relationships among churches in East Germany. As an ecumenical process, the Conciliar Process linked various religious traditions and institutions throughout East Germany and involved them in discussing problems confronting their country. According to Catholic advisor Professor Lothar Ullrich, the Conciliar Process brought the Roman Catholic Church out of a decades-long abstinence from participating in East German society. "For us Catholics in East Germany, Dresden and Basel [the site of the European meetings for the Conciliar Process] are an ecumenical learning process to bring us out of our often self-made ghetto. Through the Process our Protestant sister churches in East Germany and churches in the European context have offered us valuable assistance."[455]

Detlef Pollack, Theology Professor at the University of Leipzig, assessed the ecumenical process as very important because "for the first time in over twenty years massive dissatisfaction was articulated in the churches."[456] According to Hagen Findeis, Leipzig group member and observer of groups, the Conciliar Process "brought many people into the movement who weren't there earlier"[457] and helped spread a shared perception concerning broad ideas and the need for societal renewal beyond core activists. In this way the Conciliar Process helped create a mass base that could be mobilized in fall 1989. In the opinion of Leipzig theology professor Kurt Nowak, who had conducted the Pleisse worship service the previous month at Paul Gerhardt Church, "The church's role grew. It was a process."[458]

Although familiar with the Conciliar Process, East German activists differed in their assessments of its importance. A few of the persons I interviewed viewed it as important because it provided ideas for their groups; however, most saw it as significant primarily because it carried ideas already important for their groups to a broader segment of the church population. A total of 27 persons, or 63 percent of the 46 persons answering the question about the Conciliar Process ranked it as important. This included ten in Berlin, six in Leipzig, nine in Erfurt, and two others. Group members viewed several other church programs as important for groups and group members, but no other programs received nearly so much support as the Conciliar Process.[459]

Group members in Leipzig who viewed the Conciliar Process as important included Oliver Kloß of Working Group Human Rights, who argued, "The Process provided justification for the groups, although quite a few group members did not participate."[460] Gisela Kallenbach of Working Group Environmental Protection viewed the Conciliar Process as important for her personally, for the groups, and for the church.[461] She had worked on the Conciliar Process at the local level, responding to the invitation from Dresden Evangelical Church Superintendent Christof Ziemer, one of three members of the organizing committee for East Germany. Kallenbach felt that the Process was important because many ideas from groups such as hers spread beyond groups to the churches and ultimately to the European meetings in Basel, Switzerland, and the World Council of Churches meetings in Seoul, South Korea.[462] Christoph Wonneberger considered the Conciliar Process significant because it connected various ideas or themes and tied together groups and parishes in a better way.[463]

So, despite the difficulties surrounding group-church relationships, the Conciliar Process did play an important role in legitimizing the programs of groups for the broader Christian community in Leipzig and throughout East Germany. The Conciliar Process provided a structure and an organizational network that spread ideas from group activists and a small group of critical church leaders more broadly through the church population of East Germany. Because almost 40 percent of East Germans considered themselves Christians (more than five million Protestants and more than one million Catholics), the Conciliar Process represented a major network for spreading the ideas of groups to a broader audience. The Alternative Church Congress made this especially clear.

Nonviolence Prevails

On July 9, after the Stasi attempted to stop the protesters from moving from the stadium to the city center, the demonstration from the official Church Congress proceeded over Wundstrasse in the direction of Flossplatz.[464] A streetcar pulled up

Protestors carry banner *"Demokratie"* (democracy) toward city center
Photo by Christoph Motzer/Archiv Bürgerbewegung Leipzig e. V.

beside the group and stopped next to the demonstrators carrying the sign "Democracy" before they reached the square. Several Stasi employees jumped out, ripped down the sign, and jumped back inside the streetcar as the doors closed. Prevented from entering the streetcar, the demonstrators proceeded without the sign. Ahead, police blocked their progress toward the city center, so the demonstrators changed course again and turned onto Riemannstrasse, heading toward St. Peters Church, which was open because of the official Church Congress meetings. Rainer Müller and several other organizers of the Alternative Church Congress talked with church leaders there, who agreed to shelter the demonstrators. Inside St. Peters, about 700 participants from the Alternative Congress concluded their day of nonviolent protests with discussion sessions and a prayer service.[465]

Streetcar surrounded by demonstrators from the Church Congress closing meetings
Photo by Christoph Motzer/Archiv Bürgerbewegung Leipzig e. V.

The grassroots groups had succeeded by almost every measure. They had held a successful three-day congress that attracted group members from throughout the country. Even more importantly, a number of people from the official Church Congress had attended some of their alternative events. Most of these church members were not members of political groups. Some were just curious about the alternative program and the church's groups, while others disapproved of church and state restrictions on groups. The groups had succeeded in exposing the broader church community to their demands for democratic changes in East Germany, and a thousand church members had even joined group members in their protest demonstration.

Kathrin Walther assessed the Alternative Church Day events as "the most important action planned by groups in 1989."[466] "Although we didn't reach the city center, the service at Peter's Church was a powerful conclusion. We still had the worship service, the shared prayers, and the joint singing in Peter's Church.

St. Peter's Church, where Alternative Church
Congress demonstrators took shelter and held closing
worship services
Photo by Patricia Smith

We had the feeling that we had come a long way with this demonstration. We had carried the demands for democracy out of the Church Congress and into society and into the *Öffentlichkeit*. And it had all been carried out without violence."[467]

PART

TWO

Revolutionary Autumn

CHAPTER 7

Leaving versus Staying:
Mass Emigrations and Demonstrations,
August and September 1989

For me personally, the greatest moment was when, totally alone, totally for myself, I ran into the crowd and, at first quietly and then louder and louder, I called out, "We are the people! We are the people!"... I had seen police but had no fear. I felt strong and threw my arms high into the air and my soul cried out. [468]

—Eva Günther, Housewife,
September 25, Leipzig

The intention of the groups was to popularize the peace prayers and to build a larger following for group ideas and activities. [469]

—Jochen Lässig,
Initiative Group Living, Leipzig

Leaving East Germany: Mass Emigration

On August 2 Hungary began dismantling the barbed-wire fence between Hungary (in the east) and Austria (in the west). This set off a massive flight from East Germany in anticipation of the Hungarian border opening, as thousands of dissatisfied East Germans attempted to leave the country and move permanently to West Germany. This mass migration created a sense of urgency about the need for changes within East Germany and further delegitimized the East German government in the eyes of many citizens.

Hungary's decision to open its border with Austria had provided the impetus for a new wave of emigration and a concrete method for expressing dissatisfaction with conditions in East Germany. Some of those wanting to emigrate traveled to Hungary and crossed from there into Austria, planning to make their way on to West Germany from there. Others decided to go to the embassies and permanent missions of West Germany in various East European states, including Czechoslovakia, Hungary, Poland, and East Germany. These thousands of East German refugees created not only political problems for East Germany and the states where they fled in search of asylum but also created health and safety problems.

159

Map 7-1 Eastern Europe, 1989
Destinations of East German emigrés: East Berlin, Warsaw, Prague, Budapest,
Sopron, Vienna, Munich, and Bonn

In late July from Budapest, Prague, and Berlin came the first news reports of East German refugees wishing to emigrate to the west "occupying" the West German embassies and missions. On August 3, 80 East Germans inhabited the West German permanent mission in East Berlin, 130 were in the West German embassy in Budapest, and 20 in Prague.[470] The wave of would-be emigrés continued, and soon the embassies were forced to close from overcrowding. Already on August 8 West Germany closed its Berlin mission. In Budapest, more than a thousand East Germans wanting to emigrate sought refuge in the West German Embassy, forcing it to close because of overcrowding on August 14. The Maltese relief organization set up several tent camps in Budapest for the growing number of refugees no longer willing to return to East Germany, and on September 24, in a one-time action, the Red Cross flew 108 refugees from the West German embassy in Hungary to Vienna.[471]

*   *   *

Leipzig opposition groups also carried out programs to highlight the continued existence of the Berlin Wall and the need for fundamental changes in East Germany.[472] On August 13 several representatives of East German human rights groups, including Johannes Fischer of Leipzig's Working Group Human Rights, participated in a European action day program in Budapest. Organized by Fidesz and other Hungarian opposition groups in consultation with Leipzig groups, the program included a demonstration protesting against the Berlin Wall. Hungarian groups also protested against recent actions of Hungarian authorities that did not meet European human rights standards: Hungarian officials had sent refugees seeking temporary asylum in Hungary on their route to West Germany back to East Germany, where they were subject to persecution. At the gathering representatives from parties and groups from Hungary, Poland, Great Britain, and East Germany spoke about the significance of the cross-national event. Johannes Fischer brought greetings from East German groups, thanking the Hungarian groups for organizing the demonstration protesting the Berlin Wall. The event really should be held in East Germany, he said, but unfortunately at the time that was possible there only on a much smaller scale. As the event ended, protestors formed a human chain representing the Berlin Wall to protest its continued existence. Demonstrators then tore the paper ribbons they carried into thousands of pieces, symbolically tearing down the Berlin Wall and the divisions that it represented.

*   *   *

In Hungary, thousands more East Germans camped at Lake Balaton, the largest lake in central Europe and a favorite East German vacation spot, just as they did every summer. But 1989 was different. Some East Germans had gone to Hungary just to vacation, while others had gone with the specific intention of crossing to the west when Hungary opened its border with Austria. They waited at Lake Balaton and in other camping spots near the border—ready to cross to Austria and the west when the border opened. Northwest of Lake Balaton lay Sopron, a border crossing between Hungary and (Mörbisch) Austria—an entry to Austria, Vienna, and beyond to West Germany. Many East Germans there in Hungary prepared to abandon everything—jobs, family, friends—as they crossed the border to the west, and throughout Hungary thousands of abandoned East German cars—Trabis and Wartburgs—dotted the landscape.

To celebrate the opening of the border, Hungarian and other activists planned for a pan-European picnic on August 19 near the border crossing in Sopron. The Hungarian opposition group Hungarian Democratic Forum organized the pan-European picnic, along with the Pan-European Movement, whose president Otto von Habsburg was also a member of the European Parliament.[473] The organizing group invited groups from throughout Europe "to the place where the Iron Curtain used to stand."[474] They also circulated invitations among East Germans vacationing in Hungary, who copied the invitations and passed them on to others. And on August 19 thousands attended the picnic to commemorate the beginning of the end of the divisions between Eastern and Western Europe and between east and west.

✳   ✳   ✳

Ildikó Bódvai, a participant in the Pan European Picnic on August 19, 1989, remembered an East German family that crossed the border that day.[475] His story illustrates the difficult choices that confronted them.

A young father carrying a small child went first. His wife followed, accompanied by the grandfather. The two hesitated and fell farther behind. When the young man reached the border, he waited.

> Only a few steps separated him from Austria and freedom. He stopped there for the first time since I had been observing them. He looked around quickly. He noticed that a Hungarian border soldier walked nearby, but he didn't allow himself to be afraid. His decisiveness didn't waver for a moment. Deep in his soul he had already made his decision; he knew that he had strength and belief enough and that nothing could stop him. . . . He

could not or, rather, would not understand what battle played out in the soul of his wife. . . . He knew that this was the moment to act. . . . He called, "Come!" Or maybe it was a voiceless cry. I no longer know. They—the two who lagged behind—pulled themselves together and marched ahead with decisive steps.

When they reached the Austrian side, exhausted, they embraced and fell to the ground. . . . They stayed there a moment. Then they stood up and, keeping close together, they walked in the direction of the Red Cross tents—[that promised hope].[476]

That day, approximately 900 East German residents without visas took advantage of the temporary one-day border opening to cross over to the west—the most persons to flee East Germany in a single day since the Berlin Wall was built in 1961.[477] But the stream of East Germans going to the west did not end with the picnic on August 19. Although Hungary later attempted to control the border at Sopron by adding more border patrols, between 200 and 500 East German refugees managed to cross illegally into Austria every day until the border officially opened. (On September 10 Hungary officially opened its borders, allowing East Germans with valid documents to leave for the west.)

On August 21, oppositional groups throughout Eastern Europe held events to commemorate and condemn the invasion of tanks and troops by five Warsaw Pact states that had crushed Czechoslovakia's Prague Spring 21 years earlier, in 1968.[478] State authorities in various countries reacted to these 1989 protests differently. Authorities in Hungary and Poland, states receptive to democratic reforms in the late 1980s, condemned the 1968 invasion by Warsaw Pact members. The Polish Senate called the 1968 invasion an injury to the right of the Czechoslovak state to self-determination and of the people to democracy, freedom, and human rights. In Prague, security forces broke up a demonstration involving several thousand protestors. Later in the day, Charter 77 and three other Czech civil rights groups called for solidarity with the 370 persons arrested that day, including 50 foreigners. In Leipzig, Frank Richter prepared a letter to the Warsaw Pact states on behalf of East German opposition groups, including Leipzig's Working Group Human Rights and Working Circle Justice, protesting the invasion of Czechoslovakia by Warsaw Pact member states.[479]

Meanwhile, throughout August and September, East Germans in Hungary and elsewhere waited for a diplomatic solution among East Germany,

West Germany, and other countries that would allow them to immigrate to West Germany. (See Table 7-1 Highlights of Emigration from East Germany, 1989.) Anticipating such a solution, many East Germans in Czechoslovakia, the only state where East Germans could travel without a visa, moved on to Hungary in hopes of improving their chances of crossing to the west.

In an attempt to defuse protest from emigration groups and hoping to encourage East Germans to immigrate legally, on August 10 West Germany announced that 46,343 East German citizens had legally immigrated to West Germany during the first seven months of 1989. Many thousands more left illegally, and others without valid documents continued to risk illegal routes to the west.

The mass emigration continued throughout September and into October, putting pressure on all the states involved—East Germany, West Germany, Hungary, Austria, Czechoslovakia, and Poland. As pressures built both inside and outside East Germany, state officials in all the countries involved looked for political solutions. In some cases, special trains carried the refugees through East German territory on the way to West Germany. Others still residing in several East German cities but wishing to emigrate stopped the trains and fought with the police in attempts to board, and tensions escalated. On September 30, a special train passed through East Germany transporting 6,400 would-be emigrés to the west. At train stations in Dresden and Karl-Marx-Stadt, East Germans tried to board the train cars as they passed through, and police and demonstrators clashed. In the meantime, hundreds of other East Germans waited elsewhere for an opportunity to cross to the west. The mass emigrations would continue throughout October and into November, but East Germany again attempted to crack down and to control the exodus of its citizens.

Table 7-1
Highlights of Emigration from East Germany, 1989[480]

May 2, 1989	Hungary announces it will open its border with Austria.
August 2	Hungary begins dismantling barbed-wire fence between Hungary and Austria.
August 3	80 would-be emigrés reside in West German permanent mission in East Berlin, 130 in West German embassy in Budapest, and 20 in Prague.
August 8	West German permanent mission in Berlin closes because of overcrowding; 131 East Germans in mission.
August 10	Appealing to would-be emigrés to use legal rather than diplomatic means, West German officials announce that 46,343 East German citizens had immigrated during first seven months of 1989 using legal channels.
August 14	West German embassy in Budapest closes because of overcrowding.
August 19	Approximately 900 East Germans cross to west through checkpoint at Austrian–Hungarian border during Pan-European Picnic.
August 22	Since beginning of August, more than 10,000 East Germans have registered as immigrants in Austria.
August 23	West German embassy in Prague closes because of overcrowding. Since August 1, more than 3,000 East German citizens have fled over Hungarian border.
August 29	Bavaria in West Germany reports that it will accept up to 5,000 refugees.
September 10	Hungary opens border to Austria and allows thousands of East Germans with valid documentation to leave for west.
September 28	More than 2,000 East German residents occupy West German embassy in Prague, endangering health and safety. More than 400 are in Warsaw.
September 30	6,400 East Germans waiting in Warsaw and Prague are allowed to go to west. Train passes through East Germany, and those trying to board the train clash with police.
October 3	East Germany ends visa-free travel to Czechoslovakia.
October 4	7,600 East German refugees from Prague taken to West Germany by special train passing through East Germany. Police and demonstrators clash.
October 17 and 24	Special flights take East German refugees from Warsaw to West Germany.

October 27   East Germany announces amnesty for refugees and par-
                           ticipants in demonstrations not approved by the state.
November 1   New travel regulations allow visa-free travel to Czecho-
                           slovakia.
November 9   Berlin Wall falls and East German borders open. West
                           Germany announces that in 1989, 225,233 East German
                           citizens arrived in West Germany, including 48,177 since
                           the opening of the Czech border on November 3.

Who Were These East German Emigrants and Refugees?

Working in conjunction with the West German state ministry for inner German conditions, the research organization Infratest surveyed both legal emigrants and refugees from East Germany residing in West Germany during the end of August and the beginning of September 1989 to find out why so many East Germans left.[481]

More than half (56 percent) of these East German emigrants and refugees were young—between 18 and 30 years old. Most were relatively well educated. Eighty-six percent had completed an apprenticeship, 16 percent had gone to college, and 8 percent were college graduates. The vast majority, 87 percent, had jobs in East Germany, including 33 percent in industry, 25 percent in the service sector, 18 percent in trade, 7 percent in administration, and 4 percent in education. The economic condition of most was relatively good: 61 percent owned a car; 57 percent a color television; and 15 percent a *Datscha,* a weekend or vacation home. Most earned a relatively good income in comparison with other East Germans. A large majority of these East Germans were men—70 percent—and 40 percent of the men were single.

Why did these emigrants and refugees want to leave East Germany? According to the Infratest survey, the most frequently mentioned reasons for leaving, with 74 percent each, were because they lacked freedom of expression and they lacked travel possibilities. Seventy-two percent said they wanted a life of their own choosing, and 69 percent mentioned the lack of prospects for the future. For 65 percent of the respondents, the patronizing and overly directive East German state authorities provided a reason for leaving.

For the majority of those interviewed, 73 percent, it was the first time they had ever been in West Germany. Of those fleeing rather than emigrating legally, twenty percent had applied for a visa to emigrate, but without success. More than 90 percent of those interviewed believed that they would have a higher living standard in West Germany.

Media Coverage and Emigration

For years the East German press in Berlin had tried to ignore the massive flight of East Germans to the west. On August 7 the East German media acknowledged for the first time the swelling numbers of East German citizens wishing to emigrate to West Germany, and East German Foreign Minister Oskar Fischer warned of possible new restrictions on travel to Hungary. He also spoke of a "slander campaign" against East Germany.[482]

Throughout September 1989 the media "war" over coverage of East German emigration continued. In a commentary by ADN, the East German state news agency, and also reported in *Aktuelle Kamera,* the news program of East German television, East German officials accused West Germany of meddling in East German state affairs by failing to uphold agreements, and they accused politicians and the western media of trying to discredit East Germany and spreading false reports about emigrations problems.[483] East German press announcements also accused Hungary of failing to abide by international agreements. One report noted, "In violation of treaties and agreements under international law East German citizens are being permitted to emigrate to West Germany illegally and in the dead of night via the border with Austria."[484]

The official East German newspaper *Neues Deutschland* published numerous letters from East German readers criticizing West Germany's media campaign and foreign interference in East German affairs. One reader, Detlef Ottinger from Wismut, wrote: "What does West Germany really think of our bilateral treaties? I saw with my own eyes in Hungary how certain people talked to our vacationers at the camping sites and tried to persuade them to illegally leave East Germany. They also distributed the *BILD* newspaper [West German] with its disgusting demagogic reports. In my opinion, this is a severe interference in our affairs."[485]

Still, for an increasing proportion of the population the mass emigrations provided confirmation of fundamental problems in East German state and society.

Monday Night Peace Prayers and Demonstrations

By fall 1989, when the massive Monday demonstrations developed after the traditional Monday night peace prayers at Nikolai Church, many activists already had a long personal history of organizing and participating in demonstrations. (See Table 7-2 Demonstrations in Leipzig, January-October 1989.) In addition, they had already demonstrated their abilities to mobilize large crowds composed of diverse groups and individuals. Consequently, as the summer recess ended, the question in the minds of many Leipzigers was: What will happen in September when the peace prayers resume?

Monday, September 4

When the Monday night peace prayers resumed on September 4, 1989, after the summer recess, demonstrators wanting to leave East Germany competed for space and publicity with those wanting to stay and reform East Germany. After the services 1,200 demonstrators gathered in the church courtyard and paraded through central Leipzig. The majority called for exit visas, open borders, and free passage out of East Germany.[486]

As emigration group members demonstrated for unhindered passage to the west, opposition and alternative groups launched new initiatives for a more democratic East Germany, putting their programs before the people every Monday night at the peace prayer services. Their ideas and programs represented an alternative to emigration, and shouts of "We're staying," "Democracy," and "Reform" competed with cries of "We want out." In many ways, the mass exodus and the mass demonstrations drew strength from each other, as both pressed claims, promoted concerns, and raised issues that further destabilized the East German government.

The initial peace prayer service after the summer recess coincided with the fall trade fair in Leipzig, one of the few times the international media was allowed in the city. Well aware of the media's presence, several members of Initiative Group Living decided it was important to bring the messages of those wanting to stay and reform East Germany to the Monday night peace prayers and demonstrations in order to counter those of demonstrators wanting to leave.[487] Gesine Oltmanns recalled one group effort. On the afternoon of September 4, Uwe Schwabe, Katrin Hattenhauer, and Oltmanns had painted several

Demonstrators in Nikolai Church courtyard with
photographer in background, September 4, 1989
Photo by Rainer Kühn/Archiv Bürgerbewegung Leipzig e. V.

Photographer filming demonstration
Photo by Rainer Kühn/Archiv Bürgerbewegung Leipzig e. V.

banners at a residence at 46 Marianne Street. Because the Stasi had blocked many streets leading to Nikolai Church in an attempt to control the size of the demonstration, Oltmanns and Hattenhauer knew it would be difficult to get the banners to the church without being stopped, so they decided to wrap the banners around their stomachs and cover them with jackets. Then they boarded the streetcar and proceeded toward Nikolai Church without being detained.

As 1,200 demonstrators gathered in the church courtyard that evening after the peace prayer services, Oltmanns and Hattenhauer were among those carrying banners. They held their painted banner—"For an Open Land with Free People"—high above their heads, but for only a few moments before the Stasi ripped it away. But that was enough. West German journalists allowed in Leipzig during trade fair weeks had captured the image of police tearing the banner away from Oltmanns and Hattenhauer on film. Because western media filmed the incident, the Stasi did not arrest the two activists at that time as they customarily did during demonstrations without media coverage.

Demonstrators leaving Nikolai Church courtyard, September 4, 1989
Photo by Rainer Kühn/Archiv Bürgerbewegung Leipzig e. V.

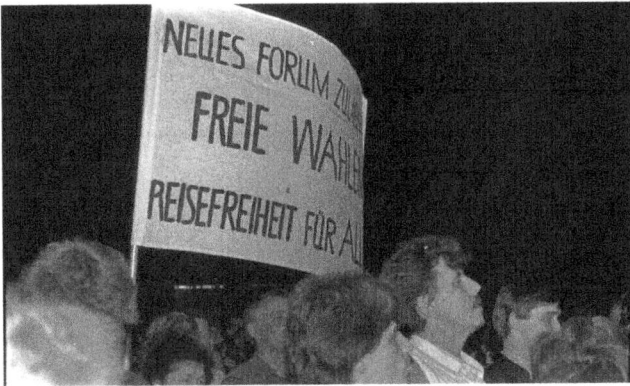

Sign, "New Forum, free elections, and free travel for all"
*Photo by Christoph Motzer/Archiv Bürgerbewegung
Leipzig e. V.*

According to Jochen Lässig of Initiative Group Living and later spokesman for the East German citizens group New Forum, the September 4 demonstration was particularly significant because the media focused on people carrying signs with slogans and, consequently, publicized and articulated the demands of the movement for political changes.[488] The footage played repeatedly on West German television and was watched by millions of East Germans who could receive television broadcasts out of West Berlin. The demands of demonstrators in Leipzig wanting to stay rather than emigrate reached a broad audience throughout East Germany and around the world.

Table 7-2
Demonstrations in Leipzig
January-October 1989[490]

Date	Occasion	Number of Participants
1/15/89	Rosa Luxemburg demonstration	800 attend; 500 participate in march
3/12/89*	Spring Industrial Fair	Bike demonstration; several dozen demonstrators
3/13/89*	After peace prayers	600 participate in silent march
5/7/89	After local election monitoring	1500 gather; 1000 marchers; 120 arrested
5/8/89	After peace prayers	550 protest election fraud
5/15/89	No peace prayers, but gathering	150 would-be emigrés
5/22/89	After peace prayers	350 demonstrators attempt to march
5/29/89	After peace prayers	Group members arrested
6/4/89	Second Pleisse Memorial March	500 demonstrators; many arrested
6/5/89	Peace prayers	1250 attend, biggest group ever
6/10/89	Street music festival	2500 attend; 140 arrested
6/12/89	After peace prayers	1000 at services, 200 demonstrate
6/19/89	After peace prayers	1100 at services; 100 march
6/26/89	Peace prayers	1000 attend
July-Aug.	Peace prayers	Summer recess
7/69/89	Alternative Church Congress	2500 attend; 1000 demonstrate
9/4/89*	Peace prayers resume; trade fair	1200 demonstrate
9/7/89	Protests against election fraud	1500 demonstrate, 72 arrested
9/11/89	After peace prayers	1500 demonstrate, 89 arrested
9/18/89	After peace prayers	2500 demonstrate, 31 arrested
9/25/89	After peace prayers	8000 demonstrate, 6 arrests
10/2/89	After peace prayers	25,000 demonstrate, many injured
10/7/89	40th Anniversary of East Germany	Hundreds demonstrate, 210 arrested, many injured
10/9/89	After peace prayers	75,000 demonstrate; "Day of Decision" peaceful

* International media coverage.

Later that week, on September 7, the customary monthly protests against election fraud resulted in 40 arrests. Oppositional groups followed up by activating solidarity networks. These contact telephone lines informed both other East German groups and international groups of police brutality and of the continued detention of those arrested. That evening in Reformierte Church, Friedrich Schorlemmer, Wittenberg pastor, theologian, and articulate spokesperson for a reformed East Germany, spoke on "Renewing Socialism." On September 10 activists signed and publicized the founding of the broad-based citizens movement New Forum, an organization that would capture the popular imagination and play an essential role in spreading the movement for democratic reforms across East Germany. On September 10 Hungary opened its border with Austria, and during the next few days 15,000 East Germans crossed to West Germany.[489]

Monday, September 11

Tensions built during the peace prayer services on September 11. Those attending worried about what would happen after the services, because the international media was not in town to cover the events and protect the demonstrators. Security forces formed a ring around the church courtyard and attempted to prevent a demonstration through the city. Even before everyone attending the service had left the church, police called out with bullhorns, "This is the East German People's Police. Leave the square immediately!"

Security forces had blocked the streets in every direction, and they instructed the demonstrators to leave the area via Ritter Street. Stasi personnel broke through the chain and pulled men and women from the crowd, targeting group activists, and led them away to the waiting police wagons. That day, more than 1,500 people demonstrated after the peace prayers, and calls for reforms and staying predominated over those for leaving. That evening police violently confronted demonstrators, arresting 89.[491]

Among those arrested that day was Katrin Hattenhauer, who had carried the banner "For an Open Land with Free People" the previous week.[492] Earlier Hattenhauer had applied for a visa to immigrate to West Germany, but when state authorities finally offered her a chance to emigrate, she had turned down the opportunity. By then she had decided to stay and work for reform, and she became a target for arrest because of her oppositional activities.

State authorities reacted to the growing opposition in Leipzig with harsh penalties for all those arrested. Those released received heavy fines ranging from 1,000 to 5,000 marks. Eleven of those arrested remained in police custody until the middle of October.[493] State authorities, however, had misjudged the impact of their action. The fines and arrests elicited a wave of protests and angry

Police wagons waiting to take away arrested demonstrators; police beatings
Photo by Rainer Kühn and Stefan Walter/Archiv Bürgerbewegung Leipzig e. V.

responses from an increasing proportion of the population.

During the following week Leipzig grassroot groups set up a contact telephone line at the office of Markus Church in support of those arrested. This was also the Leipzig office for the recently formed citizens movement group New Forum. From this office, Leipzig activists contacted groups and churches throughout East Germany as well as the media and oppositional groups in other countries.

Parents of those arrested, many of whom had never attended church or group meetings, represented a new element in the movement for a reformed East Germany.[494] Although many were skeptical about the protests initially, they knew their children were not criminals, and for many, police action against their children pushed them to take to the streets.

In Leipzig, daily services were set up for those arrested. In addition to the peace prayers in Nikolai Church on Monday, Reformierte Church held services on Tuesday, Michaelis Church on Wednesday, and Lukas Church on Thursday. Members of Leipzig oppositional groups took responsibility for these services.

According to Hans-Jürgen Sievers, pastor of Reformierte Church and chronicler of the revolution, "To everyone who participated, it was clear that this was not only a worship service, but a form of resistance and protest."[495] Sievers complimented the high quality of the services and the responsibilities that these young group members took for them, the money they raised for those with large fines and in prison, and the fact that they were the first ones involved in the demonstrations. "The twenty-year-olds" were "the motor of the movement,"[496] according to Sievers. Looking back, Sievers pointed to the critical role played by this small group of young Leipzig activists and called it "the revolution of the twenty-year-olds that brought the forty-year-olds to power."[497]

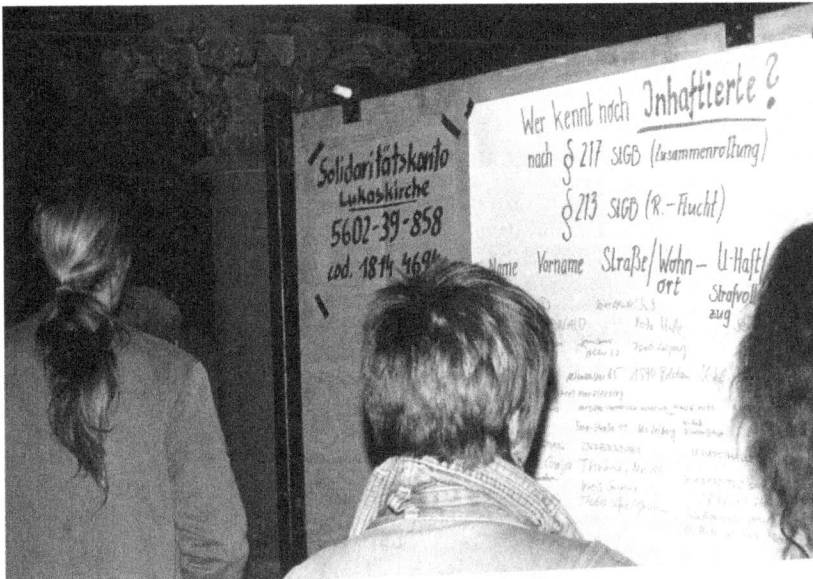

Solidarity exhibits and program at Lukas Church for those arrested
Photo by Bernd Heinze/Archiv Bürgerbewegung Leipzig e. V.

At a service in Reformierte Church Jochen Lässig of Initiative Group Living suggested that a memorial be set up at Nikolai Church. Candles were lit (and kept burning) in a window near the side door and decorated with flowers to demonstrate solidarity with those arrested.[498] A wave of solidarity followed in churches throughout East Germany as they conducted prayer services for those arrested and collected offerings to help pay for the gigantic fines levied on group members in Leipzig.

Candles in solidarity with those arrested
Photo by Bernd Heinze/Archiv Bürgerbewegung Leipzig e. V.

Monday, September 18

On September 18, Pastor Christian Führer of Nikolai Church conducted the service.[499] In his message he emphasized nonviolence. He also called for understanding for the young police force, because most had not asked for the job of policing the demonstrations and did not want it. The arrests and violence the previous week had resulted in a wave of solidarity bringing new participants into the movement, and twice as many people attended the peace prayers as the week before.[500] During the service the names of those arrested the previous week were read aloud. Those attending were advised to go directly home as soon as the services ended, but most did not follow that advice, and 2,500 demonstrators turned out that night. As participants left the peace prayers, they confronted a police chain around the Nikolai Church courtyard. Attempting to prevent a demonstration, police attacked and arrested 31 protestors as they moved toward Ritter Street. Three demonstrators received prison sentences, and five received fines of up to 10,000 marks.[501]

Police block streets near Nikolai Church.
Photo by Rainer Kühn and Stefan Walter/Archiv Bürgerbewegung Leipzig e. V.

Police in Nikolai Church courtyard, September 18, 1989
Photo by Rainer Kühn and Stefan Walter/Archiv Bürgerbewegung Leipzig e. V.

Demonstrators in Nikolai Church courtyard, September 18, 1989
Photo by Rainer Kühn and Stefan Walter/Archiv Bürgerbewegung Leipzig e. V.

By September 18 the tone of the demonstrators had changed. Rather than wanting to exit, most now demanded democratic reforms in East Germany, and citizens from other cities joined the protests. For example, a number of citizens from Kreis Auerbach drove about sixty miles north to Leipzig to participate in the Monday demonstrations, and they organized carpools so they could attend in future weeks.[502]

The following week vigils for those arrested continued in Leipzig and in numerous other cities, including Dresden, Berlin, and Halle. On September 22 the state rejected New Forum's petition to legalize the organization, declaring New Forum an enemy of the state. At the demonstrations following the peace prayers, many new demonstrators took to the streets demanding legalization of New Forum.

Demonstrators with sign demanding legalization of New Forum
Photo by Bernd Heinze/Archiv Bürgerbewegung Leipzig e. V.

Uwe Schwabe of Initiative Group Living reported that it was often difficult to estimate the number of participants in the peace prayers and in the demonstrations following the services.[503] Every Monday several members of the coordination committee went around trying to count demonstrators. Afterward they would all meet together to try to arrive at a number. There was much discussion, and the group would always choose a number in the middle for their reports. Despite disagreements, there was one thing they could all agree on: it was important that more people attend the services each week than had attended the previous week, so they redoubled their efforts to bring new participants to the peace prayers and the demonstrations.

Monday, September 25

Oppositional pastor Christoph Wonneberger of Lukas Church and Working Group Human Rights took responsibility for the September 25, 1989, peace prayer service.[504] Because of the arrests and the violence the previous Monday, the organizing group emphasized nonviolence throughout the service, drawing on Jesus' sermon on the mount and especially Matthew 5:9, "Blessed are the peacemakers." That evening Wonneberger preached on nonviolence and on confronting one's fears in what has been called "the definitive sermon of revolution." Wonneberger said that the Stasi, their dogs, and their weapons were only paper tigers and that the people should not fear them. The emotional service ended with Christa Mihm singing "We Shall Overcome," with the congregation joining in as they filed out of Nikolai Church and into the courtyard and the street.

*   *   *

In the Nikolai Church courtyard, demonstrators again encountered police and other security forces, whose number had grown larger each week. After a few minutes in the courtyard, a voice called out, "Let's go!" and demonstrators attempted to move as a group along their customary route toward Market Square next to Old City Hall. Security forces blocked their route along Grimmaische Street, however, so the demonstrators changed course. They headed in the opposite direction, from Nikolai Church toward Karl Marx Square. An estimated 8,000 demonstrators joined together in the huge square between the Opera House and the Gewandhaus, which housed Leipzig's symphony, and proceeded toward Leipzig's inner ring. The group entered the ringed boulevards for the first time that day. Stretching across the many lanes of the thoroughfare, the huge group blocked traffic. Thousands strong, they followed the ring past the train station, past the Konsument department store, and past Reformierte Church before turning around at the pedestrian overpass on Friedrich Engels Square. (See Map I-1 Leipzig, 1989, in the Introduction.) On the way back, around a thousand of the demonstrators stopped at the west hall of the train station, which they "occupied" for several minutes before the police intervened, attacking demonstrators and arresting six people.

Demonstrators waiting on Karl Marx Square before marching along Leipzig's ring.
Photo by Christoph Motzer/Archiv Bürgerbewegung Leipzig e. V.

The significance of September 25 is hard to overstate. With 8,000 demonstrators marching through the inner city, September 25 was the first great demonstration in Leipzig and the largest independent, unauthorized demonstration in East Germany since 1953. Demonstrators had entered the Leipzig Ring and marched for more than a mile along Leipzig's central ring (the length of the entire ring is approximately two and a half miles) before turning back. The demonstrators had overcome their fear of the Stasi and the police.

Security forces were prepared. Approximately 500 attack troops stood ready at Nikolai Church. The support troops at Nikolai Church carried nightsticks, but their leaders carried weapons with extra ammunition, and they were supported with police dogs. But the security forces did not attack.

Why did the security forces allow the gigantic demonstration to proceed along Leipzig's ring without attempting to stop it? Rainer Tetzner argues that the security forces could have prevented the demonstration if they had wanted to.[505] Instead, police opened a space in their human chain around Nikolai Church and allowed the demonstrators to pass through to Karl Marx Square and the ring. Because security forces prevented demonstrations that week in Halle, Magdeburg, Dresden, and Berlin, Tetzner speculates that perhaps Leipzig was a special case. When he interviewed Leipzig's Major General Strassenburg many years later, Strassenburg would only say that the Leipzig People's Police made the decision themselves that day and did not receive special orders from Berlin. Perhaps they decided not to attack because no one had expected thousands of demonstrators.[506]

CHAPTER 8

Organizing across East Germany:
New Forum and Citizen Movements

*New Forum was "a symbol for the coming together of the popula-
tion against the communist party."*[507]

—Detlef Pollack, Theology Professor
Karl Marx Univerity, Leipzig

*There was very little that people previously had in common, other
than their opposition to the [communist] party. That's why we
tried to build a sort of replica of the entire society within New
Forum, to set up groups dealing with literally every aspect of the
organization of a society."*[508]

—Ingrid Köppe,
New Forum representative
Central Round Table, Berlin

Citizen Movement Organizations and Independent Political Parties

As the peace prayers resumed in fall 1989, a number of Leipzig oppositional and other group members were also involved on another front. They had joined with other key activists throughout the country to establish East German citizens movement organizations. (See Table 8-1 East German-Wide Citizens Organizations and Independent Political Parties.) Many people were members of more than one of these groups, and the organization that held most of the power during fall 1989—and antipathy from the establishment—called itself New Forum.[509]

The founding of East German-wide citizens movements helped increase the momentum for fundamental changes in state and society. Founded with at least a core of persons who had previously been active in the political opposition,[510] these citizen movement organizations incorporated many of the ideas and programs advocated by political and oppositional groups into their founding statements.

181

Table 8-1
East German-Wide Citizens Organizations and Independent Political Parties[511]

Date	Organization/Platform/Event
March 1989	Initiative for Peace and Human Rights, founded in Berlin in January 1986, calls for an East German-wide organization
August 1989	Declaration of Intent to found New Forum
September 4	Organizational call for a United Left; Bohlener Platform
September 9/10	New Forum founded; appeal titled "Departure '89"
September 12	Democracy Now founded; calls for "fundamental democratic restructuring of East Germany"
September 24	Secret meeting in Leipzig of representatives of New Forum, Democratic Awakening, Democracy Now, and United Left
October 1	Initiative for a Green Party presented at Berlin meeting of Greenway, an organization of East European environmental groups Founding of citizens movement Democratic Awakening
October 6	"Common Declaration" of East German citizen movement organizations and parties—Democracy Now, Democratic Awakening, Initiative for Peace and Human Rights, Social Democratic Party, New Forum, and representatives of peace circles
October 7	Founding of Initiative Group for a Social Democratic Party in East Germany
October 14	New Forum with 25,000 members calls for East German-wide organizational structure at coordinating meeting in Berlin
October 28	Initiative for Peace and Human Rights builds East German-wide organization recognized by state
October 30	Formal founding of Democratic Awakening as a political party
November 8	New Forum recognized by East German state

New Forum viewed itself as a mass movement and directed its appeals to varied segments of the population. In contrast, Initiative for Peace and Human Rights did not view itself as a mass movement but targeted a narrower audience and demanded "a high degree of commitment and active participation" from its members.[512]

The most successful of the citizens movement groups, New Forum, would become the largest citizens group in East Germany before the end of the year. Founded over the weekend of September 9–10 with 30 opposition members from across East Germany, New Forum publicized an appeal, "Departure '89,"[513] inviting all East German citizens to join their movement. The objective was to open up communications between state and society concerning economic, political, environmental, and societal problems.

Jochen Lässig collecting signatures for New Forum at Nikolai Church, October 6, 1989
Photo by Martin Jehnichen/Archiv Bürgerbewegung Leipzig e. V.

Although neither New Forum nor other citizen movement organizations were initially recognized by the East German state, New Forum managed to attract relatively broad-based popular support. Initiatives and petition drives throughout East Germany called for the legalization of New Forum. At demonstrations across the country, protestors called out "New Forum," and signs for the legalization of New Forum appeared with increasing frequency during Leipzig's Monday night demonstrations. By October 14 New Forum already had a membership of 25,000, and membership would reach 200,000 before the end of the year.[514] Detlef Pollack, chronicler of the opposition, especially in Leipzig, characterized New Forum as "a symbol for the coming together of the population against the communist party."[515]

The government determined that New Forum was an enemy of the state.

New Forum
and
Citizen Movement Organizations (*Bürgerbewegungen*)

New Forum (NF)
- One of several citizens' movements founded in summer 1989 with intent of organizing at grassroots level throughout East Germany.
- Thirty founding members came primarily from East German oppositional groups in several cities, including Leipzig and Berlin.
- Viewed self as mass movement; directed appeal to wide spectrum of East German population.
- Founding declaration, "Departure '89," called for dialogue among East German citizens and the state and for democratic reforms.
- Did not have a fixed program but represented change, an alternative to the current system in the direction of more freedom and citizen participation.
- Symbolized "a coming together of the population against the communist party."*
- Used petition drives and signs and calls for legalization during demonstrations and other public events throughout East Germany to promote organization.
- 25,000 members by October, although state viewed New Forum as illegal and an enemy of the state; 200,000 members by year's end.
- Declaration of intent to found, August 1989; founded September 9–10, 1989. State recognized New Forum as a legal organization on November 8, 1989, the day before the Berlin Wall fell.

Citizen Movement Organizations in East Germany**
- Included Initiative for Peace and Human Rights (IFM), New Forum, the United Left (VL), Democratic Awakening (DA), Democracy Now (DJ), and the Greens.
- Differed in organizational structure, tactics, and members they attracted.
- Connected through core of basic ideas and shared beliefs concerning democratic reform.

* Pollack, author interview.
** Several of these organized later as political parties, but New Forum retained its looser organizational structure as a citizens' movement.

How was it possible in Leipzig, a city of half a million people, for half a million people to take to the streets, demanding democratic changes? The quick and dramatic growth of New Forum in Leipzig and the surrounding area helps us understand how the massive demonstrations—growing larger almost every Monday night in Leipzig—were possible. The growth of New Forum illustrates how these demonstrations could spread within Leipzig, from city to city, from region to region, and, ultimately, throughout the country. And given New Forum's "enemy of the state" status, it took a fair amount of courage to become a member or sign a petition in support of New Forum. These were essentially illegal acts and designated the signers as supportive of the political opposition.

* .*   *

Already on September 12, just two days after New Forum's founding, a citizens movement group was established in Königsbrück.[516] Although it had no name initially, the group later affiliated with New Forum. By September 30 this Königsbrück group had gathered signatures of 250 persons willing to work together for social, political, economic, and environmental change.

On September 13 a church environmental group in Penig linked itself to New Forum.[517] In Wilsdruff, the words "New Forum" were written on the train station, and a petition drive supporting New Forum attracted broad support. On September 17 a large number of residents of Auerbach drove to Leipzig to participate in the Monday night demonstration, and they also organized car pools to Leipzig for future demonstrations. On September 18 in the main bakery in Auerbach, the letters NF for New Forum were written in chalk on the newspaper posted on the wall.[518]

On September 19 New Forum applied to the state to be legally recognized as a group. The next day, East German authorities denied the application on the grounds that New Forum was an enemy of the state. The state's action unleashed a flood of supportive actions throughout the region calling for the state to legalize New Forum. In Oberwiesenthal several businesses began gathering signatures backing New Forum, and churches carried the project further. At a church meeting in Kittlitz on September 22, backers of New Forum gave a presentation on New Forum and collected signatures supporting the organization.[519] That same day church superintendents from throughout Saxony meeting in Dresden prepared a proclamation protesting the state's refusal to recognize New Forum and sent the proclamation to state authorities.

On September 23 at a worship service in Großschönau supporters gathered signatures calling for the legalization of New Forum. That same day signatures were also collected in Meerane and a letter of protest was sent to state authorities. Also in Meerane, physicians who were members of the state mass organization for health (FDGB-Kreis) used their monthly report to the organization to demand more democracy.

On September 27 in Königbrück at a meeting about New Forum and how to respond, the church decided to hold regular peace prayers and to follow the services with candlelight demonstrations through the city.[520] In Sosa citizens began gathering signatures calling for the legalization of New Forum. In Crottendorf citizens made contact with the New Forum organization in Berlin and requested information; they also quickly gathered 1,000 signatures calling for New Forum's legalization. In Jonsdorf, 299 people signed petitions for legalization—one out of every six persons in the small village. Signatures were also gathered in Neustadt in Saxony, and a citizen in Wittichenau received a copy of a petition from her brother who had received it from a pastor in Coswig. New Forum organizations were established in cities and villages throughout Saxony, including Zittau, Bautzen, Niederoberwitz, Raschau, and Thalberg/Erzgebirge.[521]

*   *   *

Even from its early days New Forum held a lot of appeal and influence, but there was no way to predict the pivotal role New Forum would play in the days leading up to the fall of the Berlin Wall.

CHAPTER 9

Promoting Nonviolence:
The Decisive October 9 Demonstration

*"The people" were split. While the one side celebrated the birth-
day of the Republic, the other side carried out a great demonstration against the Republic in eighteen cities: in Berlin and Leipzig,
in Karl-Marx-Stadt, Plauen, Dipoldiswalde, and other cities.*[522]

—October 7, 1989,
40th anniversary of East Germany

*Under the guidance of groups, demonstrators practiced nonvio-
lence, sitting and singing, but refusing to respond to security-force
provocation.*[523]

—Gabrielle Heide
Women for Peace, Leipzig

We live from Monday to Monday.[524]

—Helmut Hackenberg, head of
Communist Party, Leipzig district

October brought increasing unrest and escalating violence to many cities throughout East Germany, but especially to cities in Saxony. Hungary had opened its border with Austria on September 10, allowing thousands of East Germans with valid documents to leave for the west. Nevertheless, on September 28 more than 2,000 East Germans occupied the West German embassy in Prague, and 400 waited in Warsaw, unwilling to return to East Germany.[525] (See Map 7-1 Eastern Europe, 1989.) A diplomatic agreement had allowed about 6,000 East Germans in Czechoslovakia and Poland to receive papers to emi-grate, traveling to West Germany via six special trains. The trains left every two hours and passed through Dresden, Karl-Marx-Stadt, and Plauen in East Ger-many on their way to Hof on the West German border. On October 1 the last of these trains carrying emigrants with papers left East Germany and passed through to the west. However, the emigration problem was not solved. Almost

187

immediately those who had left were replaced in the West German embassies with new East German refugees seeking passage to the west.

In an attempt to control the massive flight of its citizens, on October 3 the East German government ended all visa-free travel to Czechoslovakia.[526] But state authorities had grossly underestimated the negative reaction this change in travel regulations would elicit both from those wanting to emigrate and from the public at large. All over the country, East Germans reacted with anger to the news that they could no longer travel to Czechoslovakia without passports or visas.[527] East Germans had lost the last attractive socialist country where they could travel freely. Moreover, the next day, October 4, the East German Politburo ended free travel to Romania and Bulgaria. The government had ended visa-free travel to all socialist "brother" states, essentially ending the ability of "normal" East German citizens to leave the country.

The Stasi reported widespread dissatisfaction within East Germany, noting, "The population now feels fully locked up." Citizens' reports included: "We felt we were handled like slaves; East Germany had become a prison; the last possibility of traveling outside the country was taken away; we sat, finally, in a cage."[528] Almost everywhere in East Germany citizens reacted angrily to the new regulations. Communist party members left the party, workers protested with strikes, and hundreds filed new applications to emigrate.

Monday, October 2, Peace Prayers and Demonstrations in Leipzig[529]

Meanwhile, in Leipzig tensions continued to mount as Leipzig groups, citizens, and churches prepared for the October 2 Monday night peace prayers and demonstrations. Efforts by Leipzig oppositional groups to increase the numbers participating in the demonstrations continued with obvious success, as three times as many demonstrators turned out October 2 as had the previous week.

They were, of course, warned not to participate. Heads of firms demanded that workers not participate, and students were warned that they would be kicked out of the university.[530] Hospitals made certain they had enough blood, and medical personnel were told they needed to be available in case of attacks and numerous injuries. Also in nearby cities and towns, authorities informed residents of possible violence in Leipzig. At Martin Luther University in Halle students and teachers were warned not to go to Leipzig because "blood would flow."

Following the September 25 demonstration state authorities had ordered Bishop Hempel to stop the peace prayers and threatened Pastors Christoph Wonneberger and Christian Führer with prison and loss of their jobs if they did not end their participation in the prayers.[531] But all declined to follow the orders to not participate, and plans proceeded for the following week and the peace prayer services in Leipzig.

∗   ∗   ∗

On October 2 Nikolai Church was filled to capacity by 4:20 p.m., with 2,000 congregants; however, Stasi and communist party members also occupied some of the seats. At Nikolai Church Youth Pastor Klaus Kaden and Working Group Environmental Protection conducted the service, focusing on the catastrophic situation in East Germany and the need for reform. Kaden's message clearly emphasized that everyone was responsible for the current situation and called for civil courage in making the reforms necessary in the country.[532]

That day, for the first time, Reformierte Church also held peace prayers services. The church board had agreed unanimously to the request by the church district superintendent to hold services because Nikolai Church could no longer accommodate the growing crowds of peace prayer participants, and

Demonstrating solidarity with candles and flowers
Photo by Martin Jehnichen/Archiv Bürgerbewegung Leipzig e. V.

most church members supported the decision. By 5 p.m. on October 2 Reformierte Church was filled and the crowd spilled out onto the nearby streets. Dominican Father Bernhard Venzke and a Catholic peace group conducted the services, a sign of growing support for political changes in East Germany from the broader ecumenical community. During the services, the names of the 11 activists arrested in September and still held in prison were read and remembered, and peace prayer participants who had brought flowers and candles were instructed to take them to the Nikolai Church courtyard. There, the courtyard filled with flowers and candles provided an ongoing reminder to Leipzigers of their fellow citizens still in prison.

Demonstrators gather in front of Nikolai Church.
Photo by Christoph Motzer/Archiv Bürgerbewegung Leipzig e. V.

That day—October 2—25,000 demonstrators marched along the Leipzig Ring. After the services the 3,000 to 4,000 people waiting in the Nikolai Church courtyard joined the crowd leaving the church.[533] Another huge group marched through Leipzig's old city center from Reformierte Church to join them. These combined groups, already numbering at least 5,000 demonstrators, wound their way along the streets for several blocks from Nikolai Church until they reached Karl Marx Square. There, thousands more waited. Twenty-five thousand strong, they left

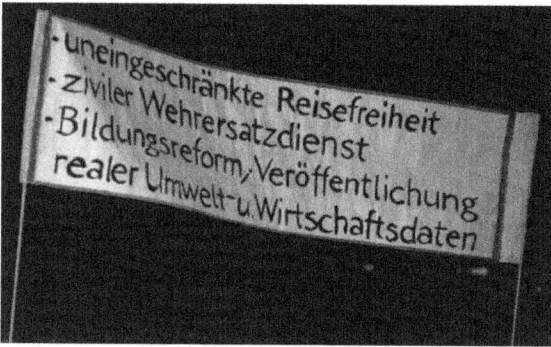

Banner calling for freedom to travel, alternatives to military service, education reform, and environmental data
Photo by Christoph Motzer/Archiv Bürgerbewegung Leipzig e. V.

the square and entered the Leipzig Ring, marching along the Georgi Ring to the central train station. As they proceeded, demonstrators called out their demands: "No violence," "No new China," "Allow New Forum," "Gorbi, Gorbi!" "We're staying here," "Freedom for the arrested," "Freedom to travel," "Democracy—Now or Never."[534]

As they proceeded along Tröndlin Ring near Nordstrasse and Reformierte Church, demonstrators encountered a police blockade stretching across all lanes of the ring and blocking their progress. A row of combat troops stood directly behind the police. The protestors attempted to break through the line, but without success. A policeman called out by loudspeaker, "This is the People's Police speaking" (*"Hier spricht die Volkspolizei"*).

"Wir sind das Volk!"—"We are the people!"

But the crowd responded spontaneously, "We are the people!" (*"Wir sind das Volk!"*), dismissing the police's claim to represent the people, and introducing their own claim. This chant—"We are the people"— would be heard over and over again in demonstrations throughout East Germany, as more and more ordinary East Germans took to the streets.

Finally the demonstrators broke through the police blockade and reached Friedrich Engels Square. At that point some left the demonstration, while others turned the corner and continued along Dittrich Ring to Runde Ecke, the round-cornered building that housed Leipzig's Stasi. About 1,500 demonstrators kept going along the ring until they reached Thomas Church, where the demonstration ended at 8:20 p.m. Many from this group of demonstrators wanted to

Kurt Masur, conductor of Leipzig Symphony and later New York Philharmonic
Photo by Frank Sellentin/ Archiv Bürgerbewegung Leipzig e. V.

return to the center city, but the police prevented them. Supported by dogs, special police forces outfitted with helmets and shields and carrying billy clubs attacked the demonstrators. The demonstration ended with 20 arrests.

The *Leipziger Volkszeitung*, the state newspaper in Leipzig, defended police violence that day as necessary to maintain order, but others were appalled.[535] In an interview carried on West German television, Kurt Masur, the conductor of the acclaimed Leipzig symphony (and later of the New York Philharmonic), said he was ashamed of the violence, and he called for dialogue.

"The sympathy of the public for those arrested grew in these weeks,"[536] according to Evangelical Church Superintendent Friedrich Magirius. People brought flowers to the churches daily, lit candles nightly to remember the arrested, and brought placards signifying solidarity, which the Stasi removed.

October 4–5

The largest number of applicants to emigrate had come from Saxony—especially Dresden and Karl-Marx-Stadt—the cities where the most violent and extensive protests also occurred. And with the news of border closings, the number of East Germans attempting to flee across the borders increased. (See Table 7-1.) During the night of October 4 East German border guards, supported by their counterparts in Poland and Czechoslovakia, arrested 111 persons in the Dresden district.[537] By the next day the border was fortified and reinforced with additional troops and helicopters. Nevertheless, attempts to cross the borders to Poland, Czechoslovakia, and West Germany continued, with arrests and imprisonment awaiting many who tried to flee.

In Prague, on October 4 the situation in the West German embassy had reached a crisis point. Thousands of East Germans pressed to be let in. Even in the garden, there was hardly a free spot, so only women with children were admitted. Because the Czechoslovak authorities had refused to provide other lodging, many East German refugees not allowed in the embassy spent the night on the street. That morning head of the Czechoslovak government Ladislav Adamec informed Erich Honecker that if East Germany did not do something about the refugees, Czechoslovakia was prepared to transport them to West Germany. Honecker and the Politburo decided to send the 7,600 East Germans from Prague to Hof in West Germany by special trains through East Germany during the night from October 4 through 5. The first secretaries of the communist party in Dresden and Karl-Marx-Stadt, Modrow and Lorenz, were warned of the upcoming trains, because trouble was expected.

Informed by the western media reports of the trains traveling through East Germany that night, thousands who wanted to emigrate came from all over East Germany. Would-be emigrés lined the tracks along the route, and as trains passed through the stations on their way west, demonstrators stormed the platforms.[538] In just one city—Karl-Marx-Stadt—on that one day—October 5—authorities estimated that 3,500 persons attempted to climb onto the trains.

In Dresden, groups began gathering around 3 p.m. on October 4, and by 6 p.m. a gigantic group gathered around the Lenin memorial, shouting chants and singing "The Internationale."[539] At 6:45 security forces tried to clear the demonstrators from the station, rounding up 1,000, but shortly afterward another 2,500 appeared, plus 6,000 more outside. At 8:15 p.m. the situation escalated. The protest turned violent, as demonstrators threw cobblestones and Molotov cocktails and also destroyed railroad property, breaking hundreds of windows. Authorities feared that the situation would spiral out of control.

Police barricaded the station, and in spite of the cold weather they turned fire hoses on the demonstrators. The gathering grew to 20,000 demonstrators. They called out "We want out" and "We want Gorbachev." Militant demonstrators attempted to break down the doors to the station, but thanks to support from a company of police troops from Halle, security forces managed to temporarily bring the demonstrators under control.

At 9 p.m. local officials received permission from officials in Berlin with Honecker's approval to use tear gas on the demonstrators, which led to further escalation. Demonstrators destroyed hundreds of plate-glass windows, along with other furnishings and equipment. At 10:10 p.m. three additional police companies from Halle arrived at the station. To bring the situation under control, police

Cleaning up after emigration protests at central train station, Dresden
Photo by Martin Jehnichen/Archiv Bürgerbewegung Leipzig e. V.

announced over the loudspeaker system that those wanting to emigrate should go home and their visas to emigrate would be prepared within three days. Fearing that this would not really happen, many who left returned to Dresden on October 6, strengthening the forces protesting there for emigration and for democratic change. That evening 700 demonstrators were arrested. Rumors suggested that the most aggressive demonstrators came from Leipzig; however, it was later proven that many "provocateurs" did not come from Leipzig but were civilian employees of the Stasi.

October 6 and 7—East German 40th-Anniversary Celebration

As the 40th-anniversary celebration for East Germany approached, the degree of dissatisfaction among East German citizens had reached a dangerous point, especially in Leipzig.[540] Recent events in the city had led to a polarization between "progressive forces" that supported the government (and no longer included all communist party members) and the majority of the population. Rather than deescalate the conflict, the regime had decided in recent weeks to consolidate its forces and use them against the population, labeling the protestors class enemies and arresting their leaders. But, the state's decisions had backfired. Many more Leipzigers joined the movement for democratic change and took to the streets. The situation had reached a standoff. It seemed that the security forces could no longer control the demonstrations with small steps. The crowds had become too large and the momentum too strong to stop without extreme measures. As October 7 and the 40th-anniversary celebration of East Germany approached—followed just two days later by Leipzig's traditional Monday night peace prayers and accompanying demonstrations—tensions in Leipzig peaked.

Would There Be a Chinese Solution?

On October 7, demonstrations broke out in 18 cities,[541] and in many cities security forces attacked the demonstrators and sometimes the passersby. In Dresden, 30,000 demonstrated, with 129 arrests. In Berlin, thousands of demonstrators attempted to march from the center of Berlin to Schönhauser Allee, leading to 700 arrests. In Berlin the police employed nightsticks, dogs, and brutality as they chased down demonstrators. A young girl was knocked down, and police beat her as she lay screaming on the ground. Captured on video and shown around the world, this picture of police violence contradicted any pictures of peace and prosperity that East German officials tried to portray. And for East German citizens, pictures of police violence against their own citizens further undermined the state's claims of peace.[542]

In Plauen on October 7, 10,000 demonstrators marched from Theater Square to the Town Hall; security forces attacked with water cannons and held those arrested for up to a week. In Karl-Marx-Stadt, police dissolved the 1,000-strong demonstration with force. In Magdeburg, authorities arrested 130, and in Potsdam, 106. Demonstrators turned out on October 7 in many other cities and towns, including Arnstadt, Erfurt, Guben, Dippoldiswalde, Torgau, Jena, Dessau, and Suhl, leading to hundreds more arrests.

Leipzig took part as well. On Saturday, October 7, 10,000 Leipzigers demonstrated. Police had blocked the courtyard of Nikolai Church, the customary meeting place for the Monday night demonstrations. Hans Jürgen Sievers reported seeing a young army draftee standing near the church with tears streaming down his face as he watched people placing candles and flowers in the church courtyard to remember those in prison. That evening police turned water cannons on the relatively small group of demonstrators and hunted them through the city streets. They arrested 210 that day and held them in horse stalls at the Leipzig fairgrounds.[543]

Police turn water on demonstrators and lead protestors away.
Photo by Martin Jehnichen/Archiv Bürgerbewegung Leipzig e. V.

Police beat protestors.
Photo by Martin Jehnichen/Archiv Bürgerbewegung Leipzig e. V.

Young demonstrator bleeding from beating
Photo by Martin Jehnichen/Archiv Bürgerbewegung Leipzig e. V.

People run from police; young child falls.
Photo by Martin Jehnichen /Archiv Bürgerbewegung Leipzig e. V.

Toward evening on October 7 Gisela Kallenbach was on her way to central Leipzig and to Nikolai Church, wanting to attend prayer services to remember civil rights demonstrators still in prison in Leipzig and in other cities in East Germany.[544] When she found that there was no service that day, Kallenbach headed on to join members of Ökodorf (Ecological Village), an ecology group from West Berlin that Working Group Environmental Protection had invited to Leipzig for the weekend.

Police with dogs and batons, on standby
Photo by Frank Sellentin/Archiv Bürgerbewegung Leipzig e. V.

Although that week Dresden had seen numerous violent encounters between police and demonstrators, Kallenbach had not personally encountered violence in Leipzig. However, earlier that evening, as Kallenbach made her way through the city, near Nikolai Church she saw for the first time police outfitted with helmets, shields, and nightsticks. As the group proceeded through central Leipzig, they ran into a huge gathering on Grimmaische Street. Police turned fire hoses on the crowd to disband the demonstration, and Kallenbach and her colleagues ran toward the opera house. Later that evening members of Working Group Environmental Protection met together and decided that they had to take some action against violence to prevent a bloodbath at the Monday night demonstration on October 9.

Monday, October 9—The Decisive Demonstration

Fearing a bloodbath in Leipzig, communist party secretary Kurt Meyer had called Leipzig symphony conductor Kurt Masur the morning of October 9 and asked him what they could do "to avoid the worst." Sitting with Meyer that morning were two other civic leaders, cabaret performer Bernd-Lutz Lange and theologian Peter Zimmermann. They and Masur joined with three Leipzig district communist party officials—Kurt Meyer, Jochen Pommert, and Roland Wötzel—to try to prevent violence. The appeal of this so-called Group of Six—a call for nonviolence—was read to the peace prayer congregations, broadcast on Leipzig's radio station, and carried over loudspeaker during the demonstration.[545] Although the Group of Six's appeal may have influenced some newcomers to the demonstrations, many other participants were already fully committed to demonstrating and to nonviolence. Nevertheless, the participation of the three state and communist party officials in calling for nonviolence likely did influence the decisions of security forces leaders not to attack the demonstrators.

In Leipzig on October 9, 75,000 persons demonstrated, the largest independent demonstration in East Germany since the people's rebellion of June 17, 1953, and almost three times as large as the previous week.[546] Tanks and troops had moved into central Leipzig, and the commander of the security forces had announced in the newspaper that the state would attack demonstrators with weapons, if necessary, to maintain order.[547] The threat of violence conjured up memories of the recent Tiananmen Square massacre and of Czechoslovakia in 1968.

In Berlin that day Erich Honecker continued to insist that the Leipzig demonstrations must be put down, whatever the cost. At a meeting in Berlin with a Chinese delegation under the leadership of deputy minister president Yao Yilin, Honecker reiterated his support for the Chinese action in Tiananmen Square to put down "counterrevolutionary uprisings."[548]

State authorities determined to contain the demonstrations in Leipzig had sent in additional forces from surrounding cities. The goal was to have 8,000 troops, combined units from the police, military reserves, Stasi uniformed forces, citizen reserves (drawn from firms and factories), and the national army. Another 5,000 civilian forces drawn from the Stasi, the communist party, and other state organizations supplemented these troops.[549]

Security forces assembled throughout Leipzig as the state prepared to suppress the demonstration with force, and they amassed arms in preparation for an attack. In the courtyard of the district police, two water cannons and several armored cars stood ready.[550] Watch posts were armed with machine guns and ammunition. Behind the Stasi building, Runde Ecke, military police forces with tear gas were posted along with ten armed tanks. Troops had orders to break up any demonstrations and to arrest the "ringleaders" regardless of the consequences. Helicopters were also on standby to defend the city.

Some Leipzig authorities had doubts about the wisdom of this plan of attack, however, and feared disastrous consequences. One doubter maintained, "The demonstrations should not be prevented everywhere, because no one wants to risk a civil war in the inner city."[551] Leipzig authorities decided they would not attack in the pedestrian-only zone of the central city. Instead, they would wait until the demonstration entered the Leipzig Ring. Then they would attack and dissolve the demonstrations.

Another problem concerned state and city authorities: They could not count on all the forces to carry out orders. As more and more Leipzig citizens took to the streets, security forces, too, questioned the wisdom and authority of the state. One member of a military reserve unit ordered into service voiced the opinion of many in his group regarding weapons: "We will only go out with nightsticks. Workers don't shoot other workers."[552]

Word spread throughout the city that security forces had orders to shoot. On the blackboard in the foyer of the university for music written in bold lettering, a warning appeared—"order to shoot!" High schools sent students home early, warning them not to go to the city center.

In some cities and towns, authorities tried to discourage demonstrators from going to Leipzig. In Crimmitschau, authorities photographed would-be demonstrators as they climbed onto the train (another piece of information for their Stasi files).[553] In Halle, the Stasi arrested a number of oppositional group members to prevent them from joining the Monday night demonstrations in Leipzig.[554]

Police with nightsticks and shields
Photo by Martin Jehnichen/Archiv Bürgerbewegung Leipzig e. V.

Nevertheless, many demonstrators from outside Leipzig did manage to reach Leipzig. For weeks, demonstrators from throughout Saxony and elsewhere in East Germany had joined in. Leipzig authorities estimated that at least 5,000 demonstrators came to Leipzig by train from other cities for the October 9 demonstration, including Dresden, Karl-Marx-Stadt, Cottbus, and East Berlin.[555] Thousands of demonstrators came to Leipzig every week from smaller towns throughout the country as well.[556]

As evening approached, tensions grew, and Leipzigers feared a massive attack that would end the demonstrations once and for all. American historian Robert Darnton observed, "Everyone present at that demonstration was convinced that the government had prepared to commit something comparable to China's Tiananmen Square massacre."[557] Nevertheless, despite warnings to avoid the inner city, thousands turned out for the peace prayer services in central Leipzig.

To prevent a Chinese solution, oppositional and alternative groups had worked tirelessly to promote and maintain nonviolence during all the Leipzig demonstrations, but now on October 9 the stakes seemed higher. Sensing the danger of the situation, three Leipzig groups, Working Circle Justice, Working Group Human Rights, and Working Group Environmental Protection, issued a joint proclamation appealing both to demonstrators and state forces for a non-violent demonstration. The groups had produced 25,000 mimeographed copies of the document, hand-turning them on the mimeograph machine in Christoph Wonneberger's office at Lukas Church.[558]

The proclamation from the three Leipzig groups called upon both the people and the security forces to avoid violence. Part of the proclamation read as follows:

> Last Monday ended with violence. We are afraid. We are afraid for ourselves, we are afraid for our friends and those near us; we are afraid for those in uniform who stand across from us. We are afraid for the future of our country.
>
> Violence always creates violence. Violence solves no problems. Violence is inhumane. Violence cannot be the sign of a newer, better society.
>
> We are the people. . . . The party and the government must be made responsible for the continuing seriousness of the situation. However, today it is on us to prevent a further escalation of violence, because our future depends on it.[559]

Kallenbach decided to distribute these flyers before the peace prayer services began.[560] She made her way from the Youth Bureau at Thomas Church toward Nikolai Church, distributing the flyers along the route. Kallenbach knew that violence could come from any side—not just from the general population and the groups, but also from state security forces. She approached a group of Stasi employees, handed them flyers, asked them to read the proclamation, and moved on toward Nikolai Church.

In Grimmaische Street Kallenbach felt a tap on her shoulder. A police officer asked her to come with him. Kallenbach asked where she should go, and, when he wouldn't answer, Kallenbach told him she wouldn't go with him. Then the policeman put his fist into her back and shoved Kallenbach to move her along.

By that time a crowd had gathered. A man spoke up: "We won't move until we know what is going to happen to the woman. We are coming along." So the growing crowd followed the officer to a group of plain-clothed police officers, although the officer himself wore a uniform. Then Kallenbach was asked about the flyers, and she said she had distributed them, although she still had more fly-ers in her bag. The police also asked whether Kallenbach would give the flyers calling for nonviolence to demonstrators like those in Dresden who had attacked the police earlier that week. Kallenbach answered, "Of course"—she was against violence as a matter of principle. She wanted everyone to know that all the group members promoting the proclamation were totally against vio-lence of any kind and that none would resort to violence. By then a large crowd had gathered and Kallenbach realized that she had an opportunity to deliver a plea for nonviolence.

Then someone asked the officer in charge whether he would arrest Kallen-bach. He shook his head no, and Kallenbach was allowed to go on her way again. As she remembered, there was such a large crowd there that the police certainly could not afford to arrest her at that time. Kallenbach continued distributing the flyers in the city center before going to the peace prayers in Reformierte Church where she participated in the service that evening.

That evening in Reformierte Church Pastor Hans-Jürgen Sievers preached on nonviolence, pointing to the role of Martin Luther King in the U.S. civil rights movement in the 1960s and drawing parallels with that movement and East Germany in 1989.[561] In both movements, there had been arrests, fines, prison. Sievers acknowledged that, as in the U.S. civil rights movement, it might take a long time to achieve their goals. But he assured them that, as they con-tinued to come together calling for change, change would come. He ended his sermon with a plea for total nonviolence during the demonstrations.

Anticipating larger crowds, two additional churches, Thomas Church and Michaelis Church, held services along with Nikolai Church and Reformierte Church. At all four churches, the appeals of the Leipzig groups as well of the community leaders were read during the service. At Thomas Church, newly opened for the peace prayers, Johannes Richter, Leipzig West district superin-tendent and pastor of Thomas Church, urged the peace prayer participants to go straight home after the service. Most, however, disregarded his advice and instead joined other demonstrators heading toward Karl Marx Square and on to the Leipzig Ring.

Security forces prevented the western media from entering Leipzig and filming the demonstration. Nevertheless, oppositional group members Siegbert

Schefke and Aram Radomski managed to enter Leipzig undetected and, with the permission of pastor Hans-Jürgen Sievers, filmed the events from the tower of Reformierte Church.[562] If the demonstration involved violence with security forces attacking, as expected, or if the demonstrators managed to carry out the demonstration totally without violence, it was important for the world to witness these events.

New Forum also handed out flyers calling for nonviolence as participants left the peace prayer services at the four Leipzig churches that evening.

✻   ✻   ✻

When the peace prayers ended at Nikolai Church, the church courtyard was filled with people, and all the streets in the entire city inside Leipzig's central ring were packed with demonstrators. Slowly the mass moved toward Karl Marx Square.[563] Police with dogs stood watch throughout the inner city, but the demonstration remained peaceful and police held back.

After the peace prayers, demonstrators from the various churches converged at Karl Marx Square and around 6 p.m. entered the Georgi Ring. The

Massive demonstration on Leipzig Ring
Photo by Bernd Heinze/Archiv Bürgerbewegung Leipzig e. V.

massive demonstration proceeded unhindered, picking up new demonstrations from the side streets along the way. By the time they reached the central train station the demonstrators numbered 75,000.[564]

Around 6 p.m. General Major Günter Straßenburg, head of the police in Leipzig, called Interior Minister Friedrich Dickel in Berlin to inform him of the huge, totally peaceful demonstration.[565] Straßenburg demanded a decision on how the forces should proceed. Dickel, however, deferred and said the decision should remain in Leipzig. At 6:25 Straßenburg gave the order: Security forces should retreat and defend only themselves.

Toralf Dörre was at the central train station with other police that day, waiting for orders.[566] Around Georgi Ring came the first of 75,000 demonstrators, although security forces had expected, at most, 30,000. As the first demonstrators stood within 30 yards of the police, the order came: Retreat. So as demonstrators reached the central train station, security forces began to fall back. At 6:30 Helmut Hackenberg, head of the Leipzig district communist party, had received a call from Berlin informing him of the decision to deescalate. At 6:45, as tensions were already relaxing in Leipzig, Hackenberg

Demonstrators on Leipzig Ring passing opera house, October 9, 1989
Photo by Heinz Löster/Gedenkstätte und Museum Runde Ecke, Leipzig

telephoned Egon Krenz in Berlin to tell him that security forces had retreated in Leipzig.

The demonstrators proceeded past the central train station, undeterred. They moved along the Tröndlin Ring and the Dittrich Ring, past the Stasi head-quarters building, to Martin Luther Ring, and on to Ross Platz. By 8:30 that evening demonstrators had made their way around the entire Leipzig Ring before the demonstration dissolved. Almost unbelievably, the 75,000 demonstrators and the thousands of security forces confronting them had remained peaceful throughout the entire route.

Later Stasi head Mielke would say of the Leipzig demonstrations: "We were prepared for everything except for candles and prayers."[567]

CHAPTER 10

Cracking Open the System and Spreading Revolution:
The Berlin Wall Falls November 9 and the World Changes

*We preferred to go to Leipzig [to participate in demonstrations],
because it was clear to us that the history of Germany would be
decided in Leipzig.*[568]

—Father with son from Merseberg

*We realized we were in a position to overthrow the govern-
ment.*[569]

—Gudula Ziemer and Holger Jackisch,
New Forum, Leipzig

*This ninth of November is a historic day: the GDR [East Ger-
many] has announced its borders are open to everyone, with
immediate effect, and the gates of the Wall stand wide open.*[570]

—News Report, ARD Television, late-night show

After October 9 there was a new sense of freedom—a new atmosphere—throughout East Germany. Before October 9, East Germans attending demonstrations or other events critical of the state feared beatings, interrogations, arrests by the police or the Stasi or other security forces. But Leipzig's nonviolent Monday night demonstrations, especially October 9, had achieved what had seemed impossible. The state had backed down, security forces stood down, and the overwhelming mass of demonstrators prevailed. A precedent was set, and after October 9 people in Leipzig and throughout East Germany could participate in peaceful demonstrations without fear. As Martin Jankowski described it, "Overnight it became possible—to go freely, to breathe, to speak."[571]

The successful outcome of the October 9 demonstration empowered the people. Thanks to the videos smuggled to the west by opposition group member Siegbert Schefke through a diplomatic contact in Berlin, Leipzig demonstrators could see themselves on television as western stations carried the story along with photos in the evening news.[572] From the bird's-eye view of the

Reformierte Church showing tower
overlooking parade route
Photo by Patricia Smith

Reformierte Church tower, they could see the massive demonstrations—with all lanes of the broad Leipzig Ring overflowing with demonstrators. Many demonstrators reported that that night they sensed the inevitability of change. And all over East Germany, citizens watched the events in Leipzig with disbelief.

On October 13 Leipzig groups held an auction at Lukas Church to raise money for those arrested during earlier demonstrations. That same day, state authorities released many of the demonstrators who still remained in prison.[573] Katrin Hattenhauer, who had been arrested September 4, was among those released that day. Later Hattenhauer reported that she'd had no idea about what had happened in Leipzig while she spent more than a month in a cell in the underground prison on Peterssteinweg, but she had feared the worst.

"While I was in prison I had heard thunder and believed that tanks were rolling through the streets. I couldn't know that the noises came from the steps of thousands of demonstrators."[574]

With the success of the October 9 demonstration and the release of most political prisoners, a major demand of the demonstrators was at least partially achieved—freedom of assembly. The laws had yet to change, but in practice authorities now allowed citizens to demonstrate without fear of arrest. However, the state still refused to recognize New Forum, the citizens movement that was spreading rapidly across East Germany, and its right to exist.

Monday, October 16

The Monday night demonstrations—by now automatic in Leipzig—continued. On October 16, 150,000 demonstrators marched around the Leipzig Ring, more than double the number only one week earlier. (See Table 10-1 Demonstrations in Leipzig, October-December 1989.) Some pastors and local authorities protested the use of the peace prayers for political purposes, calling out on the city's sound system, "The street is no place for dialogue, for solving problems." [575] But demonstrators ignored the calls. Parading through the streets, protestors presented their demands as they raised their banners and called out their slogans: "Allow New Forum." "Freedom of the Press." "Freedom of Expression." "Freedom to Travel for Everyone." "Election Reform."

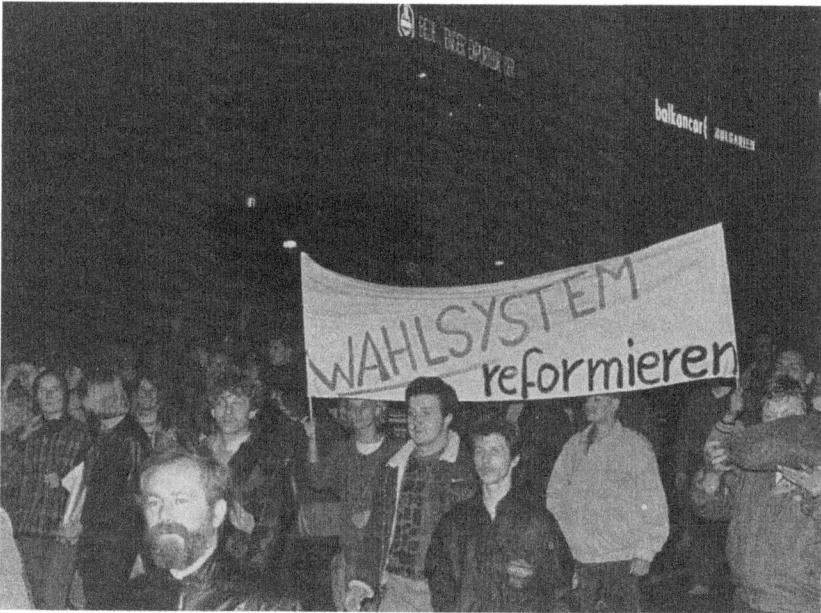

Demonstrators with banner calling for election system reform
Photo by Bernd Heinze/Archiv Bürgerbewegung Leipzig e. V.

Table 10-1
Demonstrations in Leipzig
October–December 1989*[578]

Date	Occasion	Number of Participants
10/2/89	After peace prayers	25,000 demonstrators, many injuries
10/7/89	40th anniversary of East Germany	Hundreds of demonstrators; 210 arrests; injuries
10/9/89	After peace prayers	75,000 demonstrators
10/16/89	After peace prayers	150,000 demonstrators
10/18/89	**Resignation of Erich Honecker as leader of East Germany; selection of Egon Krenz**	
10/23/89	After peace prayers	300,000 demonstrators
10/30/89	After peace prayers	400,000 demonstrators
11/3/89	**Resignation of Leipzig Mayor Bernd Seidel**	
11/4/89	Berlin demonstration; "Leipzig, City of Heroes"	1,000,000 demonstrators
11/6/89	After peace prayers	500,000 demonstrators
11/7/89	**Resignation of government**	
11/8/89	**Resignation of Central Committee and Politburo**	
11/9/89	**Fall of Berlin Wall**	
11/13/89	After peace prayers	200,000 demonstrators
11/20/89	After peace prayers	250,000 demonstrators
11/24/89	**Proposal by Krenz to eliminate leading role of the party**	
11/27/89	After peace prayers	200,000 demonstrators
12/3/89	**Resignation of new Central Committee and Politburo; Krenz out**	
12/4/89	After peace prayers	150,000 demonstrators; attempts to occupy Stasi building
12/7/89	**First negotiations held by Central Round Table of East Germany**	
12/11/89	After peace prayers	150,000 demonstrators
12/18/89	After peace prayers	200,000 demonstrators

*Entries in bold refer to actions in government and broader society

Banner calling for opposition parties, democratic elections,
and independent media
*Photo by Christoph Motzer/Archiv Bürgerbewegung
Leipzig e. V.*

The East German regime once again readied the security forces in Leipzig—police, military, and reserves, along with the Stasi. In addition, thousands of backup troops stood ready and armed nearby.[576] But this time, because of Order No. 9, signed by Honecker under pressure from other East German leaders, the forces were instructed not to attack unless the demonstration turned violent. (He'd had to be convinced. Just that afternoon Honecker had argued for violently breaking up the demonstration, including attacking the demonstrators with tanks.) Once again demonstrators marched around the entire Leipzig Ring—a two-and-a-half-mile loop—again that evening, unhindered by police or Stasi or tanks or troops.[577]

Figure 10-1 illustrates the dramatic growth in the size of Leipzig demonstrations during fall of 1989.

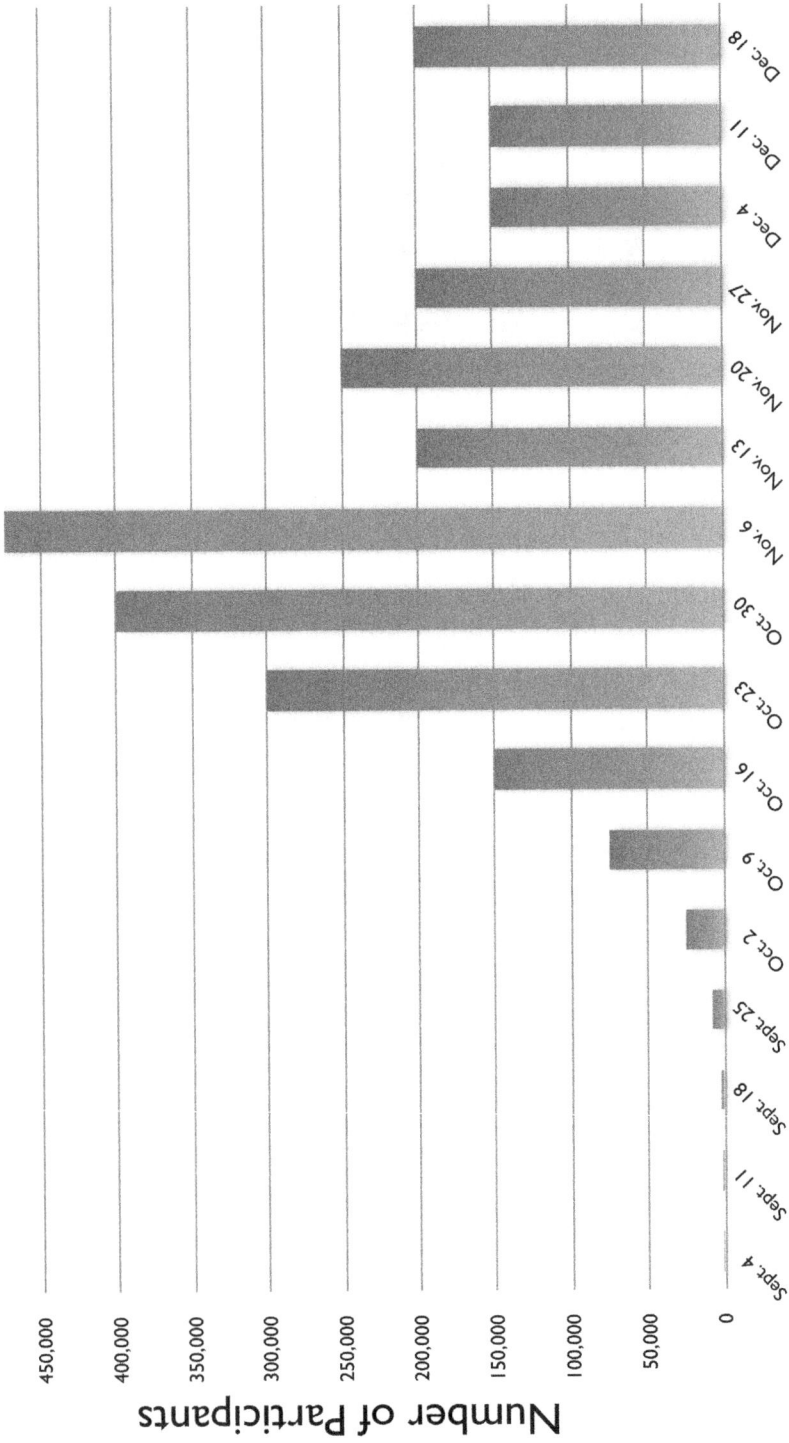

Figure 10-1 Monday Night Demonstrations in Leipzig: October-December 1989

October 18, Honecker Resigns

On October 18, East German leader Erich Honecker resigned. Egon Krenz was chosen as his replacement.[579] Pressure from demonstrations and emigrations as well as pressure from within his own party and government precipitated Honecker's fall. Already before the October 9 demonstrations Egon Krenz and other East German party and state leaders had strategized to push Honecker out. Honecker had refused to institute reforms in East Germany despite changes in the Soviet Union and throughout the east bloc, and his statements in favor of a Chinese solution to end the demonstrations alienated an increasingly large proportion of the East German public. If Honecker had been directly involved in the decisions during the October 9 demonstrations, they almost certainly would have ended with bloodshed. As Gorbachev had suggested during East Germany's 40th-anniversary celebrations just two weeks earlier, "Life punishes those who come too late."[580]

That same day, October 18, the Central Committee of the communist party issued a statement calling New Forum the enemy of socialism and reinforcing the decision not to recognize the group, despite increasing calls from the people for recognizing New Forum during demonstrations in Leipzig and elsewhere.[581]

The next day, representatives of New Forum were not allowed to participate in a meeting of city leaders (at Moritz Bastei) attended by 1,500 Leipzigers because Roland Wötzel of the city's communist party leadership refused to sit at the same table as an organization that was an enemy of the state.[582]

Other meetings among government authorities and representatives of the church and the people (including grassroots groups) had similar challenges. City authorities tried to keep control of the meetings—restricting the participants and the topics of conversation, and they continued to deny New Forum recognition and a place at the table. So no real dialogue took place—and many demands for changes promoted initially by groups and now taken up by tens of thousands of demonstrators went undiscussed. Opposition leaders Thomas Rudolph and Christoph Wonneberger, also pastor of Lukas Church, both attended the meeting with local party and government leaders and Leipzig citizens but left disappointed. Despite the success of the demonstrations, local leaders continued to ignore the demands of groups and demonstrators.

Monday, October 23

On October 23, the number of participants in the Monday night demonstrations doubled again from the previous week. Leipzigers witnessed the biggest demonstrations up to that point—300,000—and that evening thousands of the demonstrators carried candles as they marched around Leipzig's ring.[583] That day, for the first time, demands were heard for the end of the Berlin Wall, as demonstrators called out "Open the border" and "The Wall must go." Even more explicit calls were heard for the end of East Germany: "Egon, be smart—40 years are enough."[584]

Demonstrators with candles
Photo by Martin Jehnichen/Archiv Bürgerbewegung Leipzig e. V.

Candlelight demonstration through streets of Leipzig
Photo by Martin Jehnichen/Archiv Bürgerbewegung Leipzig e. V.

Although by now demonstrations were held in many cities throughout East Germany, many demonstrators from outside the area preferred to demonstrate in Leipzig. Marching alongside 300,000 demonstrators in Leipzig inspired and empowered many. A visitor from Neubrandenburg, located north of Berlin in the region of Mecklenburg-Vorpommern (Pomerania) 200 miles from Leipzig, returned home euphoric after participating in the Leipzig demonstration. He wrote down all the slogans that he had heard during the demonstrations in Leipzig and then copied them onto small notes that he gave to friends. These demonstrators then trusted themselves to call out the slogans they had heard in Leipzig during their own demonstrations. In Neubrandenburg, a city with a population of about 90,000, 15,000–20,000 people showed up for the demonstration, almost a quarter of the population.[585]

The Leipzig demonstrations snowballed, spreading to other cities throughout East Germany. Halle, Dresden, Jena, Schwerin, Weimar, Karl-Marx-Stadt, Erfurt, Plauen. By the end of October more than 170 cities and towns had held demonstrations during October, and more than 65 followed Leipzig's lead and convened demonstrations every week. (See Map 10-1.) The momentum was impossible to stop.

Oct. 2
Berlin
Leipzig
Oct. 3
Dresden
Bad Schandau
Oct. 4
Freiberg
Heidenau
Karl-Marx-Stadt
Neubrandenburg
Pirna
Plauen
Reichenbach
Werdau
Zwickau
Oct. 5
Magdeburg
Wilthen
Oct. 6
Aschersleben
Bautzen
Zwönitz
Oct. 7
Dessau
Dippoldiswalde
Erfurt
Gehlsdorf-
Rostock
Guben
Hainichen
Jena
Lindow
Markneukirchen
Rosslau
Suhl
Torgau
Oct. 8
Bischofswerda
Grossröhrsdorf
Meerane
Plessow-Potsdam
Treuen
Guben
Oct. 9
Halle
Oct. 10
Ilmenau
Nordhausen
Wernigerode
Oct. 11
Halberstadt
Oct. 13
Klingenthal
Oct. 16
Waren-Müritz
Wurzen
Oct. 18
Eberswalde-Finow
Mühlhausen
Oct. 19
Greifswald

Leinefeld
Stendal
Zeulenroda
Zittau
Oct. 20
Dessau
Gotha
Oederan
Olbernhau
Camburg
Langebrück-Dresden
Oct. 21
Gera
Oct. 22
Stavenhagen

Oct. 23
Aue
Ballenstadt-
Halle
Colditz
Eisenach
Glauchau
Greiz
Heilgenstadt
Marienberg
Merseburg
Mühltroff-
Plauen
Oelsnitz
Pössneck
Schwerin
Stralsund
Templin
Oct. 24
Anclam

Aschersleben
Demmin
Meinigen
Meissen
Weimar
Oct. 25
Altenburg
Bad Doberan
Bad Elster
Bad Lausick
Calbe
Coswig-Halle
Eisenberg
Genthin
Halberstadt

Limbach-Oberfrohna
Penzlin
Senftenberg
Wittstock
Oct. 26
Adorf
Boitzenburg
Grossenhain
Hagenow
Leinefelde
Ludwigslust
Parchim
Quedlinburg
Röbel
Wittenberg
Wittenburg
Worbis
Zossen
Oct. 27
Dorfchemnitz

Eibenstock
Görlitz
Grossräschen
Lauchhammer
Milmersdorf
Osterwieck
Pockau
Saalfeld
Schmölln
Tambach-Dietharz
Teterow
Triptis
Oct. 28
Bad Langensalza
Frauenstein
Friedland
Kirchberg
Münchenberndorf
Schönberg
Schönheide
Sebnitz
Ueckermünde
Zschopau
Oct. 30
Anklam
Burgstädt
Delitzsch
Dingelstedt
Ehrenfriedersdorf
Flöha
Gerberhausen
Grimma
Hennigsdorf
Kohren-Sahlis
Leisnig
Lychen
Malchin
Neustadt
Nossen
Oschatz
Ribnitz-
Damgarten
Schneeberg
Schwarzenberg
Sonneberg
Weisswasser
Wittichenau
Oct. 31
Bad Brambach
Bad Salzungen
Bad Wilsnack
Goldberg
Lobenstein
Naumburg
Neuhaus
Penig
Plau am See
Stadtroda
Waltershausen
Wolfe

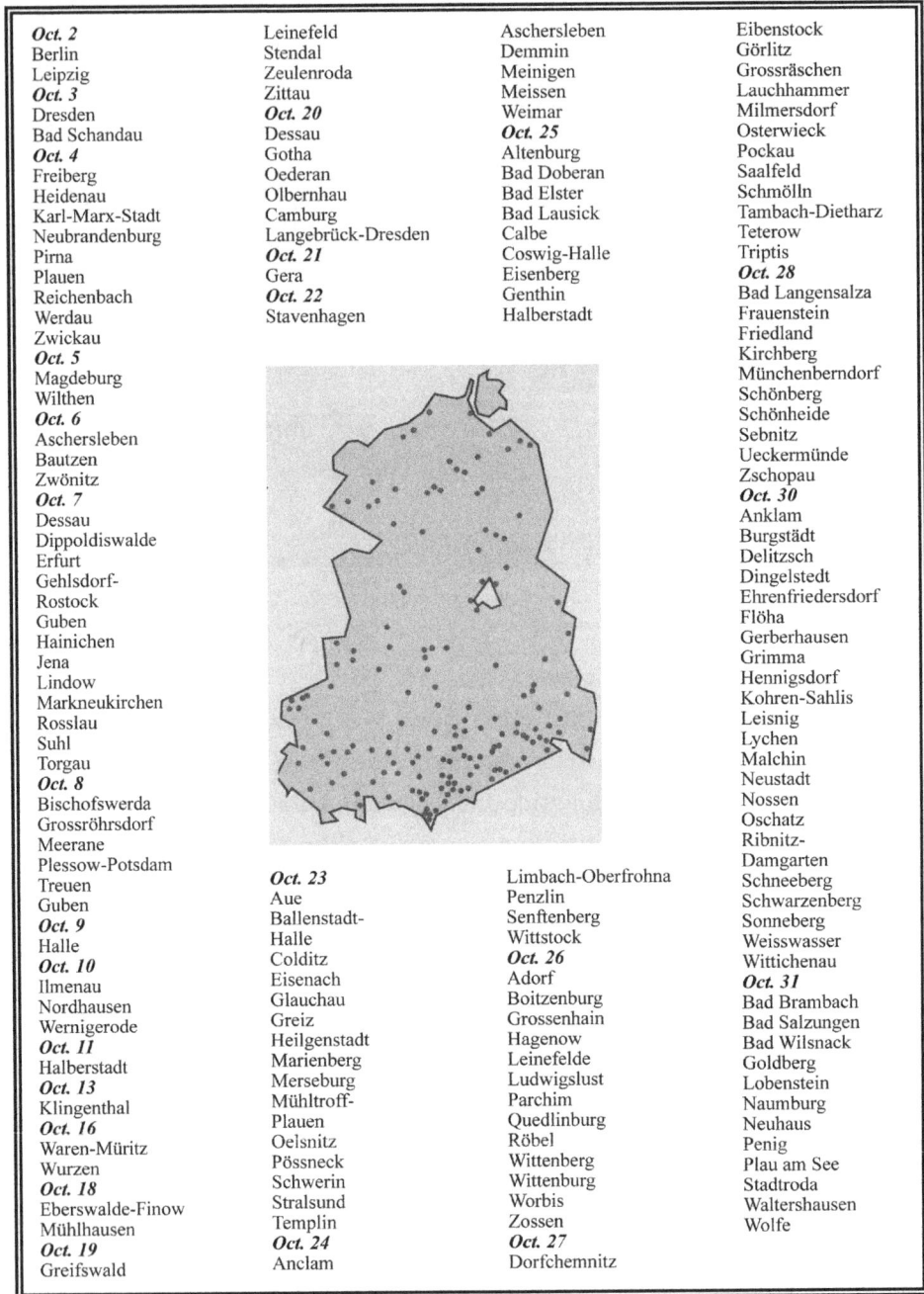

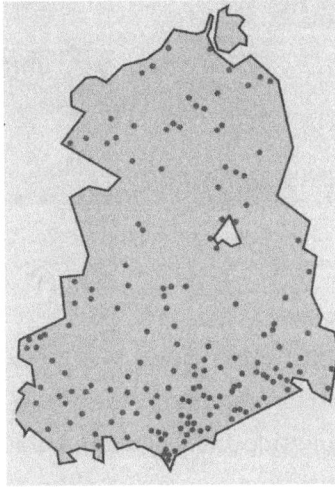

Map 10-1 Demonstrations in East Germany, October 1989
East German cities holding demonstrations during October 1989
(Dates on map denote first demonstration in October for city)

The Leipzig demonstrations included prominent figures who did not support the current communist party-dominated political system.[586] Participants recognized more and more family, friends, and coworkers among the demonstrators. A well-known artist asked rhetorically how much longer would they need to keep demonstrating—they had already been demonstrating for five weeks. But the response—"Nothing has changed yet"—meant that they would keep demonstrating as long as they needed to in order to change the system. By then *das Volk*—the people—sensed their power. On their own initiative the people joined these gigantic weekly gatherings of like-minded citizens, made one circle around the ring, and then went home again. The larger the crowd marching around the Leipzig Ring, the more strength the demonstrators gained from each other to keep going and to come back the following week.

Demonstrators gather on Karl Marx Square.
Photo by Martin Jehnichen/Archiv Bürgerbewegung Leipzig e. V.

Others from outside Leipzig sensed the significance of the events taking place in Leipzig and wanted to be part of it. Jankowski tells the story of a father and son from Merseberg who went to Leipzig regularly to join the Monday night demonstrations. Even though by that time Merseburg had its own demonstrations, they continued their trips to Leipzig, saying, "We preferred to go to Leipzig because it was clear to us that the history of Germany would be decided in Leipzig."[587]

*   *   *

As the weeks passed and the size of the demonstrations grew, participants began sensing their power and their possibilities. Many in Leipzig and throughout the country felt what some New Forum members in Leipzig articulated: "We realized we were in a position to overthrow the government."[588] By the end of October, the more radical demands seemed achievable. The impossible—like getting rid of the Berlin Wall or overturning the entrenched communist government—seemed possible. And the rhetoric and the demands of demonstrators changed.

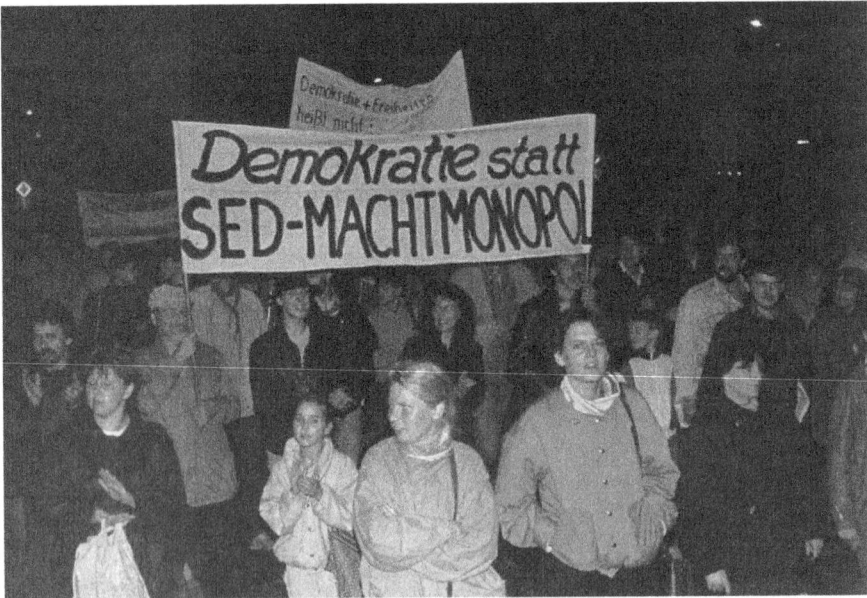

Sign calling for "Democracy instead of SED [communist party] monopoly"
Photo by Bernd Heinze/Archiv Bürgerbewegung Leipzig e. V.

Monday, October 30

In Leipzig seven churches opened for peace prayers on October 30, and afterward 400,000 demonstrators paraded through the streets of the city. Most of them circled the entire Leipzig Ring.[589] A number of demonstrators called for reform, and others demanded more radical changes. Cries of "Tear down the Wall" sounded through the crowd, along with previously heard calls of "Free elections," "A clean environment," and "Allow New Forum."[590] Banners demanded "Democracy, Now or Never" and "The Power of the Land—Not in One Hand." And many called for the resignation of Egon Krenz.

Banner, *"Keine Gewalt"* (No violence)

During the demonstration one of New Forum's speakers, Jochen Lässig (also a member of Initiative Group Living), called out the demands of New Forum and was answered by a group of thousands chanting their responses.[591] Lässig emphasized that their demonstrations had had an effect—the people now had an opportunity for dialogue with government authorities—but if the citizens of East Germany wanted real changes, they needed to keep demonstrating. "Demonstrators, demonstrators, this is New Forum speaking," called Lässig through a megaphone. The crowd responded with applause. "Down with the party that claims the leading role but doesn't allow free elections!" Thousands answered, "We are the people! We are the people!" Ten times Lässig shouted out a New Forum demand—for free elections, freedom of the press, freedom of assembly, freedom to travel— and ten times the crowd of thousands responded, "Allow New Forum." The exchange ended with a call for absolute nonviolence: Don't damage anything; prevent any provocation that could lead to violence.

That evening the East German television program *Aktuelle Kamera* broadcast live footage of the demonstration for the first time.[592] October 30 also marked the last broadcast from the hated East German television program *Der*

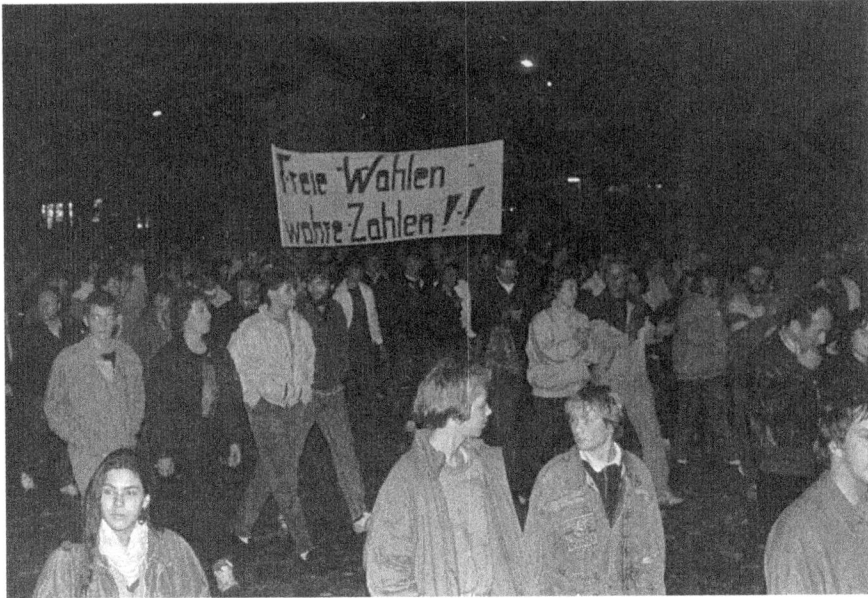

Demonstrators with sign calling for free elections and accurate numbers
Photo by Bernd Heinze/Archiv Bürgerbewegung Leipzig e. V.

Schwarze Kanal (the Black Channel).[593] The program had played every Monday evening for decades, just before the evening movie, presumably in hopes of reaching an audience tuning in for the movie. The program covered West German broadcasts—and then added an East German commentary to show the errors of those western reports. Viewing it as political propaganda, most East Germans ignored the program, and now the state had decided to drop the propaganda program, perhaps finally acknowledging its ineffectiveness.

The next day, October 31, the Leipzig newspaper *Sächsisches Tageblatt* published an article that accurately described the previous evening's events, an astonishing change from most previous press coverage in East Germany.[594] The headlines noted that 300,000 had demonstrated—calling for deeds instead of words.[595] The article described the exchange between Lässig of New Forum and the responses of the demonstrators and mentioned the main demands of the demonstrators: free elections, freedom of the press, and freedom to travel, as well as allowing New Forum.

The newspaper also reported that, for the first time, Leipzig's Mayor Bernd Seidel and other city authorities had spoken with demonstrators.[596] Acknowledging problems in the city, Seidel responded that groups could not solve all problems; however, he recognized demonstrations as "a legitimate means" for raising issues. With the publication of this news story, a degree of press freedom had been achieved in Leipzig, and a party and government leader had acknowledged the right to assemble in a demonstration as legitimate. But some demonstrators remained in prison, and New Forum still had not been recognized.

As October ended, the revolution lost one of its most important strategists. On October 30, Christoph Wonneberger, a central figure of the political opposition and pastor of Lukas Church, suffered a massive stroke.[597] He lay in a coma, no longer able to play a role in how the revolution played out. When he awoke from the coma, he had lost his speech and spent several years relearning how to speak and how to function in society. During that period the Evangelical Church forced him into retirement.

*   *   *

By November, the massive opposition rallies in Leipzig and throughout East Germany had achieved more results. Travel became freer, as the East German government announced on November 1 the resumption of visa-free travel to Czechoslovakia,[598] but these new travel regulations satisfied no one. New Forum suggested that instead of making small changes to travel regulations, the government should give each East German citizen an exit visa valid for travel to any country in the world.[599] Besides, by now almost everyone marching wanted much more than revised travel regulations—they wanted new leaders and major political changes. Demonstrators kept up their protests, without having any idea that they were days away from the fall of the Berlin Wall and that the travel provisions would be the tipping point.

The travel regulations failed to stem the pressures from those wanting to leave East Germany permanently. Many took advantage of the freedom to travel to Czechoslovakia without a visa, but then they had no valid documents to travel beyond. These refugees put tremendous pressure on the Czech government, which threatened to close the Czech border with East Germany. The Czechoslovaks were unwilling, they said, to provide a refugee camp for East Germans.[600]

Although made somewhat haphazardly, the new travel regulations—and the hasty changes to them that would come a week later—had a monumental impact. Ultimately, they opened the Berlin Wall, allowing free movement between east and west.

* * *

Every day brought new developments, new pressures. On November 2, for the first time a local newspaper—the *Mitteldeutschen Neuesten Nachrichten*—published a catalog of New Forum's demands.[601] That same day formerly secret data on air pollution in Leipzig was published for the first time, and citizens could also finally get data on whether water was drinkable.[602] On November 3, Bernd Seidel—mayor of Leipzig—refused dialogue with the people, then resigned.[603]

Demonstration on Alexanderplatz, Berlin, November 4, 1989
Photo by Frank Sellentin/Archiv Bürgerbewegung Leipzig e. V.

In Berlin on November 4 more than a million people participated in a state-approved demonstration organized by artists in Berlin—for freedom of expression, press, and assembly. Speaking there, prominent East German author Christoph Hein called Leipzig the "City of Heroes"—Leipzigers took risks that others failed to take.[604]

City of Heroes, Leipzig (Heldenstadt)
Photo by Bernd Heinze/Archiv Bürgerbewegung Leipzig e. V.

Monday, November 6

In comparison with the demands of the Berlin demonstration, Reiner Tetzner assessed the Leipzig demands on November 6 as much more radical.[605] In Leipzig, demonstrators called for the communist party to give up its power and become, instead, part of the opposition.[606] And while thousands in Leipzig called out, "The Wall must go! The Wall must go!" no such demands were heard in Berlin. [607]

Despite heavy rain, 500,000 Leipzigers came out for this demonstration, making it the largest independent demonstration in the history of the city.[608] Before marching around the Leipzig Ring, a crowd gathered in Karl Marx Square and listened to various speakers call for revolutionary changes in East Germany. Bernd-Lutz Lange of the Group of Six called on government leaders to look at the signs that demonstrators carried to find a good agenda for action. Roland Wötzel, communist party leader in Leipzig and one of the Group of Six, was also scheduled to speak. But demonstrators whistled him off the podium, indicating their dissatisfaction with his recent selection as first secretary (head)

500,000 demonstrate in Leipzig on November 6, despite heavy rain.
Photo by Bernd Heinze/Archiv Bürgerbewegung Leipzig e. V.

of the Leipzig district government.[609] In addition to customary calls for free elections and a true multiparty system, the speakers demanded the resignation of the government and the Central Committee members then in power.[610]

The quality of the sound system in Karl Marx Square was terrible, and the crowd grew impatient.[611] Restless demonstrators stood waiting for the march to begin, their umbrellas dripping. A speaker for New Forum stepped to the podium and called for the communist party to give up its privileged position. Thousands of cries interrupted the speech—"Allow New Forum! Allow New Forum!"

An ever-increasing number of Leipzig demonstrators believed that not only the leaders but also the system needed to change. The crowd became unruly, eager to start marching around the ring, and some participants feared that the demonstration would turn violent that day. But nonviolence prevailed.

Demonstrators carrying sign with words "Democracy never, without New Forum"
Photo by Bernd Heinze/Archiv Bürgerbewegung Leipzig e. V.

November 7

Stasi Chief Erich Mielke's last report to the Politburo in Berlin on November 7 summarized the situation that East German political and government authorities faced.[612] In the period from October 30 to November 5 the number of demonstrators in East Germany almost tripled, climbing to 1.35 million participants in more than 210 demonstrations. The previous week there had been only 145 demonstrations with 540,000 participants. Mielke wrote, "Demonstrations in the *Kreisstädten* [smaller cities—county seats] have increased and reached the number of participants comparable to those in *Bezirksstädten* [seats of the larger districts—comparable to state capitals][613]—in Plauen (30,000 demonstrators), Dessau (35,000), Nordhausen (25,000), Hoyerswerda and Quendlinburg (15,000). What government still has the power to be able to resist this pressure from the people?"

On November 7 numerous communist party organizations throughout East Germany demanded the resignation of the Politburo, the highest communist party organization in East Germany, and 500 persons protested in front of the building of the party's Central Committee. Elsewhere, the people kept the pressure on the government, demonstrating that evening in 30 cities throughout East Germany. [614]

That same day, November 7, the entire East German government led by Willi Stoph resigned. The next day, November 8, Erich Mielke along with the entire Politburo resigned, the only time that the entire leadership had resigned in the history of communist parties. These mass resignations, along with the continuing pressures from those wanting to emigrate, provided a context for the decisions on November 9, the day the Berlin Wall would fall.

Without the pressures of these demonstrations that began in Leipzig and spread throughout East Germany, the East German government may have limped along and resisted reform for many more years. But Mielke's statement about his powerlessness in the face of so many demonstrators makes clear that the continuing pressures of the demonstrations led directly to the resignation of the government and the Politburo members (and to the fall of the Berlin Wall). Even the notorious Stasi chief Erich Mielke found it impossible to attack his fellow East Germans.

November 9

Despite the resignations of the previous two days, citizens continued their pressures on the communist party and government. In East Berlin on November 9 the government again attempted to revise the travel regulations, hoping to quell protests and stem the flow of East Germans leaving the country.[615] Although accounts of what transpired that day vary, by the end of the day it was clear that the world had changed.

On the morning of November 9 a group of four officials worked hurriedly on a new draft of the travel regulations that Egon Krenz would take to the Politburo for discussion and approval later that day. As proposed, the regulations would allow all East Germans in possession of valid papers to apply to leave the country, temporarily or permanently. Authorities would review and quickly approve the applications for almost everyone without a waiting period, except for a few extraordinary circumstances. The new regulations would take effect the next day, November 10.

Krenz then carried the newly drafted travel regulations to the Politburo for their immediate consideration. Reportedly, because many of the Politburo members were new appointees following the mass resignations on November 8, they were not familiar with previous versions of the travel regulations and were not fully aware of the implications of approving the new proposal. Nevertheless, the Politburo approved the proposal with relatively little discussion or concern.

According to some reports, Krenz then took the proposed travel regulations to the Central Committee of the communist party, which was holding its 10th Congress in Berlin that week. The unrest in East Germany weighed on Central Committee members, who recognized that changes had to be made to bring some stability to the country. Consequently, the Central Committee, too, approved the regulations with only a cursory review and, seemingly, without considering the immediate implications of the proposed changes.

Under Krenz's leadership East Germany had instituted daily press conferences, and Krenz wanted the new regulations mentioned in the news report that evening. Half an hour before the press conference Günter Schabowski, head of the press team of four presenters, stopped by Krenz's office to see if there was anything else to put on the agenda for the press conference. Krenz briefed Schabowski on the day's developments and gave him a copy of the new travel regulations. The two agreed that Schabowski would report on the changes in travel regulations at the day's briefing.

The press conference began at 6 p.m., with reporters from East and West Germany as well as many other countries attending.[616] For the past month East German news organizations had begun reporting accurately what was happening in East Germany. Also, in the new era of relative openness, the press conference was televised live.

Near the end of the press conference, Günter Schabowski stepped to the podium and gave his report. He briefly updated the developments on the travel front and read aloud the new temporary travel regulations that would be published the next day. The document was confusing. The title indicated that the regulations addressed emigration through Czechoslovakia, but obviously by the time they had been approved and read at the press conference, the broad regulations addressed almost all East German travel and emigration issues.

Schabowski read the document that outlined the significant provisions: (1) those who wanted to travel abroad no longer needed to present a reason, and applications would generally be approved quickly, with very few grounds for denial; (2) the district offices of the police would promptly issue visas for those who wanted to leave East Germany permanently; (3) those wanting to leave permanently could cross directly into West Berlin and West Germany at any border crossing; and (4) East German consulates and embassies in other states would no longer issue visas allowing East German citizens to emigrate via a third state.[617] The document stated that the new regulations would take effect immediately and that the press release explaining the temporary regulations would be published November 10.

After Schabowski's report, a journalist asked if there was some mistake. Schabowski reaffirmed that East Germans wanting to travel could apply for visas without proving a need to travel and that East Germans wanting to emigrate could apply to their district police and receive visas without delay. Another reporter asked when the regulations would take effect. Schabowski, who had not had an opportunity to read the regulations before the press conference, looked at the document again and said he guessed immediately, not noticing that the regulations would not be published until the following day.

Confusion and contradictory reports accompanied the press conference and continued throughout the evening and the next day. Initially, almost no one present at the press conference recognized the significance of Schabowski's announcement, and afterward reporters discussed among themselves what the new rules meant. Reuters and DPA (German Press Agency) broadcast the first reports just after 7 p.m. and noted only that East Germans could soon leave the country through the appropriate border crossings.[618] Then at 7:05 p.m. the Associated Press reported simply: "According to information supplied by SED [communist party] Politburo member Günter Schabowski, the GDR [East Germany] is opening its borders." Soon all other press agencies present at the press conference followed suit. West Germany's ARD broadcast an 8 p.m. news bulletin noting simply that East Germany was opening its borders. As soon as they heard the announcement, East Germans headed for the Wall, and soon a growing crowd of East Germans waited for the Wall to open at the crossing points leading to West Berlin.

Because the regulations were not scheduled for publication until the next day, November 10, the border guards were taken by surprise by the crowds standing at their gates. The border patrols had no prior knowledge of the new regulations and no instructions about how they should implement them. Some consulted with other guards. Others called for advice but were told to tell the crowd to come back the next morning. Clearly that was not a solution, given the building pressures of the growing crowds wanting to cross to West Berlin. At most crossings guards decided to allow their fellow citizens to cross rather than risk violence, but some stamped "no return" on the passports. At Bornholmer Street, the commander in charge decided that he would not risk injury to his men from increasingly impatient crowds that had already pushed through a fenced enclosure. He ordered his men to open the crossing and allow the crowd to pass freely without even showing their identification papers.[619]

When Krenz and other East German authorities learned about the impact of the revised travel regulations and the press conference, they initially tried to bring the situation under control. On the evening news, the announcer reminded East Germans that passport offices would be open the next day. But the announcement came too late. Thousands of East Germans already waited at the Wall for their opportunity to cross to the west. Rather than provide a pressure release valve for those wanting to emigrate, the new regulations had opened up new opportunities and new pressures from a much broader segment of the East German population.

Krenz considered his options. He would need to use tanks to close the wall crossings so tightly that they could not be stormed. Or he could let things run their course. He didn't see any other choices. He decided, then, to let the people—his fellow citizens—cross.[620]

The Berlin Wall had opened, allowing East Germans to cross to West Berlin. And the next day, November 10, all East German borders opened. East Germans had achieved their goal. They could travel freely and live wherever they chose. The Berlin Wall had fallen.

The breadth and depth of change was almost unimaginable—from the elimination of the leading role of the communist party to a new state and party leadership and the participation of citizen representatives in the central government and in cities across the country to the abolition of the dreaded Stasi and the opening of their files to democratic elections, free speech, and human rights—a new Germany. These revolutionary changes—initiated by a small group of political activists who believed they could make a difference—would continue to astonish East German participants and the entire world.

The world had changed dramatically, in just one year, and without violence.

Photo by Martin Jehnichen/Archiv Bürgerbewegung Leipzig e. V.
Cars lined up at border to cross into West Germany

Border guards and crowds greet East Germans crossing to West Germany.
Photo by Martin Jehnichen/Archiv Bürgerbewegung Leipzig e. V.

On November 9, 1989, the Berlin Wall opened.
(Photo of Brandenburg Gate taken from east side twenty years later.)
Photo by Patricia Smith

AFTERWORD:

Heroes of Leipzig's Peaceful Revolution

A hero is a person with special capabilities or characteristics that they put to use in remarkable performances—the so-called heroic acts. . . . The "Heroes of the Peaceful Revolution" . . . are for us heroes in the extraordinary sense of the word. Each in his/her own way, they have contributed courageously, so that in fall 1989 the East German dictatorship ended.[621]

—Thomas Mayer, author
Helden der Friedlichen Revolution
(Heroes of the Peaceful Revolution)

In the end they were successful in a way that hardly any of the activists could have imagined. . . . Without them, the peaceful revolution would not have taken place, not in Leipzig and not anywhere else.[622]

—Michael Beleites, activist and investigator
Foreword, *Heroes of the Peaceful Revolution*

In 10 years—the world has changed. The impossible became possible—from peace prayers with candles in our hands to the stones of the Berlin Wall now in the museum. [623]

—Beate Schelmat, pastor
Kirchbach

O f course the work of Leipzig's activists didn't end with the fall of the Berlin Wall. Most continued to play roles in the political, social, and economic lives of their community after the revolution,[624] even if their sphere of influence may have diminished.

Many of these activists continued their involvement in political issues after the revolution—most as members of New Forum. But New Forum, like most of the oppositional groups earlier, was not able to attract a large enough following to play a major role in state and national politics. New Forum, like the opposition, was composed of idealists—"early adapters" or the "vanguard" in diffusion theory—while later leadership roles were played by persons more closely tied to mainstream institutions, including western political parties and the church—

233

"late adaptors" or "influentials."[625] For example, Superintendent Friedrich Magirius, a "thorn in the side" of political groups, headed up Leipzig's Round Table (the forum set up after November 9 where Leipzig government representatives met with representatives of citizens movements and new political parties to discuss and advance reforms), and several church pastors joined mainstream political parties with counterparts in the west (or absorbed into the West German parties).

After reunification, however, it was not East Germans who played the key political roles in the former territory of East Germany.[626] Politicians and government officials from West Germany put their own people in many important government and political positions in what was formerly East Germany. For example, in the early years after reunification, both the mayor of Leipzig and the head of the state of Saxony came from West Germany. Also, at universities and research institutes, West Germans were sent in to fill administrative, research, and teaching positions, while former East German administrators, researchers, and professors lost their jobs.

In the first (and only) free elections for the East German legislature (*Volkskammer*) on March 18, 1990, Alliance 90, the combined political grouping representing New Forum, Initiative for Peace and Human Rights, and other citizens movement groups, received only 2.9 percent of the vote. The Green Party had an even poorer showing, with only 2 percent of the national vote.[627] (In contrast, the Party of Democratic Socialism [PDS], the successor to the East German communist party, received 16.4 percent of the vote.) Already in late 1989, established West German parties had come into East Germany and organized sister parties in the east that dominated the elections. The Christian Democrats won 40.8 percent of the vote, the Social Democrats 21.9 percent.

A number of the activists interviewed for this study were involved in politics after the 1989 revolution. Many participated in the Round Tables held at local as well as national levels in East Germany. Some were elected to city councils and a few to state, national, and European legislatures. Others played leadership roles in citizens groups, served as staff assistants to legislators, and held administrative positions in government.

In Leipzig, Thomas Rudolph played roles as one of the initiators of the Round Table and as staff. Other oppositional group members working on

Leipzig's Round Table as staff or in elected positions included Brigitte Moritz, Jochen Lässig, Gisela Kallenbach, and Roland Quester.

Also at the local level in Leipzig, Jochen Lässig of Initiative Group Living and later New Forum was elected to the Leipzig city council and headed up the regional delegation of New Forum. (In 1995 Lässig was awarded the *Bundesverdienstkreuz* [order of merit] by the Federal Republic of Germany for his role in the 1989 revolution.) Brigitte Moritz of Working Group Peace Service and editor of *Kontakte* also served on the Leipzig city council as a representative of Alliance 90 from 1990 to 1999. Gisela Kallenbach of Working Group Environmental Protection was a city council member from 1990 to 1991, before she was selected to head Leipzig's newly created agency for environmental protection, a position she held until 2000. Roland Quester, also of Working Group Environmental Protection, is currently on Leipzig's city council, where he has responsibilities for planning and environmental issues.

Several group members served as elected officials or staff members in the Saxony state legislature in Dresden. Michael Arnold, earlier of Initiative Group Living and New Forum, represented Alliance 90/the Greens in the state legislature before he turned to dentistry full time, and Thomas Rudolph of Working Circle Justice and later Initiative for Peace and Human Rights served as his administrative/legislative assistant. Gisela Kallenbach currently serves as an elected representative in the state legislature, and prior to that she was a member of the European Parliament from 2004 to 2009. Kallenbach has also worked as a United Nations representative in Albania. (In 2001 Kallenbach received Germany's *Bundesverdienstkreuz*.)

A number of Leipzig activists worked at archives and organizations that furthered the political goals of movement groups after 1989. Roland Quester of Working Group Environmental Protection cofounded environmental group Eco-Lion (Ökolöwe), created from a union of church and state environmental groups in 1989, and since 1994 he has headed up Leipzig's Umweltbibliothek (Environmental Library). Rainer Müller and Oliver Kloß, respectively of Working Circle Justice and Working Group Human Rights, worked on the local staffs of the Initiative for Peace and Human Rights and at the group's archive. Uwe Schwabe cofounded and worked at Archiv Bürgerbewegung Leipzig researching and preserving the memory of the peaceful revolution in Leipzig.

Thomas Rudolph, Brigitte Moritz, and Gabriele Heide all worked for years in social service agencies—Rudolph heading up a program helping to house and feed low-income residents of Leipzig, and Moritz and Heide in a program to counter discrimination against immigrants and others from abroad and to help integrate them into society.

Kathrin Walther moved to Berlin, where she heads up a foundation, the European Academy for Women in Politics and the Economy (*Europäische Akademie für Frauen in Politik und Wirtschaft*), promoting women in the workforce and in politics and society. Gesine Oltmanns took several years off from paid employment to marry and to raise eight children, but she now works for a church foundation promoting the nonviolent revolution and recently published a 25th-anniversary calendar commemorating the revolution of 1989.

Christoph Wonneberger had a long recovery period following the stroke he suffered on October 30, 1989, a little more than a week before the East German government and the Berlin Wall fell. Wonneberger had to relearn to speak, but before he fully recuperated, the church forced the oppositional pastor into retirement. In his retirement Wonneberger has turned to new endeavors, among them participating in a bicycle tour from Paris, France, to Moscow, Russia, a trip covering more than 2,000 miles. Two books documenting his life and his experiences in East Germany were published in spring 2014 commemorating his seventieth birthday.[628] In the late 1990s and in the 21st century Wonneberger has received several awards, including the 2014 German National Prize, awarded in the 25th anniversary year of the East German Revolution in recognition of his courageous role.

After reunification, a number of oppositional group members studied and completed degrees that most had not been allowed to pursue in East Germany because of their critical stances and oppositional involvements. Jochen Lässig went to law school and completed his degree in 1998, and he currently works as an attorney in private practice in central Leipzig. Michael Arnold completed his dentistry studies and practices dentistry in Dresden. Rainier Müller studied political science and history. He currently works as a freelance historian, and his work has frequently focused on the role of the political opposition in the late 1980s as well as on educational issues.

Uwe Schwabe became one of the important chroniclers of Leipzig's role in the East German revolution in 1989. Initially after the revolution he cofounded and headed up Archiv Bürgerbewegung Leipzig, an important repository for documentation of Leipzig groups and the East German citizens movement, and he continues to serve on the group's board. Currently, Schwabe works for the German government's museum of contemporary history (*Zeitgeschichtliches Forum*) with responsibilities for collecting materials to document East German times. He has also researched and written extensively on the roles of political groups in the East German revolution of 1989 and has provided numerous researchers, including this author, with crucial materials. In 1995 Schwabe was awarded the *Bundesverdienstkreuz* for his role in the 1989 revolution. In recognition of multiple contributions, in spring 2014 Schwabe, along with Archiv Bürgerbewegung Leipzig, was awarded the German National Prize for 2014 for work in carrying out the memory of East Germany's peaceful revolution.

Many of the activists I interviewed were initially disappointed in the period immediately after 1989 and during the early years of German reunification. Although all had fought for a more democratic society, most wanted a more democratic East Germany rather than a reunified Germany that absorbed East Germany into the political and economic structures of the Federal Republic of Germany (West Germany). Many were most disappointed by the inequalities built into western market economies and the lack of social justice. Over the years since 1989, I have interviewed several of these activists more than once, and most appreciate many of the freedoms and benefits offered by a market system (capitalism) and western-style representative democracy, although most wanted a grassroots, more participatory democracy. Many remain disappointed by certain aspects of the economic system, especially, and by the fact that so few people remained actively involved in politics after 1989.

In my interviews I asked activists to assess the contributions that their groups made to the East German revolution of 1989. Brigitte Moritz viewed Working Group Peace Service and other Leipzig groups as important for the revolution, particularly because through the peace prayers the groups spread important ideas and prepared people to carry out the revolution without violence. In addition, Moritz pointed to groups in East Germany as "the exit point for the formation of the first democratic parties, New Forum, Democratic Awakening, the Social Democratic Party, and so forth."[629] She says, "We have accomplished our goal."

Although Working Group Environmental Protection did not fully achieve its goals in the early years after the revolution, because environmental destruction continued, Roland Quester pointed out, "Something important in the area of consciousness building did occur. People in East Germany became much more aware of environmental problems, and our group itself became strong and not insignificant."[630] Also, according to Gisela Kallenbach, after the revolution, "environmental groups in East Germany have totally different opportunities to work more effectively and to influence what happens,"[631] and both Kallenbach and Quester have worked on environmental issues in Leipzig city government following the revolution. Since reunification, enormous changes have occurred in the environmental arena—in Leipzig, Saxony, and East Germany. Money from Germany and from the European Union has supported major environmental cleanups and infrastructure improvements throughout the country, and air and water quality have improved dramatically.

When I interviewed Jochen Lässig shortly after the revolution, he pointed to Initiative Group Living's and other human rights groups' roles in the Initiative for the Renewal of Society as particularly important.[632] The Initiative had spearheaded a number of the events covered in this book that led to the revolutionary fall, and Lässig personally felt that the Rosa Luxemburg march in January 1989 and the street music festival in June were especially effective. Initiative Group Living also played a major role in founding the citizens movement group New Forum. Lässig and many other group members, however, were disappointed that after the massive demonstrations people did not continue to participate in politics, and years after the revolution the political vacuum remained.

Twenty years later as Lässig looked back on 1989, he felt that the primary importance of oppositional groups and civil rights activists was that they sped up the revolution.[633] "We were important for the revolution. It would have happened without us. But we accelerated the process. . . . Like a house of cards . . . someone has to push. And we were the ones—the civil rights activists."

Christoph Wonneberger,
Pastor of Lukas Church,
Working Group Human
Rights
Photo by Patricia Smith

Jochen Lässig, Initiative
Group Living
Photo by Patricia Smith

Gesine Oltmanns, Initiative
Group Living
Photo by Patricia Smith

Uwe Schwabe, Initiative
Group Living
Photo by Patricia Smith

Rainer Müller, Working
Circle Justice
Photo by Patricia Smith

Kathrin Walther, Working
Circle Justice
Photo by Thomas Mayer

Thomas Rudolph,
Working Circle Justice
Photo by Thomas Mayer

Gabriele Heide,
Women for Peace
Photo by Patricia Smith

Brigitte Moritz, Working
Group Peace Service and
Women for Peace
Photo by Patricia Smith

Gisela Kallenbach, Working
Group Environmental
Protection
Private photo

Roland Quester, Working
Group Environmental
Protection
Photo by Patricia Smith

APPENDIX A

Cast of Characters[634]

Leipzig Activists
(in alphabetical order)

Arnold, Michael

Cofounder of oppositional human rights group Initiative Group Living (IGL) and, later, cofounder of New Forum in East Germany; arrested during Rosa Luxemburg affair and on several other occasions; after revolution, elected to Saxony state legislature; currently a dentist in Dresden.

Hattenhauer, Katrin

Working Circle Justice (AKG); arrested for distributing flyers for Rosa Luxemburg demonstration; co-organizer of street music festival; in fall 1989 held in Stasi prison for more than a month; cofounder of Archiv Bürgerbewegung; freelance artist in Berlin and Pella, Italy.

Heide, Gabriele

Cofounder of Women for Peace (*Frauen für den Frieden*), Leipzig oppositional group; concerned about militarization of East Germany and especially in education system, and produced informational exhibits and studies; after 1989 worked in social service agency on intercultural issues and with youth.

Kallenbach, Gisela

Working Group Environmental Protection (AGU); member of group since 1982; initially didn't consider self oppositional but became more involved in oppositional activities; participated in ecumenical Conciliar Process; worked to promote nonviolence on October 9; after revolution served on Leipzig's Round Table and city council before heading up city environmental agency; elected to European Parliament and later Saxony state legislature.

Kloß, Oliver

> Working Group Human Rights (AGM); a conscientious objector to military service and connected to other construction-soldier and draft-resister groups in East Germany.

Kowasch, Fred

> Initiative Group Living (IGL); spoke at Rosa Luxemburg demonstration; applied to emigrate to west and from there worked on media efforts of East German groups.

Lässig, Jochen

> Initiative Group Living (IGL) and later cofounder of New Forum, Leipzig; arrested during Rosa Luxemburg affair; street musician and organized street music festival; a spokesman for New Forum during fall 1989 demonstrations; served on Leipzig city council and headed coalition Alliance 90/Greens (1990–96); earned law degree and currently in private practice in Leipzig.

Moritz, Brigitte

> Cofounder of Working Group Peace Service (AGFD) and Women for Peace (*Frauen für den Frieden*); editor of *Kontakte,* newsletter of Leipzig groups sent throughout country; as New Forum representative, worked on Leipzig Round Table and elected to city council; currently heads social service agency working on intercultural issues and with youth.

Müller, Rainer

> Working Circle Justice (AKG), Working Group Human Rights (AGM), Solidarity Church, and environmental groups; oppositional since youth; refused military service; participated in most oppositional group activities in Leipzig; arrested during Rosa Luxemburg affair; in 1989 member of citizens movement organization Initiative for Peace and Human Rights and later active in New Forum; after revolution studied history and political science and currently works as freelance historian.

Oltmanns, Gesine

> Initiative Group Living (IGL) and, earlier, Working Circle Justice (AKG); arrested during Rosa Luxemburg affair; worked with persons wanting to emigrate; involved in contact networks promoting solidarity for those arrested; after 1989 worked for agency handling dissolution

of Stasi headquarters and release of Stasi files; during break from political involvements, raised eight children; now works for a foundation promoting the nonviolent revolution and peaceful reforms.

Quester, Roland

Working Group Environmental Protection (AGU); cofounder and staff of Umweltbibliothek and editor of *Streiflichter,* newsletter connecting environmental groups across East Germany; organizer and participant in Pleisse memorial march and other oppositional activities; after 1989 founded environmental union and heads Leipzig's environmental library; currently serves on Leipzig city council.

Richter, Frank

Working Group Human Rights (AGM); part of media effort of Leipzig and East German opposition getting reports to Eastern Europe and the west; contacts in East European opposition.

Rudolph, Thomas

Cofounder Working Circle Justice (AKG); responsible for media efforts of opposition, including international contacts; coordinated network of oppositional groups; viewed as one of masterminds of revolution; cowrote many letters and publications of Leipzig human rights groups; cofounder of movement organization Initiative for Peace and Human Rights and later worked with New Forum and Alliance 90/Green coalition; initiator and staff of Leipzig Round Table; staff to Michael Arnold in Saxony state legislature; currently heads social service agency providing food and shelter and raising profile of low-income inhabitants of Leipzig.

Schwabe, Uwe

Cofounder of Initiative Group Living (IGL); helped organize and participated in Rosa Luxemburg demonstration, Pleisse march, street music festival, peace prayers, and Monday demonstrations; cofounder of Archiv Bürgerbewegung Leipzig; currently works at Forum for Contemporary History; has written extensively on revolution.

Tallig, Jürgen

Cofounder of Marxist group Dialog; arrested for painting pro-democracy signs; coordinated election-monitoring efforts of Marxist, communist party, and student groups; cofounded New Forum and served as speaker; later a social worker in Berlin-Weissensee.

Walther, Kathrin

Working Circle Justice (AKG); coordinated contact bureau solidarity efforts; with Rudolph, responsible for media efforts of Leipzig and East German oppositional groups; co-organizer of Alternative Church Congress; cowrote many documents published by human rights groups; currently heads Berlin foundation promoting women in economic and political spheres.

Wonneberger, Christoph

Founder of Working Group Human Rights (AGM); as oppositional pastor of Lukas Church, sheltered groups and made rooms, telephones, mimeograph equipment available; co-organized Alternative Church Congress; connections to groups throughout East Germany (also West Germany and Eastern Europe) through conscientious objector, peace, human rights, and various church networks; called most important figure in fall revolution by some; suffered stroke on October 30, 1989, and in 1991 was forced into early retirement by church.

Other East German Activists

Beleites, Michael

Environmental activist; produced *Pechblende,* exposé on uranium mining.

Schefke, Siegbert

Videographer; filmed demonstration from Reformierte Church tower and smuggled film to western television.

Sengewald, Matthias

Previously member of Leipzig's Working Group Peace Service and pastor at Leipzig Youth Bureau; moved to Erfurt and connected to wide variety of groups across country.

Templin, Regina (Lotte)

Member of Initiative for Human Rights (IFM), Berlin, and Solidarity Church; worked with emigration groups and others wanting to emigrate.

Pastors and Other Church Officials, Leipzig

Berger, Matthias

Pastor of Erlöser Church, head of church-group coordinating committee for peace prayers; Stasi informer with code name Carl.

Führer, Christian

Head pastor, Nikolai Church; sponsored emigration group Hope.

Kaden, Klaus

Pastor at Church Youth Bureau located next to Thomas Church; worked with Working Group Environmental Protection and emigration group, Kaden's Circle.

Magirius, Friedrich

Superintendent, Leipzig East Church District; involved groups in coordinating committee for peace prayers in Leipzig, but later banned them from participating; later, head of Leipzig's Round Table.

Richter, Johannes

Superintendent, Leipzig East Church District; pastor of Thomas Church in city center.

Sievers, Hans-Jürgen

Pastor of Reformierte Church on northwest edge of Leipzig Ring; allowed oppositional/controversial meetings in church and photographers to film demonstrations from church tower; opened church for peace prayers, fall 1989; wrote account of revolutionary period.

Turek, Rolf-Michael

Pastor of Markus Church in Leipzig-Reudnitz, south of city center; supported groups with use of facilities and equipment; involved with monitoring May 1989 local elections.

Wonneberger, Christoph

Pastor of Lukas Church in Leipzig-Volkmarsdorf, east of center; cofounded oppositional Working Group Human Rights; developed East German-wide initiative for social peace service and model for peace prayers; supported oppositional groups; lost speech after stroke on October 30, 1989, and church forced him into early retirement.

Pastors and Other Church Leaders, Elsewhere in East Germany

Domsch, Kurt

> President, Saxony Church District, which includes Leipzig; failed to support proposal for social peace service and many group-initiated activities.

Falcke, Heino

> Evangelical Church provost for Erfurt district; supporter of grassroots groups; cochaired ecumenical Conciliar Process for East Germany bringing together groups and churches.

Gensichen, Hans-Peter

> Head of the Evangelical Church's Environmental Research Center in Wittenberg; until mid-1980s informally coordinated church-based environmental groups throughout East Germany.

Hempel, Johannes

> Bishop, Saxony Church District, which includes Leipzig with district offices in Dresden; under pressure from East German state, failed to support Christoph Wonneberger's proposal for a social peace service and many activities of alternative and oppositional groups in Leipzig.

Government Officials, East Germany

Honecker, Erich

> Head of East German state and communist party from 1976 until October 18, 1989; resisted reform and favored attacking demonstrators; forced out by members of communist party leadership, including Egon Krenz.

Krenz, Egon

> Replaced Erich Honecker as East German state and party leader on October 18, 1989; resigned under pressure on December 6, 1989; Krenz's initial support for Chinese solution—attacking demonstrators—doomed his administration from beginning.

Mielke, Erich

Head of East German Ministry for State Security, the Stasi; resigned November 7, 1989, two days before fall of Berlin Wall; remembered for quote "We were prepared for everything except for candles and prayers."

Schabowski, Günter

Member of central communist party leadership with responsibilities for media; at press conference on November 9, 1989, Schabowski, who had not been informed about the contents of the press release on travel regulations, mistakenly provided the press with information that resulted in immediate opening of Berlin Wall.

Government Officials and Civic Leaders, Leipzig

Group of Six

Group of Leipzig governmental and cultural leaders who called for nonviolence in Leipzig on October 9. Among the six were Lange, Masur, Meyer, Pommert, Wötzel, and Zimmerman (see below).

Hackenberg, Helmut

Head of the communist party leadership in district of Leipzig; involved with decision not to attack demonstrators on October 9.

Hummitzsch, Manfred

Head of the Ministry for State Security, the Stasi, in district of Leipzig; involved with decision not to attack demonstrators on October 9.

Lange, Bernd-Lutz

Leipzig cabaret performer and author; as part of Group of Six, called for nonviolence during October 9 demonstration.

Masur, Kurt

Head of Leipzig symphony; as part of Group of Six, called for nonviolence during October 9 demonstration and for dialogue; after revolution also conductor and music director of New York Philharmonic.

Meyer, Kurt

Part of communist party leadership for district of Leipzig; as one of Group of Six, called for nonviolence during October 9 demonstration.

Pommert, Joachim

Part of communist party leadership for district of Leipzig; responsible for propaganda; as one of Group of Six, called for nonviolence during October 9 demonstration.

Seidel, Bernd

Mayor of Leipzig; resigned on November 3, 1989.

Strassenburg, Gerhard

Head of police in Leipzig district, which includes city of Leipzig; along with Helmut Hackenberg, involved in decision not to attack demonstrators on October 9.

Wötzel, Roland

Part of communist party leadership for district of Leipzig and head of planning commission; as part of Group of Six, called for nonviolence during October 9 demonstration.

Zimmerman, Peter

Theologian on faculty at University of Leipzig; as part of Group of Six, called for nonviolence during October 9 demonstration.

Oppositional and Alternative Groups and Organizations, Leipzig

Human Rights

Initiative Group Living (IGL)

Working Circle Justice (AKG)

Working Group Human Rights (AGM)

Peace

Women for Peace (*Frauen für den Frieden*—FfdF)

Working Group Peace Service (AGFD)

Environment

Working Group Environmental Protection (AGU)

Marxist

Dialog

Citizen Movement Organizations, East Germany
> Initative for Peace and Human Rights (IFM)
> New Forum (NF)

Leipzig Churches
(involved in peace prayers and other events in 1989)

Church Youth Bureau—Located in city center next to Thomas Church; meeting spot for some church groups; solidarity telephones.

Lukas Church—Located east of city center; focal point of oppositional group activity in Leipzig; site of Alternative Church Congress; solidarity telephones.

Michaelis Church—Located north of center city; facilities used for some controversial activities; despite location outside central city, opened for peace prayers on October 16.

Markus Church—Located south of city center at crossroads of transportation lines; facilities used for election monitoring and other group activities.

Nikolai Church—Located in Leipzig center; primary site for peace prayers since 1982; gathering point for demonstrations during 1989.

Paul Gerhard Church—Located in south Leipzig; starting location for worship service and Pleisse memorial march.

Peters Church—Located just south of central Leipzig; demonstration after Alternative Church Congress ended there.

Propstei Catholic Church—One of five churches and the first Catholic Church opened for peace prayers on October 16.

Reformierte Church—Second church opened for peace prayers; held controversial environmental meetings, including Pleisse memorial march and A Mark for Espenhain.

Thomas Church—One of last churches opened for peace prayers; generally not supportive of controversial or oppositional activities.

APPENDIX B

Explaining the East German Revolution of 1989

Most explanations for the East German revolution of 1989—Reagan won the Cold War, communism collapsed, it was a "spontaneous" revolution—fail to account for the role of demonstrations and demonstrators. They exclude people, their ideas, and their actions from the equation.[635]

Many in the west view Ronald Reagan as playing the key role in bringing down the Berlin Wall and winning the Cold War. But in reality, Reagan gave his "Mr. Gorbachev, tear down this wall" speech in 1987, two years after Gorbachev began advocating for major changes in the Soviet bloc.

Collapse and other economic explanations—East Germans wanted bananas and other material goods—may help explain the demands of one group of protesters, those wanting to emigrate to the west. However, economic explanations ignore the demands for a more democratic East Germany articulated by political activists and a continually increasing share of the East German population. And they fail to explain how the demonstrations originated, developed, and spread.

Others argued that it was a church revolution. However, although the church did play a role by providing meeting places for groups and sheltering them from the state, the church played a mixed role. When pressured by the state, church authorities clamped down on group activities and prevented groups from promoting controversial programs within churches. For example, for almost a year groups were prohibited from organizing the peace prayers at Leipzig's Nikolai Church, so they took their demands to the streets, a critical factor in the 1989 revolution. Churches jumped on the bandwagon late in the revolution, but earlier they pressured activists to moderate or stop their activities and criticisms.

Still others point to the massive demonstrations in East Germany throughout fall 1989 as a "spontaneous" revolution. Research shows, however, that the demonstrations that ultimately brought down the East German state were neither a centrally directed movement composed exclusively of activists

251

nor a spontaneous uprising of totally unorganized individuals. Rather, the demonstrations included a core of activists with a history of political involvement as well as a variety of groups and individuals mobilized to action through numerous and varied informational channels and through the example of public action.

Most chroniclers of the East German revolution have overlooked or downplayed the role of activists in the East German revolution of 1989. This oversight may be understandable. In East Germany, no dominant countrywide leader or group emerged—in actuality or in the media. No one comparable in name recognition to poet, playwright, and dissident Vaclav Havel in Czechoslovakia or Solidarity leader Lech Walesa in Poland developed in East Germany. Although no famous leaders emerged in East Germany, a loose, underlying organization did exist, tying together alternative and oppositional groups throughout the country. Small groups of committed activists existed in most major East German cities. They met mainly in churches and had links to other activists primarily through peace, environmental, and human rights groups. Church networks, a few oppositional networks, and other informal networks joined these groups together within cities and from city to city. These links occurred through periodic face-to-face meetings of groups, *samizdat* and church-based newsletters and other publications, and telephone chains informing individuals and groups of events and arrests in other areas. These activist groups provided the underlying organization for a mass movement and the huge demonstrations that spread from Leipzig throughout East Germany in fall 1989.

APPENDIX C

Coordinating Groups and Movements

Group-Based Communication Networks

A number of networks served to loosely coordinate information and activities of group members from throughout East Germany. These networks were particularly effective in crisis situations and for involving a wide variety of groups and individuals in solidarity demonstrations, but they also provided channels for communicating more routine information. They also proved effective for organizing the East German-wide election-monitoring campaign that proved election fraud. As Sebastian Pflugbeil of citizens movement New Forum stated:

> Whenever we had heard, for example, that people had been arrested, one could find out specifics about who had been arrested and where with the help of these contact phones; about what was planned in terms of how best to respond; who was organizing something in solidarity with the arrestees; and so forth. For such purposes, communication was organized exceedingly well.[636]

Relevant networks ranged from broad, general networks such as Peace Concrete, coordinating a wide variety of groups, to more narrowly focused networks coordinating groups within particular thematic areas such as draft resistance or the environment. The East German state was aware of these networks, and officials worried about the capability of these networks to coordinate broad-based programs involving a wide variety of groups. In a June 1989 report, the East German Stasi pointed to more than ten networks "with specific coordination and assignment functions" that tied together groups from throughout East Germany.[637] More than half of the networks were established before 1985, but several were founded or expanded in 1988 and 1989. The networks highlighted in the Stasi report and discussed briefly below include Peace Concrete, Environmental Library, Green Network Ark, Initiative for Peace and Human Rights, Peace Circle Total Refusers (conscientious objectors), Solidarity Church, and

Church from Below. Although none of these networks utilized a tight, centralized organizational structure that sent orders from the center out to the regions,
all of the networks did provide channels for communicating ideas and information among groups throughout East Germany. Taken together, the networks
provided the means for contacting and loosely coordinating most East German
activists plus an expanding circle of sympathizers within a relatively short
period.

Although some of these groups utilized Evangelical Church facilities,
equipment, or supplies for some of their functions, the networks were not
church networks. Nor were most even condoned by the official leadership structure of the church. Various networks, however, did have the support of critical
or oppositional pastors. Moreover, a number of group activists who played coordinative roles in networks were employed by churches in various positions and,
consequently, could use church telephones, a vital channel for networks in a
society where access to telephones and other means of communication was
restricted by the state.

Several critical or oppositional pastors served on the coordinating committees of group networks. For example, the 10–15-member coordinating committee for Peace Concrete comprising representatives from all church regions
included pastors Meckel, Albani, Eppelmann, Tschiche, and Lietz.[638] (Ehrhart
Neubert of the Evangelical Church Federation staff estimated that of the 4,500
Evangelical Church pastors in East Germany, 20 percent were critical, 60–70
percent were cautious, and 10 percent were state-conforming.[639]) These critical
East German pastors played a crucial supportive role for groups and facilitated
group organization.

Although the various East German networks together did not promote
any single, tightly coordinated program (and only seldom did individual networks do so), they did possess the ability to inform their constituent group
members about events or programs carried out by groups in other areas. Consequently, the networks enabled groups in other areas to choose to take (or not
to take) supportive actions or to participate in broader joint projects. The May
1989 election campaign, discussed in Chapter 4, demonstrated how a relatively
small number of oppositional groups from throughout East Germany succeeded in developing and successfully carrying out a loosely coordinated plan

with the common goal of proving election fraud. This election-monitoring campaign, which would have been impossible without preexisting networks, had a major impact on the subsequent involvement of groups and the broader population as activists called for more democracy in East Germany throughout fall 1989.

In June 1989, the Stasi estimated that there were about 160 grassroots groups in East Germany, with about 2,500 members, with about 150 of the groups connected to churches.[640] Groups included 35 peace, 39 ecology, 23 mixed peace and ecology, 10 human rights, 7 women's, 3 doctors' circles, and 39 third world groups. The Stasi estimated that about 600 of these members served in leadership committees and assessed perhaps 60 of these group members—the "hard-core"—as "fanatical enemies of socialism."[641] According to the Stasi, the most active and the most dangerous groups were in Berlin. The report pointed to the Initiative for Peace and Human Rights (IFM), particularly, as an enemy of the state, in part because the Berlin group had expanded and in 1989 it linked together oppositional groups throughout East Germany. (Not reported by the Stasi was the fact that in 1989 Leipzig human rights groups played important coordinating roles for IFM.) According to the Stasi report, Leipzig, Karl-Marx-Stadt, Dresden, Gera, and Erfurt—cities in the southern tier of East Germany—also contained concentrations of oppositional groups.[642]

Nevertheless, according to Ulrike Poppe, a group activist who served on the steering committee for Peace Concrete, the Stasi had greatly underestimated the number of active groups in East Germany. Actually, just one network, Peace Concrete, coordinated 325 groups throughout the country—more than double the number the Stasi had estimated—and linked by this network were 90 groups in Saxony alone.[643] So, as state authorities and security forces attempted to maintain control of the streets in fall 1989, they made their decisions on the basis of inaccurate information.

Peace Concrete (*Konkret für den Frieden*)

Founded in 1982 and organized by groups, this network was not a church network, although it developed under the roof of the church. According to Ulrike Poppe, who kept information cards containing telephone numbers and addresses for contacting groups throughout East Germany, "Most peace, human rights, women's, ecological, and third world groups could be reached over the network Peace Concrete."[644] Ehrhart Neubert, author of a major study on the history of the opposition in East Germany, emphasized, "Essentially Peace Concrete was the only network that tied together all groups in the land."[645]

Central to the network was a steering committee composed of both Christian and non-Christian activists who represented various regions as well as movements in East Germany. The steering committee met every three months. In addition, representatives of groups in the network met together annually as well as in periodic regional meetings. Representatives came from each of the seven Peace Concrete regions, which corresponded to the regions for the Evangelical Church. In addition, the coordinating committee included representatives of human rights, environmental, and third world groups. Leipzig was tied into the network through Ralf Elsässer, a member of Leipzig's Working Group Environmental Protection, who participated in the coordinating committee as a representative for environmental groups. Because Elsässer's group in Leipzig produced the newsletter *Streiflichter,* which was distributed to all environmental groups in East Germany, Elsässer could link information from Peace Concrete to environmental networks throughout the country.

Peace Concrete worked well as a communication network coordinating almost all grassroots groups in East Germany. In addition, Peace Concrete held East German-wide gatherings every year. These meetings helped to build a common awareness of important ideas and to forge a broad group identity.

As a network, however, Peace Concrete also had weaknesses. Newer networks of groups working in thematic areas, such as Network Ark on environmental issues, had taken over part of Peace Concrete's communication functions. Also, because Peace Concrete was so closely tied to church structures, it was susceptible to pressures of the church leadership as the church responded to pressures from the state, so in fall 1989 the network did not always work well, especially for oppositional activities.[646]

Environmental Library (*Umweltbibliothek*)

In 1986 the group Environmental Library (*Umweltbibliothek des Friedens—und Umweltkreises der Zionskirchgemeinde*) formed in Berlin, and through its publication *Umweltblätter* and by making its facilities available to other groups, the Environmental Library played a crucial informational and coordinating role for environmental as well as other groups in East Germany. The group used its "press" to produce materials for other East German groups that did not have access to printing facilities.[647]

The Environmental Library played a major role in the election-monitoring campaign by printing materials for a wide variety of groups in a number of East German cities. However, the rooms, equipment, and staff of the Environmental Library not only facilitated the election campaign but also supported many other group-supported activities. In fall 1989, the Environmental Library's computer was used around the clock to produce informational leaflets and assist in organizing public events for groups from across East Germany.

Green Network Ark (*Grünes Netzwerk "Arche"*)

Founded in January 1988 technically within the Evangelical Church structure with the intent of coordinating church-related environmental groups, Network Ark's goal was "improving the exchange of information, coordinating common activities for the protection of the environment, and overcoming organizational problems and conceptual weaknesses" in the environmental movement.[648] Among its founding members were four former members of Berlin's Environmental Library,[649] a much more loosely structured organization, and the founding of the Network Ark led to considerable strife among the two organizations and their leading members.[650] Founders of Network Ark wanted an organization with a firmer structure that would facilitate more intentional and effective coordination.[651] The network was organized into seven regions that corresponded to the structure of the Evangelical Church. Coordination occurred within regions, as representatives of groups met together, and among regions, through meetings of regional representatives. In theory, Network Ark promoted considerable independence among the regions. However, because many environmental groups in the other regions viewed the network as Berlin-dominated, many groups resisted these coordinative efforts.[652] Network Ark's publication, *Arche Nova,* provided additional sources of information and means of coordination for network members as well as for other groups in East Germany.

Network Ark was intensively involved in organizing and protesting the May 1989 election and distributed various materials on the subject, and its regional structure provided a network for coordinating election monitoring in cities throughout East Germany.[653] For example, in Erfurt, election monitoring locally occurred through a broad coalition of church-based groups, Catholic and Protestant; however, members of the Erfurt environmental group Oasis, along with its sponsor pastor Aribert Rothe, a regional representative of Network Ark, were primary organizers of the Erfurt monitoring campaign.

Nevertheless, Network Ark was only one of many networks involved in organizing the election-monitoring effort throughout East Germany. The monitoring campaign illustrates how many groups in major cities throughout East Germany—linked informally through a number of networks, including Network Ark—could successfully carry out a national campaign and prove election fraud. In fall 1989 this coalition of networks, some tightly structured like Network Ark and others much more loosely organized like the Environmental Library, was in place to communicate information about demonstrations and various other actions in Leipzig, Berlin, and other cities.

Initiative for Peace and Human Rights [*Initiativ Frieden und Menschenrechte* (IFM)]

Established initially in 1985, the Berlin group Initiative for Peace and Human Rights (IFM) played a crucial organizational and coordinative role among *oppositional* groups.[654] Viewing itself as oppositional, IFM was tied into a clandestine network composed of approximately twenty oppositional groups that organized and met outside of church structures. Then, in 1989, IFM organized itself as an East German-wide network. In January 1988, after the arrest and forced emigration of many of IFM's members after the Rosa Luxemburg demonstrations in Berlin, the coordination of oppositional groups shifted to Leipzig. The network, informally known as the Saturday Circle (*Sonnabend Kreis*), met every month in Leipzig. By coordinating media and other international contacts for most oppositional East German groups, Thomas Rudolph and several Leipzig members of this network played a critical role in publicizing oppositional activities, e.g., the Rosa Luxemburg marches, the May 7 election results, the Pleisse demonstrations, and other demonstrations, arrests, and solidarity actions.

IFM also cooperated with other networks that spread information and coordinated activities throughout East Germany. As Berlin member Reinhard Weißhuhn reported,

Members of IFM worked together with other groups and with church workers on the establishment of a contact telephone system that would serve the
information exchange between various project groups and initiatives. This
work quickly expanded: Solidarity actions with those in prison were organized, contacts arranged, informational meetings convened. Also, the local
election campaign in May 1989 was overseen with the help of these contact
telephones.[655]

This network, coordinated primarily through Leipzig in late 1989, provided critical organizational support for the fall revolution.

Friendship Circle Draft Resisters (*Freundeskreis Totalverweigerer*)

From early on conscientious objectors, including both draft resisters and
construction soldiers who served alongside the military but did not carry
weapons, developed camaraderie and informal networks of support. With the
formation of the Berlin Friendship Circle Draft Resisters in 1986, however, conscientious objectors to military service developed a more formalized network. A
primary objective of the Berlin group was to encourage ties with similar groups
in other regions of East Germany. As part of this goal, the group organized
annual meetings, took action to promote the civil rights of conscientious objectors, and pushed for a social peace service. Friendship Circle Draft Resisters was
also closely tied into the broad-based network Peace Concrete through Heiko
Lietz, who served on its steering committee and held responsibilities there for
coordinating activities related to problems of military service. East German
draft resisters and construction soldiers also developed connections with similar groups in West Germany, England, Spain, Sweden, Poland, and Hungary,
and with War Resisters International.[656]

Several Leipzig group members were linked into East German networks
involved with military service problems. Oliver Kloß of Working Group Human
Rights was part of the coordination circle for military service problems associated with Samariter Church in Berlin, a group that met at least every three
months.[657] As a result of his experiences as an early construction soldier, draft
counselor, and initiator of the program for a social peace service, Christoph
Wonneberger had numerous contacts within the network, including addresses
and phone numbers of prominent activists and groups throughout East Germany.[658] Leipzig's Initiative Group Living and its subgroup on conscientious

objection also had close connections to groups of draft resisters, including ties with subgroups of Initiative for Peace and Human Rights and Working Circle Friedrichsfelder in Berlin and with several other groups in Dresden, Berlin, and elsewhere.[659]

A number of members of draft-resister groups had participated actively in the election-monitoring campaign. Mario Schatta, a member of the Weissensee Peace Group in Berlin and a key figure in the draft resisters' network, also played a central role in election monitoring. Earlier he had initiated election projects in the Weissensee district of Berlin, and in 1989 he was a key organizer of the monitoring campaign throughout East Germany.

As a group, draft resisters had been radicalized by their experiences and their oppositional stance, and in 1989 their formal and informal networks linked them to demonstrations and other activities promoting a more democratic East Germany.

Church from Below (*Kirche von Unten*)

Founded in response to the 1987 decision of the Evangelical Church leadership to cancel the annual Peace Workshop in Berlin to avoid friction with the state,[660] grassroots group members organized, financed, and convened the Church Congress from Below (*Kirchentag von Unten*) where concerns of grassroots groups could be discussed openly.[661] The first regional grouping of the Church from Below originated in Berlin-Brandenburg, and additional regional Church Congresses from Below formed later in conjunction with official church congresses in other cities including Jena, Halle, Saalfeld, Dresden, Leipzig, and Greifswald.[662] These meetings organized by the Church from Below provided a model for the Alternative Church Congress held at Lukas Church in Leipzig in July 1989.

The Church from Below invited the participation of a wide variety of alternative groups including peace, environmental, human rights, third world, women's, lesbian, and homosexual groups from throughout East Germany to these meetings. The Berlin group was a center for Open Work (*Offene Arbeit*), part of the Evangelical Church's youth program (*Junge Gemeinde*), and, like Open Work, the Church from Below had an anarchist orientation and a flexible organizational structure. A primary objective of the Church from Below was to secure representation of the grassroots base of the church in church affairs, because members felt that the church leadership often failed to represent their interests.[663] Group members from the Church from Below also promoted fundamental changes in East German society. Through their network they organized solidarity actions for those arrested in the Rosa Luxemburg march and other demonstrations and also protested state censorship of church publications.

The contact network of the Church from Below included communication links among regions as well as within regions. The group's regular meetings also provided a forum for grassroots groups in East Germany to join together, and according to Stasi estimates, the monthly gatherings of the Berlin network attracted between 50 and 250 members. Members of the Church from Below were also tied in to other networks such as Peace Concrete and the Conciliar Process.[664]

Working Circle Solidarity Church (*Arbeitskreis Solidärische Kirche*)

Although Solidarity Church groups originated earlier, such as Leipzig's group in 1983,[665] the network was activated in 1987. The network of Working Circle Solidarity Church tied together church workers with a critical or political stance toward society.[666] Composed of 500–600 persons, the network was organized within the structures of the Evangelical Church into 12 regional groups and coordinated through an elected coordinating committee.[667]

A major goal of Solidarity Church was to become part of the official structure of the Evangelical Church so group members could have an impact on church decisions.[668] Solidarity Church understood itself as a grassroots or basis group and promoted "the democratization of the Evangelical Church and the socialistic society in East Germany."[669] The group promoted "new thinking," worked to erase the "democratic deficit" through political and governmental reforms, and struggled with the *Absage and Abgrenzung* paper that questioned the division of Germany.[670] Group members also worked with emigration groups and published a report on the problems of those wanting to emigrate.[671]

According to Lotte Templin, "the *program* of Solidarity Church was not so important. *Solidarity* was most important thing—not documents."[672] In an effort to promote critical thinking and a broader solidarity throughout society, in 1988

Solidarity Church organized a summer academy for group members and others from throughout East Germany with radical political ideas and oppositional leanings. To further coordinate the work of East German grassroots groups, the network organized monthly information "kiosks," loosely organized meetings where representatives from all groups could quickly exchange information.[673] Solidarity Church also instituted contact telephones for information and coordination of various activities, especially during crisis situations.[674] Through this contact network members of Solidarity Church provided support for and demonstrated solidarity not just with their own members, but also with other oppositional group members from throughout East Germany and beyond.

In May 1989 Solidarity Church joined with groups throughout East Germany to monitor local elections.[675] In part, the coordination for broad efforts such as the election-monitoring campaign occurred through persons with memberships in multiple groups and networks. For example, Berliner Marianne Birthler, a member of the coordinating committee for Solidarity Church's network, was also a member of Initiative for Peace and Human Rights, another network that played a key role in the election-monitoring campaign.

Leipzig's Solidarity Church, a group with 15–20 members in 1988, participated in various Leipzig group actions and programs. As cofounder and leader of the Working Group Solidarity Church in Leipzig,[676] Edgar Dusdal, with his deputy Bernd Oehler, worked closely with oppositional groups in Leipzig. Many members of Solidarity Church were linked through multiple memberships in various groups and networks. Oehler and Rainer Müller, another member of Solidarity Church, were both members of the Leipzig oppositional human rights group Working Circle Justice, one of the organizing groups for Leipzig's election-monitoring campaign. Solidarity Church-Leipzig had also participated in the organizing committee for the peace prayers at Nikolai Church from its beginning and in 1988 signed the group letter to Bishop Hempel protesting the exclusion of groups from the peace prayers.

Ten Days of Peace (*Friedensdekaden*)

The Ten Days of Peace meetings tied together peace and other grassroots groups from throughout East Germany, and a number of Leipzig groups and their members participated. The meetings, held in churches in various cities, were organized around a new theme every year, and individual groups prepared information and exhibits on some current aspects of the theme.[677] Themes in the 1980s included "create peace without weapons" and "peace grows out of justice."[678] Leipzig's Working Group Social Peace Service had regularly assumed organizational responsibilities for the meetings.

An important informational and coordinative structure for groups, Ten Days of Peace meetings provided intensive and extensive contact with group members from throughout East Germany. Held every year during the same week in November and lasting an entire week, the meetings could be counted on to regularly bring groups together. According to Heino Falcke, Erfurt provost and one of the church leaders most supportive of groups, preparation for the event was important for most East German groups, and the meetings provided a "crystallization point" for group work because representatives of almost all groups attended. During this ten-day period participants joined together for meals, lectures, entertainment, and action programs.[679]

Several other regularly scheduled East German-wide meetings provided group members the opportunity to meet face-to-face with others from across the country and to share information. For example, women's groups organized under church auspices from throughout East Germany also met together once a year.[680] While many participants in church-based women's organizations were quite conservative and uninterested in reform, some members of alternative grassroots groups did participate in the meetings. As they shared their ideas with others, the meetings helped to spread an awareness of ideas and issues for societal reform to a broader range of church members and more conservative groups.

Besides meetings at the national level, meetings also took place at the regional level. For example, all grassroots groups in the Saxony Church district, including peace, third world, environmental, and women's groups, were invited to meet together once a year.[681] These meetings, coordinated by the youth minister for the Saxony Church district, involved more than 80 grassroots groups.[682]

Ulrike Poppe lists many other types of meetings in addition to major gatherings of groups and organizations that spread Öffentlichkeit and fostered solidarity among groups and their members.[683] These appeared in Leipzig, Berlin, and most major East German cities during the late 1980s. Types of meetings and meeting places included peace and environmental libraries, cafes, exhibitions, informational meetings, blues masses, political prayer services, worship services, workshops, seminars, readings, literature evenings, films and videos, lectures, and much more.[684]

Samizdat and Other Publications

To counter state controls on information, groups also produced their own publications and distributed them—locally, regionally, and frequently throughout East Germany. These publications of various groups spread information about important group issues, activities, solidarity programs, etc., to members of their own groups as well as to other activists. Some were published under church auspices using the stamp "For Inner Church Use Only," which offered a measure of protection, while other *samizdat* publications were produced fully outside the church and therefore totally illegal.

The number and range of these group publications increased dramatically in the late 1980s. An objective of all was to create *Öffentlicheit* and to bring the various concerns of groups into the public arena. Almost all of these group publications promoted changes in the East German society and state, although the themes and demands varied, and their programs for change frequently brought them into conflict with church and state authorities that tried to prevent their publication and distribution.

Particularly important publications intended for groups throughout East Germany included the Berlin Environmental Library's *Umweltblätter,* the Initiative for Peace and Human Rights' *Grenzfall,* and several environmental publications including Green Network Ark's *Arche Nova* and Leipzig Working Group Environmental Protection's *Streiflichter.* The Leipzig newsletter *Kontakte,* edited by Brigitte Moritz, distributed throughout Leipzig and to others in East Germany, also provided group members with essential information about group activities.[685]

In a chapter on *samizdat* in his book on the East German opposition published after the revolution, Erhart Neubert provides an 11-page table listing almost 200 publications of East German alternative and oppositional groups and networks in East Germany in the 1980s.[686] The table lists 16 publications in

Leipzig alone, including the newsletters *Kontakte* and *Streiflichter,* which alone produced 60 separate issues. In addition to newsletters, various Leipzig groups published other documents to promote their goals and programs. For example, Working Circle Justice researched and published materials on the emigration problem and human rights, military service issues, a secret plan of the state to build an atomic power plant, and information about opposition groups in Czechoslovakia.[687] These publications were distributed in Leipzig through personal contact, at meetings of groups, and by mail to persons and groups in East Germany and abroad.

Initiative Group Living published a document on refusing military service in fall 1988 that was distributed to East German groups through the Ten Days of Peace meetings, and the group also published a report along with photographs of the street music festival.[688] Working together, several Leipzig groups documented the Pleisse march and pollution in the area in a report, *The Pleisse,* and other Leipzig alternative groups produced papers on a number of subjects. Artists and the cultural opposition in Leipzig also published several journals, all entailing multiple issues.[689] Additionally, Leipzig groups publicized their programs locally and organized specific events through the distribution of handbills, and they periodically used open letters to publicize their goals.[690]

Writing in 1988, Ulrike Poppe assessed the development of group publications and their impact on groups themselves and on the broader East German society.[691] As a steering committee member of Peace Concrete, the network that linked 325 groups, Poppe had a broad overview of the group scene throughout the country. Poppe noted, "Increasingly these journals are also appearing outside of the church—legitimate and necessary, but illegal."[692] She continued, "Repeatedly these publications, whether published with the '*inner church use*' mark or not, have been subjected to repressive measures by state authorities. There have been searches of church rooms (e.g., November 1987 at the Environmental Library in Berlin), arrests, fines, threats." Nevertheless, Poppe concluded, "I think one thing is certain: the process is no longer reversible. So many information journals can no longer be prohibited; so many authors, printers, distributers can't be imprisoned. Only five years ago such a situation was hardly imaginable."[693]

Citizen Movement Organizations and Independent Political Parties

Although still illegal at the time, East German-wide citizens movement groups (*Bürgerbewegungen*) and independent political parties began to publicly organize in August and September 1989. A number of important citizens organizations publicized their founding in relatively quick succession, and later in the fall most reorganized as political parties (see Table 8-1). These groupings represented another type of network that connected a broad range of individuals and groups within and among various regions in East Germany. Citizen movement organizations and political parties founded or expanded during the second half of 1989 included New Forum, Democracy Now, Democratic Awakening, the United Left, the Greens, and the Social Democratic Party.[694] Founded in 1986, Initiative for Peace and Human Rights, the most oppositional of these groupings, had already organized as a statewide citizens movement in March 1989.

Many of these organizations built upon previous group, church, and other contacts, and to some extent, they utilized preexisting communication networks. For example, a number of founding members of both Democratic Awakening and the Social Democratic Party were Evangelical pastors previously involved with critical or oppositional groups. Many members of New Forum and Democracy Now had previously been members of one or more oppositional or church-based grassroots groups, e.g., peace, environmental, or human rights groups.[695] The United Left consisted primarily of reform-minded Marxists and other left-leaning socialists. The existence of these earlier memberships, contact networks, and other connections—formal and informal, church-based and private—meant that much of the groundwork had already been laid for developing communication channels within these new organizations and connecting them to other groups throughout East Germany.

The founding of East German-wide citizens movements helped increase the momentum for fundamental changes in state and society. Founded with at least a core of persons who had previously been active in the political opposition, these citizen movement organizations incorporated many of the ideas and programs advocated by political and oppositional groups into their founding statements. Moreover, these organizations represented a further step in the campaign of political groups to promote *Öffentlichkeit* by making public statements and taking public action, as they organized and stepped into public view in spite of their illegal status. Through these public actions, the movement organizations moved away from the protection of the church, but they also set themselves on a more independent course, with fewer dangers of co-optation.

Many prominent Leipzig activists joined these statewide groupings, and at the same time they continued to promote demonstrations and other actions for democratic reforms through grassroots groups in Leipzig. My interviews with members of Leipzig oppositional groups and other materials document that a number of Leipzig oppositional and other group members participated actively in various newly formed social movement organizations and that a number served in leadership positions.

Leipzig group member Thomas Rudolph of Working Circle Justice was a key member of the East German-wide citizens group Initiative for Peace and Human Rights, and Michael Arnold of Leipzig's Initiative Group Living signed the founding document for the citizens group New Forum. Others, including Jochen Lässig, Edgar Dusdal, and Jürgen Tallig—who belonged to three very different Leipzig grassroots groups with links to many others—played central roles in regional organization of New Forum in Leipzig.

*   *   *

Like the earlier oppositional groups from which they emerged, these citizens organizations followed similar patterns. They were generally broad-based and attempted to attract members from a wide range of individuals and other groups in East Germany. Although members of many of these groups and movements came from within the church or from church-supported groups, the organizations were clearly separate from the church and took on their own unique forms. At the founding of the Social Democratic Party on October 7, 1989, spokesman and cofounder of the party and Evangelical pastor Markus Meckel stated, "With this initiative we have left the church *[den Raum der Kirche]*. Personally, I have not left the church, but the space for this kind of political activity is society."[696]

The various parties and movement organizations were distinct from each other, and as a result, these differentiated groups appealed to diverse parts of the broader populace. New Forum viewed itself as a mass movement and directed its appeals to varied segments of the population. In contrast, Initiative for Peace and Human Rights did not view itself as a mass movement but targeted a narrower audience and demanded "a high degree of commitment and active participation" from its members.[697] Democratic Awakening appealed especially to pastors and committed church members, while the Greens attracted East Germans concerned about the environment.[698]

All of these organizations pointed to the need for fundamental reforms in East Germany and directed their appeals to the broad East German population dissatisfied with conditions as they were. Moreover, despite their separate status, these groups also emphasized general areas of agreement concerning basic ideas and beliefs in joint appeals to the East German public. These organizations attempted to coordinate their actions, and most of these movement groups and parties, along with representatives of a number of peace groups, signed a "Common Declaration" emphasizing their common goals.

Because of differences within and among organizations—involving goals, methods, tactics, and personalities—this coordination had its shortcomings. In a telephone interview in early October 1989 Bärbel Bohley, a leading oppositional figure and spokeswoman for the citizens group New Forum, said that she did not believe that there would be a union of the various opposition groups in East Germany because they had different goals. The common ground was that they all wanted to change things and were making the same demands.[699] As Bohley's statement suggests, the citizens movement organizations were connected primarily through a core of basic ideas and shared beliefs that served as a loose coordination mechanism.

The most successful of the citizens movement groups, New Forum, would become the largest citizens group in East Germany before the end of the year. Following an earlier announcement of intent, over the weekend of September 9–10 30 opposition members from across East Germany founded New Forum and signed and publicized an appeal, "Departure '89," calling for dialogue and democratic reforms. Although neither New Forum nor other citizens groups were initially recognized by the East German state, especially New Forum managed to attract relatively broad-based popular support. Initiatives and petition drives throughout East Germany called for the legalization of New Forum. At demonstrations across the country, protestors called out "New Forum," and signs for the legalization of New Forum appeared with increasing frequency during Leipzig's Monday night demonstrations. By October 14 New Forum already had a membership of 25,000, and membership would reach 200,000 by the end of the year.[700] Although New Forum did not have a firm program but rather called for dialogue among East German citizens, it represented opposition or an alternative to the system as it was and symbolized the desire for change. Detlef Pollack, chronicler of the opposition, especially in Leipzig, characterized New Forum as "a symbol for the coming together of the population against the communist party."[701]

New Forum's development in Leipzig and in Saxony illustrates how this mass movement spread throughout the region, involving diverse groups and individuals from various localities. The quick and dramatic growth of New Forum in Leipzig and the surrounding area (See Chapter 8.) also helps us understand how the massive demonstrations—growing larger almost every Monday night in Leipzig—were possible, and how, in Leipzig, a city of half a million people 500,000 people could take to the streets, demanding democratic changes. The growth of New Forum illustrates how these demonstrations could spread from city to city, from region to region, and ultimately throughout the entire country.

Together, New Forum and the other newly established citizens movement groups played a huge role in creating a broader movement culture throughout East Germany. They helped to legitimize opposition to the state and communist party leadership and to mobilize broad segments of the population. Central to this movement culture were action programs that pushed these movement groups into the political arena. The cumulative effect of various ideas, programs, and actions stemming from all these heterogeneous groups—parts of a diversified social movement—contributed immensely to the mobilization of a mass movement and to the revolution of 1989 in East Germany.

Spreading a Social Movement:
Diffusion of Innovation

D iffusion of innovation, particularly as it relates to the role of ideas and to the communication process, is especially relevant for explaining how ideas important to a social movement develop and spread among activists, to other groups, and beyond to mobilize the broader population. In diffusion of innovation or cultural diffusion literature as it relates to social movements, ideas or social movements are the innovations, and political groups help explain how a shared perception concerning ideas develops and is translated into grievances. Diffusion also helps explain how a social movement spreads to other groups and beyond during the mobilization phase, in part through influential leaders as well as through other channels such as the media. Diffusion also sheds light on the cross-national and cross-cultural spread of ideas and movements.

An early work that influenced much of the later work on diffusion is Everett M. Rogers' *Diffusion of Innovation*.[702] Rogers identifies four crucial elements in the diffusion process: "(1) the *innovation*, (2) its *communication* from one individual to another (3) in a *social system* (4) over *time*."[703] He defines *innovation* as "ideas perceived as new by the individual," noting that it does not matter whether an idea is "objectively" new, and *diffusion* as "the process by which an innovation spreads."[704] The *social system* includes individuals who are functionally differentiated,[705] and adoption decisions are made *over time*.

McAdam and Rucht argue that to make a case for diffusion of social movements, three facts must be established: (1) the *temporal sequence* must support the case, with the transmitter preceding the adopter in time; (2) the two movements share identifiable *common elements*; and (3) the *channels of diffusion* can be specified and documented empirically.[706] Building on these factors specified by McAdam and Rucht,[707] my work on the East German revolution emphasizes that ideas provide a common element linking a wide variety of groups and individuals in a social movement.[708] This study looks at how ideas come to be held in common, the channels that serve to spread the ideas both cross-nationally and domestically, and the time and developmental aspects involved in the construction of ideas and the mobilization of a movement.

Diffusion helps explain how a grassroots movement spreads from a relatively small group of activists and followers to a mass movement involving widespread participation.[709] In part, the spread of an innovation beyond a small group involves an extension of ideas important to the movement from "innovators," activists viewed as marginal to the broader community, to "key communicators" and "influentials," persons generally more conservative and less willing to adopt new ideas or innovations, but whose opinion is listened to and who are respected by a broad spectrum of the community.[710]

Analyzing the channels through which ideas and other relevant information spread provides insights into the mobilization phase of a social movement as well as into its earlier development. In East Germany, the ecumenical Conciliar Process for Peace, Justice, and the Preservation of Creation spread and legitimized ideas previously held primarily by group members to a large proportion of the church population. Also, in Leipzig, the participation of Kurt Masur, then the acclaimed director of the Leipzig symphony and later of the New York Philharmonic, and other respected Leipzig leaders prior to the October 9, 1989, demonstration, when the state threatened to use whatever force necessary to contain the demonstrators, helped to legitimate the Leipzig protests for a broader segment of the population.

The mass media provides an additional communication channel that is particularly useful for both the spread of relevant ideas and the mobilization of a social movement, because it enables individuals or small groups to reach a larger audience.[711] In this respect, global communications play increasingly important roles in social movements, particularly where the state controls access to the domestic mass media. The mass media's contribution to the diffusion process involves providing knowledge about an idea or innovation and can help explain movement activity in geographically distant locations.

Diffusion represents a central concept for explaining the emergence, development, and spread of social movements. In part, the diffusion of ideas through broad-based organizations helps explain how ideas spread, as they did in East Germany through the Evangelical Church and other churches, e.g., through the ecumenical Conciliar Process. Diffusion also helps explain how an oppositional identity was created and spread in Leipzig, first among activists and later more broadly throughout East Germany and beyond.

Spreading the Movement for Democracy

How did the grassroots movement for democracy in Leipzig spread from a relatively small group of activists and followers in early fall 1989 to involve a huge popular base of supporters? In part, the spread involved the diffusion of the ideas and activities important to the movement from *activists* viewed as marginal to the broader population to *community leaders* generally more conservative and less willing to adopt new ideas or innovations but who were listened to and respected by a broad spectrum of the community.

The Connectors

Malcolm Gladwell has popularized diffusion of innovation theory in *The Tipping Point: How Little Things Can Make a Big Difference.*[712] In his book Gladwell points to certain types of persons with special gifts who play roles in spreading innovations, ideas, or movements: Mavens, Connectors, and Salesmen.[713] Although Gladwell looks at these persons as spreading innovations through the broader community, they can also carry out the same functions within and among groups and the activist community.

Mavens are the idea people. They accumulate knowledge and control information.[714] Within Leipzig groups Thomas Rudolph of Working Circle Human Rights was a Maven. He wrote many of the group initiatives and declarations and headed the media campaign of East German groups. Jochen Lässig of Initiative Group Living was also a Maven, particularly as he articulated the ideas of the movement for democratic reform verbally, first as he spoke up for oppositional groups in Leipzig during the peace prayers and demonstration. Later, he was a spokesman for the citizens movement New Forum, first in Leipzig and then regionally and beyond. Uwe Schwabe of Initiative Group Living was a Maven, too, particularly after the revolution as he compiled and distributed information, set up archives, wrote about group and movement ideas, and made materials available to researchers, authors, filmmakers, and the like after the revolution.[715]

Connectors take the ideas or innovation articulated by Mavens and spread them. Connectors "know lots of people" and have "a special gift for bringing the world together."[716] According to Gladwell, "The point about connectors is that by having a foot in so many different worlds, they have the effect of bringing them all together."[717] Among East German groups, Ulrike Poppe was a Connector. As a steering committee member of the important network Peace Concrete and through multiple group memberships and church connections, Poppe helped link various groups into the loosely connected East German movements for democratic reform. Christoph Wonneberger, oppositional pastor and group member, was also a connector both in Leipzig and throughout East Germany. In Leipzig, he was an "integration figure" and made Lukas Church available for a wide range of oppositional group meetings. He also had regional and East German connections to peace, draft resister, human rights, and other groups as well as connections to the network Peace Concrete and with oppositional pastors. Among Leipzig group members, Rainer Müller was also a Connector, with multiple group memberships in Leipzig and the Saxony region in peace, environmental, and human rights groups. He also had connections to East German-wide groups and networks, e.g., draft resisters, as well as to oppositional groups and movements in Eastern Europe.

In summer 1989, Leipzig groups still concentrated their efforts within the group milieu, although they were connected to most of the networks discussed above. However, by fall, the movement for democratic reform would spread to the broader community. Carried by other sets of "influentials"—other Mavens, Connectors, and Salesmen—they interpreted and spread movement ideas and helped incorporate a new set of supporters into the movement for democratic reform.

Diffusion of innovation theory contributes to our understanding of how ideas for democratic reforms spread from a handful of group members to involve millions of supporters in mass demonstrations throughout East Germany. It provides insights about how contagious ideas spread throughout a society. The example of Matthias Sengewald, a group member and church worker, illustrates how innovations, ideas, and information can spread from one area to another as well as throughout a community.

The Example of Matthias Sengewald

The involvements of Matthias Sengewald illustrate the interlocking web of connections among members actively engaged in groups and movements at the local, regional, state, and international levels.[718] In the case of Sengewald, these connections occurred primarily within church structures. A proponent of a reformed socialism, Sengewald joined oppositional groups and participated in oppositional activities throughout East Germany. He felt that to save socialism, it was necessary to change the state and the conditions within the country.

Sengewald earlier lived in Leipzig, but in 1986 he moved to Erfurt. In Leipzig, Sengewald had been active in church and group programs and served as staff for the Evangelical Church's Youth Bureau. He had been a member of Leipzig's Working Group Peace Service, and his wife had belonged to Leipzig's Women for Peace, an oppositional peace group that had sister groups in other cities, including Berlin and Halle. (Prior to that, Sengewald had worked outside the church, but after he refused military service, nonchurch employment was difficult to find.)

In Erfurt, Sengewald worked with the group City and Living Environment to save Erfurt's historic inner city, and he was well connected to church and personal networks in Erfurt, in Leipzig, and throughout East Germany. Through his work in Erfurt, which was supported by the church but not directly tied to church structures, Sengewald had links to other church workers, both clergy and lay, such as Helmut Hartmann, pastor at the Evangelical Mission in Erfurt. Sengewald also had a long history of involvement with peace groups, and in Erfurt he was associated with Working Group Nonviolence and the peace library at Michaelis Church. Sengewald's local connections extended beyond the groups with which he was directly involved, and persons from a variety of other groups mentioned him as someone playing an important role in relation to groups in Erfurt, e.g., Aribert Rothe, who worked with environmental groups, and Gerlinde Harbig, a Catholic who worked at the church's Ecumenical Bureau.[719] The peace prayer services in Erfurt, held every Thursday since 1978 at the Catholic Lorenz Church, also provided a network for conveying information and organizing events. In addition to his contacts with groups associated with the Evangelical Church and with Catholics and other Protestants through ecumenical connections, Sengewald maintained contacts with critical Marxists in Erfurt who had earlier participated in meetings to establish a Christian-Marxist dialogue. Sengewald characterized himself as "always doing something a little bit political, but within the church."[720]

Sengewald's regional contacts took place partly through the twice-yearly meetings of grassroots groups in Thuringia, the region that included Erfurt. In addition, he continued to keep in contact with group members in Leipzig, in Saxony. In my interviews in Leipzig when I mentioned I was also talking with group activists in Erfurt and Berlin, several persons suggested that I contact Matthias Sengewald.

Through his work in church-related positions and his involvement with peace and other issues, Sengewald had developed an extensive network of contacts with group members in East German-wide group and church activities. As a draft resister, he had connections with groups composed of both persons who had previously totally resisted military service and those who had served as construction soldiers. The groups met at least annually, and members continued to be intensively involved in peace work and to support others in East Germany wishing to resist military service. The church's youth work (*Jugendarbeit*) provided another East German-wide network of contacts for Sengewald, with staff and with group members, because most alternative groups were part of the church's youth program. Staff for youth work met together at least annually with their colleagues from throughout East Germany. Sengewald also had country-wide connections with others who worked in the church's advisory work (*Beratungsarbeit*) counseling youth about their options for military or alternative service, and he played a key role in organizing the first advisory meetings (*Beratertag*) in Thuringia.

Through his peace involvements Sengewald also had close connections with the East German-wide peace movement and other broad group networks. In three different years, Sengewald served in the leadership for the Ten Days of Peace workshops (*Friedensdekaden*). Sengewald ranked the Ten Days of Peace meetings, the network Peace Concrete, and the Conciliar Process as very important factors in influencing the activity levels of groups he worked with and the movements for change in East Germany.

In addition to face-to-face meetings, *samizdat* or church-supported group publications including *Umweltblätter* and *Arche Nova* from Berlin and *Kontakte* from Leipzig represented important connections for Sengewald with groups throughout East Germany and kept him informed about ideas and events in other regions.

Matthias Sengewald was a Connector. His contacts, both formal and informal, kept Sengewald tied into ideas and developments important to groups throughout East Germany. Sengewald's previous involvements in Leipzig and his connections with other outside groups, plus his integration into Erfurt groups and networks, served to loosely connect Erfurt into East German-wide group activities. These connections provided contacts with a wide variety of persons who, if not regularly and directly involved in oppositional activities, had at least participated in programs or action that in some ways opposed positions of the East German state.

The example of Matthias Sengewald illustrates how, through multiple and overlapping personal connections as well as through more formal networks, information spread from person to person, group to group, and community to community throughout East Germany. The information available through these channels included specific contact information about meetings, workshops, demonstrations, solidarity actions, and other events. In addition, information about various themes such as peace, conscientious objection to military service, environmental problems, human rights, and democratic reforms spread through these channels. In this way, a growing awareness of societal problems and the need for changes spread throughout East German group and church communities. These connections and this shared awareness provided communication channels and paved the way for the mass demonstrations during fall 1989 in Leipzig and throughout East Germany.

BIBLIOGRAPHY

A. Interviews by Author

Bohley, Bärbel. Berlin, 17 March 1992.

Böttger, Martin. Dresden, 14 April 1992.

Burghardt, Barbara. Erfurt, 6 April 1992.

Burghardt, Hermann-Josef (Knopf). Erfurt, 6 April 1992.

Cooper, Belinda. Berlin, 15 November 1991 and 23 November 1991.

DeHaas, Joachim. Berlin, 15 November 1991.

Elmer, Karin. Berlin, 25 February 1992.

Elmer, Konrad. Berlin, 25 February 1992.

Falcke, Heino. Erfurt, 10 April 1992.

Findeis, Hagen. Leipzig, 26 March 1992.

Fischer, Werner. Berlin, 25 February 1992.

Gensichen, Hans-Peter. Berlin, 6 April 1992.

Glaeßner, Gert-Joachim. Berlin, 12 November 1991.

Grützmacher, Peter. Berlin, 18 February 1992.

Harbig, Gerlinde. Erfurt, 4 May 1992.

Hartmann, Helmut. Erfurt, 23 April 1992.

Hayner, Otto-Fritz. Berlin, 28 April 1991.

Heide, Gabriele. Leipzig, 24 March 1992, 5 November 1999, and 23 September 2009.

Hofmann, Michael. Leipzig, 23 March 1992.

Jahn, Roland. Berlin, 30 March 1992.

Jordan, Carlo. Berlin, 15 November 1991 and 11 March 1992.

Kallenbach, Gisela. Leipzig, 22 April 1992 and 13 March 2010.

Kloß, Oliver. Leipzig, 21 April 1992.

Kukutz, Irena. Berlin, 22 January 1992.

Ladstetter, Mathias. Erfurt, 23 April 1992.

Lässig, Jochen. Leipzig, 26 March 1992 and 25 September 2009.

Lietz, Heiko. Güstrow, 11 November 1999.

Lewek, Christa. Berlin, 10 February 1992 and 10 March 1992.

Magirius, Friedrich. Leipzig, 21 April 1992.

Mehlhorn, Ludwig. Berlin, 6 May 1992.

Metzner, Karl. Erfurt, 10 April 1992.

Moritz, Brigitte. Leipzig, 22 April 1992 and 23 September 2009.

Müller, Rainer. Leipzig, 24 March 1992, 21 April 1992, and 22 September 2009.

Müller, Silvia. Berlin, 27 January 1992.

Musigmann, Wolfgang. Erfurt, 23 April 1992 and 2 November 1999.

Neubert, Ehrhart. Berlin, 19 March 1992 and 16 February 1999.

Neumann, Ulrich. Berlin, 25 February 1992.

Nowak, Kurt. Leipzig, 23 March 1992.

Oltmanns, Gesine. Leipzig, 9 October 2013.

Pahnke, Rudi. Berlin, 6 May 1992.

Passarge, Andreas. Berlin, 28 April 1992.

Pollack, Detlef. Leipzig, 25 March 1992.

Poppe, Ulrike. Berlin, 3 March 1992.

Quester, Roland. Leipzig, 25 March 1992 and 23 September 2009.

Rink, Dieter. Leipzig, 25 February 1992.

Rothe, Aribert. Erfurt, 9 April 1992.

Rüddenklau, Wolfgang. Berlin, 27 January 1992.

Rudolph, Thomas. Dresden, 15 April 1992.

Schatta, Mario. Berlin, 16 March 1992.

Schefke, Siegbert. Dresden, 14 April 1992.

Schorlemmer, Friedrich. Weimar, 3 April 1992.

Schulz, Marianne. Berlin, 20 October 1991, 28 February 1992, 29 April 1992, and 1 May 1992.

Schwabe, Uwe. Leipzig, 22 April 1992, 5 November 1999, and 10 March 2010.

Sengewald, Matthias. Erfurt, 23 April 1992.

Templin, Regina (Lotte). Berlin, 6 May 1992.

Templin, Wolfgang. Berlin, 4 February 1992.

Truckenbrodt, Frank. Erfurt, 6 April 1992.

Ullmann, Wolfgang. Berlin, 26 February 1992 and 18 February 1999.

Walther, Kathrin. Leipzig, 24 March 1992.

Weißhuhn, Barbara. Erfurt, 4 May 1992.

Weißhuhn, Reinhard. Berlin, 4 February 1992.

Wonneberger, Christoph. Leipzig, 25 March 1992, 15 March 2010, and 11 October 2013.

B. Social Movements, Eastern Europe, and General Sources

Abel, Elie. *The Shattered Bloc: Behind the Upheaval in Eastern Europe.* Boston: Houghton Mifflin, 1990.

Albrow, Martin, and Elizabeth King, eds. *Globalization: Knowledge and Society: Readings from International Sociology.* Newbury Park, CA: Sage Publications, 1990.

Alinsky, Saul D. *Rules for Radicals: A Pragmatic Primer for Realistic Radicals.* New York: Vintage Books, 1989.

Almond, Gabriel A., and James S. Coleman. *The Politics of Developing Areas.* Princeton, NJ: Princeton University Press, 1960.

Almond, Gabriel A., and G. Bingham Powell. *Comparative Politics: A Developmental Approach.* Boston: Little, Brown and Co., 1966.

Amnesty International. *Der regionale Menschenrechtsschutz in Afrika, Amerika und Europa.* Frankfurt am Main: Fischer Taschenbuch Verlag GmbH, 1988.

Anderson, Benedict. *Imagined Communities: Reflections on the Origin and Spread of Nationalism.* New York: Verso, 1983.

Applebaum, Anne. *Iron Curtain: The Crushing of Eastern Europe, 1944–1956.* New York: Doubleday, 2012.

Arato, Andrew. "Interpreting 1989." *Social Research* 60, no. 3 (fall 1993): 609–646.

Ascherson, Neal. *The Polish August: The Self-Limiting Revolution.* Middlesex: Penguin, 1981.

Ash, Timothy Garton. *The Magic Lantern: The Revolution of '89 Witnessed in Warsaw, Budapest, Berlin, and Prague.* New York: Random House, 1990.

_____. *The Polish Revolution: Solidarity.* New York: Vintage Books, 1985.

_____. *The Uses of Adversity: Essays on the Fate of Central Europe.* New York: Vintage Books, 1990 (originally published 1983).

Bahro, Rudolf. David Fernbach, trans. *The Alternative in Eastern Europe*. London: Verso, 1981. (Europäische Verlagsanstalt, 1977).

Bahro, Rudolf. Mary Tyler, trans. *Building the Green Movement*. Philadelphia: New Society Publishers, 1986.

Bahro, Rudolf. Gus Fagan and Richard Hurst, trans. *From Red to Green: Interviews with the New Left Review*. London: Verso, 1984.

Baloyra, Enrique A., ed. *Comparing New Democracies: Transition and Consolidation in Mediterranean Europe and the Southern Cone*. Boulder, CO: Westview, 1987.

Banac, Ivo, ed. *Eastern Europe in Revolution*. Ithaca, NY: Cornell University Press, 1992.

Barry, Charles L., ed. *The Search for Peace in Europe: Perspectives from NATO and Eastern Europe*. Washington, DC: National Defense University Press, 1993.

Benn, David Wedgwood. *From Glasnost to Freedom of Speech: Russian Openness and International Relations*. New York: Council on Foreign Relations Press, 1992.

Bermeo, Nancy, ed. *Liberalization and Democratization: Change in the Soviet Union and Eastern Europe*. Baltimore: Johns Hopkins University Press, 1991.

Bermeo, Nancy. "Rethinking Regime Change." Review Article, *Comparative Politics* 22, no. 3 (April 1990): 359–377.

Betz, Hans-Georg. *Postmodern Politics in Germany: The Politics of Resentment*. New York: St. Martin's Press, 1991.

————. "Value Change in Postmaterialist Politics: The Case of West Germany." *Comparative Political Studies* 23, no. 2 (July 1990): 239–256.

Boggs, Carl. *Social Movements and Political Power: Emerging Forms of Radicalism in the West*. Philadelphia: Temple University Press, 1986.

Bonime-Blanc, Andrea. *Spain's Transition to Democracy: The Politics of Constitution-making*. Boulder, CO: Westview Press, 1987.

Boulding, Elise. *Building a Global Civic Culture: Education for an Interdependent World*. New York: Teachers College Press, 1988.

————. "The Old and New Transnationalism: An Evolutionary Perspective." *Human Relations* 44, no. 8 (1991): 789–805.

Brackley, Peter. *World Guide to Environmental Issues and Organizations*. Harlow, Essex, UK: Longman Group UK Limited, 1990.

Brinton, William M., and Alan Rinzler, eds. *Without Force or Lies: Voices from the Revolution of Central Europe in 1990*. San Francisco: Mercury House, 1990.

Brogan, Patrick. *Eastern Europe 1939–1989: The Fifty Years War*. London: Bloomsbury, 1990.

Bromke, Adam. *Poland: The Last Decade*. Oakville, Ontario, Canada: Mosaic Press, 1981.

Brown, Archie, ed. *Political Culture and Communist Studies*. London: The Macmillan Press, Ltd., 1984.

Brown, Archie, and Jack Grey, eds. *Political Culture and Political Change in Communist States*. New York: Holmes and Meier Publishers, Inc., 1979.

Brown, J.F. *Surge to Freedom: The End of Communist Rule in Eastern Europe*. Durham, NC: Duke University Press, 1991.

Bruns, Wilhelm, ed. *Die Ost-West-Beziehungen am Wendepunkt? Bilanz und Perspektiven*. Bonn: Verlag Neue Gesellschaft, 1988.

Bukowski, Charles J., and Mark A. Cichock, eds. *Prospects for Change in Social Systems: Challenges and Responses*. New York: Praeger, 1987.

Bunce, Valerie, and Dennis Chong. "The Party's Over: Mass Protest and the End of Communist Rule in Eastern Europe." Paper presented at the American Political Science Association annual meeting, San Francisco, CA, 30 August–2 September 1990.

Calhoun, Craig, ed. *Habermas and the Public Sphere*. Cambridge, MA: MIT Press, 1993.

Camiller, Patrick, and Jon Rothschild, trans. *Power and Opposition in Post-Revolutionary Societies*. London: Ink Links, 1979.

Cantor, Norman F. *The Age of Protest: Dissent and Rebellion in the Twentieth Century*. New York: Hawthorn, 1969.

Chalidze, Valery. *The Soviet Human Rights Movement*. New York: The American Jewish Committee, 1984.

Chatfield, Charles, and Peter van den Dungen, eds. *Peace Movements and Political Cultures*. Knoxville: University of Tennessee Press, 1988.

Chilcote, Ronald et al. *Transitions from Dictatorship to Democracy: Comparative Studies of Spain, Portugal, and Greece.* New York: Taylor and Francis, 1990.

Chirot, Daniel, ed. *The Crisis of Leninism and the Decline of the Left: The Revolutions of 1989.* Seattle: University of Washington Press, 1991.

Chong, Dennis. *Collective Action and the Civil Rights Movement.* Chicago: University of Chicago Press, 1991.

Clark, Susan L., ed. *Gorbachev's Agenda: Changes in Soviet Domestic and Foreign Policy.* Boulder, CO: Westview Press, 1989.

Claude, Richard Pierre, and Burns H. Weston, eds. *Human Rights in the World Community: Issues and Action.* Second Edition. Philadelphia: University of Pennsylvania Press, 1992.

Claudin, Fernando. *L'Opposition dans les pays du socialisme réel.* Paris: Presses Universitaires de France, 1983.

Cocks, Joan. *The Oppositional Imagination: Feminism, Critique, and Political Theory.* New York: Routledge, 1989.

Cohen, Jean. "Strategy or Identity: New Theoretical Paradigms and Contemporary Social Movements." *Social Research* 52, no. 4 (Winter 1985): 663–716.

The Conference on Security and Cooperation in Europe: An Overview of the CSCE Process, Recent Meetings and Institutional Development. Washington, DC: Commission on Security and Cooperation in Europe, 1992.

Coutin, Susan Bibler. *The Culture of Protest: Religious Activism and the U.S. Sanctuary Movement.* Boulder, CO: Westview Press, 1993.

Curry, Jane Leftwich, ed. *Dissent in Eastern Europe.* New York: Praeger Publishers, 1983.

_____. trans. and ed. *The Black Book of Polish Censorship.* New York: Vintage, 1984.

Dahl, Robert A. *Polyarchy: Participation and Opposition.* New Haven: Yale University Press, 1971.

Dalton, Russell J. *Citizen Politics in Western Democracies: Public Opinion and Political Parties in the United States, Great Britain, West Germany, and France.* Chatham, NJ: Chatham House Publishers, 1988.

Dalton, Russell J., and Manfred Kuechler, eds. *Challenging the Political Order: New Social and Political Movements in Western Democracies.* New York: Oxford University Press, 1990.

D'Anieri, Paul, Claire Ernst, and Elizabeth Kier. "New Social Movements in Historical Perspective." *Comparative Politics* 22, no. 4 (July 1990): 445–458.

Day, Alan J. *Peace Movements of the World.* Essex, UK: Longman Group UK Limited, 1991.

DeBardeleben, Joan. *The Environment and Marxism-Leninism: The Soviet and East German Experience.* Westview Special Studies on the Soviet Union and Eastern Europe. Boulder, CO: Westview Press, 1985.

Degenhardt, Henry W. *Revolutionary and Dissident Movements: An International Guide.* Essex, UK: Longman Group UK Limited, 1988.

Diamond, Larry, Juan J. Linz, and Seymour Martin Lipset, eds. *Democracy in Developing Countries.* Boulder, CO: Lynne Rienner Publishers, 1988.

Di Palma, Giuseppe. *To Craft Democracies: An Essay on Democratic Transitions.* Berkeley: University of California Press, 1990.

Donnelly, Jack. *Universal Human Rights in Theory and Practice.* Ithaca, NY: Cornell University Press, 1989.

Downs, Charles. *Revolution at the Grassroots: Community Organizations in the Portuguese Revolution.* Albany: State University of New York Press, 1989.

East, Roger. *Revolutions in Eastern Europe.* New York: Pinter Publishers, 1992.

Ehrmann, Henry W., ed. *Interest Groups on Four Continents.* Pittsburg, PA: University of Pittsburgh Press, 1958.

Eisinger, Peter. "The Conditions of Protest Behavior in American Cities." *American Political Science Review* 67 (March 1973): 11–28.

Epstein, Barbara. "Rethinking Social Movement Theory." *Socialist Review* 20 (1990): 35–66.

Eyerman, Ron, and Andrew Jamison. *Social Movements: A Cognitive Approach.* University Park: Pennsylvania State University Press, 1991.

Fantasia, Rick. *Cultures of Solidarity: Consciousness, Action, and Contemporary American Workers.* Berkeley: University of California Press, 1988.

Feldbrugge, F.J.M. *Samizdat and Political Dissent in the Soviet Union.* Leyden: A.W. Sijthoff, 1975.

Feldman, Elliot J. *A Practical Guide to the Conduct of Field Research in the Social Sciences.* Boulder, CO: Westview Press, 1981.

Finifter, Ada W., and Ellen Mickiewicz. "Redefining the Political System of the USSR: Mass Support for Political Change." *American Political Science Review* 86, no. 4 (December 1992): 857–874.

Finkle, Jason L., and Richard W. Gable, eds. *Political Development and Social Change.* New York: John Wiley & Sons, 1966.

Fitzpatrick, Catherine. *From Below: Independent Peace and Environmental Movements in Eastern Europe and the USSR.* New York: Helsinki Watch Committee, October 1987.

_____. *The Moscow Helsinki Monitors: Their Vision, Their Achievement, The Price They Paid, May 12, 1976–May 12, 1986.* New York: Helsinki Watch Committee, 1986.

Forsythe, David P. *Human Rights and World Politics.* Lincoln: University of Nebraska Press, 1989.

Foss, Daniel A., and Ralph Larken. *Beyond Revolution: A New Theory of Social Movements.* South Hadley, MA: Bergin and Garvey Publishers, Inc., 1986.

Foweraker, Joe. *Making Democracy in Spain: Grassroots Struggle in the South, 1955–1975.* New York: Cambridge University Press, 1979.

Fraser, Ronald. *1968: A Student Generation in Revolt.* New York: Pantheon, 1988.

Frederick, Howard H. *Global Communication and International Relations.* Belmont, CA: Wadsworth, 1993.

Friedgut, Theodore H. *Political Participation in the USSR.* Princeton, NJ: Princeton University Press, 1979.

French, Hilary F. *Green Revolutions: Environmental Reconstruction in Eastern Europe and the Soviet Union.* World Watch Institute: Worldwatch Paper 99, November 1990.

Fry, John. *The Helsinki Process: Negotiating Security and Cooperation in Europe.* Washington, DC: National Defense University Press, 1993.

Gamson, William. *The Strategy of Social Protest.* Second Edition. Belmont, CA: Wadsworth Publishing, 1990.

Gamson, William A., and Gadi Wolfsfeld. "Movements and Media as Interacting Systems." *Annals of the American Academy of Political and Social Science* 528 (July 1993): 114–125.

Garson, G. David. *Group Theories of Politics.* Sage Library of Social Research, 61. Beverly Hills: Sage Publications, 1979.

Gaventa, John. *Power and Powerlessness: Quiescence and Rebellion in an Appalachian Valley.* Urbana: University of Chicago Press, 1980.

Gerlach, Luther P., and Virginia H. Hine. *People, Power, Change: Movements of Social Transformation.* Indianapolis and New York: Bobbs-Merrill Company, Inc., 1970.

Gitlin, Todd. *The Whole World Is Watching: Mass Media in the Making and Unmaking of the New Left.* Berkeley: University of California Press, 1980.

Gladwell, Malcolm. *The Tipping Point: How Little Things Can Make a Big Difference.* New York: Back Bay Books, Little, Brown and Co., 2000.

Golan, Galia. *The Czechoslovak Reform Movement: Communism in Crisis, 1962–1968.* Cambridge: Cambridge University Press, 1971.

Goldstein, Judith, and Robert O. Keohane, eds. *Ideas and Foreign Policy: Beliefs, Institutions, and Political Change.* Ithaca: Cornell University Press, 1993.

Goldstone, Jack A., Ted Robert Gurr, and Farrokh Moshiri, eds. *Revolutions of the Late Twentieth Century.* Boulder, CO: Westview Press, 1991.

Goodwyn, Jeff. *No Other Way Out: States and Revolutionary Movement, 1945–1991.* Cambridge: Cambridge University Press, 2001.

Goodwyn, Lawrence. *Breaking the Barrier: The Rise of Solidarity in Poland.* New York: Oxford University Press, 1991.

————. "Organizing Democracy: The Limits of Theory and Practice." *Democracy* 1, no. 1 (January 1981): 41–60.

Gramsci, Antonio. Quinton Hoare and Geoffrey Nowell-Smith, ed. and trans. *Selections from the Prison Notebooks of Antonio Gramsci.* New York: International Publishers, 1971.

Gurr, Ted Robert. "The Revolution—Social-Change Nexus: Some Old Theories and New Hypotheses." *Comparative Politics* 5, no. 3 (April 1973): 359–392.

Gwertzman, Bernard, and Michael T. Kaufman, eds. *The Collapse of Communism.* New York: Random House, 1990.

Gyorgy, Andrew, and James Kuhlman, eds. *Innovation in Communist Systems.* Westview Special Studies on the Soviet Union and Eastern Europe. Boulder, CO: Westview Press, 1978.

Habermas, Jürgen. Thomas Burger, trans. *The Structural Transformation of the Public Sphere: An Inquiry into a Category of Bourgeois Society*. Cambridge, MA: MIT Press, 1991.

Hager, Carol J. "Environment and Democracy in the Two Germanies." Paper presented at the American Political Science Association annual meeting, San Francisco, CA, 30 August –2 September 1990.

Hahn, Jeffrey W. *Soviet Grassroots: Citizen Participation in Soviet Government*. Princeton, NJ: Princeton University Press, 1988.

Hall, Peter, ed. *The Political Power of Economic Ideas: Keynesianism across Nations*. Princeton, NJ: Princeton University Press, 1989.

Hankiss, Elemér. "The 'Second Society': Is There an Alternative Social Model Emerging in Contemporary Hungary?" *Social Research* 55, no. 1–2 (Spring/Summer 1988): 13–42.

Hanson, Russell L. *The Democratic Imagination in America: Conversations with Our Past*. Princeton, NJ: Princeton University Press, 1985.

Haraszti, Miklós. Katalin Landesmann and Stephen Landesmann, trans. *The Velvet Prison: Artists under State Socialism*. New York: Farrar, Straus, and Giroux, 1989.

Hauf, Volker. *Lokal Handeln: Ein politisches Fazit*. Köln: Kiepenheuer und Ulitsch, 1992.

Havel, Václav. Ed. Paul Wilson. *Open Letters: Selected Writings, 1965–1990*. New York: Vintage Books, Random House, 1992.

Heinrich, Hans-Georg. *Hungary: Politics, Economics, and Society*. Boulder, CO: Lynne Rienner, 1986.

Huntington, Samuel. *Political Order in Changing Societies*. New Haven, CT: Yale University Press, 1968.

Inglehart, Ronald. *Culture Shift in Advanced Industrial Society*. Princeton, NJ: Princeton University Press, 1990.

_____. "The Silent Generation in Europe: Intergenerational Change in Post-Industrial Societies," *American Political Science Review* 65, no. 4 (1971): 991–1017.

_____. *The Silent Revolution: Changing Values and Political Styles among Western Publics*. Princeton, N.J.: Princeton University Press, 1977.

_____. "Value Change in Advanced Industrial Societies," *American Political Science Review* 81, no. 4 (1987): 1289–303.

Jancar-Webster, Barbara, ed. *Environmental Action in Eastern Europe: Responses to Crises.* Armonk, NY: M.E. Sharpe, 1993.

Johnson, Chalmers. *Revolutionary Change.* Boston: Little, Brown, and Co., 1966.

Kamieniecki, Sheldon. *Environmental Politics in the International Arena: Movements, Parties, Organizations, and Policy.* Albany: State University of New York Press, 1993.

Kaldor, Mary, ed. *Europe from Below: An East-West Dialogue.* New York: Verso, 1991.

_____. *The New Detente.* New York: Verso, 1989.

Kelly, Petra. *Nonviolence Speaks to Power.* Honolulu: Center for Global Nonviolence Planning Project, 1992.

Keohane, Robert O., and Joseph S. Nye, eds. *Transnational Relations and World Politics.* Cambridge, MA: Harvard University Press, 1971.

_____. *Power and Interdependence: World Politics in Transition.* Boston: Little, Brown, 1977.

Key, V.O., Jr. *Politics, Parties, and Pressure Groups.* New York: Thomas Y. Crowell Co., 1964.

Kittrie, Nicholas N., and Ivan Volgyes, eds. *The Uncertain Future: Gorbachev's Eastern Bloc.* New York: Paragon House, 1988.

Kitschelt, Herbert. *The Logics of Party Formation: Ecological Politics in Belgium and West Germany.* Ithaca: Cornell University Press, 1989.

_____. "Political Opportunity Structures and Political Protest: Anti-Nuclear Movements in Four Democracies," *British Journal of Political Science* 16, no. 1 (January 1986): 57–85.

_____. "Political Regime Change: Structure and Process-Driven Explanations?" *American Political Science Review* 86, no. 4 (December 1992): 1028–1034.

Kitschelt, Herbert. Maurice Zeitlin, ed. "New Social Movements in West Germany and the United States." *Political Power and Social Theory* 5. A Research Annual. Greenwich, CT: JAI Press, 1985.

Klandermans, Bert. "Mobilization and Participation: Social-Psychological Expansions of Resource Mobilization Theory." *American Sociological Review* 49, no. 5 (October 1984): 583–600.

_____. "New Social Movements and Resource Mobilization: The European and American Approach." *International Journal of Mass Emergencies and Disasters* 4, no. 2 (August 1986): 13–37.

Klandermans, Bert, ed. *Organizing for Change: Social Movement Organizations in Europe and the United States.* International Social Movement Research: A Research Annual, vol. 2. Greenwich, CT: JAI Press, Inc. 1989.

Klandermans, Bert, Hanspeter Kriesi, and Sidney Tarrow, eds. *From Structure to Action: Comparing Social Movement Research across Cultures.* International Social Movement Research: A Research Annual, vol. 1. Greenwich, CT: JAI Press, 1988.

Klandermans, Bert, and Dirk Oegema. "Potentials, Networks, Motivations, and Barriers: Steps towards Participation in Social Movements." *American Sociological Review* 52, no. 4 (August 1987): 519–531.

Knabe, Hubertus. "Neue Soziale Bewegungen im Sozialismus: Zur Genesis alternativer politischer Orientierungen in der DDR." *Kölner Zeitschrift für Soziologie und Sozialpsychologie* 40 (1988): 551–569.

Knoke, David. *Political Networks: The Structural Perspective.* New York: Cambridge University Press, 1990.

Kochanek, Stanley A. "Perspectives on the Study of Revolution and Social Change." *Comparative Politics* 5, no. 3 (April 1973): 313–319.

Kohler, Beate. Frank Carter and Ginnie Hole, trans. *Political Forces in Spain, Greece, and Portugal.* Boston: Butterworth Scientific, 1982. Published in association with European Center for Political Studies.

Kolinsky, Eva, ed. *Opposition in Western Europe.* London: Croom Helm, 1987.

Kovrig, Bennett. *Of Walls and Bridges: The United States and Eastern Europe.* A Twentieth Century Fund Book. New York: New York University Press, 1991.

Kriesberg, Louis. Bronislaw Misztal and Janusz Mucha, eds. *Social Movements as a Factor in the Change of the Contemporary World.* Research in Social Movements, Conflicts, and Change, vol. 10. Greenwich, Conn.: JAI Press, 1988.

Kriesi, Hanspeter. "The Political Opportunity Structure of New Social Movements: Its Impact on their Mobilization." Abteilung Öffentlichkeit und soziale Bewegung, Wissenschaftszentrum Berlin für Sozialforschung (February 1991): 40 pages.

Laba, Roman. *The Roots of Solidarity: A Political Sociology of Poland's Working-Class Democratization.* Princeton, NJ: Princeton University Press, 1991.

Ladrech, Robert. "Social Movements and Party Systems: The French Socialist Party and New Social Movements." *West European Politics* 12, no. 3 (July 1989): 262–279.

Lane, Robert E. *Political Ideology: Why the American Common Man Believes What He Does.* New York: The Free Press, 1962.

Laqueur, Walter, and Robert Hunter, eds. *European Peace Movements and the Future of the Western Alliance.* New Brunswick, NJ: Transaction Books, 1985.

Lawson, Stephanie. "Conceptual Issues in the Comparative Study of Regime Change and Democratization." *Comparative Politics* 25, no. 2 (January 1993): 183–203.

Lebahn, Axel. "Political and Economic Effects of Perestroika on the Soviet Union and Its Relations to Eastern Europe and the West." *The International Spectator* 9, no. 2 (2004): 107–125.

Legters, Lyman H. *Eastern Europe: Transformation and Revolution, 1945–1991: Documents and Analyses.* Lexington, MA: D. C. Heath and Co., 1992.

Lewin, Moshe. *The Gorbachev Phenomenon: An Historical Interpretation.* Berkeley: University of California Press, 1988.

Lewis, Paul G. *Democracy and Civil Society in Eastern Europe.* Selected Papers from the Fourth World Congress for Soviet and East European Studies, Harrogate, 1990. New York: St. Martin's Press, 1992.

Lionberger, Herbert F. *Adoption of New Ideas and Practices.* Ames, IA: Iowa State University, 1960.

Lipschutz, Ronnie D., and Ken Conca, eds. *The State and Social Power in Global Environmental Politics.* New York: Columbia University Press, 1993.

Lipsky, Michael. "Protest as a Political Resource." *American Political Science Review* 62, no. 4 (1968): 1144–158.

Littell, Robert, ed. *The Czech Black Book.* New York: Avon, 1969.

Lohmann, Susanne. "A Signaling Model of Informative and Manipulative Political Action." *American Political Science Review* 87, no. 2 (June 1993): 319–333.

Ludmilla, Alexeyeva. *Soviet Dissent: Contemporary Movements for National, Religious, and Human Rights.* Middletown, CT: Wesleyan University Press, 1985.

MacIntyre, Alasdair. "Ideology, Science, and Revolution." *Comparative Politics* 5, No. 3 (April 1973): 321–342.

Malecki, E.S., and H.R. Mahood. *Group Politics: A New Emphasis.* New York: Scribners, 1972.

Mänicke-Gyöngyösi, Krisztina. "Sind Lebensstile politisierbar? Zu den Chancen einer 'zivilen' Gesellscarft in Ost- und Ostmitteleuropa," *Politische Vierteljahresschrift* 20, no. 30 (1989): 335–350.

Mannheim, Karl. Louis Wirth and Edward Shils, trans. *Ideology and Utopia: An Introduction to the Sociology of Knowledge.* New York: Harcourt Brace Jovanovich, 1985 (first published in 1936).

Markovits, Andrei S., and Philip S. Gorski. *The German Left: Red, Green, and Beyond.* New York: Oxford University Press, 1993.

Marks, Michael P. "Researching the Origins of Ideas in Foreign Policy: The Case of Spain." *International Studies Notes* 20, no. 1 (Winter 1995): 21–31.

Marx, Gary T., and Douglas McAdam. *Collective Behavior and Social Movements: Process and Structure.* Englewood Cliffs, NJ: Prentice Hall, 1994.

Mason, David S. "Glasnost, Perestroika, and Eastern Europe." *International Affairs* 64, no. 3 (Summer 1988): 431–448.

_____. *Revolution in East-Central Europe: The Rise and Fall of Communism and the Cold War.* Boulder, CO: Westview Press, 1992.

Mastny, Vojtech. *The Helsinki Process and the Reintegration of Europe, 1986–1991.* New York: New York University Press, 1992.

Mayer, Margit. "Social Movement Research and Social Movement Practice: The U.S. Pattern." Dieter Rucht, ed. *Research on Social Movements: The State of the Art in Western Europe and the USA,* 47–120. Boulder CO: Westview Press, 1991.

Mazrui, Ali A. *Cultural Forces in World Politics.* Portsmouth, NH: Heinemann, 1990.

McAdam, Doug. *Freedom Summer.* New York: Oxford University Press, 1988.

_____. *Political Process and the Development of Black Insurgency 1930–1970.* Chicago: University of Chicago Press, 1982.

McAdam, Doug, John D. McCarthy, and Mayer N. Zald. *Comparative Perspectives on Social Movements: Political Opportunities, Mobilizing Structures, and Cultural Framings*. New York: Cambridge University Press, 1996.

McAdam, Doug, John D. McCarthy, and Mayer N. Zald. "Social Movements." Neil J. Smelser, ed. *Handbook of Sociology,*695–737. Beverly Hills, CA: Sage Publications, 1988.

McAdam, Doug, and Dieter Rucht. "The Cross-National Diffusion of Movement Ideas." *Annals of the American Academy of Political and Social Science*, No. 528 (July 1993): 56–74.

McCann, Michael W. *Rights at Work: Pay Equity Reform and the Politics of Legal Mobilization*. Chicago: University of Chicago Press, 1994.

————. *Taking Reform Seriously: Perspectives on Public Interest Liberalism*. Ithaca, NY: Cornell University Press, 1986.

McCarthy, John D. "Resource Mobilization and Social Movements: A Partial Theory," *American Journal of Sociology* 82, no. 6 (1977): 1212–1241.

McCrea, Barbara P., Jack C. Plano, and George Klein, eds. *The Soviet and East European Political Dictionary*. Santa Barbara, CA: ABC-CLIO, 1984.

McLaughlin, Barry, ed. *Studies in Social Movements: A Social Psychological Perspective*. New York: The Free Press, 1969.

McLellan, David. *Ideology*. Minneapolis: University of Minnesota Press, 1986.

Meadows, Donella H. *The Global Citizen*. Washington, DC: Island, 1991.

Melucci, Alberto. "The New Social Movements: A Theoretical Approach." *Social Science Information* (SAGE) 9, no. 2 (1980): 199–226.

Melucci, Alberto. John Keane and Paul Mier, eds. *Nomads of the Present: Social Movements and Individual Needs in Contemporary Society*. Philadelphia: Temple University Press, 1989.

Menschenrechte in der Welt: Dokumentation. Bonn: Auswärtiges Amt, 1978.

Meyer, Alfred G. "Political Change through Civil Disobedience in the USSR and Eastern Europe," J. Roland Pennock and John W. Chapman, eds. *Political and Legal Obligation* 12: Yearbook of the American Society for Political and Legal Philosophy. New York: Atherton Press (1970): 421–439.

Michalowski, Bernhard, Christine Proske, and Günther Fetzer, eds. *Freiheit '90: Osteuropa im Aufbruch*. München: Wilhelm Heyne Verlag, 1990.

Michnik, Adam. Maya Latynski, trans. *Letters from Prison and Other Essays.* Berkeley: University of California Press, 1985.

Milbrath, Lester W. *Political Participation.* Chicago: Rand McNalley Co., 1965.

Ministerium für Auswärtige Angelegenheiten der Deutschen Demokratischen Republik. *Dokumente des KSZE Prozesses, 1973–1989.* Berlin: Staatsverlag der Deutschen Demokratischen Republik, 1990.

Miszlivetz, Ferenc. "The Unfinished Revolutions of 1989: The Decline of the Nation-State?" *Social Research* 58, no. 4 (Winter 1991): 781–804.

Misztal, Bronislaw, ed. *Poland after Solidarity: Social Movements versus the State.* New Brunswick, NJ: Transaction Books, 1985.

Modelski, George. "Is World Politics Evolutionary Learning?" *International Organization* 44, no. 1 (Winter 1990): 1–24.

Moe, Terry M. *The Organization of Interests: Incentives and the Internal Dynamics of Political Interest Groups.* Chicago: University of Chicago Press, 1980.

Moore, Barrington, Jr. *Injustice: The Social Bases of Obedience and Revolt.* Armonk, NY: M.E. Sharpe, 1978.

Morris, Aldon D. *The Origins of the Civil Rights Movement: Black Communities Organizing for Change.* New York: The Free Press, 1984.

Morris, Aldon D., and Cedric Herring. "Theory and Research in Social Movements: A Critical Review." Samuel Long, ed., *Annual Review of Political Behavior* 2, 138–198. Boulder, CO: Westview Press, 1988.

Morris, Aldon D., and Carol McClurg Mueller, eds. *Frontiers in Social Movement Theory.* New Haven: Yale University Press, 1992.

Mosse, George L. *The Nationalization of the Masses: Political Symbolism and Mass Movements in Germany from the Napoleonic Wars through the Third Reich.* New York: Howard Fertig, 1975.

Moxon-Brown, Edward. *Political Change in Spain.* New York: Routledge, 1989.

Müller-Rommel, Ferdinand, ed. *New Politics in Western Europe: The Rise and Success of Green Parties and Alternative Lists.* New Directions in Comparative and International Politics. Boulder, CO: Westview, 1989.

Naisbitt, John. *Megatrends: Ten New Directions Transforming Our Lives.* New York: Warner Books, Inc., 1982.

Naisbitt, John, and Patricia Aburdene. *Megatrends 2000.* New York: William Morrow and Co., 1990.

Neidhardt, Friedhelm, and Dieter Rucht. "The Analysis of Social Movements: The State of the Art and Some Perspectives for Further Research." Dieter Rucht, ed., *Research on Social Movements: The State of the Art in Western Europe and the USA*, 421–464. Boulder, CO: Westview Press, 1991.

Neubert, Ehrhart. "Religiöse Aspekte von Gruppen der Neuen Sozialen Bewegungen," *Berliner Journal für Soziologie* 3 (1991): 393–411.

Neue Soziale Bewegungen (Forschungsjournal) 3, no. 2 (1990). Sonderheft über Soziale Bewegungen und politischer Wandel im Osten.

Oberschall, Anthony. *Social Conflict and Social Movements*. Englewood Cliffs, NJ: Prentice-Hall, 1973.

————. *Social Movements: Ideologies, Interests, and Identities*. New Brunswick: Transaction Publishers, 1993.

O'Donnell, Guillermo, Philippe C. Schmitter, and Laurence Whitehead. *Transitions from Authoritarian Rule: Tentative Conclusions about Uncertain Democracies*. Baltimore: Johns Hopkins University Press, 1986.

Olson, Mancur. *The Logic of Collective Action: Public Goods and the Theory of Groups*. Cambridge: Harvard University Press, 1965.

Ostoja-Ostaszewski, A, et al. *Dissent in Poland: Reports and Documents in Translation, December 1975–July 1977*. London: Association of Polish Students and Graduates in Exile, 1977.

Overby, L. Marvin. "West European Peace Movements: An Application of Kitschelt's Political Opportunity Structure Thesis," *West European Politics* 13, no. 1 (January 1990): 1–11.

Papadakis, Elim. *The Green Movement in West Germany*. New York: St. Martin's Press, 1984.

Parkin, Sara, ed. *Green Light on Europe*. London: Heretic Books, 1991.

Pateman, Carole. *Participation and Democratic Theory*. New York: Cambridge University Press, 1970.

Pehe, Jiri. "An Annotated Survey of Independent Movements in Eastern Europe." *Radio Free Europe Research*. RAD Background Report 100 (13 June 1989).

Pestalozzi, Hans A., Ralf Schlegel, and Adolf Bachmann, eds. *Frieden in Deutschland: Die Friedensbewegung: wie sie wurde, was sie ist, was sie werden kann*. München: Wilhelm Goldmann Verlag, 1982.

Pinard, Maurice. *The Rise of a Third Party: A Study in Crisis Politics.* Englewood Cliffs, NJ: Prentice Hall, 1971.

Pipa, Arshi, ed. *Perestroika in Eastern Europe.* Special Issue: *Telos* 79 (Spring 1989).

Piven, Frances Fox, and Richard A. Cloward. *Poor People's Movements: How They Succeed and How They Fail.* New York: Vintage Books, 1977.

Presthus, Robert, ed. "Interest Groups in International Perspective." *Annals of the American Academy of Social and Political Science* 413 (May 1974).

Pridham, Geoffrey, and Pippa Pridham. *Toward Transnational Parties in the European Community.* London: Policy Studies Institute. Studies in European Politics 2 (May 1979).

————. *Transnational Party Co-operation and European Integration.* Boston: George Allen and Unwin, 1981.

Prins, Gwyn, ed. *Spring in Winter: The 1989 Revolutions.* Manchester: Manchester University Press, 1990.

Pye, Lucian W., and Sidney Verba, eds. *Political Culture and Political Development.* Princeton, NJ: Princeton University Press, 1965.

Raina, Peter. *Independent Social Movements in Poland.* London: London School of Economics and Political Science (distributed by Orbis books), 1981.

Rakowska-Harmstone, Teresa, ed. *Perspectives for Change in Communist Societies.* Westview Special Studies on the Soviet Union and Eastern Europe. Boulder, CO: Westview Press, 1979.

Ramet, Pedro, ed. *Religion and Nationalism in Soviet and East European Politics.* Durham, NC: Duke University Press, 1989.

Ramet, Sabrina Petra, ed. *Adaptation and Transformation in Communist and Post-Communist Systems.* Boulder, CO: Westview Press, 1992.

Ramet, Sabrina P. *Social Currents in Eastern Europe: The Sources and Meaning of the Great Transformation.* Durham, NC: Duke University Press, 1991.

Reich, Jens. "Intelligentsia and Class Power in Eastern Europe before and after 1989." *Aussenpolitik* 43, no. 4 (1992): 315–323.

Renon, Karin D. "Social Movement." William Outhwaite and Tom Bottomore, eds. *The Blackwell Dictionary of Twentieth-Century Social Thought,* 597–600. Cambridge, MA: Blackwell, 1993

Rensenbrink, John. *Poland Challenges a Divided World.* Baton Rouge: Louisiana State University Press, 1988.

Rogers, Everett M. *Diffusion of Innovations.* New York: The Free Press, 1962.

_____. *Diffusion of Innovations.* Third Edition. New York: The Free Press, 1983.

Rosenau, James N., ed. *The Scientific Study of Foreign Policy.* New York: Nichols, 1971.

_____. *The Study of Global Interdependence: Essays on the Transnationalisation of World Affairs.* New York: Nichols, 1980.

Rothfels, Hans. *The German Opposition to Hitler.* London: Oswald Wolff, 1961.

Rubenstein, Joshua. *Soviet Dissidents: Their Struggle for Human Rights.* Boston: Beacon, 1980.

Rucht, Dieter, ed. *Research on Social Movements: The State of the Art in Western Europe and the USA.* Boulder, CO: Westview Press, 1991.

Rudé, George. *Ideology and Popular Protest.* New York: Pantheon Books, 1980.

Rüdig, Wolfgang, ed. and compiler. *Anti-Nuclear Movements: A World Survey of Opposition to Nuclear Energy.* Essex, UK: Longman Group UK Limited, 1990.

Rustow, Dankwart A. "Transitions to Democracy: Toward a Dynamic Model." *Comparative Politics* 2, no. 3 (April 1970): 337–364.

Samisdat, Unabhängige Literatur in Osteuropa und der Sowjetunion. Köln: Stadtbibliothek Köln und Osteuropäisches Kultur- und Bildungs-Zentrum IGNIS, 1985.

Sanders, Robert E. "The Role of Mass Communication Processes in Producing Upheavals in the Soviet Union, Eastern Europe, and China." Sarah Sanderson King and Donald P. Cushman, eds. *Political Communication: Engineering Visions of Order in the Socialist World,* 143–162. Albany: State University of New York Press, 1992.

Saunders, George, ed. *Samizdat: Voices of the Soviet Opposition.* New York: Monad Press, 1974.

Schapiro, Leonard, ed. *Political Opposition in One-Party States.* New York: John Wiley and Sons, 1972.

Schattschneider, E. E. *The Semisovereign People: A Realist's View of Democracy in America.* New York: Harcourt Brace Jovanovich, 1975 (originally published 1960).

Scheingold, Stuart A. *The Politics of Rights: Lawyers, Public Policy, and Political Change.* New Haven: Yale University Press, 1974.

Schmitter, Philippe C. *Interest Conflict and Political Change in Brazil.* Stanford, CA: Stanford University Press, 1971.

Schöpflin, George, ed. *Censorship and Political Communication in Eastern Europe.* London: Frances Pinter, 1983.

Scott, Alan. *Ideology and the New Social Movements.* Boston: Unwin Hyman, 1990.

Scott, James C. *Domination and the Arts of Resistance: Hidden Transcripts.* New Haven: Yale University Press, 1990.

_____. *Weapons of the Weak: Everyday Forms of Peasant Resistance.* New Haven: Yale University Press, 1985.

Share, Donald. *The Making of Spanish Democracy.* New York: Praeger, 1986. Co-published with Center for the Study of Democratic Institutions.

Shipley, Peter. *Patterns of Protest in Western Europe.* Boston: Boston University, Institute for the Study of Conflict. Conflict Studies, no.189 (1986).

Sicinski, Andrzej, and Monica Wemegah, eds. *Alternative Ways of Life in Contemporary Europe.* Tokyo: The United Nations University, 1983.

Skilling, Gordon. "Interest Groups and Communist Politics Revisited." *World Politics* 36, no. 1 (October 1983): 1–27.

_____. *Samizdat and an Independent Society in Central and Eastern Europe.* Columbus: Ohio State University Press, 1989.

Skilling, Gordon and Franklyn Griffiths, eds. *Interests Groups in Soviet Politics.* Princeton, NJ: Princeton University Press, 1971.

Skocpol, Theda. *Social Revolutions in the Modern World.* New York: Cambridge University Press, 1994.

_____. *States and Social Revolutions: A Comparative Analysis of France, Russia, and China.* New York: Cambridge University Press, 1979.

Smith, Patricia J. "Contributions of the Conference on Security and Cooperation in Europe to the Democratization of Eastern Europe." Paper presented at the Women in International Security Studies Summer

Symposium, "Future Directions in International Security," Summer 1990.

_____. "The Environmental Movement in the Soviet Union." Paper presented at the Soviet and East European Studies Conference, Seattle: University of Washington, Spring 1990.

Smolla, Rodney A. *Free Speech in an Open Society.* New York: Alfred A. Knopf, 1992.

Snow, David A., and Robert D. Benford. "Ideology, Frame Resonance, and Participant Mobilization." Bert Klandermans, Kriesi, and Tarrow, eds. *From Structure to Action: Comparing Social Movement across Cultures,* 197–218. Greenwich, CT: JAI, 1988.

_____. "Master Frames and Cycles of Protest." Morris and Mueller, eds. *Frontiers in Social Movement Theory,* 133–155. New Haven: Yale University Press, 1992.

Snow, David A., E. Burke Rochford, Jr., Steven K. Worden, and Robert D. Benford. "Frame Alignment Processes, Micromobilization, and Movement Participation." *American Sociological Review* 51, no. 4 (August 1986): 464–481.

Solomon, Susan Gross, ed. *Pluralism in the Soviet Union: Essays in Honour of Gordon Skilling.* London: Macmiilan Press, 1984.

Spretnak, Charlene, and Fritjof Capra. *Green Politics.* Santa Fe: Bear and Co., 1986.

Starr, Harvey. "Democratic Dominoes: Diffusion Approaches to the Spread of Democracy in the International System." *Journal of Conflict Resolution* 35, no. 2 (June 1991): 346–381.

Stiefel, Matthias, and Marshall Wolfe. *A Voice for the Excluded: Popular Participation in Development: Utopia or Necessity?* London: Zed Books, 1994. Published in association with the United Nations Research Institute for Social Development, Geneva.

Stokes, Gale. *The Walls Came Tumbling Down: The Collapse of Communism in Eastern Europe.* New York: Oxford University Press, 1993.

Tarrow, Sidney. "'Aiming at a Moving Target': Social Science and the Recent Rebellions in Eastern Europe." *PS: Political Science and Politics* 24, no. 1 (March 1991): 12–20.

_____. *Power in Movement: Social Movements, Collective Action and Politics.* New York: Cambridge University Press, 1994.

_____. "Social Protest and Policy Reform." *Comparative Political Studies* 25, No. 4 (January 1993): 519–607.

_____. *Struggle, Politics, and Reform: Collective Action, Social Movements, and Cycles of Protest.* Western Societies Program. Occasional Paper no. 21. Ithaca, NY: Center for International Studies, Cornell University, 1991.

_____. *Struggling to Reform: Social Movements and Policy Change During Cycles of Protest.* Western Societies Program. Occasional Paper no. 15. Ithaca, NY: Center for International Studies, Cornell University, 1983.

Taylor, Michael. "Rationality and Revolutionary Collective Action." Michael Taylor, ed. *Rationality and Revolution*, 63–97. Cambridge: Cambridge University Press, 1988.

_____. "Structure, Culture, and Action in the Explanation of Social Change," *Politics and Society* 17, no. 2 (1989): 115–162.

Tilly, Charles. *From Mobilization to Revolution.* New York: Random House, 1978.

Tilly, Lousie A., and Charles Tilly, eds. *Class Conflict and Collective Action.* Beverly Hills: Sage Publications, 1981.

Tismaneanu, Vladimir, ed. *In Search of Civil Society: Independent Peace Movements in the Soviet Bloc.* New York: Routledge, 1990.

Tismaneanu, Vladimir. *Reinventing Politics: Eastern Europe from Stalin to Havel.* New York: The Free Press, 1992.

Toffler, Alvin. *The Third Wave.* New York: Bantam Books, 1980.

Tökés, Rudolf L., ed. *Dissent in the USSR: Politics, Ideology, and People.* Baltimore: Johns Hopkins University Press, 1975.

_____. *Opposition in Eastern Europe.* London: Macmillan, 1979.

Touraine, Alain, Francois Dubet, Michel Wieviorka, and Jan Strzelecki. Trans. David Denby. *Solidarity: The Analysis of a Social Movement: Poland 1980–1981.* New York: Cambridge University Press, 1983.

Triska, Jan F., and Paul M. Cocks, eds. *Political Development in Eastern Europe.* Praeger Special Studies in International Politics and Government. New York: Praeger, 1977.

United Nations. *The International Bill of Human Rights*. New York: United Nations, 1985.

Volgyes, Ivan. *Political Socialization in Eastern Europe: A Comparative Framework*. New York: Praeger Publishers, 1975.

Volgyes, Ivan, ed. *Social Deviance in Eastern Europe*. Boulder, CO: Westview Press, 1978.

Waller, Michael. *Peace, Power and Protest: Eastern Europe in the Gorbachev Era*. London: Institute for the Study of Conflict. Conflict Studies, no. 209, 1988.

Wasserstrom, Jeffrey N., and Elizabeth J. Perry. *Popular Protest and Political Culture in Modern China: Learning from 1989*. Politics in Asia and the Pacific: Interdisciplinary Perspectives, Haruhiro Fukui, series editor. Boulder, CO: Westview Press, 1992.

Weigel, George. *The Final Revolution: The Resistance Church and the Collapse of Communism*. New York: Oxford University Press, 1992.

Whetten, Lawrence L. *Interaction of Political and Economic Reforms within the East Bloc*. New York: Crane Russak, 1989.

Wiarda, Howard J. *Transcending Corporatism? The Portuguese System and the Revolution of 1974*. Institute of International Studies, University of South Carolina, Essay Series no. 3. 1976.

————. *The Transition to Democracy in Spain and Portugal*. Washington, DC: American Enterprise Institute for Public Policy Research, 1989.

Willetts, Peter, ed. *Pressure Groups in the Global System: The Transnational Relations of Issue-Oriented Non-Governmental Organizations*. London: Francis Pinter, 1972.

Wilson, James Q. *Political Organizations*. New York: Basic Books, 1973.

Winch, Peter. *The Idea of a Social Science and Its Relation to Philosophy*. London: Routledge and Kegan Paul, 1958.

Wiseman, H.V. *Political Systems: Some Sociological Approaches*. New York: Fredrick A. Praeger, 1966.

Wolin, Sheldon, S. "The Politics of the Study of Revolution." *Comparative Politics* 5, no. 3 (April 1973): 343–358.

Woods, Lawrence T. "Non-Governmental Organizations and the United Nations System: Reflecting upon the Earth Summit Experience." *International Studies Notes* 18, no. 1 (Winter 1993): 9–15.

Wronski, Tadeusz. *A Troubled Transition: Poland's Struggle for Pluralism.* London: Institute for European Defence and Strategic Studies, Alliance Publishers, European Security Study, no. 9, 1990.

Young, Crawford, ed. *The Rising Tide of Cultural Pluralism: The Nation-State at Bay?* Madison: University of Wisconsin Press, 1993.

Zald, Mayer N., and Roberta Ash. "Social Movement Organization: Growth, Decay and Change." *Social Forces* 44, no. 1 (September 1965): 327–340.

Ziegler, Charles E. *Environmental Policy in the USSR.* Amherst: University of Massachusetts Press, 1987.

Ziegler, Harmon. *Interest Groups in American Society.* Englewood Cliffs, NJ: Prentice-Hall, 1964.

Zinner, Paul E., ed. *National Communism and Popular Revolt in Eastern Europe: A Selection of Documents on Events in Poland and Hungary, February–November, 1956.* New York: Columbia University Press, 1956.

Zuzowski, Robert. *Political Dissent and Opposition in Poland: The Workers' Defense Committee "KOR."* Westport, CT: Praeger, 1992.

C. Sources on Groups, the Church, and Change in East Germany

Abgeordnetengruppe Bündnis 90/DIE GRÜNEN im Bundestag, eds. *Ein Jahr Bündnis 90/DIE GRÜNEN im Bundestag.* Bonn: Bundeshaus, Februar 1992.

Ahbe, Thomas, Michael Hofmann, and Volker Stiehler, eds. *Wir bleiben hier! Erinnerungen an den Leipziger Herbst '89.* Leipzig: Gustav Kiepenheuer Verlag, 1999. Albrecht, Jannette, et al., eds. *Stattbuch Ost: Adieu DDR oder die Liebe zur Autonomie: ein Wegweiser durch die Projektlandschaft.* Berlin: Stattbuch Verlag, 1991.

Allen, Bruce. *Germany East: Dissent and Opposition.* Montreal: Black Rose, 1991.

Ammer, Thomas. "The Emerging Democratic Party System in the GDR." *Außenpolitik* 41, no. 4 (1990): 377–389.

Arbeitsgruppe Menschenrechte and Arbeitskreis Gerechtigkeit, eds. (Kathrin Walther, Thomas Rudolph, and Frank Wolfgang Sonntag). "Was war los in Leipzig?" *Die Mücke: Dokumentation der Ereignisse: Leipzig*

Chronik vom 13. Februar bis 5. September 1988, Part I (Leipzig: *Samizdat,* March 1989), 1–7, published in *Ost-West-Diskussionsforum* 6 (April 1989), 8–11. *Leipzig Chronik vom 11. September bis 27. Januar,* Part II (Leipzig: *Samizdat,* March 1989), 7–17, published in *Ost-West-Diskussionsforum* 7 (June 1989), 7–10. *Leipzig Chronik vom 23. Februar bis 29. Mai 1989,* Part III (Leipzig: *Samizdat,* June 1989) published in *Ost-West-Diskussionsforum* 8/9 (October 1989), 14–15. *Leipzig Chronik vom 4. Juni bis 4. September 1989,* Part IV (Leipzig: *Samizdat,* September 1989) published in *Ost-West-Diskussionsforum* 10 (February 1990), 18–20.

Asmus, Ronald D. "Is There a Peace Movement in the GDR?" *Orbis* 27, no. 2 (Summer 1983): 301–341.

Bahrmann, Hannes, and Christoph Links, eds. *Bilderchronik der Wende: Erlebnisse aus der Zeit des Umbruchs 1989/90.* Berlin: Ch. Links Verlag, 1999.

Baister, Stephen, and Chris Patrick. *Guide to East Germany.* Bucks, England: Bradt, 1990.

Bartee, Wayne C. *A Time to Speak Out: The Leipzig Citizen Protests and the Fall of East Germany.* New York: Praeger, 2000.

Baumann, Eleonore, et al. *Der Fischer Weltalmanach. Sonderband DDR.* Frankfurt am Main: Fischer Taschenbuch Verlag, 1990.

Beleites, Michael. *Untergrund: Ein Konflikt mit der Stasi in der Uran-Provinz.* Berlin: BasisDruck Verlag, 1991.

Besier, Gerhard, and Stephan Wolf, eds. *"Pfarrer, Christen und Katholiken": Das Ministerium für Staatssicherheit der ehemaligen DDR und die Kirchen.* Second edition. Neukirchen-Vluyn: Neukirchener Verlag des Erziehungsvereins GmbH, 1992 (first edition 1991).

Blanke, Thomas, and Rainer Erd, eds. *DDR: Ein Staat vergeht.* Frankfurt am Main: Fischer Taschenbuch Verlag, 1990.

Bock, K. H. *DDR Transparent: Parlament, Regierung.* Bad Honnef: Verlag Karl Heinrich Bock, 1990.

Bódvai, Ildikó. Péter Sulányi, trans. "Paneuropäisches Picknick—der lautlose Aufschrei." Hans Kaiser, ed. *Norbert Lobenwein 89–90: Momente, die die Welt bewegten,* 19–21. Konrad Adenauer Stiftung. Budapest: Volt, 2009.

Bohse, Reinhard, et al. *Gewindet denen, die am 9. Oktober in Leipzig demonstri-erten*. Leipzig: Forum Verlag Leipzig, 1989.

Buescher, Wolfgang, Hans-Peter Wensierski, and Klaus Wolschner, eds. *Schw-erter zu Pflugscharen: Friedensbewegung in der DDR*. Vol. 2. Hattingen: Scandia Verlag, 1982.

Buhl, Susanne, and Tobias Gohlis. *Leipzig*. Ostfildern: DuMont Reiseverlag, 2009.

Bürger, Wolfram, and Michael Weichenhan, eds. *Wolfgang Ullmann: Demokratie—jetzt oder nie! Perspektiven der Gerechtigkeit*. München: Kyrill & Method Verlag, 1990.

Bürgerbewegungen für Demokratie in den Kommunen. Berlin: Staatsverlag der Deutschen Demokratischen Republik, 1990.

Bürgerkomitee Leipzig. *Stasi intern: Macht und Banalität*. Leipzig: Forum Ver-lag Leipzig, 1991.

Childs, David. *The GDR: Moscow's German Ally*. London: George Allen & Unwin, 1983.

Childs, David, Thomas A. Baylis, and Marilyn Rueschemeyer. *East Germany in Comparative Perspective*. New York: Routledge, 1989.

Childs, David, and Richard Popplewell. *The Stasi: The East German Intelligence and Security Service, 1917–89*. New York: New York University Press, 1996.

Club of Rome. *Die erste globale Revolution*. Spiegel Spezial 2, 1991.

Dale, Gareth. *The East German Revolution of 1989*. Manchester, UK: Manches-ter University Press, 2006.

Darnton, Robert. *Berlin Journal: 1989–1990*. New York: W.W. Norton and Co., 1991.

DDR Journal zur Novemberrevolution: August bis Dezember 1989. 2. Erweiterte Auflage. Die tageszeitung (taz). Berlin: Henke Pressedruck, 1989.

Dennis, Mike. *The Stasi: Myth and Reality*. London: Pearson Education Limited, 2003.

Deutsche Demokratische Republik: Handbuch. Leipzig: VEB Verlag Enzyk-lopädie, 1979.

Dieckmann, Friedrich, Annette Müller, et al. *Demo-Reminiszenzen: Friedens-feier, Gedichte, Ansprachen auf der Kundgebung des Neuen Forum am 18. November 1989 in Leipzig*. Berlin: Union Verlag, 1990.

Dietrich, Christian, and Uwe Schwabe, eds. *Freunde und Feinde: Dokumente zu den Friedensgebete in Leipzig zwischen 1981 und dem 9. Oktober 1989.* Leipzig: Evangelischer Verlag, 1994. Also online version.

Dittman, Uta, ed. *10 Jahre friedliche Revolution: Ein Weg der Erinnerung. Ausstellungskatalog.* Dresden: Sächsischer Landtag, 1999.

Dokumente des KSZE—Prozesses 1973–1989. Berlin: Staatsverlag der Deutschen Demokratischen Republik, 1990.

Draheim, Dirk, Hartmut Hecht, Dieter Hoffmann, Klaus Richter, and Manfred Wilke, eds. *Robert Havemann: Dokumente eines Lebens.* Berlin: Christoph Links Verlag, 1991.

Ehring, Klaus, and Martin Dallwitz. *Schwerter zu Pflugscharen.* Hamburg: Rowohlt Taschenbuch Verlag, 1982.

Elvers, Wolfgang, and Hagen Findeis. *Was ist aus den politischen alternativen Gruppen geworden? Eine soziologische Auswertung von Interviews mit ehemals führenden Vertretern in Leipzig und Berlin.* Unpublished thesis, Religionssoziologisches Institut Emil Fuchs an der Theologischen Fakultät der Karl Marx-Üniversität. Leipzig, 1990.

Falcke, Heino. *Die unvollendete Befreiung: Die Kirchen, die Umwälzung in der DDR und die Vereinigung Deutschlands.* Ökumenische Existenz Heute 9. München: Chr. Kaiser Verlag, 1991.

Fensch, Helmut, ed. *Olle DDR: Eine Welt von gestern.* Berlin: Henschel Verlag, 1990.

Findeis, Hagen, Detlef Pollack, and Manuel Schilling, eds. *Die Entzauberung des Politischen: Was ist aus den politisch alternativen Gruppen der DDR geworden? Interviews mit führenden Vertreten.* Leipzig: Evangelische Verlagsanstalt, 1994.

Fischbach, Günter, ed. *DDR-Almanach '90: Daten, Information, Zahlen.* Stuttgart: Verlag Bonn Aktuell, 1990.

Flemming, Thomas. *Die Berliner Mauer: Grenze durch eine Stadt.* Berlin-Brandenburg: be.bra Verlag, 2009.

Förster, Peter, and Günter Roski. *DDR zwischen Wende und Wahl: Meinungsforscher analysieren den Umbruch.* Berlin: LinksDruck Verlag, 1990.

Francisco, Ronald. "Leadership and the Crisis of State in the GDR." Paper presented at the American Political Science Association annual meeting. San Francisco, CA, August 1990.

Fricke, Karl Wilhelm. *Opposition und Widerstand in der DDR: Ein politischer Report.* Köln: Verlag Wissenschaft und Politik, 1984.

Fricke, Karl Wilhelm. "The State Security Apparatus of the Former GDR and Its Legacy." *Außenpolitik* 45, no. 2 (1994): 153–163.

Friedheim, Daniel V. "Bringing Society Back into Democratic Transition Theory after 1989: Pact Making and Regime Collapse." *East European Politics and Society* 7, no. 3 (Fall 1993): 482–512.

_____. "Regime Collapse in the Peaceful East German Revolution: The Role of Middle-Level Officials." *German Politics* 2, no. 1 (April 1993): 97–112.

Gauck, Joachim. With Margarethe Steinhausen and Hubertus Knabe. *Die Stasi-Akten: Die unheimliche Erbe der DDR.* Reinbeck bei Hamburg: Rowohlt Taschenbuch Verlag, 1991.

Gedmin, Jeffrey. *The Hidden Hand: Gorbachev and the Collapse of East Germany.* Washington, DC: AEI Press, 1992.

Glaeßner, Gert-Joachim. "Vom 'realen Sozialismus' zur Selbstbestimmung: Ursachen und Konsequenzen der Systemkrise in der DDR." *Aus Politik und Zeitgeschichte* 1–2, no. 5 (Januar 1990): 3–20.

Glaeßner, Gert-Joachim, and Ian Wallace, eds. *The German Revolution of 1989: Causes and Consequences.* Providence, RI: Berg, 1992.

Goeckel, Robert F. "The Luther Anniversary in East Germany." *World Politics* 37, no. 1 (October 1984): 112–133.

_____. *The Lutheran Church and the East German State: Political Conflict and Change under Ulbricht and Honecker.* Ithaca, NY: Cornell University Press, 1990.

Gohlis, Thomas. *Leipzig.* Köln: DuMont, 1998.

Grabner, Wolf-Jürgen, Christiane Heinze, and Detlef Pollack, eds. *Leipzig im Oktober: Kirchen und alternative Gruppen im Umbruch der DDR— Analysen zur Wende.* Berlin: Weichern, 1990.

Greenwald, C. Jonathan. *Berlin Witness: An American Diplomat's Chronicle of East Germany's Revolution.* University Park: Pennsylvania State University Press, 1993.

Grunenberg, Antonia. *Aufbruch der inneren Mauer: Politik und Kultur in der DDR, 1971–1990.* Bremen: Edition Temmen, 1990.

Harenberg, Bodo, ed. *Chronik '89: Die Wende in der DDR*. Dortmund: Chronik Verlag, 1989.

Haufe, Gerda, and Karl Bruckmeier, eds. *Die Bürgerbewegungen in der DDR und in den Ostdeutschen Bündesländern*. Opladen: Westdeutscher Verlag, 1993.

Heber, Norbert, and Johannes Lehmann, eds. *Keine Gewalt: Der friedliche Weg zur Demokratie: Eine Chronik in Bildern*. Berlin: Verbum Druck Verlagsgesellschaft, 1991.

Helwig, Gisela, and Detlaf Urban, eds. *Kirchen und Gesellschaft in beiden deutschen Staaten*. Edition Deutschland Archiv. Köln: Verlag Wissenschaft und Politik, 1987.

Hertel, Hans-Hermann. *Chronik des Mauerfalls: Die dramatischen Ereignisse um den 9. November 1989*. 11th edition. Berlin: Ch. Links Verlag, 2009.

Hildebrandt, Jörg, and Gerhard Thomas, eds. *Unser Glaube mischt sich ein. . . : Evangelische Kirche in der DDR 1989: Berichte, Fragen, Verdeutlichungen*. Berlin: Evangelische Verlagsanstalt, 1990.

Hildebrandt, Rainer. *From Gandhi to Walesa: Nonviolent Struggle for Human Rights*. Berlin: Verlag Haus am Checkpoint Charlie, 1987.

_____. *It Happened at the Wall*. 18th edition. Berlin: Verlag Haus am Checkpoint Charlie, 1992.

Hille, Barbara, and Walter Jaide. *DDR-Jugend: Politisches Bewußtsein und Lebensalltag*. Opladen: Leske und Budrich, 1990.

Hirsch, Ralf, and Lew Kopelew, eds. *Initiative Frieden und Menschenrechte: Grenzfall*. Berlin: Selbstverlag, 1989.

Hirschman, Albert O. "Exit, Voice, and the Fate of the German Democratic Republic: An Essay in Conceptual History." *World Politics* 45, no. 2 (January 1993): 173–202.

Hollitzer, Tobias, "'Heute entscheidet es sich: Entweder die oder wir'—zum 9. Oktober 1989 in Leipzig." *Horch und Guck* 7, no. 23 (1998 (2)), 22–37.

Hollitzer, Tobias, and Reinhard Bohse, eds. *Heute vor 10 Jahren: Leipzig auf dem Weg zur Friedlichen Revolution*. Fribourg/New York: InnoVatio Verlag, 2000.

Hollitzer, Tobias, and Sven Sachenbacher, eds. *Die Friedliche Revolution in Leipzig: Bilder, Dokumentation, und Objekte*, vols. 1 and 2. Leipzig: Leipzig Universität Verlag, 2012.

Holzapfel, Klaus-J. *Sächsischer Landtag: 1. Wahlperiode, 1990–1994: Volkshand-buch.* Rheinbreitbach: NDV Neue Darmstädter Verlagsanstalt, 1991.

Israel, Jürgen. *Zur Freiheit Berufen: Die Kirche in der DDR als Schutzraum der Opposition 1981–1989.* Berlin: Aufbau Taschenbuch Verlag, 1991.

James, Harold, and Marla Stone, eds. *When the Wall Came Down: Reactions to German Unification.* New York: Routledge, 1992.

Janka, Walter. *Schwierigkeiten mit der Wahrheit.* Berlin: Aufbau-Verlag, 1990.

Jankowski, Martin. *Der Tag, der Deutschland veränderte: 9. Oktober 1989.* Leipzig: Evangelische Verlaganstalt, 2007 (second edition, 2009).

Joas, Hans, and Martin Kohli, eds. *Der Zusammenbruch der DDR.* Frankfurt am Main: Suhrkamp, 1993.

Johnson, Carsten. *Massenmobilisierung in der DDR im Jahre 1989: Der Wandel der politischen Opportunitätsstruktur und die Dynamik des Massen-protestes.* Freie wissenschaftliche Arbeit zur Erlangung des Grades eines Diplom-Politologen, Freie Universität Berlin, Fachbereich Politische Wissenschaft, Berlin, Oktober 1992.

Jones, Merrill Elaine. *Greens under God and the Gun: The East German Envi-ronmental Movement, the Lutheran Church, and the East German State.* B.A. Honors Thesis, Harvard College, March 1991.

Joppke, Christian. *East German Dissidents and the Revolution of 1989: Social Movement in a Leninist Regime.* Washington Square, NY: New York University Press, 1995.

_____. "Why Leipzig? 'Exit' and 'Voice' in the East German Revolution." *German Politics* 2, no. 3 (December 1993): 393–414.

Jung, Heinz, and Fritz Krause. *Abschied von einer Realität: Zur Niederlage des Sozialismus und zum Abgang der DDR: Ein politisches Tagebuch—Som-mer 1989 bis Herbst 1990.* Frankfurt am Main: IMSF, 1990.

Kahlau, Cordula, ed. *Aufbruch! Frauenbewegung in der DDR: Dokumentation.* München: Verlag Frauenoffensive, 1990.

Kamenitsa, Lynn. "The Process of Political Marginalization: East German Social Movements after the Wall." *Comparative Politics* 3, no. 3 (April 1998): 313–333.

Keefe, Eugene K., ed. *East Germany: A Country Study.* Area Handbook Series. Washington DC: US Government Printing Office, 1982.

Keithly, David M. *The Collapse of East German Communism: The Year the Wall Came Down, 1989.* Westport, CT: Praeger, 1989.

Keller, Dietmar, and Matthias Kirchner, eds. *Biermann und kein Ende: Eine Dokumentation zur DDR-Kulturpolitik.* Berlin: Dietz Verlag, 1991.

Kleines Politisches Wörterbuch. Berlin: Dietz Verlag, 1988.

Knabe, Hubertus, ed. *Aufbruch in eine andere DDR: Reformer und Oppositionelle zur Zukunft ihres Landes.* Reinbek bei Hamburg: Rowohlt Taschenbuch Verlag, 1989.

————. "Politische Opposition in der DDR: Ursprünge, Programmatik, Perspektiven." *Aus Politik und Zeitgeschichte* 2, no. 90 (5 Januar 1990): 21–32.

Kolinsky, Eva. "Everyday Life Transformed: A Case Study of Leipzig since German Unification." *World Affairs* 156, no. 4 (Spring 1994): 159–174.

Komitee für Grundrechte und Demokratie, ed. *Freiheit, Gleichheit, Geschwisterlichkeit: Text zur außerparlamentarischen Arbeit der basispolitischen sozialen Bewegung, 1979–1989.* Sonderdruck für die Aktiven in den basisdemokratischen Friedens-, Umwelt- und Menschenrechtsgruppen und Sozialen Bewegungen in der DDR. Einhausen: hbo druck, 1990.

Konrad Adenauer Stiftung. *Norbert Lobenwein 89–90: Momente, die die Welt bewegten.* Budapest: Volt, 2009. Trans. from Hungarian to German. German editor, Hans Kaiser. Trans., Dr. Péter Sulányi.

Koordinierungsgruppe Wahlen, ed. "*Wahlfall 89: Eine Dokumentation,*" 1989.

Kreuzer, Markus. "New Politics: Just Post-Materialist? The Case of the Austrian and Swiss Greens." *West European Politics* 13, no. 1 (January 1990): 12–30.

Krisch, Henry. "Changing Political Culture and Political Stability in the German Democratic Republic." *Studies in Comparative Communism* XIX, no. 1 (Spring 1986): 41–53.

————. *The German Democratc Republic: The Search for Identity.* Boulder, CO: Westview Press, 1985.

Kroh, Ferdinand, ed. "*Freiheit ist immer Freiheit. . .': Die Andersdenkenden in der DDR.*" Berlin: Ullstein Sachbuch, 1988.

Kuhn, Ekkehard. *Der Tag der Entscheidung: Leipzig, 9. Oktober 1989.* Berlin: Verlag Ullstein, 1992.

Kuhn, Ekkehard. *"Wir Sind Das Volk!" Die friedliche Revolution in Leipzig, 9. Oktober 1989.* Berlin: Verlag Ullstein, 1999.

Kühnel, Wolfgang, Jan Weilgohs, and Marianne Schulz. "Die neuen Gruppierungen auf dem Wege vom politischen Protest zur parlamentarischen Interessenvertretung. Soziale Bewegungen im Umbruch der DDR-Gesellschaft." *Zeitschrift für Parlamentsfragen* 1 (1990): 22–37.

———. "Politische Opposition in der DDR: Urspringe, Programmatik, Perspektiven." *Aus Politik und Zeitgeschichte* 1–2 (1990): 21–32.

Kukutz, Irena, and Katja Havemann. *Geschützte Quelle. Gespräche mit Monika H. alias Karin Lenz.* Berlin: BasisDruck, 1990.

Kuran, Timur. "Now out of Never: The Element of Surprise in the East European Revolution of 1989." *World Politics* 44, no. 1 (October 1991): 7–48.

Land, Rainer, and Rolf Possekel. *Fremde Welten: Die gegensätzliche Deutung der DDR durch SED-Reformer und Bürgerbewegung in den 80er Jahren.* Berlin: Ch. Links, 1998.

Lange, Bernd-Lutz. *Gebrauchsanweisung für Leipzig.* München: Piper Verlag, 2008.

Lange, Horst, and Uwe Matthes. "Mit Vordenkern und Akteuren der Wende im Gespräch." *Deutschland Archiv* 23, no. 12 (December 1990): 1935–1941.

Langer, Kai. *"Ihr sollt wissen, daß der Norden nicht schläft. . . ." Zur Geschichte der "Wende" in den drei Nordbezirken der DDR.* Bremen, Rostock: Ed. Temmen, 1999.

Lasky, Melvin J. *Voices in a Revolution: The Collapse of East German Communism.* New Brunswick, NJ: Transaction Publishers, 1992.

Lehmbruch, Gerhard. "The Process of Regime Change in East Germany: An Institutionalist Scenario for German Unification." *Journal of European Public Policy* 1, no. 1 (June 1994): 115–141.

Leipziger Menschenrechtsgruppen 1989. *Heute vor 10 Jahren,* Papers 1–9. January–October 1999.

Lemke, Christiane. "New Issues in the Politics of the German Democratic Republic: A Question of Political Culture?" *Journal of Communist Studies* 2, no. 4 (December 1986): 341–358.

———. *Die Ursachen des Umbruchs 1989: Politische Sozialisation in der ehemaligen DDR.* Opladen: Westdeutscher Verlag, 1991.

Lewek, Christa, Manfred Stolpe, and Joachim Garstecki, eds. *Menschenrechte in christlicher Verantwortung.* Berlin: Evangelische Verlaganstalt, 1980.

Lieberwirth, Steffen. *Wer eynen spielmann zu tode schlaegt . . . Ein mittelalterliches Zeitdokument anno 1989.* Leipzig: Edition Peters, 1990.

Lindner, Bernd. *Die demokratische Revolution in der DDR 1989/90.* Bonn: Bundeszentrale für politische Bildung, 1998.

_____. "Die politische Kultur der Straße als Medium der Veränderung." *Aus Politik und Zeitgeschichte 17* (29 June 1990): 16–28.

Lindner, Bernd, and Ralph Grüneberger, eds. *Demonteure: Biographien des Leipziger Herbst.* Bielefeld: Aisthesis Verlag, 1992.

Links, Christoph, and Hannes Bahrmann. *Wir Sind das Volk: Die DDR im Aufbruch: Eine Chronik.* Wuppertal: Peter Hammer Verlag, 1990 (published earlier in DDR, Aufbau Verlag).

Lohmann, Susanne. "The Dynamics of Informational Cascades: The Monday Demonstrations in Leipzig, East Germany, 1989–91." *World Politics 47,* no. 1 (October 1994): 42–101.

Löw, Konrad, ed. *Ursachen und Verlauf der deutschen Revolution 1989.* Berlin: Duncker & Humblot, 1991.

Lutz, Peter C. *The Changing Party Elite in East Germany.* Cambridge, MA: MIT Press, 1972.

Lyons, Matthew Nemiroff. *The "Grassroots" Network: Radical Non-Violence in the Federal Republic of Germany, 1972–1985.* Lanham, MD: University Press of America, 1989.

Maaz, Hans-Joachim. *Der Gefühlsstau: Ein Psychogramm der DDR.* Berlin: Argon Verlag GmbH, 1990.

Macrakis, Kristie. *Seduced by Secrets: Inside the Stasi's Spy-Tech World.* New York: Cambridge University Press, 2008.

Maleck, Bernard. *Wolfgang Ullmann: "Ich werde nicht schweigen": Gespräche mit Wolfgang Ullmann.* Berlin: Dietz Verlag, 1991.

Mallinckrodt, Anita. *The Environmental Dialogue in the GDR.* Lanham, MD: University Press of America, 1987.

Mayer, Thomas. *Der nicht aufgibt. Christoph Wonneberger—eine Biographie.* Leipzig: Evangelische Verlagsanstalt, 2014.

_____. *Helden der Friedlichen Revolution: 18 Porträts von Wegbereitern aus Leipzig.* Leipzig: Evangelische Verlaganstalt, 2009.

McAdams, A. James. *Germany Divided: From the Wall to Reunification.* Princeton, NJ: Princeton University Press, 1993.

McFalls, Laurence H. "Changing Political Culture in Postcommunist Central Europe: Lessons from the East German Case." Paper presented at the American Political Science Association annual meeting, New York, 1–4 September 1994.

_____. *Communism's Collapse, Democracy's Demise? The Cultural Context and Consequences of the East German Revolution.* Washington Square, NY: New York University Press, 1995.

Menge, Marlies. *"Ohne uns läuft nichts mehr": Die Revolution in der DDR.* Stuttgart: Deutsche Verlags-Anstalt, 1990.

Michalowski, Bernhard, et al. *9. November 1989: Der Tag der Deutschen.* Munchen: Wilhelm Heyne Verlag, 1990.

Mitter, Armin, and Stefan Wolle, eds. *"Ich liebe euch doch alle!" Befehle und Lageberichte des MfS, Januar–November 1989.* Second edition. Berlin: BasisDruck, 1990.

Müller, Heiner. *Zur Lage der Nation.* Berlin: Rotbuch Verlag, 1990.

Müller, Manfred. *Protestanten: Begegnung mit Zeitgenossen.* Leipzig: Mitteldeutscher Verlag, 1990.

Müller-Enbergs, Helmut, Marianne Schulz, and Jan Wielgohs, eds. *Von der Illegalität ins Parlament: Werdegang und Konzept der neuen Bürgerbewegungen.* Berlin: LinksDruck Verlag, 1991.

Mundus, Doris. *Leipzig, 1989: Eine Chronik.* Leipzig: Lehmstedt Verlag, 2009.

_____. *Leipzig in One Day: A City Tour.* Leipzig: Lehmstedt Verlag, 2008.

Naimark, Norman M. "'Ich will hier raus': Emigration and the Collapse of the German Democratic Republic." Ivo Banac, ed. *Eastern Europe in Revolution,* 72–79. Ithaca: Cornell University Press, 1992.

Neubert, Ehrhart. *Geschichte der Opposition in der DDR, 1949–1989.* Berlin: Ch. Links Verlag, 1998.

_____. "Protestantische Kultur und DDR-Revolution." *Aus Politik und Zeitgeschichte* 19 (3 Mai 1991): 21–29.

_____. "Eine Protestantische Revolution." *Deutschland Archiv* 23, no. 5 (Mai 1990): 704–713.

_____. *Eine Protestantische Revolution*. Osnabrück: KONTEXTverlag, 1990.

Neues Forum Leipzig. *Jetzt oder nie—Demokratie! Leipziger Herbst '89*. Second edition. Leipzig: Forum Verlag, 1989.

Offene Arbeit Selbstauskünfte. Erfurt: Offene Arbeit des Evangelischen Kirchenkreises Erfurt, 1991.

"Ökumenisches Seminar über Menschenrechte." *DDR-Komitee für Menschenrechte: Schriften und Information; 40 Jahre Vereinte Nationen Priorität dem Recht auf Frieden* 11, no. 2 (1985): 93–94.

Ökumenische Versammlung für Gerechtigkeit, Frieden und Bewahrung der Schöpfung: Dresden-Magdeburg-Dresden: Eine Dokumentation. Berlin: Aktion Sühnezeichen/Friedensdienste, 1990.

Oldenburg, Fred. "The Impact of Gorbachev's Reform on the GDR." Berichte des Bundesinstituts für ostwissenschaftliche und internationale Studien, no. 25. Köln: Bundesinstitut für ostwissenschaftliche und internationale Studien, 1988.

Oltmanns, Gesine, and Hans-Jürgen Röder, eds. *Vor 25 Jahren: Die Friedliche Revolution 1989—Ein Wochenrückblick*. Leipzig: Stiftung Friedliche Revolution, 2013.

Opp, Karl-Dieter, and Christiane Gern. "Dissident Groups, Personal Networks, and Spontaneous Cooperation: The East German Revolution of 1989." *American Sociological Review* 58 (October 1993): 659–680.

Opp, Karl-Dieter, and Peter Voss. *Die volkseigene Revolution*. Stuttgart: Klett-Cotta, 1993.

Pausch, Andreas Peter. Uwe Schwabe, ed. *Widerstehen: Pfarrer Christoph Wonneberger*. Berlin: Metropol Verlag, 2014.

Philipsen, Dirk. *We Were the People: Voices from East Germany's Revolutionary Autumn of 1989*. Durham, NC: Duke University Press, 1993.

Politische Parteien und Bewegungen der DDR über sich selbst: Handbuch. Berlin: Staatsverlag der Deutschen Demokratischen Republik, 1990.

Pollack, Detlef. "Außenseiter oder Repräsentanten? Zur Rolle der politisch alternativen Gruppen im gesellschaftlichen Umbruchprozeß der DDR." *Deutschland Archiv* 23, no. 8 (August 1990): 1216–1223.

————. "Das Ende einer Organisationsgesellschaft: Systemtheoretische Über-legungen zum gesellschaftlichen Umbruch in der DDR." *Zeitschrift für Soziologie* 19, no 4 (August 1990): 292–307.

————. "Religion und gesellschaftlicher Wandel: Zur Rolle der Kirche im gesellschaftlichen Umbruch." *Übergänge* 6 (1990): 236–243.

————. "Überblick über den Stand der Forschung zum Thema Kirche und Religion in der DDR," *Zeitschrift für Evangelische Ethik* 35 (1991): 306–317. Mohn: Gütersloher Verlagshaus Gerd.

Pollack, Detlef, ed. *Die Legitimität der Freiheit: Politisch alternative Gruppen in der DDR unter dem Dach der Kirche.* Forschungen zur Praktischen Theologie 8. Frankfurt am Main and New York: Peter Lang, 1990.

Poumet, Jacques. "Die Leipziger Untergrundzeitschriften aus der Sicht der Staatssicherheit." *Deutschland Archiv* 29, no. 1 (1996): 67–85.

Presse- und Informationsstelle des Bundes der Evangelischen Kirchen in der DDR, ed. *Unterwegs: Evangelische Kirche in der Deutschen Demokratischen Republik: Eine Information.* Jena: Wartburg Verlag Max Keßler, 1981.

Probst, Lothar. "Bürgerbewegungen, politische Kultur und Zivilgesellschaft." *Aus Politik und Zeitgeschichte* 19 (3 May 1991): 30–35.

————. *Ostdeutsche Bürgerbewegungen und Perspektiven der Demokratie: Entstehung, Bedeutung, und Zukunft.* Köln: Bund-Verlag, 1993.

Ramet, Pedro. "Church and Peace in East Germany." *Problems of Communism* 33, no. 4 (1984): 44–57.

————. "Disaffection and Dissent in East Germany." *World Politics* 37, no. 1 (October 1984): 85–111.

————. "The Evangelical Church, the State, and the Peace Movement in East Germany." *Crossroads* 22 (1986): 31–48.

Reich, Jens. *Rückkehr nach Europa: Zur neuen Lage der deutschen Nation.* München: Carl Hanser Verlag, 1991.

Rein, Gerhard, ed. *Die Opposition in der DDR: Entwürfe für einen anderen Sozialismus.* Berlin: Wichern-Verlag, 1989.

————. *Die protestantische Revolution, 1987–1990: Ein deutsches Lesebuch.* Berlin: Wichern-Verlag, 1990.

Rendtorff, Trutz, ed. *Protestantische Revolution? Kirche und Theologie in der DDR: Ekklesiologische Voraussetzungen, politischer Kontext, theologische und historische Kriterien*. Göttingen: Vandenhoeck and Ruprecht, 1993.

Rexin, Manfred. "The GDR on the Way to Germany." *Außenpolitik* 41, no. 4 (1990): 318–327.

Rheinischen Merkur, ed. *Zurück zu Deutschland: Umsturz und demokratischer Aufbruch in der DDR*. Bonn: Bouvier Verlag, 1990.

Richter, Edelbert. *Christentum und Demokratie in Deutschland: Beiträge zur geistigen Verbreitung der Wende in der DDR*. Leipzig: Gustav Kiepenheimer Verlag, 1991.

Richter, Manfred, and Elsbeth Zylla, eds. *Mit Pflugscharen gegen Schwerter: Erfahrungen in der Evangelischen Kirche in der DDR, 1949–1990: Protokolle*. Bremen: Edition Temmen, 1991.

Richter, Michael. *Die Friedliche Revolution: Aufbruch zur Demokratie in Sachsen, 1989/90*. Vols. 1 and 2. Göttingen: Vandenhoeck & Ruprecht, 2009.

Riley, Kathleen Kerry. *Everyday Subversion: From Joking to Revolting in the German Democratic Republic*. East Lansing: Michigan State University Press, 2008.

Ritter, Jürgen, and Peter Joachim Lapp. *Die Grenze: Ein deutsches Bauwerk*. Berlin: Ch. Links Verlag, 2009.

Rüddenklau, Wolfgang. *Störenfried: ddr-opposition 1986–1989: mit Texten aus den "Umweltblättern."* Berlin: BasicDruck Verlag, 1992.

Rueschemeyer, Marilyn S. "Participation and Control in a State Socialist Society: The German Democratic Republic." Unpublished manuscript, 1989.

Rueschemeyer, Marilyn S., and Christiane Lemke, eds. *The Quality of Life in the German Democratic Republic*. Armonk, NY: M.E. Sharpe, Inc., 1989.

Sagurna, Michael, ed. *1989: Chronologie der Wende in Sachsen*. Dresden: Sächsische Staatskanzlei, 1999.

Sandford, John. *The Sword and the Ploughshare: Autonomous Peace Initiatives in East Germany*. END Special Report. London: Merlin Press/European Nuclear Disarmament, 1983.

Scharf, C. Bradley. *Politics and Change in East Germany: An Evaluation of Socialist Change*. Boulder, CO: Westview Press, 1984.

Schneider, Wolfgang. *Leipziger Demontagebuch*. Leipzig and Weimar: Gustav Kiepenheuer, 1990.

Schorlemmer, Friedrich. "Die Befindlichkeit der Ostdeutschen und die Offenheit für Weltprobleme." Jahrestagung der UNESCO. Weimar: 2 April 1992.

_____. *Bis alle Mauern fallen: Text aus einem verschwundenen Land*. Berlin: Verlag der Nation, 1991.

_____. *Träume und Alpträume: Einmischungen, 1982–90*. Berlin: Verlag der Nation, 1990.

_____. *Worte öffnen Fäuste: Die Rückkehr in ein schwieriges Vaterland*. München: Kindler Verlag, 1992.

Schüddekopf, Charles, ed. *"Wir sind das Volk!" Flugschriften, Aufrufe und Texte einer Deutschen Revolution*. Reinbek bei Hamburg: Rowohlt Taschenbuch Verlag, 1990.

Schulze, Rudolf, ed. *Nach der Wende: Wandlungen in Kirche und Gesellschaft*. Berlin: Wichern-Verlag, 1990.

Schumann, Frank, ed. *100 Tage die die DDR Erschütterten*. Berlin: Verlag Neues Leben, 1990.

Schwabe, Uwe. "Symbol der Befreiung: Die Friedensgebete in Leipzig." *Horch und Guck* 7, no. 23 (1998 (2)): 1–21.

Sélitrenny, Rita, and Thilo Weichert. *Das unheimliche Erbe: Die Spionageabteilung der Stasi*. Leipzig: Forum-Verlag Leipzig, 1991.

Sievers, Hans-Jürgen. *Stundenbuch einer deutschen Revolution: Die Leipziger Kirchen im Oktober 1989*. Zollikon: G2W-Verlag, 1990. (Third expanded edition, 2009.)

Smith, Patricia J., ed. *After the Wall: Eastern Germany since 1989*. Boulder, CO: Westview Press, 1998.

Smith, Patricia J. "Political Communication in the East German Revolution of 1989: Assessing the Role of Political Groups." Paper presented at Americn Political Science Association, annual meeting, New York, 1-4 September 1994.

_____. "Political Groups in the East German Revolution of 1989: Applying the Political Process Model." Paper presented at Western Political Science Association annual meeting, Albuquerque, NM, 10-12 March 1994.

_____. "Transformation in the German Democratic Republic: An Evaluation of the Role of Global Ideas and International Linkages." Paper presented at International Studies Association/West and ISSS Conference, Phoenix: 5 November 1992.

Smith, Patricia Jo. *Democratizing East Germany: Ideas, Emerging Political Groups, and the Dynamics of Change.* PhD dissertation. Seattle: University of Washington, 1995. UMI Dissertation Services, 9616673.

Sommer, Norbert. *Der Traum aber bleibt: Sozialismus und christliche Hoffnung: Eine Zwischenbilanz.* Berlin: Wichern-Verlag, 1992.

Sontheimer, Kurt. *Deutschlands Politische Kultur.* München: Piper, 1990.

Spittmann-Rühle, Ilse, and Gisela Helwig, eds. *Ideologie und Gesellschaftliche Entwicklung in der DDR: Achtzehnte Tagung zum Stand der DDR-Forschung in der Bundesrepublik Deutschland, 28. bis 31. Mai 1985.* Edition Deutschland Archiv. Köln: Verlag Wissenschaft und Politik, 1985.

Staude, Fritz. *Sie Waren Stärker: Der Kampf der Leipziger Sozialdemokratie in der Zeit des Sozialistengesetzes, 1878–1890.* Leipzig: VEB Bibliographisches Institut, 1969.

Stolpe, Manfred. *Den Menschen Hoffnung geben.* Berlin: Wichern-Verlag, 1991.

————. "Zum Verständnis der Prinzipien VI und VII der Schlußakte von Helsinki—Juristische und politische Implikationen—Anmerkungen aus christlicher Verantwortung für die Menschenrechte." *DDR-Komitee für Menschenrechte: Schriften und Information. 40 Jahre Vereinte Nationen Priorität dem Rechte auf Frieden* 11, no. 2 (1985): 95–106.

Süß, Walter. "Revolution und Öffentlichkeit in der DDR." *Deutschland Archiv* 23, no. 6 (June 1990): 907–921.

Taylor, Frederick. *The Berlin Wall: A World Divided, 1961–1989.* New York: Harper Collins, 2006.

Templin, Wolfgang. "Ins Netz gegangen und rausgesprungen." *quer*, no. 2 (February 1992): 10–11.

————. "Zivile Gesellschaft—Osteuropäische Emanzipationsbewegungen und unabhängiges Denken in der DDR seit Beginn der Achtziger Jahre." Ilse Spittmann and Gisela Helwig, eds. *Die DDR im vierzigsten Jahr - Geschichte. Situationen. Perspektiven. 22. Tagung zum Stand der DDR-Forschung in der Bundesrepublik Deutschland, 16–19 May 1989.* Köln: Edition Deutschland Archiv: 58–65.

Tetzner, Reiner. *Kerzen-Montage verändern die Welt: Warum die Waffen wirklich schweigen.* Leipzig: Edition Vulcanus, 2009.

_____. *Leipziger Ring: Aufzeichnungen eines Montagsdemonstranten.* Leipzig: Edition Vulcanus, 2004.

Thaysen, Uwe. *Der Runde Tisch. Oder: Wo Blieb Das Volk?* Opladen: Westdeutscher Verlag, 1990.

Tietzel, Manfred, Marion Weber, and Otto F. Bode. *Die Logik der sanften Revolution: Eine ökonomische Analyse.* Tübingen: Mohr, 1991.

Torpey, John. "Two Movements, Not a Revolution: Exodus and Opposition in the East German Transformation." *German Politics and Society* 26 (1992): 21–42.

Unterberg, Peter. *"Wir sind erwachsen, Vater Staat!" Vorgeschichte, Entstehung und Wirkung des Neuen Forum in Leipzig.* Diplomarbeit an der Fakultät für Sozialwissenschaft der Ruhr-Universität Bochum, March 1991.

URANIA (Gerhard Banse, Nina Hager, Klaus Buttker, eds.). *Verantwortung aus Wissen: Beiträge von DDR-Wissenschaftlern zu Friedensforschung und Friedenskampf.* Berlin: Dietz Verlag, 1989.

Urban, Detlef. "Die Umweltarbeit der Kirchen," 131-136. Gisela Helwig und Detlef Urban, eds. *Kirchen und Gesellschaft in beiden deutschen Staaten.* Edition Deutschland Archiv. Köln: Verlag Wissenschaft und Politik, 1987.

Veränderungen in Gesellschaft und Politischem System der DDR: Ursachen, Inhalte, Grenzen: Einundzwanzigsten Tagung zum Stand der DDR-Forschung in der Bundesrepublik Deutschland, 24. bis 27. Mai 1988. Edition Deutschland Archiv. Köln: Verlag Wissenschaft und Politik, 1988.

40 [Vierzig] Jahre DDR . . . und die Bürger melden sich zu Wort. Berlin: Büchergilde Gutenberg & Carl Hanse Verlags, 1989.

Walther, Joachim, Wolf Biermann, and Günter de Bruyn. *Protokoll eines Tribunals: Die Ausschlüsse aus dem DDR-Schriftstellerverband, 1979.* Reinbek bei Hamburg: Rowohlt Taschenbuch, 1991.

Wielgohs, Jan, und Marianne Schulz. "Reformbewegung und Volksbewegung: Politische und soziale Aspekte im Umbruch der DDR-Gesellschaft." *Aus Politik und Zeitgeschichte* 16–17 (April 1990): 15–24.

_____. "Die revolutionäre Krise am Ende der 80er Jahre und die Formierung der Opposition: Expertise im Auftrag des Deutschen Bundestages, Enquete-Kommission." Aufarbeitung von Geschichte und Folgen der SED-Diktatur in Deutschland. Berlin: January 1994.

_____. "Von der illegalen Opposition in die legale Marginalität: Zur Entwicklung der Binnenstruktur der ostdeutschen Bürgerbewegung." *Berliner Journal für Soziologie* 3 (1991), 383–392, and 1 (1992), 119–128.

Wilms, Dr. Dorothee. *Essays on Intra-German Policy.* Bonn: Press and Information Office of the Government of the Federal Republic of Germany, 1989.

Wimmer, Micha, and Christine Proske, eds. *"Wir Sind das Volk!" Die DDR im Aufbruch: Eine Chronik in Dokumenten und Bildern.* München: Wilhelm Heyne Verlag, 1990.

Wittstock, Uwe. *Von der Stalinallee zum Prenzlauer Berg: Wege der DDR-Literatur 1949–1989.* München: Piper, 1989.

Woods, Roger. *Opposition in the GDR under Honecker, 1971–85.* New York: St. Martin's Press, 1986.

Wuttke, Carola, and Bernd Musiolek, eds. *Parteien und politische Bewegungen im letzten Jahr der DDR.* Berlin: BasisDruck, 1991.

Zimmerling, Zeno, and Sabine Zimmerling. *Neue Chronik DDR: Berichte, Fotos, Dokumente. 1. Folge: 7. August–18. Oktober 1989.* Berlin: Verlag Tribüne Berlin GmbH, 1990.

_____. *Neue Chronik DDR: Berichte, Fotos, Dokumente. 2. Folge: 19. Oktober–23. November 1989.* Berlin: Verlag Tribüne Berlin GmbH, 1990.

_____. *Neue Chronik DDR: Berichte, Fotos, Dokumente. 3. Folge: 24. November–22. Dezember 1989.* Berlin: Verlag Tribüne Berlin GmbH, 1990.

Zwahr, Harmut. *Ende einer Selbstzerstörung: Leipzig und die Revolution in der DDR.* Göttingen: Vandenhoeck und Ruprecht, 1991. (Second edition 1993.)

D. Group Documents

Periodicals
Anstösse
Arche Nova
Briefe
Friedrichfelder Feuermelder
Gegenstimmen
Grenzfall
Kontakte
MoAning stAr
Streiflichter
Umweltblätter
Umweltbrief

Secondary Sources on German and East European Groups
Across Frontiers
Dissent
Eastern Europe Newsletter
East European Reporter
Kirche in Sozialismus
Ost-West Diskussionsforum
Radio Free Europe Research

ENDNOTES

1. Letter from University of Kansas Summer Language Institute to parents.

2. Thanks to an agreement demanded by the major grocery chains. See Patricia J. Smith, ed., *After the Wall: Eastern Germany since 1989* (Boulder, CO: Westview Press, 1998).

3. Most groups in East Germany developed under the auspices of the Evangelical (Protestant) Church, a church body that combined both Lutheran and Reformed (Calvinist) traditions. The German word *evangelisch* means "Protestant" and does not have the connotation of proselytizing generally associated with evangelical churches in the United States. The East German Evangelical Church had more than 5,000,000 members, the vast majority of the slightly more than 6 million East Germans who claimed religious affiliation. (Pedro Ramet, "Religious Distribution in Eastern Europe," lecture at University of Washington, Seattle: 26 January 1989.) See Chapters 3 and 6 as well as Robert F. Goeckel, *The Lutheran Church and the East German State: Political Conflict and Change under Ulbricht and Honecker* (Ithaca: Cornell University Press, 1990) for more information regarding churches in East Germany.

4. *Samizdat* referred to the government-censored literature and other information reproduced clandestinely by dissident groups throughout Eastern Europe. Activists copied the material by hand or with typewriters using carbon paper and distributed the material through friends and other underground contacts.

5. Doris Mundus, *Leipzig, 1989: Eine Chronik* (Leipzig: Lehmstedt, 2009), 25.

6. Rainer Land and Ralf Possekel, *Fremde Welten: Die gegensätzliche Deutung der DDR durch SED Reformer und Bürgerbewegung in den 80er Jahren* (Berlin: Ch. Links Verlag, 1998), 297–98.

7. Sources used to compile the story of the 1989 Rosa Luxemburg demonstration in Leipzig include author interviews with Jochen Lässig (Leipzig: 26 March 1992), Rainer Müller (Leipzig: 24 March 1992 and 21 April 1992), Gesine Oltmanns (Leipzig: 9 October 2013), Thomas Rudolph (Dresden: 15 April 1992), and Uwe Schwabe (Leipzig: 22 April 1992); Arbeitsgruppe Menschenrechte (AGM) and Arbeitskreis Gerechtigkeit (AKG), eds., "Was war los in Leipzig?" *Die Mücke: Dokumentation der Ereignisse: Leipzig Chronik vom 13. Februar bis*

5. *September 1988,* Part I, (Leipzig: *Samizdat,* March 1989), published in *Ost-West Diskussionsforum* 6 (April 1989) 8–11; Part II, *Chronik vom 11. September bis 27. Januar,* (Leipzig: *Samizdat,* March 1989), published in *Ost-Westdiskussionsforum* 7 (June 1989), 7–10; Leipziger Menschenrechtsgruppen 1989, *Heute vor 10 Jahren,* Paper 1, 2–3; Tobias Hollitzer and Reinhard Bohse, *Heute vor 10 Jahren: Leipzig auf dem Weg zur Friedlichen Revolution* (Fribourg/New York: InnoVatio Verlag), 13–59; Bernd Lindner, *Die demokratische Revolution in der DDR 1989/90* (Bonn: Bundeszentrale für politische Bildung, 1998), 7–11; Thomas Mayer, *Helden der Friedlichen Revolution: 18 Porträts von Wegbereitern aus Leipzig,* Schriftenreihe des Sächsischen Landesbeauftragten für die Stasi-Unterlagen (Leipzig: Evangelische Verlagsanstalt, 2009); Armin Mitter and Stefan Wolle, eds., *"Ich liebe euch doch alle!" Befehle und Lageberichte des MfS, Januar-November 1989* (Berlin: BasisDruck, 1990), 8–16; Ehrhart Neubert, *Geschichte der Opposition in den DDR, 1949–1989* (Berlin: Ch. Links Verlag, 1998), 786, 789, 805; Kerry Kathleen Riley, *Everyday Subversion: From Joking to Revolting in the German Democratic Republic* (East Lansing: Michigan State University Press, 2008), 180–89; Wolfgang Rüddenklau, *Störenfried: ddr opposition, 1986–1989* (Berlin: BasisDruck Verlag, 1992), 313–22; and Uwe Schwabe, "Symbol der Befreiung," *Horch und Guck* 7, no. 23 (1998 (2)), 9.

8. C. Bradley Scharf, *Politics and Change in East Germany: An Evaluation of Socialist Change* (Boulder, CO: Westview Press, 1984), 25.

9. Other parties included the Christian Democratic Union (CDU), the Liberal Party of Germany (LDPD), the National Democratic Party of Germany (NDPD), and the Democratic Farmers' Party (DBD).

10. Barbara Donovan, "Crackdown on Dissidents in the GDR," Radio Free Europe/Radio Liberty, *RAD Background Report* 22, GDR (17 February 1988), 4.

11. Jiri Pehe, "Independent Activity in Eastern Europe," Radio Free Europe/Radio Liberty, *RAD Background Report* 1, Eastern Europe (4 January 1989), 5.

12. The details surrounding these negotiated settlements have been the focus of considerable strife among oppositionists such as Bärbel Bohley, Wolfgang and Lotte Templin, and Reinhard Schult, on the one hand, and Evangelical Church officials such as Manfred Stolpe, on the other. The controversy reached a climax on April 26, 1992, when the sides confronted each other in a public meeting in

Gethsemane Church. See also issues of *Berliner Zeitung* for April and May 1992.

13. http://www.cnn.com/SPECIALS/cold.war/episodes/23/interviews/gorbachev/. Honecker was apparently referring to the new economic system, a series of economic reforms introduced in East Germany in the mid-1960s that provided some decentralization and some acknowledgment of markets.

14. Mayer, *Helden*, 52–53.

15. Land and Possekel, *Fremde Welten*, 297–98.

16. Land and Possekel, *Fremde Welten*, 297–98.

17. Lässig, author interview.

18. Schwabe, author interview.

19. Schwabe, author interview.

20. Schwabe, author interview; Mayer, *Helden*, 146.

21. Mayer, *Helden*, 68.

22. Information on Müller and on Working Circle Justice came from author interviews with Müller, Rudolph, and Kathrin Walther (Leipzig: 24 March 1992); Mayer, *Helden*, 30–37, 72–79, 110–17.

23. *The Holy Bible*, Revised Standard Version.

24. Mayer, *Helden*, 74; Müller, author interview.

25. Mayer, *Helden*, 78.

26. Müller, author interview. The term, the Greens, refers to the West German political party as well as, more generally, to environmental groups and the environmental movement.

27. AGM and AKG, *Die Mücke*, Part I; Part II; *Die Mücke, Leipzig Chronik vom 23. Februar bis 29. Mai 1989*, Part III (Leipzig: *Samizdat*, June 1989), published in *Ost-West Diskussionsforum* 8/9 (October 1989), 14–15; *Die Mücke, Leipzig Chronik vom .4 Juni bis .4 September 1989*, Part IV (Leipzig: *Samizdat*, September 1989), published in *Ost-West Diskussionsforum* 10 (February 1990), 18–20. In conjunction with the 20th anniversary of Leipzig's peaceful revolution, a special exhibition, "Leipzig auf dem Weg zur Friedlichen Revolution" provided documentation of Leipzig events during 1989. Supported by the state of Saxony as part of the program, "20 Jahre Friedliche Revolution und Deutsche Einheit" and the Bürgerkomitee Leipzig e. V. with the Gedenkstätte Museum in der "Runden Ecke" and the Museum in the Stasi Bunker, the catalog to the special exhibition also provides documentation. See Tobias Hollitzer and Sven Sachen-

bacher, eds., *Die Friedliche Revolution in Leipzig: Bilder, Dokumente, und Objekte,* Vols. 1 and 2 (Leipzig: Leipziger Universitätsverlag, 2012).

28. Rudolph, author interview.

29. Rudolph, author interview.

30. Rudolph, author interview.

31. Lässig, author interview.

32. Rudolph, author interview.

33. Information on Working Group Human Rights and on Wonneberger compiled from author interviews with Wonneberger (Leipzig: 25 March 1992), Oliver Kloß (Leipzig: 21 April 1992), Gabriele Heide (Leipzig: 24 March 1992), Heiko Lietz (Gustrow: 11 November 1999), Ehrhart Neubert (Berlin: 19 March 1992); Archiv Bürgerbewegung Leipzig interviews with Christoph Wonneberger, transcribed (Leipzig: 25 November 2008 and 2 December 2008); Mayer, *Helden,* 14–21.

34. After moving from Dresden to Leipzig, Wonneberger spent some time settling into his new parish, taking care of family responsibilities (a sick grandmother lived with him until she died) and getting a sense of what was happening in the Leipzig group scene before founding Working Group Human Rights.

35. Author interviews with Kloß and Wonneberger.

36. Wonneberger, author interview.

37. Article 19 of the United Nations' International Covenant on Civil and Political Rights provided, "Everyone shall have the right to freedom of expression; this right shall include the freedom to seek, receive, and impart information and ideas of all kinds regardless of borders, either orally, in writing or in print, in the form of art, or through any other media of his [or her] choice." Similarly, Basket III of the Helsinki Final Act dealing with Cooperation in Humanitarian and Other Fields instructed participating states "to facilitate the freer and wider dissemination of information of all kinds [and] to encourage cooperation in the field of information and the exchange of information with other countries."

38. When used in this book, unless otherwise specified, "the church" generally refers to the Evangelical [Protestant] Church, a church body that combined both Lutheran and Reformed (Calvinist) traditions. In Leipzig and the Saxony region, most Protestant churches were Lutheran. Five million of the six million East

Germans claiming religious affiliation were connected to the Evangelical Church.

39. As used in this book, "group" and "group member" frequently refers to activist or oppositional groups, especially in Leipzig. However, "group" is sometimes used to refer to the range of groups (church and nonchurch) organized under the umbrella of East German churches. (Many of these groups grew more activist and oppositional during 1989.)

40. Land and Possekel, *Fremde Welten*, 295–96.

41. Mayer, *Helden*, 111–17.

42. Mayer, *Helden*, 114.

43. Author interviews with Walther and Rudolph; Archiv Bürgerbewegung interview with Kathrin Mahler Walther (Leipzig: no date); Mayer, *Helden*, 30–37, 111–17.

44. Mayer, *Helden*, 114.

45. Rudolph, author interview. Members of the steering committee included Rudolph, Müller, Walther, Richter, and Quester.

46. Author interviews with Kloss and Rudolph.

47. Author interviews with Müller, Rudolph, Kloß, and Hagen Findeis (Leipzig: 26 March 1992). Previously the group Initiative for Peace and Human Rights in Berlin had coordinated this oppositional network, but after the arrests and forced emigration of many Berlin activists following the 1988 Rosa Luxemburg demonstration in Berlin, responsibilities shifted to Leipzig. Network meetings were important for creating common goals and objectives and building a shared perception among member groups concerning important ideas and a sense of themselves as linked together by these shared concerns.

48. Mayer, *Helden*, 34.

49. Rudolph, author interview; Mayer, *Helden*, 34.

50. Rudolph, author interview; Mayer, *Helden*, 34.

51. Leipziger Menschenrechtsgruppen 1989, *Heute*, Paper 1, 2–4.

52. Leipziger Menschenrechtsgruppen 1989, *Heute*, Paper 1, 3.

53. Leipziger Menschenrechtsgruppen 1989, *Heute*, Paper 1, 3.

54. AGM and AKG, *Die Mücke*, Part II, 10–11; Hollitzer and Bohse, *Heute*, 20–24, 28; Leipziger Menschenrechtsgruppen 1989, *Heute*, Paper 1, 3–4.

55. Hollitzer and Bohse, *Heute*, 21.

56. Hollitzer and Bohse, *Heute,* 24–25.

57. Rüddenklau, *Störenfried,* 319–20.

58. Human Rights Watch, *The Persecution of Human Rights Monitors, December 1988 to December 1989, A World Wide Survey,* published December 1989 by Human Rights Watch/Africa Watch/Americas Watch/Asia Watch/Helsinki Watch/Middle East Watch; New York, New York; section on German Democratic Republic, 130–36.

59. Hollitzer and Bohse, *Heute,* 25–26.

60. Letter from Berlin groups in Rüddenklau, *Störenfried,* 321–22.

61. Lässig, author interview.

62. Regina (Lotte) Templin, author interview (Berlin: 6 May 1992).

63. Michael Richter, *Die Friedliche Revolution: Aufbruch zur Demokratie in Sachsen, 1989/90,* vol. 1 (Göttingen: Vandenhoeck & Ruprecht, 2009), 80–83.

64. Richter, *Die Friedliche Revolution,* 80.

65. Richter, *Die Friedliche Revolution,* 80–83.

66. Norman M. Naimark, "'Ich will hier raus': Emigration and the Collapse of the German Democratic Republic," in Ivo Banac, ed., *Eastern Europe in Revolution* (Ithaca: Cornell University Press, 1992), 72–95; Malcolm Byrne, ed., *Uprising in East Germany, 1953: Shedding Light on a Major Cold War Flashpoint,* A National Security Archive Electronic Briefing Book, compiled by Gregory F. Domber, 15 June 2001.

67. Naimark, "Emigration," 78–79.

68. Thomas Flemming, *Die Berliner Mauer: Grenze durch eine Stadt* (Berlin-Brandenberg: be.bra verlag, 2009); Frederick Taylor, *The Berlin Wall: A World Divided, 1961–1989* (New York: Harper Collins, 2006); Bill Holland, "Five Interesting Facts about the Berlin Wall," 5 August 2011, Listosaur.com; Jennifer Rosenberg, "The Rise and the Fall of the Berlin Wall," History 1900s, *About.com.*

69. Basket III of the Helsinki Final Act dealt with Cooperation in Humanitarian and Other Fields, and Section I provided that the participating states would facilitate freer movement and contacts.

70. Wolfgang Ullmann, author interview (Berlin: 26 February1992), and Bernard Maleck, *Wolfgang Ullmann: "Ich werde nicht schweigen": Gespräche mit Wolfgang Ullmann* (Berlin: Dietz Verlag, 1991), 25–38.

71. Maleck, *Ullmann,* 38.

72. *Neues Deutschland* (14 December 1988), 6, trans. in FBIS (Foreign Broadcast Information Service), *Daily Report* (East Europe: 19 December 1988), 20–25; Barbara Donovan, "East Germany Planning New Travel and Emigration Regulations," *Radio Free Europe Research*, RAD Background Report/241/GDR (8 December 1988), 2. Invalids and persons above retirement age were not subject to the travel restrictions.

73. *Neues Deutschland* (14 December 1988), 6, trans. in FBIS, *Daily Report* (East Europe: 19 December 1988), 21.

74. See "Under Country Arrest," *East European Reporter* 3, no. 1 (November 1987) for an article by Carlo Jordan, an environmental activist, about his experiences.

75. Lotte Templin, author interview.

76. Barbara Donovan, "New East German Travel Regulations," *Radio Free Europe Research*, RAD Background Report/61 (6 April 1989), 2.

77. Sources for March 13 demonstration include author interviews with Schwabe, Rudolph, Lässig, and Oltmanns; AGM and AKG, *Die Mücke,* Part I; Leipziger Menschenrechtsgruppen 1989, *Heute,* Paper 2, 3–4; Hollitzer and Bohse, *Heute,* 61–111; Lindner, *Die demokratische Revolution,* 39–47; Mitter and Wolle, *"Ich liebe euch,"* 28; Neubert, *Opposition,* 671–77; Richter, *Die Friedliche Revolution: Saxony,* vol. 1, 80–83; Riley, *Everyday Subversion,* 167–68, 189–91; and Rüddenklau, *Störenfried,* 122–24, 171–203.

78. Trade and trade fairs had played an important role in Leipzig for centuries and continued to shape Leipzig into the 20th century. For much of its history Leipzig lay on the crossroads for both east-west trade and north-south trade, and already in the 12th century Leipzig was an important trading town ("Leipzig Trade Fair," www.enwikipedia.org). During the communist era, the spring and fall trade fairs in Leipzig provided major venues for producers from throughout the east bloc, and Leipzig was one of the most important markets for COMECON (Council for Mutual Economic Assistance), the Soviet bloc trade organization.

79. Hollitzer and Bohse, *Heute,* 100.

80. A block west of Nikolai Church on Grimmaische Street stood the renowned Mädler's Passage, featuring 70 vaults for shops and corridors almost 20 feet wide and more than 400 feet long, longer than a football field. In 1989 these shops carried luxury goods, and Mädler's Passage was famous throughout Europe as

an upscale shopping area patronized especially during trade fairs [Doris Mundus, *Leipzig in One Day: A City Tour* (Leipzig: Lehmstedt Verlag, 2009), 10–11]. Few Leipzigers and none of Leipzig's oppositional group members could have afforded to shop there, but Jochen Lässig, a member of Initiative Group Living and one of the activists imprisoned for his role in distributing leaflets for the Rosa Luxemburg demonstration, earned his living by playing guitar and singing for tips at the entrance to Mädler's Passage (Lässig, author interview; Meyer, *Helden*, 22–29). Because Lässig was not licensed by the city or state, he was arrested periodically for performing illegally. On March 11 the Stasi arrested him and fined him for playing music in the streets of Leipzig's central city. Later in 1989 he would play a central role in organizing the illegal Street Music Festival and other oppositional activities—and he would become a key spokesman for New Forum and other groups during Leipzig's fall revolution.

81. Leipziger Menschenrechtsgruppen 1989, *Heute*, Paper 2, 3.

82. Leipziger Menschenrechtsgruppen 1989, *Heute*, Paper 2, 3.

83. Author interviews with Wonneberger, Rudolph, and Schwabe; Rüddenklau, *Störenfried*, 221–22.

84. Author interviews with Oltmanns, Schwabe, and Lässig.

85. Müller, author interview.

86. Rudolph, author interview.

87. Author interviews with Müller and Rudolph.

88. Leipziger Menschenrechtsgruppen 1989, *Heute*, Paper 2, 3.

89. Hollitzer and Bohse, *Heute,* 101.

90. Lässig, author interview.

91. Author interviews with Oltmanns, Rudolph, Schwabe, and Lässig; Mayer, *Helden*, 50–54.

92. Mayer, *Helden*, 54.

93. See "Erklärung" in Mayer, *Helden*, 55.

94. Author interviews with Rudolph, Lässig, and Oltmanns.

95. Dirk Philipsen, *We Were the People: Voices from East Germany's Revolutionary Autumn of 1989* (Durham, NC: Duke University Press, 1993), 141–46; author interviews with Roland Quester (Leipzig: 25 March 1992) and Rudolph.

96. Philipsen, *We Were the People*, 143.

97. Philipsen, *We Were the People*, 143.

98. Neubert, *Opposition*, 676–77; Gerhard Besier and Stephan Wolf, *"Pfarrer, Christen, und Katholiken,": Das Ministerium für Staatssicherheit der ehemaligen DDR und die Kirchen,* second edition (Vluyn: Neukirchener Verlag des Erziehungsvereins GmbH, 1992), 664–77; Schwabe, "Symbol der Befreiung," 9; Dietrich and Schwabe, *Freunde und Feinde,* 220-35.

99. Besier and Wolf, *"Pfarrer, Christen, und Katholiken,"* 668-69.

100. Konrad Elmer, author interview (Berlin: 25 February 1992).

101. Hollitzer and Bohse, *Heute,* 99.

102. Brigitte Moritz, author interview.

103. Jochen Lässig, author interview.

104. Moritz, author interview.

105. Mayer, *Helden,* 18.

106. Schwabe, "Symbol der Befreiung," 6.

107. Mayer, *Helden,* 18,

108. Friedrich Magirius, author interview (Leipzig: 21 April 1992).

109. Magirius, author interview.

110. AGM and AKG, *Die Mücke,* Part III, 14–15.

111. Robert F. Goeckel, "Historical Legacies and 'Mature Socialism,'" in Marilyn S. Rueschemeyer and Christiane Lemke, eds., *The Quality of Life in the Germany Democratic Republic* (Armonk, NY: M.E. Sharpe, Inc., 1989), 224.

112. Krisch, Henry, *The German Democratic Republic*: The Search for Identity (Boulder, CO: Westview Press, 124.

113. Author interviews with Carlo Jordan (Berlin: 15 November 1991), Christa Lewek (Berlin: 10 February 1992), and Detlef Pollack (Leipzig: 25 March 1992); Goeckel, *Church,* 16–19.

114. Neubert, author interview.

115. Goeckel, *Church,* 65–73.

116. Goeckel, *Church,* 183.

117. Klemens Richter, "Zu einer Standortbestimmung der katholischen Kirche in der DDR," *Deutschland Archiv* 15 (August 1982), 800–803, and "Veränderte Haltung der DDR Katholiken," *Deutschland Archiv* 16 (May 1983), 454–58.

118. Pedro Ramet, "Religious Distribution in Eastern Europe."

119. Meeting with Rüdiger Minor, Bishop of the East German Methodist Church (Dresden: 7 August 1988).

120. Author interviews with Heino Falcke (Erfurt: 10 April 1992), Neubert, Friedrich Schorlemmer (Weimar: 3 April 1992), Gisela Kallenbach (Leipzig: 22 April 1992), Brigitte Moritz, and Gabriele Heide; *Ökumenische Versammlung für Gerechtigkeit, Frieden und Bewahrung der Schöpfung: Dresden—Magdeburg— Dresden: Eine Dokumentation* (Berlin: Aktion Sühnezeichen/Friedensdienste, 1990). The English translation of the title for this ecumenical effort of the World Council of Churches is "Conciliar Process for Justice, Peace, and the Integrity of Civilization."

121. Goeckel, *Church*, 190–95.

122. Goeckel, *Church*, 244–46.

123. "Dokumente zur Kirchenpolitik in Sachsen," 3.

124. Unlike most other alternative groups, Leipzig's human rights groups met primarily outside of church facilities.

125. John Sandford, *END Special Report: The Sword and the Ploughshare: Autonomous Peace Initiatives in East Germany* (London: END/Merlin Press, 1983), 27–28; "Conscientious Objection in East Germany," en.wikipedia.org.

126. Sandford, *The Sword and the Ploughshare*, 29.

127. The East German draft recalls the U.S. draft during the Vietnam era, when potential draftees searched for exemptions and some draft resisters chose to go to Canada.

128. Sandford, *The Sword and the Ploughshare*, 30.

129. Sandford, *The Sword and the Ploughshare*, 74.

130. Neubert, *Opposition*, 300.

131. Sandford, *The Sword and the Ploughshare*, 31.

132. I draw this conclusion in part from my interviews with Leipzig group activists and others throughout East Germany, and from written sources on the East German revolution, including Neubert, *Opposition*, and Mayer, *Helden*. In recent years Wonneberger's role has been recognized with various awards, and two new books on Wonneberger appeared in conjunction with his 70th birthday in March 2014: Thomas Mayer, *Der nicht aufgibt. Christoph Wonneberger— eine Biographie* (Leipzig: Evangelische Verlagsanstalt, 2014), and Andreas Peter Pausch, *Widerstehen: Pfarrer Christoph Wonneberger*, Uwe Schwabe, ed. (Berlin: Metropol Verlag, 2014).

133. Sandford, *The Sword and the Ploughshare*, 70–75.

134. Scharf, *Politics and Change in East Germany*, 176. This contrasted with only 40,000 Soviet troops in Poland, 65,000 in Hungary, 80,000 in Czechoslovakia, and none in Romania.

135. Krisch, *The German Democratic Republic*, 133.

136. *Christian Science Monitor* (21 February 1990), 6.

137. *Christian Science Monitor* (29 March 1990), 5.

138. "Jugendweihe," en.wikipedia.org.

139. Goeckel, *Church*, 256; author interviews with Heide and Moritz.

140. Sandford, *The Sword and the Ploughshare*, 32–33.

141. Sources used to develop the section on a social peace service include Neubert, *Opposition*, 389–95; biography of Christoph Wonneberger and transcribed interviews with Wonneberger, Archiv Bürgerbewegung Leipzig; and author interviews with Wonneberger.

142. Neubert, *Opposition*, 295–99.

143. Neubert, *Opposition*, 392.

144. Neubert, *Opposition*, 395.

145. Neubert, author interview; Wonneberger, transcribed interviews, Archiv Bürgerbewegung, 6–9.

146. Neubert, *Opposition*, 394.

147. This section is based on author interviews with Wonneberger, Magirius, Lässig, Schwabe, Rudolph, Müller, Heide, and Moritz; Neubert, *Opposition*, 783–88; Sebastian Feydt, Christiane Heinze, and Martin Schanz, "Die Leipziger Friedensgebete," in Wolf-Jürgen Grabner, Christiane Heinze, and Detlef Pollack, eds., *Leipzig im Oktober: Kirchen und alternative Gruppen im Umbruch der DDR—Analysen zur Wende* (Berlin: Weichern, 1990), 123.

148. The formal name for the coordinating committee was *Ausschuß der Bezirkssynode Leipzig "Frieden und Gerechtigkeit."*

149. Author interviews with Moritz, Heide, Müller, Schwabe, and Magirius. By 1989 approximately 60 groups from the Leipzig area were tied into this church network. Moritz edited *Kontakte*, the newsletter of Leipzig church-based alternative groups.

150. Heide, author interview. The excluded groups included Women for Peace, an environmental group, a Nicaragua support group, and a group opposing military service.

151. Wayne C. Bartee, *A Time to Speak Out: The Leipzig Citizen Protests and the Fall of East Germany* (Westport, CT: Praeger Publishers, 2000), 184.

152. Magirius, author interview.

153. Neubert, *Opposition*, 582–83.

154. Neubert, *Opposition*, 582.

155. Neubert, *Opposition*, 583.

156. Philipsen, *We Were the People*, 147.

157. Philipsen, *We Were the People*, 146–49.

158. Philipsen, *We Were the People*, 147.

159. Philipsen, *We Were the People*, 147.

160. Philipsen, *We Were the People*, 148.

161. *Die Mücke*, Part III, 14.

162. Lässig, author interview.

163. Moritz, author interview. Moritz provided much of the information for this section on Working Group Peace Service; other sources include Neubert, *Opposition*, 400, 463–65, 580, and Mayer, *Helden*, 38–43.

164. Moritz, author interview.

165. Neubert, *Opposition*, 400.

166. A number of persons interviewed mentioned Moritz and *Kontakte* as important to the Leipzig group scene.

167. Moritz, author interview.

168. Mayer, *Helden*, 39–43.

169. Mayer, *Helden*, 41.

170. Moritz, author interview.

171. Moritz, author interview.

172. Mayer, *Helden*, 41.

173. Heide, author interview. Heide provided most of the information for this section on Women for Peace. Other material came from author interviews with Moritz, Bärbel Bohley (Berlin: 17 March 1992), Ulrike Poppe (Berlin: 3 March 1992), and Irene Kukutz (Berlin: 22 January 1992) as well as Neubert, *Opposition*, 580–81, and Mayer, *Helden*, 38–43.

174. Heide, author interview.

175. Heide, author interview.

176. Ulrike Poppe, "Das kritische Potential der Gruppen in Kirche und Gesellschaft," Detlef Pollack, ed., *Die Legitimität der Freiheit: Politisch alternative Gruppen in der DDR unter dem Dach der Kirche* (Frankfurt am Main: Peter Lange, 1990), 75. The East German state had placed the church—particularly the Evangelical Church, which had sheltered and sometimes even fostered groups—in a role as mediator between the state and the grassroots groups. The state expected churches to be responsible for the actions of "their" groups and to "legitimatize" and "regulate" the groups. Although the church had not chosen this relationship, the state-church agreement frequently put church leaders in the position of speakers for the groups, generally an unsatisfactory situation for both churches and groups; however, by and large the state was not willing to accept groups as dialogue partners, so the church had continued to walk the tightrope, mediating between the state, on the one hand, and grassroot groups, on the other. Churches frequently pressured grassroots groups to moderate and even stop their activities so the church could maintain its fragile agreement with the state.

177. "Dokumente zur Kirchenpolitik in Sachsen," 2–3.

178. "Dokumente zur Kirchenpolitik in Sachsen," 1–2.

179. Magirius, author interview.

180. Wonneberger, author interview.

181. "Dokumente zur Kirchenpolitik in Sachsen," 3.

182. The Stasi viewed Wonneberger and Führer as particularly reactionary, that is, as opposed to the state and its programs or, in other words, the most supportive of social and political changes in East Germany. Those who supported state programs were seen as progressive. See Stasi report in Besier und Wolf, *"Pfarrer, Christen und Katholiken,"* 565.

183. Rudolph, author interview.

184. Heide, author interview.

185. Wonneberger, author interview.

186. Wonneberger, author interview.

187. Müller, author interviews.

188. Pollack, author interview.

189. Besier and Wolf, *"Pfarrer, Christen und Katholiken,"* 878.

190. Moritz, author interview.

191. Schwabe, author interview.

192. Magirius, author interview.

193. Author interviews with Moritz, Magirius, Lässig, Schwabe, and Müller.

194. Magirius, author interview.

195. Magirius, author interview.

196. Moritz, author interview.

197. Rudolph, author interview.

198. Müller, author interview.

199. Heide, author interview.

200. Heide, author interview.

201. Müller, author interview.

202. Lässig, author interview.

203. Some observers of East Germany have argued that the events of 1989 were spontaneous. See Appendix B, about explanations for the 1989 revolution.

204. Bartee, *A Time to Speak Out*, 184.

205. Magirius, author interview.

206. *Die Mücke,* Part IV, 20.

207. Malcolm Gladwell, *The Tipping Point: How Little Things Can Make a Big Difference* (New York: Back Bay Books, Little, Brown, and Co., 2000), 192.

208. Land and Possekel, *Fremde Welten*, 294.

209. Author interview with Martin Böttger (Dresden: 14 April 1992).

210. Sources for the election-monitoring campaign include author interviews with Mario Schatta (Berlin: 16 March 1992), Pollack, Schwabe, Lässig, Heide, Findeis, Wonneberger, Kallenbach, Aribert Rothe (Erfurt: 9 April 1992), Wolfgang Rüddenklau (Berlin: 27 January 1992), Carlo Jordan (Berlin: 15 November 1991), Wolfgang Musigmann (Erfurt: 23 April 1992), Gerlinde Harbig (Erfurt: 23 April 1992), and Helmut Hartmann (Erfurt: 23 April 1992); AGM and AKG, *Die Mücke,* Part III, *Ost-West Diskussionsforum* 8/9, 14–15; Koordinierungsgruppe Wahlen (ed.), "Wahlfall 89: Eine Documentation" (no publication date or location listed), 37 pages; Hollitzer and Bohse, *Heute,* 113–68; Mitter and Wolle, *"Ich liebe euch,"* 97–107; Leipziger Menschenrechtsgruppen 1989, *Heute,* Paper 3, 4; Lindner, *Die demokratische Revolution,* 25–32.

211. Lässig, author interview.

212. Mayer, *Helden*, 68.

213. Leipziger Menschenrechtsgruppen 1989, *Heute*, Paper 3, 4.

214. Lindner, *Die demokratische Revolution*, 26.

215. Lindner, *Die demokratische Revolution*, 26.

216. Neubert, *Opposition*, 605–607.

217. Hollitzer and Bohse, *Heute*, 116.

218. Lindner, *Die demokratische Revolution*, 27.

219. Lindner, *Die demokratische Revolution*, 27.

220. Lindner, *Die demokratische Revolution*, 27.

221. Group members pointed to the right of East German cities to monitor elections provided for under Section 43, Paragraph 1 of the East German Election Law.

222. Barbara P. McCrea, Jack C. Plano, and George Klein, eds., *The Soviet and East European Political Dictionary* (Santa Barbara, CA: ABC-CLIO, 1984), 295–97.

223. Lindner, *Die demokratische Revolution*, 24. At a meeting at the end of October, Warsaw Pact foreign ministers formally took action to end the Brezhnev Doctrine [*Los Angeles Times* (28 October 1989), latimes.com].

224. Philipsen, *We Were the People*, 392.

225. Lindner, *Die demokratische Revolution*, 24.

226. "Polish Round Table Agreement," en.wikipedia.org. Top government authorities met in Warsaw with representatives of the political opposition in the first Round Table discussion in the Soviet bloc. The government initiated the discussion with the banned trade union Solidarity and other opposition groups in an attempt to defuse growing social unrest.

227. "Elections in Poland," en.wikipedia.org.

228. Lindner, *Die demokratische Revolution*, 24.

229. Lindner, *Die demokratische Revolution*, 24. Partially because of the pressures from the international media, Havel was released from prison on parole in May 1989.

230. Charles Gati, "East and West in Eastern Europe," *Soviet-American Relations after the Cold War*, Robert Jervis, Seweryn Bialer, eds. (Durham, NC: Duke University Press, 1991), 148-49. See also Charles Gati, "Eastern Europe on Its Own," *Foreign Affairs*, America and the World, 1988 Issue, online version.

231. Marilyn Rueschemeyer and Christiane Lemke, "The Transformation of a State Socialist Society," in Marilyn S. Rueschemeyer and Christiane Lemke, eds., *The Quality of Life in the German Democratic Republic* (Armonk, NY: M.E. Sharpe, Inc., 1989), 236.

232. Alfred Kosing, "Zur Dialektik der weiteren Gestaltung der entwickelten sozialistischen Gesellschaft," in *Deutsche Zeitschrift für Philosophie* 36, no. 7 (1988–89), 577–87.

233. Interview with Wolfgang Templin (Berlin: 4 February 1992).

234. *Der Spiegel* (8 November 1988), 27. Optimistic that East Germany, too, would finally change, reform-oriented East Germans had eagerly followed news from the Soviet Union through the Soviet press digest, *Sputnik;* however, on November 19, 1988, East German censors suddenly banned *Sputnik.* Many Leipzigers who read the publication regularly were shocked to learn that East Germans would no longer be allowed to read a magazine published in and circulated freely throughout the Soviet Union, and more than 200,000 East Germans protested the censors' action. That same month, East German censors banned four Soviet films scheduled to show at Berlin's Soviet Film Festival [Author interviews with Lässig and Schwabe; Jonathan Grix, "Non-Conformist Behaviour and the Collapse of the GDR," in Paul Cooke and Jonathan Grix, eds., *German Monitor: East Germany: Continuity and Change* (January 2000), 69–79].

235. The Leninist principle of democratic centralism specified that policies would be decided by central authorities who were, at least nominally, democratically elected. Members and organizations at all levels were bound by decisions made at the center.

236. "Although other parties nominally continued to exist, the Soviet occupation authorities forced them to join in the National Front of Democratic Germany, a nominal coalition of parties that was for all intents and purposes controlled by the SED [the communist party]. By ensuring that Communists predominated on the list of candidates put forward by the National Front, the SED effectively predetermined the composition of legislative bodies in the Soviet zone, and from 1949 in East Germany" ("Socialist Unity Party of Germany," en.wikipedia.org).

237. Sandford, *The Sword and the Ploughshare*, 8–12.

238. Sandford, *The Sword and the Ploughshare*, 11.

239. Scharf, *Politics and Change in East Germany*, 25.

240. This section on group roles in the elections was compiled from author interviews with Rudolph, Lässig, Shatto, Rüddenklau, Jordan, Neubert, Rothe, and Musigmann; Neubert, *Opposition*, 810–15; Rüddenklau, *Störenfried*, 287–93; Bettina Röder, "Es bogen sich die morschen Balken: Der Wahlbetrug vom 7. Mai," Jörg Hildebrandt and Gerhard Thomas, eds., *Unser Glaube mischt sich ein. . . : Evangelicshe Kirche in der DDR 1989: Berichte, Fragen, Verdeutlichungen* (Berlin: Evangelische Verlaganstalt, 1990), 22-29; "Wahlfall 89;" Mitter and Wolle, *"Ich liebe euch,"* 97–107.

241. See Stasi documentation in Mitter and Wolle, *"Ich liebe euch,"* 101–107, for a comparison of 1989 nonparticipation with earlier elections.

242. Both protest tactics were successful in mobilizing group members and a broader populace, with nonvoting levels rising and "no" votes also increasing, according to monitoring reports. Election boycotts can be viewed as similar to the everyday forms of resistance discussed by James C. Scott in *Weapons of the Weak: Everyday Forms of Peasant Resistance* (New Haven, CT: Yale University Press, 1985), with nonvoters dropping out but not actively causing problems. In comparison, voting "no" was more oppositional in that it involved taking a public stance, and monitoring the "no" votes required a more coordinated effort. This latter tactic also provided more opportunity to confront the state and to demonstrate to the public the extent of the state's deception regarding the election process.

243. Rüddenklau, *Störenfried*, 288.

244. Rüddenklau, *Störenfried*, 288. Groups included Initiative Group "Refusing the Practice and Principal of Division" (*Absage an Praxis und Prinzip der Abgrenzung*), the peace circles of Batholomäus and Golgatha churches, and Project Group Ecology and Human Rights of Network Ark.

245. Compiled from Rüddenklau, *Störenfried*, 288–89; Mitter and Wolle, *"Ich liebe euch,"* 97–98; Röder, "Der Wahlbetrug," 22–25; and "Wahlfall 89."

246. Röder, "Der Wahlbetrug," 25-26.

247. *Arche Nova* (February 1989), 61.

248. *Arche Nova* (April 1989), 79.

249. Author interviews with Rudolph and Lässig; Leipziger Menschenrechts-gruppen 1989, *Heute,* Paper 3, 4; Mayer, *Helden,* 118–25; Hollitzer and Bohse, *Heute,* 113–68; and Mitter and Wolle, "Ich liebe euch," 28-39.

250. Hollitzer and Bohse, *Heute,* 154–55.

251. Mayer, *Helden,* 118–25.

252. Mayer, *Helden,* 18, 123.

253. Hollitzer and Bohse, *Heute,* 148.

254. Leipziger Menschenrechtsgruppen 1989, *Heute,* Paper 3, 3.

255. Leipziger Menschenrechtsgruppen 1989, *Heute,* Paper 3, 3; Hollitzer and Bohse, *Heute,* 147; author interview, Rudolph.

256. Leipziger Menschenrechtsgruppen, *Heute,* Paper 3, 3.

257. Mayer, *Helden,* 57-62.

258. *Die Mücke,* Part III, 14; Mitter and Wolle, *"Ich liebe euch,"* 35–36.

259. Mitter and Wolle, *"Ich liebe euch,"* 38.

260. Lindner, *Die demokratische Revolution,* 26.

261. Lindner, *Die demokratische Revolution,* 27.

262. *Die Mücke,* Part III, 14; Mitter and Wolle, *"Ich liebe euch,"* 36.

263. Leipziger Menschenrechtsgruppen 1989, *Heute,* Paper 3, 3.

264. Hollitzer and Bohse, *Heute,* 156–57.

265. Richter, *Die Friedliche Revolution,* 111–116; Hollitzer and Bohse, *Heute,* 156–57.

266. Richter, *Die Friedliche Revolution,* 111–116; Hollitzer and Bohse, *Heute,* 156–57.

267. "Wahlfall 89," 24.

268. "Wahlfall 89," 20–22.

269. Mayer, *Helden,* 60.

270. "Wahlfall 89," 33.

271. Even this letter listed only a portion of the groups that had participated in the election monitoring campaign (for example, Open Work Erfurt was not listed) and the variety of communication networks involved.

272. Leipziger Menschenrechtsgruppen, *Heute,* Paper 3, 4.

273. Leipziger Menschenrechtsgruppen, *Heute,* Paper 3, 4.

274. Lindner, *Die demokratische Revolution,* 30–31.

275. Lindner, *Die demokratische Revolution,* 30.

276. Letter from Evangelisches Ministerium Erfurt to Nationalrat der Nationalen Front der Deutschen Demokratischen Republik (Erfurt: 11 May 1989). (Copy from Karl Metzner.)

277. Evangelisches Ministerium, "Kanzelabkündigung" (Erfurt: 27 May 1989). See also Gerhard Rein, *Die protestantische Revolution, 1987–1990: Ein deutsches Lesebuch* (Berlin: Wichern-Verlag, 1990), 139–140.

278. Rothe, author interview.

279. Neubert, *Opposition*, 814.

280. Neubert, *Opposition*, 814–15.

281. Heide, author interview.

282. Hollitzer and Bohse, *Heute*, 173.

283. Account of Pleisse River drawn in part from Anonymous, "Die Pleisse-Pilgerweg," Hans-Peter Gensichen, "Kritisches Umweltengagement in den Kirchen," Jürgen Israel, ed., *Zur Freiheit Berufen: Die Kirche in der DDR als Schutzraum der Opposition, 1981–1989* (Berlin: Aufbau Taschenbuch Verlag, 1991), 178–83.

284. Mayer, *Helden*, 47.

285. Mayer, *Helden*, 47.

286. William Tuohy, "East German Town's Bitter Image, *Los Angeles Times* (4 March 1990).

287. Tuohy, "East German Town's Bitter Image."

288. Hans-Peter Gensichen, "Kritisches Umweltengagement in den Kirchen," Jürgen Israel, ed., *Zur Freiheit Berufen: Die Kirche in der DDR als Schutzraum der Opposition, 1981–1989* (Berlin: Aufbau Taschenbuch Verlag, 1991), 151–52.

289. Kirchliches Forschungsheim, *Die Karteibroschüre der kirchlichen Umweltgruppen in der DDR*, November 1988.

290. Mitter and Wolle, *"Ich liebe euch,"* 47.

291. Merrill Elaine Jones, *Greens under God and the Gun: The Environmental Movement, the Lutheran Church, and the East German State* (Bachelor of Arts thesis, Department of Government, Harvard College, March 1991), 70.

292. Richter, *Der Friedliche Revolution*, 91.

293. Tuohy, "East German Town's Bitter Image."

294. "Chernobyl nuclear accident: figures for deaths and cancers still in dispute," *The Guardian* (10 January 2010), web article.

295. Reuters, Greenpeace, Kiev press release, "Milk, berries still contaminated from Chernobyl: Greenpeace" (3 April 2011), web article.

296. Quester, author interview; Mayer, *Helden,* 107.

297. Mayer, *Helden,* 106.

298. Author interviews with Quester and Kallenbach; Mayer, *Helden,* 44–49, 104–109.

299. Kallenbach, author interview.

300. Author interviews with Kallenbach and Quester.

301. "Dokumente zur Kirchenpolitik in Sachsen," 2–3.

302. Author interviews with Quester and Schwabe; Riley, *Everyday Subversion,* 139–40.

303. Quester, author interview.

304. Kallenbach, author interview.

305. Ranked as the group's top concerns by both Kallenbach and Quester.

306. Kallenbach, author interview.

307. Quester, author interview.

308. Kallenbach, author interview. Sources used for the section on Kallenbach include author interviews; Mayer, *Helden,* 44–49; Kallenbach, Archiv Bürgerbewegung Leipzig interview; Gisela Kallenbach, "Arbeitsgruppe Umweltschutz beim Jugendpfarramt Leipzig," paper presented at Milyedagen, Bergen, Norway, 12–14 May 1990, 2 (mimeographed copy from Kallenbach, 7 pp.); and "Gisela Kallenbach," interview in Land and Possekel, *Fremde Welten,* 227–49.

309. Mayer, *Helden,* 46; Kallenbach, author interview.

310. Mayer, *Helden,* 48–49.

311. Kallenbach, author interview; Gisela Kallenbach, "Arbeitsgruppe Umweltschutz"; Mayer, *Helden,* 45.

312. Kallenbach, author interview; Kallenbach, "Arbeitsgruppe Umweltschutz," 2; Mayer, *Helden,* 45.

313. Mayer, *Helden,* 48.

314. Kallenbach, author interview; Kallenbach, "Arbeitsgruppe Umweltschutz," 3.

315. Kallenbach, "Arbeitsgruppe Umweltschutz," 3.

316. Mayer, *Helden,* 49. See copy of letter.

317. Mayer, *Helden,* 44–49; Kallenbach, author interviews; Kallenbach, Archiv Bürgerbewegung Leipzig interview.

318. Mayer, *Helden*, 47–48.

319. Mayer, *Helden*, 45.

320. Sources used for this section on Quester include author interviews; Mayer, *Helden*, 104–109; and Riley, *Everyday Subversion*, 138–40, 290.

321. Quester, author interview.

322. Mayer, *Helden*, 106–107.

323. Quester, author interview.

324. Kallenbach, author interview.

325. Quester, author interview.

326. Quester, author interview.

327. Kallenbach, "Arbeitsgruppe Umweltschutz," 5.

328. Independent in the sense that they were not state-sponsored; however, generally the various movement groups functioned under the protective roof of the Evangelical Church.

329. Goeckel, *Church*, 253; author interviews with Hans-Peter Gensichen (Berlin: 6 April 1992), Rüddenklau, Neubert, Jordan, and Rothe.

330. Gensichen, author interview.

331. Quester, author interview.

332. Rothe, author interview.

333. Rothe, author interview.

334. Author interviews with Müller and Quester.

335. Quester, author interview.

336. Kallenbach, author interview.

337. Quester, author interview.

338. Quester, author interview.

339. Quester, author interview.

340. Quester, author interview.

341. *Pechblende,* a play on words, refers to pitchblende, the principal ore of uranium. *Pech* can mean tar or pitch, but also bad luck or tough luck, and *Blende* can mean deception.

342. Michael Beleites, *Untergrund: Ein Konflikt mit der Stasi in der Uran-Provinz* (Berlin: BasisDruck, 1991). See pp. 97–170 on the Pechblende study.

343. Beleites, *Untergrund,* 107.

344. Falcke, author interview.

345. Beleites, *Untergrund*, 97.

346. Beleites, *Untergrund*, 104.

347. Beleites, *Untergrund*, 97.

348. Sources used for the 1988 Pleisse march include author interviews with Lässig, Schwabe, Heide, and Quester; AGM and AKG, *Die Mücke*, Part I, 9; Dietrich and Schwabe, *Freunde und Feinde*, 375–76; Hollitzer and Bohse, *Heute*, 169–74; Riley, *Everyday Subversion*, 170–72; and Schwabe, "Symbol der Befreiung," 4–5.

349. Hollitzer and Bohse, *Heute*, 173.

350. Hollitzer and Bohse, *Heute*, 173.

351. Wolfgang Elvers and Hagen Findeis. *Was ist aus den politischen alternativen Gruppen geworden? Eine soziologische Auswertung von Interviews mit ehemals führenden Vertretern in Leipzig und Berlin*, unpublished thesis, Religionssoziologisches Institut Emil Fuchs an der Theologischen Fakultät der Karl Marx-Üniversität (Leipzig, 1990), 127.

352. On innovation theory, see Gladwell, *The Tipping Point*, 197; Everett M. Rogers, *Diffusion of Innovations* (New York: The Free Press, 1962), 12, 21–23; and Herbert F. Lionberger, *Adoption of New Ideas and Practices* (Ames, IA: Iowa State University, 1960), 52–66. Also see Appendix D.

353. Ökological Arbeitkreis der Dresdner Kirchenbezirke, "Eine Mark für Espenhain," in Jürgen Israel, ed., *Zur Freiheit Berufen: Die Kirches in der DDR als Schutzraum der Opposition, 1981–1989* (Berlin: Aufbau Taschenbuch Verlag, 1991), 177–78.

354. Richter, *Die Friedliche Revolution: Sachsen*, 93; Gensichen, "Kritisches Umweltengagement," 152, 177–78.

355. Ökological Arbeitkreis," Espenhain," 177–78.

356. Ökological Arbeitkreis, "Espenhain," 177.

357. Ökological Arbeitkreis, "Espenhain," 178.

358. Author interviews with Heide, Moritz, and Quester; Sievers, *Stundenbuch*, 30–31, 156; Gensichen, "Kritisches Umweltengagement," 152.

359. Mayer, *Helden*, 74–75; Müller, author interview.

360. Mayer, *Helden*, 76.

361. Richter, *Die Friedliche Revolution*, 204–205; Sievers, *Stundenbuch*, 30–31; Hollitzer and Bohse, *Heute*, 174–78.

362. Gensichen, "Kritisches Umweltengagement," 178.

363. Dietrich and Schwabe, *Freunde und Feinde*, 487. Other sources used for the second Pleisse demonstration include interviews with Schwabe, Lässig, and Quester; Anonymous, "Der Pleisse-Pilgerweg, 178-183; Gensichen, "Kritisches Umweltengagement," 152, 182; Hollitzer and Bohse, *Heute*, 169–215; *Streiflichter* no. 54 (10 July 1989); Leipziger Menschenrechtsgruppen 1989, *Heute*, Paper 4, 14; Philipsen, *We Were the People*, 157–59; Rein, *Die protestantische Revolution*, 148; Richter, *Die Friedliche Revolution: Sachsen*, 196; Riley, *Everyday Subversion*, 195–97; *Die Mücke*, Part IV, 18.

364. Groups involved included Initiative Group Living, Working Circle Justice, Working Group Human Rights, Working Group Environmental Protection, and Christian Environmental Seminar, Rötha.

365. Anonymous, "Der Pleisse-Pilgerweg," 179–80.

366. Dietrich and Schwabe, *Freunde und Feinde*, 488–90.

367. Dietrich and Schwabe, *Freunde und Feinde*, 489.

368. *Die Mücke*, Part IV, 18; Anonymous, "Der Pleisse-Pilgerweg," 181.

369. Hollitzer and Bohse, *Heute*, 174–80.

370. Dietrich and Schwabe, *Freunde und Feinde*, 489.

371. Hollitzer and Bohse, *Heute*, 174–80.

372. Hollitzer and Bohse, *Heute*, 174–80; Riley, *Everyday Subversion*, 196.

373. *Die Mücke*, Part IV, 18; Rein, *Die protestantische Revolution*, 148; Rüddenklau, *Störenfried*, 200.

374. Hollitzer and Bohse, *Heute*, 199.

375. Hollitzer and Bohse, *Heute*, 184.

376. Anonymous, "Der Pleisse-Pilgerweg," 178–83.

377. Anonymous, "Der Pleisse-Pilgerweg," 182.

378. Anonymous, "Der Pleisse-Pilgerweg," 182; Hollitzer and Bohse, *Heute*, 185.

379. *Die Mücke*, Part IV,18.

380. Anonymous, "Der Pleisse-Pilgerweg," 183.

381. Leipziger Menschenrechtsgruppen 1989, *Heute*, Paper 4, 14.

382. *Die Mücke*, Part IV, 19; Rein, *Die protestantische Revolution,*148.

383. Hollitzer and Bohse, *Heute*, 185–86.

384. Hollitzer and Bohse, *Heute*, 186.

385. Anonymous, "Der Pleisse-Pilgerweg," 183.

386. Gabriele Heide, author interview.

387. Kathrin Walther, interview, Archiv Bürgerbewegung (no date), 2.

388. Gladwell, *The Tipping Point,* 166.

389. Lindner, *Die demokratische Revolution,* 33; official Chinese government figures give 300 dead and 2,000 injured.

390. Neubert, *Opposition,* 815-16.

391. *Neues Deutschland* (5 June1989), 1.

392. Günter Fischbach, ed., *DDR-Almanach '90: Daten, Information, Zahlen* (Stuttgart: Verlag Bonn Aktuell, 1990), 212.

393. Reported in *Neues Deutschland* (27 June 1989).

394. Rein, *Die protestantische Revolution,* 149.

395. Rein, *Die protestantische Revolution,* 149.

396. Kallenbach, author interview.

397. Rein, *Die protestantische Revolution,* 180.

398. Church Congresses were sponsored by consortiums of lay members in various church districts and were independent of the official church bureaucracy. See Philipsen, *We Were the People,* 156.

399. Schwabe, "Symbol der Befreiung," 14.

400. Neubert, *Opposition,* 817.

401. Hendrik Schröder interview with Christoph Wonneberger, Inforadio 93.1, Berlin-Brandenberg, Serie "Zeitgenossen" (4 July 2009), "Die Leipziger Pfarrer Christoph Wonneberger," 1-2, printed on www.inforadio.de/radio_zum_lesen/spezial/zeitgenossen___begegnungen/der_leipziger_pfarrer.html.

402. Walther, interview, Archiv Bürgerbewegung, 1.

403. Walther, interview, Archiv Bürgerbewegung, 1.

404. Walther, interview, Archiv Bürgerbewegung, 1.

405. Neubert, *Opposition,* 817.

406. Philipsen, *We Were the People,* 156

407. Dietrich and Schwabe, *Freunde und Feinde,* 364–365.

408. Wonneberger, author interview; *Die Mücke,* Part IV, 20; Dietrich and Schwabe, *Freunde und Feinde,* 364; Neubert, *Opposition,* 817.

409. Schröder interview with Wonneberger, Inforadio 93.1, 2.

410. Lindner, *Die demokratische Revolution,* 36.

411. Sources used about the street music festival include *Die Mücke*, Part IV, 19; Stephen Lieberwirth, *Wer einen Spielmann zu Tode schlägt: Ein mittelalterliches Zeitdokument anno 1989* (Leipzig: Edition Peters, 1990); Rüddenklau, *Störenfried*, 294; Albrecht Döhnert and Paulus Rummel, "Die Leipziger Montagsdemonstrationen," in Grabner, Heinze, and Pollack, *Leipzig im Oktober: Kirchen und alternative Gruppen im Umbruch der DDR—Analysen zur Wende* (Berlin: Weichern, 1990), 148; author interviews with Lässig and Schwabe.

412. In contrast, only an estimated 100 persons participated in the Ninth Annual Rosenthal Festival on June 24 organized by the state-sponsored youth association, Free German Youth (FDJ) [*Die Mücke*, Part IV, 19].

413. *Die Mücke,* Part IV, 19.

414. Uwe Schwabe, author interview. See Lieberwirth, *Spielmann,* for photo documentation.

415. Mundus, *Leipzig, 1989,* 9; Lindner, *Die demokratische Revolution,* 36.

416. Schwabe, "Symbol der Befreiung," 15.

417. Schwabe, "Symbol der Befreiung," 14.

418. Hans-Jürgen Sievers, *Stundenbuch,* 32.

419. Philipsen, *We Were the People,* 156, for numbers at closing ceremonies. Stasi estimates were lower: 50,000 (Mitter and Wolle, *"Ich liebe euch,"* 111).

420. Sievers, *Stundenbuch,* 32.

421. Sievers, *Stundenbuch,* 32–33.

422. Philipsen, *We Were the People,* 156.

423. Sievers, *Stundenbuch,* 30–33.

424. Mitter and Wolle, *"Ich liebe euch,"* 111, Stasi report 10 July 1989, on misuse of church events and facilities; Lindner, *Die demokratische Revolution,* 36.

425. Mayer, *Helden,* 116.

426. Sievers, *Stundenbuch,* 32.

427. Lindner, *Die demokratische Revolution,* 36; Mundus, *Leipzig, 1989,* 9; Siever, *Stundenbuch,* 31.

428. Mayer, *Helden,* 116.

429. Walther, interview, Archiv Bürgerbewegung, 1.

430. Philipsen, *We Were the People,* 156.

431. Sievers, *Stundenbuch,* 32.

432. Walther, interview, Archiv Bürgerbewegung, 1.

433. Walther, interview, Archiv Bürgerbewegung, 1-2.

434. Walther, interview, Archiv Bürgerbewegung, 2.

435. Heide, author interview.

436. Rein, *Die protestantische Revolution*, 93–98.

437. Rein, *Die protestantische Revolution*, 141–42.

438. Author interviews with Falcke, Pollack, Neubert, Schorlemmer, and Heide.

439. In *Ökumenische Versammlung;* see the unnumbered attachment at the end of the document for a history of the process.

440. *Ökumenische Versammlung*, 164–71.

441. *Ökumenische Versammlung*, 164–71.

442. For a complete list of participating denominations, see *Ökumenische Versammlung*, 182.

443. *Ökumenische Versammlung*, 184–87, 201–204.

444. *Ökumenische Versammlung*, 184.

445. *Ökumenische Versammlung*, 182.

446. *Ökumenische Versammlung*, 172.

447. Leipziger Menschenrechtsgruppen, *Heute vor 10 Jahren*, Paper 4, 4, 14.

448. Philipsen, *We Were the People*, 156.

449. Mitter and Wolle, *"Ich liebe euch,"* 22.

450. Mitter and Wolle, *"Ich liebe euch,"* 54.

451. Joachim Garstecki, "Nachwort: Umkehr in den Schalom Gottes," *Ökumenische Versammlung für Gerechtigkeit, Frieden und Bewahrung der Schöpfung: Dresden-Magdeburg-Dresden: Eine Dokumentation* (Berlin: Aktion Sühnezeichen/Friedensdienste, 1990) 198; however, Garstecki did not specify from which groups.

452. *Ökumenische Versammlung*, 199.

453. *Ökumenische Versammlung*, 198–99.

454. *Ökumenische Versammlung*, 198-99.

455. *Ökumenische Versammlung*, 194, footnote 3, 200.

456. Pollack, author interview.

457. Findeis, author interview.

458. Nowak, author interview.

459. For many group members the Conciliar Process played a more important role in spreading the ideas of groups to the broader population, especially church members, than in providing new ideas for groups.

460. Kloß, author interview.

461. Kallenbach, author interview.

462. Kallenbach, interview, Archiv Bürgerbewegung, 14.

463. Wonneberger, author interview.

464. Sievers, *Stundenbuch*, 32.

465. Sievers, *Stundenbuch*, 32; Mundus, *Leipzig, 1989*, 9.

466. Mayer, *Helden*, 116.

467. Walther, interview, Archiv Bürgerbewegung, 2.

468. Quotation from *Demonteure: Biographien des Leipziger Herbst* reprinted in Sächsischer Landtag, *Friedliche Revolution: Ein Weg der Erinnerung* (Ausstellungskatalog, 1999), 49.

469. Lässig, author interview.

470. Sources for this section on emigration include Fischbach, *DDR-Almanach '90*; Eleonore Baumann, et al., *Der Fischer Welt Almanach: Sonderband DDR* (Frankfurt am Main: Fischer Taschenbuch Verlag, 1990); Philipsen, *We Were the People*; Naimark, "Emigration"; *FBIS*; Micha Wimmer and Christine Proske, eds., *Wir Sind das Volk! Die DDR im Aufbruch: Eine Chronik in Dokumenten und Bildern* (München: Wilhelm Heyne Verlag, 1990).

471. Bobo Harenberg, ed., *Chronik '89: Die Wende in der DDR* (Dortmund: Chronik Verlag, 1990), 65-67.

472. Leipziger Menschenrechtsgruppen 1989, *Heute*, Paper 6, 1–3.

473. Harenberg, *Chronik '89*, 59.

474. Harenberg, *Chronik '89*, 59.

475. Ildikó Bódvai, "Paneuropäisches Picknick—der lautlose Aufschrei," in Norbert Lobenwein, *89–90: Momente, die die Welt bewegten* (Budapest: Konrad Adenauer Stiftung, 2009), 19–20.

476. Bódvai, "Picknick," 19-20, trans. from German by Patricia Smith.

477. Harenberg, *Chronik '89*, 58–59.

478. Leipziger Menschenrechtsgruppen 1989, *Heute*, Paper 6, 1–2.

479. Leipziger Menschenrechtsgruppen 1989, *Heute*, Paper 6, 1–2.

480. Compiled from Fischbach, *DDR-Almanach '90,* Baumann, *Der Fischer Welt Almanach: Sonderband DDR;* Philipsen, *We Were the People;* Naimark, *"Emigration"; FBIS;* Wimmer and Proske, *Wir Sind das Volk!;* Harenberg, *Chronik '89.*

481. Harenberg, *Chronik '89,* Survey by Infratest Kommunikationsforschung in "Warum ein Neubeginn?" 67.

482. Baumann, *Der Fischer Weltalmanach: Sonderband DDR,* 138.

483. Hamburg DPA in German (6 September 1989), FBIS, *Daily Report* (Eastern Europe), (11 September 1989), 15.

484. East Berlin ADN International Service, 11 September 1989, translated in FBIS, *Daily Report* (Eastern Europe), (11 September 1989), 15.

485. *Neues Deutschland* (7 September 1989), 2, translated in FBIS, *Daily Report* (Eastern Europe), (11 September 1989), 16.

486. *Die Mücke,* Part IV, 20.

487. Tetzner, *Kerzen-Montage verändern die Welt: Warum die Waffen wirklich schweigen* (Leipzig: Edition Vulcanus, 2004), 83–86.

488. Lässig, author interview.

489. Baumann, *Der Fischer Welt Almanach: Sonderband DDR,* 146.

490. Based on various sources cited in this book, including *Die Mücke,* Parts I-IV, *Ost-West Diskussionsforum;* Fischbach, *DDR-Almanach '90;* Baumann, *Der Fischer Welt Almanach: Sonderband DDR;* Grabner, Heinze, and Pollack, *Leipzig im Oktober;* Philipsen, *Wir Sind das Volk;* Wolfgang Schneider, *Leipziger Demontagebuch* (Leipzig and Weimar: Gustav Keipenheuer, 1990); Mundus, *Leipzig, 1989;* Tetzner, *Kerzen-Montage;* Reiner Tetzner, *Leipziger Ring: Aufzeichnungen eines Montagsdemonstranten* (Leipzig: Edition Vulcanus, 2004); Hollitzer and Bohse, *Heute;* Schwabe, "Symbol der Befreiung"; Linder, *Die demokratische Revolution;* Michael Sagurna, ed., *1989: Chronologie der Wende in Sachsen* (Dresden: Sächsische Staatskanzlei, 1999).

491. *Die Mücke,* Part IV, 20; Tetzner, *Kerzen-Montage,* 86–88; Sievers, *Stundenbuch,* 39–42; Lindner, *Die Demokratische Revolution,* 67.

492. Tetzner, *Kerzen-Montage,* 87–88.

493. Tetzner, *Kerzen-Montage,* 87; Sievers, *Stundenbuch,* 42.

494. Schwabe, "Symbol der Befreiung," 16.

495. Sievers, *Stundenbuch,* 43.

496. Sievers, *Stundenbuch,* 43.

497. Sievers, *Stundenbuch*, 43.

498. Schwabe, "Symbol der Befreiung," 16; Tetzner, *Kerzen-Montage*, 88.

499. Feydt, Heinze, and Schanz, "Die Leipziger Friedensgebete," 126–27.

500. Sievers, *Stundenbuch*, 45.

501. Thomas Ahbe, Michael Hoffman, and Volker Stiehler, eds., *Wir bleiben hier! Erinnerungen an den Leipziger Herbst '89* (Leipzig: Gustav Kiepenheuer Verlag, 1991), 132.

502. Sagurna, *1989, Sachsen*, 27.

503. Schwabe, author interview.

504. Sources for the September 25 peace prayer section include Sievers, *Stundenbuch*, 49–52; Hollitzer and Bohse, *Heute*, 389-406; Mitter and Wolle, *"Ich liebe euch,"* 174–76; Mundus, *Leipzig, 1989*, 14–15; Tetzner, *Kerzen-Montage*, 92–94; Riley, *Everyday Subversion*, 212–17; Schwabe, "Symbol der Befreiung," 16–17; and Lindner, *Die demokratische Revolution*, 67–68.

505. Tetzner, *Kerzen-Montage*, 92.

506. Tetzner, *Kerzen-Montage*, 93.

507. Pollack, author interview.

508. Quoted in Philipsen, *We Were the People*, 203, 321.

509. Other citizen movement organizations included Initiative for Peace and Human Rights, the United Left, Democratic Awakening, Democracy Now, and the Greens.

510. Leipzig members of political groups interviewed for this study who joined citizen movement organizations include Initiative for Peace and Human Rights' Thomas Rudolph, Rainer Müller, and Oliver Kloß; New Forum's Jochen Lässig, Uwe Schwabe, and Brigitte Moritz; and Democratic Awakening's Hagen Findeis.

511. Information compiled from Philipsen, "We Were the People"; Wimmer and Proske, *Wir Sind das Volk!*; Helmut Müller-Enbergs, Marianne Schulz, and Jan Wielgohs, eds., *Von Illegalität ins Parlament: Werdegang und Konzept der Neuen Bürgerbewegungen* (Berlin: LinksDruck, 1991); Rein, *Opposition*; Zeno and Sabine Zimmerling, *Neue Chronik DDR: Berichte, Fotos, Dokumente, .1 Folge: 7. August-.18 Oktober, 1989, second edition* (Berlin: Berlag Tribune Berlin GmbH, 1990); Gerda Haufe and Karl Bruckmeier, eds., *Die Bürgerbewegungen in der DDR und in den Ostdeutschen Bundesländern* (Opladen: Westdeutscher Verlag, 1993); Christoph Links and Hannes Bahrmann, *Wir Sind das Volk: Die DDR im*

Aufbruch: Eine Chronik (Wuppertal: Peter Hammer Verlag, 1990); Fischbach, *DDR-Almanach '90;* Baumann, *Der Fischer Welt Almanach: Sonderband DDR;* and FBIS *Daily Reports* (Eastern Europe). There is considerable disagreement in these sources about the founding dates of several groups; sometimes the dates vary by as much as a month. In part, these variations may be due to citing a date for a preliminary organizational meeting as compared with a founding date, or for the founding as a citizens' group as compared to a party.

512. FBIS, *Daily Report* (Eastern Europe) (1 November 1989), 28, from Hamburg DPA in German (31 October 1989).

513. See Lindner, *Die demokratische Revolution,* 50, for text of "Aufbruch 89—Neues Forum" ["Departure '89—New Forum"].

514. Philipsen, *We Were the People,* 395; FBIS, *Daily Reports* (Eastern Europe) (14 December 1989), 55, *Zycie Warszawy* in Polish (4 December 1989), 5.

515. Pollack, author interview.

516. Sagurna, *1989, Sachsen,* 26.

517. Sagurna, *1989, Sachsen,* 26.

518. Sagurna, *1989, Sachsen,* 27.

519. Sagurna, *1989, Sachsen,* 28.

520. Sagurna, *1989, Sachsen,* 29.

521. Sagurna, *1989, Sachsen,* 29–30.

522. Bernd Lindner and Ralph Grüneberger, eds., *Demonteure: Biographien des Leipziger Herbst,* reprinted in Sächsischer Landtag, *Friedliche Revolution: Ein Weg der Erinnerung* (Ausstellungskatalog, 1999), 54.

523. Heide, author interview.

524. Mundus, *Leipzig, 1989,* 25.

525. Richter, *Die Friedliche Revolution,* 250–52.

526. Richter, *Die Friedliche Revolution,* 255–57.

527. Richter, *Die Friedliche Revolution,* 261–62.

528. Richter, *Die Friedliche Revolution,* 262.

529. Richter, *Die Friedliche Revolution,* 253–55.

530. Richter, *Die Friedliche Revolution,* 253.

531. Mundus, *Leipzig, 1989,* 15.

532. Sources for October 2 include Mundus, *Leipzig, 1989,* 16; Feydt, Heinze, and Schanz, "Die Leipziger Friedensgebet," 126–28; Hollitzer and Bohse, *Heute,*

407–50; Sievers, *Stundenbuch*, 58–69; Ahbe, Hoffman, and Stiehler, *Wir bleiben hier!* 32; Martin Jankowski, *Der Tag, der Deutschland veränderte: 9. Oktober 1989*, second edition (Leipzig: Evangelische Verlaganstalt, 2009), 63–65; Riley, *Everyday Subversion*, 217–22; Tetzner, *Kerzen-Montage*, 119–130; Tetzner, *Leipziger Ring*, 9–13.

533. Hollitzer and Bohse, *Heute*, 416-23.

534. Hollitzer and Bohse, *Heute*, 420.

535. Hollitzer and Bohse, *Heute*, 424; Sievers, *Stundenbuch*, 64.

536. Friedrich Magirius, "Wiege der Wende," Wolfgang Schneider, *Leipziger Demontagebuch* (Leipzig and Weimar: Gustav Kiepenheuer, 1990),13.

537. Richter, *Die Friedliche Revolution*, 265.

538. Richter, *Die Friedliche Revolution*, 266–67.

539. Richter, *Die Friedliche Revolution*, 268–69.

540. Richter, *Die Friedliche Revolution*, 297, 313–98.

541. Lindner, *Die demokratische Revolution*, 82-83.

542. Sievers, *Stundenbuch*, 74.

543. Lindner, *Die demokratische Revolution*, 82–83; Sievers, *Stundenbuch*, 73–74.

544. Gisela Kallenbach, interview, Archiv Bürgerbewegung (12 May 2008), transcribed, 20–21.

545. Jankowski, *Der Tag, der Deutschland veränderte*, 77–78, 94–95; Richter, *Die Friedliche Revolution*, 379.

546. Baumann, *Der Fischer Welt Almanach: Sonderband DDR*, 151. For an hour-by-hour chronology of October 9 in Leipzig, see Jankowski, *Der Tag, der Deutschland veränderte*, 86–115. Sources for October 9 include Mundus, *Leipzig, 1989*, 20-26; Lindner, *Die demokratische Revolution*, 77, 79-81; Richter, *Die Friedliche Revolution*, 357-98; Feydt, Heinze, and Schanz, "Die Leipziger Friedensgebet," 128–35; Sievers, *Stundenbuch*, 76–94; Riley, *Everyday Subversion*, 226–33; Hollitzer and Bohse, *Heute*, 460–69, 498-502; Jankowski, *Der Tag, der Deutschland veränderte*, 73–120; Tetzner, *Kerzen-Montage*, 153–196; Tetzner, *Leipziger Ring*, 28–35.

547. Magirius, "Wiege der Wende," 23.

548. Jankowski, *Der Tag, der Deutschland veränderte*, 90.

549. Jankowski, *Der Tag, der Deutschland veränderte*, 84.

550. Jankowski, *Der Tag, der Deutschland veränderte*, 96.

551. Jankowski, *Der Tag, der Deutschland veränderte*, 86–87.

552. Jankowski, *Der Tag, der Deutschland veränderte*, 95.

553. Sagurna, *1989, Sachsen*, 38.

554. Jankowski, *Der Tag, der Deutschland veränderte*, 95.

555. Jankowski, *Der Tag, der Deutschland veränderte*, 114.

556. Sagurna, *1989, Sachsen*, 44.

557. Robert Darnton, *Berlin Journal: 1989–1990* (New York: W.W. Norton and Company, 1991), 11.

558. Jankowski, *Der Tag, der Deutschland veränderte*, 85.

559. Jankowski, *Der Tag, der Deutschland veränderte*, 99; Sievers, *Stundenbuch*, 82–83; Mundus, *Leipzig, 1989*, 20–26, *"Appell"* reprinted, 21.

560. Archiv Bürgerbewegung Leipzig interview with Kallenbach; Kallenbach, "Arbeitsgruppe Umweltschutz beim Jugendpfarramt Leipzig;" Kallenbach, author interview.

561. Sievers, *Stundenbuch*, 83–87.

562. Siegbert Schefke, author interview (Dresden: 14 April 1992); Sievers, *Stundenbuch*, 92–94.

563. Jankowski, *Der Tag, der Deutschland veränderte*, 104.

564. Sievers, *Stundenbuch*, 82.

565. Richter, *Die Friedliche Revolution*, 382–83.

566. Jankowski, *Der Tag, der Deutschland veränderte*, 106.

567. Mundus, *Leipzig, 1989*, 25.

568. Jankowski, *Der Tag, der Deutschland veränderte*, 123.

569. Gudula Ziemer and Holger Jackisch, "2. Akt: Wir sind das Volk—aber wer sind wir?" *Neues Forum Leipzig*, 26.

570. Taylor, *The Berlin Wall*, 427 (Taylor translation).

571. Jankowski, *Der Tag, der Deutschland veränderte*, 124.

572. Siegbert Schefke, author interview (Dresden: 14 April 1992); Sievers, *Stundenbuch*, 91–92; Mundus, *Leipzig, 1989*, 26, 28.

573. Mundus, *Leipzig, 1989*, 27.

574. Jankowski, *Der Tag, der Deutschland veränderte*, 111.

575. Mundus, *Leipzig, 1989*, 28.

576. Richter, *Die Friedliche Revolution*, 449; Hollitzer and Bohse, *Heute*, 469–73.

577. Tetzner, *Leipziger Ring*, 44.

578. Based on various sources cited in this book, including *Die Mücke; DDR Almanach '90; Der Fischer Welt Almanac: Sonderband DDR;* Grabner, Heinze, and Pollack, *Leipzig im Oktober;* Lindner, *Die demokratishce Revolution;* Karl-Dieter Opp and Peter Voss, *Die volkseigene Revolution* (Stuttgart: Klett-Cotta, 1993); Philipsen, *We Were the People; Leipziger Demontagebuch;* Sievers, *Stundenbuch;* Tetzner, *Der Tag, der Deutschland veränderte;* Tetzner, *Kerzen-Montage;* Mundus, *Leipzig, 1989;* Hollitzer and Bohse, *Heute;* Leipziger Menschenrechtsgruppen 1989, *Heute.*

579. Mundus, *Leipzig, 1989*, 28.

580. Mundus, *Leipzig, 1989*, 18.

581. Mundus, *Leipzig, 1989*, 28.

582. Mundus, *Leipzig, 1989*, 28; Richter, *Die Friedliche Revolution*, 442–43.

583. Mundus, *Leipzig, 1989*, 29.

584. Tetzner, *Kerzen-Montage*, 233; Lindner, *Die demokratische Revolution*, 87.

585. Jankowski, *Der Tag, der Deutschland veränderte*, 123.

586. Tetzner, *Kerzen-Montage*, 232–33.

587. Jankowski, *Der Tag, der Deutschland veränderte*, 123.

588. Ziemer and Jackisch, "2. Akt," 26.

589. Mundus, *Leipzig, 1989*, 32.

590. Tetzner, *Kerzen-Montage*, 245–46; Lindner, *Die demokratische Revolution*, 87; Neues Forum Leipzig, *Jetzt oder nie—Demokratie! Leipziger Herbst '89*, second edition (Leipzig: Forum Verlag, 1989), 167–68.

591. Neues Forum Leipzig, 167–68; Tetzner, *Kerzen-Montage*, 246; Mundus, *Leipzig, 1989*, 32.

592. Richter, *Die Friedliche Revolution*, 535; "*Aktuelle Kamera*," en.wikipedia.org: "*Aktuelle Kamera*'s main program was originally scheduled at 8 pm before being moved to 7:30 pm in the 1960s, so as not to coincide with the major West German newscasts, ZDF's *Heute* at 7 pm and the ARD's *Tagesschau* at 8 pm, both of which were widely watched in East Germany. . . . Almost a month before the opening of the Berlin Wall in 1989, *Aktuelle Kamera* loosened its fidelity to the party line and began presenting fair reports about the events transforming East Germany at the time. On October 16, 1989, it showed its first pictures of the massive opposition rallies taking place every Monday in Leipzig."

593. Sievers, *Stundenbuch*, 117; *"Der schwarze Kanal,"* en.wikipedia.org: *"Der schwarze Kanal"* (the Black Channel) "was a series of political propaganda programmes broadcast weekly between 1960 and 1989 by East German television. Each edition was made up of recorded extracts from recent West German television programmes re-edited to include a Communist commentary."

594. Neues Forum Leipzig, 169; *Sächsisches Tageblatt* (31 October1989), 1.

595. Other sources say 350,000 and 400,000 demonstrators.

596. Mundus, *Leipzig, 1989*, 32; Tetzner, *Kerzen-Montage*, 251; Neues Forum Leipzig, 183-84. At a meeting October 31 Seidel said he would suggest steps for legalizing New Forum, and on November 1 Seidel met with three representatives of New Forum.

597. Author interviews with Wonneberger and Heide; Mayer, *Helden*, 15.

598. Tetzner, *Kerzen-Montage*, 251.

599. Links and Bahrmann, *Wir sind das Volk*, 85.

600. Taylor, *The Berlin Wall*, 421.

601. Mundus, *Leipzig, 1989*, 33–34.

602. Tetzner, *Kerzen-Montage*, 251.

603. Mundus, *Leipzig, 1989*, 33; Richter, *Die Friedliche Revolution*, 660–61.

604. Mundus, *Leipzig, 1989*, 33; Tetzner, *Kerzen-Montage*, 251. Neues Forum Leipzig, 193–94 includes speech of Christoph Hein.

605. Tetzner, *Kerzen-Montage*, 261; Tetzner, *Leipziger Ring*, 70–71.

606. Mundus, *Leipzig, 1989*, 34.

607. Already on October 23, calls of "The Wall must go" were heard in Leipzig (Lindner, *Die demokratische Revolution*, 87).

608. Tetzner, *Kerzen-Montage*, 260.

609. Tetzner, *Kerzen-Montage*, 261.

610. Mundus, *Leipzig, 1989*, 34.

611. Tetzner, *Kerzen-Montage*, 260.

612. Tetzner, *Kerzen-Montage*, 267; Mitter and Wolle, *"Ich liebe euch,"* 246–51.

613. In East Germany there are three territorial levels below the national level, including 15 districts (*Bezirke*), 219 counties (*Kreise*), and about 90,000 towns and communities (*Gemeinde*); *Country Studies, East Germany*, now mongabyay, http://www.mongabay.com/history/east_germany/east_germanydistrict_and_local_government.html#LgG6OX0MeDsohRsf.99)

614. Tetzner, *Kerzen-Montage*, 265.

615. This account of Berlin Wall opening is developed from Richter, *Die Friedliche Revolution*, 727–36; Hans-Hermann Hertel, *Chronik des Mauerfalls: Die dramatischen Ereignisse um den 9. November 1989*, eleventh edition (Berlin: Ch. Links Verlag, 2009), 149ff; Mundus, *Leipzig, 1989*, 35–36; Taylor, *The Berlin Wall*, 420–28; interview with Egon Krenz, www.chronik-der-mauer.de [www.chronik-der-mauer.de/index.php/chronik/1989/November/9].

616. Taylor, *The Berlin Wall*, 422–24; Richter, *Die Friedliche Revolution*, 727–28.

617. Richter, *Die Friedliche Revolution*, 727–28.

618. Taylor, *The Berlin Wall*, 425–28.

619. Taylor, *The Berlin Wall*, 427.

620. Interview with Egon Krenz, www.chronik-der-mauer.de/index.php/chronik/1989/November/9/.

621. Mayer, *Helden*, 8.

622. Michael Beleites, "Vorwort," in Mayer, *Helden*, 10.

623. In Sievers, *Stundenbuch*, 150, Pastor Beate Schelmat from Kirchbach speaking at Reformierte Church in October 9, 1999, ten years after Leipzig's peaceful revolution.

624. Information in this chapter came primarily from author interviews with activists and from Mayer, *Helden*, and Mundus, *Leipzig, 1989*.

625. See Appendix D for more on diffusion theory.

626. Patricia J. Smith, "The Illusory Economic Miracle," *After the Wall: Eastern Germany since 1989* (Boulder, CO: Westview Press, 1998), 107–135.

627. "East German General Election, 1990," en.wikipedia.org.

628. Mayer, *Wonneberger;* Pausch, *Wonneberger.*

629. Moritz, author interview.

630. Quester, author interview. After the revolution, Working Group Environmental Protection merged with the state environmental group and became Ökolöwe.

631. Kallenbach, author interview.

632. Lässig, author interview.

633. Mayer, *Helden*, 24.

634. Compiled primarily from author interviews; Mayer, *Helden;* Mundus, *Leipzig, 1989;* and Neubert, *Opposition.*

635. For several works providing alternative explanations, see Gert-Joachim Glaeßner and Ian Wallace, *The German Revolution of 1989: Causes and Consequences* (Providence, RI: Berg, 1992); Hans Joas und Martin Kohli, eds., *Der Zusammenbruch der DDR* (Frankfurt am Main: Suhrkamp, 1993); Konrad Löw, ed., *Ursachen und Verlauf der deutschen Revolution 1989* (Berlin: Duncker und Humblot, 1991); and Andrew Arato, "Interpreting 1989," *Social Research* 60, no. 3 (Fall 1993), 609–46. For a discussion in English of a number of alternative explanations, see Laurence H. McFalls, *Communism's Collapse, Democracy's Demise: The Cultural Context and Consequences of the East German Revolution* (New York: New York University Press, 1995), Chapter 3. McFalls himself puts forth a cultural explanation, arguing that the erosion of values in the 1980s created a frustration that mobilized East Germans: 98–99.

636. Quoted in Philipsen, *We Were the People*, 165.

637. Mitter and Wolle, *"Ich liebe euch,"* 47.

638. Mitter and Wolle, *"Ich liebe euch,"* 63.

639. Neubert, author interview.

640. Mitter and Wolle, *"Ich liebe euch,"* 47.

641. Mitter and Wolle, *"Ich liebe euch,"* 48.

642. Mitter and Wolle, *"Ich liebe euch,"* 49.

643. Ulrike Poppe, "Das kritische Potential der Gruppen in Kirche und Gesellschaft: 1988," in Detlef Pollack, ed., *Die Legitimität der Freiheit: Politisch alternative Gruppen in der DDR unter dem Dach der Kirche* (Frankfurt am Main: Peter Lang, 1990), 68–69. The network Peace Concrete coordinated more than 325 groups throughout East Germany, including 70 in the Church Province of Saxony (Saxony Anhalt, including Magdeburg and Halle); 90 in Saxony (Leipzig, Karl-Marx-Stadt, and Dresden area); 60 in Thuringia (the region surrounding Erfurt); 25 in the Mecklenburg area in the north, and 80 in Berlin-Brandenburg.

644. Poppe, "Das kritische Potential," 68; Neubert, *Opposition*, 700–704, 800; author interviews with Ulrike Poppe (Berlin: 3 March 1992), Silvia Müller (Berlin: 27 January 1992), Heiko Leitz (Güstrow: 11 November 1999), and Neubert.

645. Neubert, *Opposition*, 701.

646. Neubert, *Opposition*, 793–800.

647. Ruddenklau, *Störenfried*, 286. Earlier the group had used a wax-process

mimeograph machine, which by 1989 was seldom used because they had obtained a computer with the help of West German groups. Other sources for the section on Berlin's Environmental Library include from author interviews with Wolfgang Rüddenklau (Berlin: 27 January 1992), Jordan, and Quester.

648. *Arche Nova 1* (1 January 1988), 3.

649. Among the four was Ulrich Neumann, who emigrated from East Berlin to West Berlin in June 1988 and served as a primary organizer of the east-west exchange of information [author interviews with Ulrich Neumann (Berlin: 25 February 1992), Jordan, and Belinda Cooper (Berlin: 15 and 23 November 1991)].

650. Jordan, author interview. According to Jordan, Stasi files opened after the revolution suggest that the Stasi instigated many of the problems between the two groups and their members.

651. Information in this section came from Jones, *Greens under God and the Gun*, 87–90, and from author interviews with Cooper, Jordan, Neumann, and Andreas Passarge (Berlin: 28 April 1992).

652. Quester, author interview.

653. Neubert, *Opposition*, 827.

654. Author interviews with Bohley, Poppe, Wolfgang Templin, Lotte Templin, Reinhard Weißhuhn (Berlin: 4 February 1992), and Rudolph; Mitte and Wolle, *"Ich liebe euch,"* 49; Neubert, *Opposition*, 839.

655. Reinhard Weißhuhn, "Initiative für Frieden und Menschenrechte—vor und nach der Wende," in *Burgerbewegungen für Demokratie in den Kommunen* (Berlin: Staatsverlag der Deutschen Demokratischen Republik, 1990), 25.

656. Information from author interviews with Schatta, Leitz, Wonneberger, Kloß, and Schwabe; Mitter and Wolle, *"Ich liebe euch,"* 70–71; and Neubert, *Opposition*, 577 714.

657. Kloß, author interview.

658. Wonneberger, author interview.

659. Schwabe, author interview.

660. Neubert, *Opposition*, 578.

661. Compiled from Hans-Jürgen Buntrock, "Die Kirche von Unten," in Ferdinand Kroh, ed., *"Freiheit is immer Freiheit. . . ."*, 181–209; Mitter and Wolle, *"Ich liebe euch,"* 65–66; and Helsinki Watch Report, *From Below*, 46. The *Kirchentag*

generally involved four to five days of meetings, with the first three days focusing on scriptures, sermons, and more specifically church-related information, followed by a weekend featuring information and opinion exchange in the form of workshops, symposiums, speakers, and discussions. The *Kirchentag* served as a gathering place for local Christians as well as for those from other regions, and as many as 100,000 attended some regional church congresses.

662. Buntrock, "Die Kirche von Unten," 209.

663. Buntrock, "Die Kirche von Unten," 192.

664. Mitter and Wolle, *"Ich liebe euch,"* 65–66.

665. Mayer, *Helden,* Dusdal letter, 97.

666. Lotte Templin, author interview; Neubert, *Opposition,* 710–12; Mayer, *Helden,* 97–103; Mitter and Wolle, *"Ich liebe euch,"* 64–65.

667. Mitter and Wolle, *"Ich liebe euch,"* 64.

668. Mitter and Wolle, *"Ich liebe euch,"* 65.

669. Mitter and Wolle, *"Ich liebe euch,"* 64.

670. Neubert, *Opposition,* 711–12.

671. Lotte Templin, author interview.

672. Lotte Templin, author interview.

673. Neubert, *Opposition,* 711.

674. Elvers and Findeis, *Gruppen,* 38.

675. Neubert, *Opposition,* 711–12.

676. Mayer, *Helden,* 97–103; Neubert, *Opposition,* 712.

677. Moritz, author interview.

678. Besier and Wolf, *"Pfarrer, Christen, und Katholiken,"* 831–37.

679. Falcke, author interview.

680. Heide, author interview.

681. Moritz, author interview.

682. Pollack, author interview.

683. Poppe, "Das kritische Potential," 74.

684. Poppe, "Das kritische Potential," 74.

685. Rudolph, author interview.

686. Neubert, *Opposition,* 752–68.

687. Author interviews with Müller and Rudolph.

688. Schwabe, author interview; Neubert, *Opposition,* 764–65.

689. Neubert, *Opposition,* 764–65.

690. Lässig, author interview.

691. Poppe, "Das kritische Potential," 72–74; Poppe, author interview.

692. Poppe, "Das kritische Potential," 73.

693. Poppe, "Das kritische Potential," 73

694. In German, *Neues Forum, Demokratie Jetzt, Demokratische Aufbruch, Vereinigte Linke, SozialistIn/nen, Grüne Liste* and *Grüne Partei.*

695. Elvers and Findeis, *Gruppen,* 11–15 and 86–87 provide evidence of these multiple involvements, and my interviews revealed that many leaders and activists in illegal or church-related grassroots groups later participated actively, and often as leaders, in broad-based citizens' movement groups and political parties.

696. Interview with Markus Meckel, "Markus Meckel: Wir haben den Raum der Kirche verlassen," in Rein, *Die Opposition in der DDR,* 95.

697. FBIS, *Daily Report* (Eastern Europe), (1 November 1989), 28, from Hamburg DPA in German (31 October 1989).

698. FBIS, *Daily Report* (Eastern Europe), (7 December 1989), 65 from *Gazeta Wyborcza* (23 November 1989), 6. In October 1989 Democracy Now organized a petition drive calling for a referendum to abolish the clause in the East German Constitution on the leading role of the communist party in order to create a true multiparty system.

699. FBIS, *Daily Report* (Eastern Europe), (3 October 1989), 26, from Hamburg DPA in German (2 October 1989).

700. Philipsen, *We Were the People,* 395; FBIS, *Daily Reports* (Eastern Europe), (14 December 1989), 55, *Zycie Warszawy* in Polish (4 December 1989), 5.

701. Pollack, author interview.

702. Everett M. Rogers, *Diffusion of Innovation* (New York: The Free Press, 1962).

703. Rogers, *Diffusion,* 12.

704. Rogers, *Diffusion,* 13. Rogers notes that even in the case of technological innovations, it is the *idea* about the new material product that is spread, as well as the object itself.

705. Rogers, *Diffusion,* 14.

706. Doug McAdam and Dieter Rucht, "The Cross-National Diffusion of Movement Ideas," *Annals of the American Academy of Political and Social Science,* No.

528 (July 1993), 66. McAdam and Rucht point to the significance of non-relational (television, the print media, scholarly and radical writings) channels as well as direct relational channels (person-to-person relationships) not only for domestic diffusion of social movements but also for cross-national diffusion (73–74).

707. McAdam and Rucht draw from the work on the cross-national diffusion of policy or other organizational innovations by David Strang and John W. Meyer, "Institutional Conditions for Diffusion," paper delivered at the Workshop on New Institutional Theory (Ithaca, NY: November 1991).

708. Patricia Jo Smith, *Democratizing East Germany: Ideas, Emerging Political Groups, and the Dynamics of Change,* PhD dissertation (Seattle: University of Washington, 1995), UMI Dissertation Services, 9616673.

709. Rogers' five categories of adopters—innovators, early adopters, early majority, late majority, and laggards—are applicable [Rogers, *Diffusion* (1962), 150].

710. Lionberger, *Adoption,* 52–66.

711. Rogers, *Diffusion* (1983), 18.

712. Malcolm Gladwell, *The Tipping Point: How Little Things Can Make a Big Difference* (New York: Little, Brown and Company, 2000). (Bay Back Paperback version published 2002.)

713. Gladwell, *The Tipping Point,* 196–215.

714. Gladwell, *The Tipping Point,* 60.

715. Whenever I met with Schwabe, he would bring me new articles and books or point out materials that had recently been published.

716. Gladwell, *The Tipping Point,* 38.

717. Gladwell, *The Tipping Point,* 51.

718. The information in this section came from my interview with Matthias Sengewald (Erfurt: 23 April 1992) as well as from others interviewed in Leipzig and Erfurt.

719. Author interviews with Aribert Rothe and Gerlinde Harbig (Erfurt: 4 May 1992).

720. Sengewald, author interview.

ACKNOWLEDGMENTS

Many individuals and institutions made this book possible.

Thanks especially to the activists and other East Germans who generously shared their time and experiences with me, first in the late 1980s and early 1990s and later in follow-up interviews. Their information and experiences form the heart of this book. Several Leipzig group members went out of their way to help with this project by providing additional materials, contact information for other interviewees, their own histories and overviews of the group situation in Leipzig and East Germany, and hospitality. I especially thank Uwe Schwabe, Gabriele Heide, Gisela Kallenbach, Jochen Lässig, Brigitte Moritz, Rainier Müller, Gesine Oltmanns, Roland Quester, Thomas Rudolph, and Christoph Wonneberger. (See a full list of interviews at the beginning of the Bibliography. Unless otherwise noted, all translations in the book are my own.)

Archives provided invaluable *samizdat* and other source material on groups, the political opposition, and the events of 1989 as well as copying privileges. Especially important were Archiv Bürgerbewegung Leipzig; Umweltbibliothek Leipzig; Archive of the Initiative for Peace and Human Rights; Museum in the "Runden Ecke" in Leipzig; Forschungszentrum zu den Verbrechen des Stalinismus in Dresden; and Umweltbibliothek in Berlin. Especially helpful current and previous staff members include Uwe Schwabe, Saskia Paul, Monika Keller, Rainer Müller, and Thomas Rudolph. Many photos from Archiv Bürgerbewegung Leipzig's large collection documenting events in the late 1980s appear in this book. (See "Credits" for specific information on archives, photographers, and photographs.)

Much of the information in this book *Revolution Revisited: Behind the Scenes in East Germany, 1989,* appeared initially as my PhD dissertation in political science titled *Democratizing East Germany: Ideas, Emerging Political Groups, and the Dynamics of Change* (Seattle: University of Washington, 1995). Thanks to professors on my supervisory committee at the University of Washington in Seattle who guided me: John T.S. Keeler, Sabrina Ramet, the late George Modelski, and Michael McCann.

An International Research and Exchanges Board (IREX) fellowship with funds supplied by the National Endowment for the Humanities and the United States Information Agency supported my research year in Berlin and eastern Germany, and the Deutscher Akademischer Austauschdienst (DAAD) and Humboldt University in Berlin also afforded me support. My East German advisor Dr. Marianne Schulz, earlier of the East German Academy of Sciences and after reunification at the Max Planck Institute, gave me invaluable assistance during both the dissertation and book phases of this project. Her own important research on groups and movements in East Germany provided a broad perspective as well as in-depth knowledge about political changes occurring within the country and the region, and she generously offered her materials, knowledge, time, and hospitality.

A number of persons I first met in East Berlin before the Wall came down have provided friendship and support over the past 25 years. I am especially grateful to friends Marianne Schulz and the late Peter Schulz; the late Maureen Kaufmann and Otto-Fritz Hayner; and Heidi and Harry Sabelus.

Special thanks to my Seattle editor Jessica Murphy Moos for her expert guidance in conceptualizing the book and in helping me identify and shape important stories from the masses of interviews and other research materials I have compiled over the years. Thanks also to my granddaughter Anna Smith and son-in-law Simon Dalexy for help with maps and photos; to my sister Joyce Saricks for helping with translations and proofreading German bibliographic entries; to Deborah Gooden, Bill Smith, and Kathleen Wolgemuth for reading and offering valuable comments on various chapters; to Gene Dwiggins and the 1-1 staff at the Univerity Village Apple Store in Seattle for assistance with photos and maps; and to my copy editor Stephanie and to Miles, Amber, Adrienne, Matt, and all the helpful staff at Dog Ear Publishing.

Most importantly, thanks to my husband Bill, son Mark, and daughter Jennifer for their inspiration, support, and love as I have pursued this project over many years, first as a dissertation and more recently as a book.

CREDITS

Archiv Bürgerbewegung Leipzig (ABL) e. V. made available the following images and photographs of the photographers listed below (page numbers follow names):

Bernd Heinze: 137, 144, 145, 174, 175, 178, 204, 209, 218, 220, 223, 224, 225
Martin Jehnichen: 74, 116, 127, 141, 183, 189, 194, 196, 197, 201, 214, 215, 217, 230
Rainer Kühn: 39, 142, 169, 170
Rainer Kühn and Stefan Walter: 173, 176, 177
Christoph Motzer: 52, 61, 71, 127, 131, 140, 153, 154, 170, 180, 190, 191, 211
Frank Sellentin: 20, 23, 192, 198, 222,
Images: 21, 133, 143

GMRE—"Bürgerkomitee Leipzig e.V. für die Auflösung der ehemaligen Staatssicherheit (MfS), Träger der Gedenkstätte Museum in der "Runden Ecke" mit dem Museum im Stasi-Bunker"—provided the following:

Heinz Löster: cover photo and p. 205—*GMRE Inv.-Nr.: F.A. 13018*

Mimeograph machine (Rex Rotary 490), p. 10—*GMRE Inv.-Nr.: 03000*

Bottle of water from Pleisse River, p. 125—*GMRE (Tobias Hollizter) Inv.-Nr.: 17226*

Thomas Mayer provided the photographs of Walther and Rudolph on pages 239 and 240.

I thank everyone who has provided photographs and other images for this book. Special thanks to Saskia Paul of ABL and Susanne Beutler of GMRE as well as to Gesine Oltmanns, Monica Keller, Uwe Schwabe, Gisela Kallenbach, Kathrin Walthers, and Thomas Mayer for their assistance.

CPSIA information can be obtained at www.ICGtesting.com
Printed in the USA
BVOW11s0038171014

371146BV00003B/9/P